Development and the Learning Organisation

Oxfam GB, Oxfam America, and the Institute of Development Studies

Oxfam GB, founded in 1942, is a development, humanitarian, and campaigning agency dedicated to finding lasting solutions to poverty and suffering around the world. Oxfam believes that every human being is entitled to a life of dignity and opportunity, and it works with others worldwide to make this become a reality.

From its base in Oxford, UK, Oxfam GB publishes and distributes a wide range of books and other resource materials for development and relief workers, researchers, campaigners, schools and colleges, and the general public, as part of its programme of advocacy, education, and communications.

Oxfam GB is a member of Oxfam International, a confederation of 12 agencies of diverse cultures and languages which share a commitment to working for an end to injustice and poverty – both in long-term development work and at times of crisis.

For further information about Oxfam's publishing, and online ordering, visit www.oxfam.org.uk/publications

For further information about Oxfam's development, advocacy, and humanitarian relief work around the world, visit www.oxfam.org.uk

Oxfam America is an international agency committed to developing lasting solutions to poverty, hunger, and social injustice. We achieve results through long-term partnerships with groups in poor communities that are already working successfully toward these goals, as well as through informed advocacy for policy changes that will improve the lives of poor people around the world.

Oxfam America works collectively with other members of Oxfam International, fighting poverty and related injustice around the world. Oxfam America is also committed to an extensive educational agenda that reaches all segments of the population – particularly young people. By informing Americans about the daily realities of poor communities as they are linked to economic and social policies, Oxfam seeks to expand public awareness of the injustices of poverty and to develop a citizen's movement dedicated to its eradication.

For further information, visit www.oxfamamerica.org

The Institute of Development Studies (IDS) is one of the world's leading centres for research and teaching on development. The Institute holds an international reputation for the quality of its work and the intellectual rigour with which it applies academic skills to real-world policy challenges. In all sectors of its work, IDS aims to stimulate debate and influence the way people think about international development.

For further information, visit www.ids.ac.uk

Development and the Learning Organisation

Essays from *Development in Practice*

Edited by
Laura Roper, Jethro Pettit, and Deborah Eade

A Development in Practice Reader

Series Editor
Deborah Eade

Institute of Development Studies
Sussex

Oxfam

First published by Oxfam GB in association with Oxfam America and IDS in 2003.

© Oxfam GB 2003

ISBN 0 85598 4708

A catalogue record for this publication is available from the British Library.

Available from:

Bournemouth English Book Centre, PO Box 1496, Parkstone, Dorset, BH12 3YD, UK
tel: +44 (0)1202 712933; fax: +44 (0)1202 712930; email: oxfam@bebc.co.uk

USA: Stylus Publishing LLC, PO Box 605, Herndon, VA 20172-0605, USA
tel: +1 (0)703 661 1581; fax: +1 (0)703 661 1547; email: styluspub@aol.com

For details of local agents and representatives in other countries, consult our website:
www.oxfam.org.uk/publications
or contact Oxfam Publishing, 274 Banbury Road, Oxford OX2 7DZ, UK
tel: +44 (0)1865 311 311; fax: +44 (0)1865 312 600; email: publish@oxfam.org.uk

Our website contains a fully searchable database of all our titles, and facilities for secure on-line ordering.

The Editor and Management Committee of Development in Practice acknowledge the support given to the journal by affiliates of Oxfam International, and by its publisher, Carfax, Taylor & Francis. The views expressed in this volume are those of the individual contributors, and not necessarily those of the Editor or publisher.

Published by Oxfam GB, 274 Banbury Road, Oxford OX2 7DZ, UK.

Printed by Information Press, Eynsham.

Oxfam GB is a registered charity, no. 202 918, and is a member of Oxfam International.

Contents

Section 3:
Levels of learning: organisational case studies

Contributors

Dr Jens Aagaard-Hansen is a social anthropologist and a medical doctor. Based at the Danish Bilharziasis Laboratory for the past nine years, the main focus of his work has been on applied medical anthropology in cross-disciplinary settings.

Domnic Abudho is a teacher in Nyang'oma Educational Division (Bondo District, Kenya) with a particular interest in agriculture.

Sara Ahmed worked for ten years at the Institute of Rural Management (IRMA), Gujarat, teaching courses in rural development, environmental management, and gender issues. She is currently working as an independent gender and development consultant, based in Ahmedabad.

Colin L. Beckwith has worked in international development for the past 20 years, mainly in Latin America and West Africa, focusing on strategy creation and organisational development. Since 1998 he has been a member of CARE's Latin America Regional Management Unit.

Didier Bloch is an independent consultant in information, communication, and project planning and evaluation. He has worked in this capacity for a number of international NGOs (Oxfam-Brazil, SCF, CRS, and UNICEF), as well as for various Brazilian NGOs, including Grupo Curumim, an organisation working with traditional midwives.

Nora Borges is a clinical psychologist who is also qualified in Planning and Human Resource Management. She works as an independent consultant in organisational learning and training with NGOs, including Grupo Curumim, private sector companies, and government departments.

Fred Carden is Senior Specialist in Evaluation at IDRC. He has written in the areas of evaluation, international cooperation, and environmental management. His current work includes the development of evaluation tools and methods in the areas of organisational assessment, participatory monitoring and evaluation, programme evaluation, and outcome mapping.

A. Mushtaque R. Chowdhury is a Deputy Executive Director of BRAC in Bangladesh and a Visiting Professor at Columbia University in New York City.

Barry Coates is Director of the World Development Movement (WDM), a democratic membership network based in the UK. WDM's active supporters and local groups campaign for changes in the policies of Northern governments, companies, and international institutions to counter injustice and create opportunities for the poor. Recent campaigns include the MAI, WTO and the GATS, Third World debt, and regulation of multinational corporations.

Rosalind David has been working as Head of Impact Assessment at ActionAid for the last four years. Before ActionAid she worked with Oxfam GB for three years as Natural Resources Adviser for Africa, and with SOS Sahel for four years as lead researcher on the links between migration and natural resource management.

Gelaye Debebe received her PhD in Organisational Behaviour from the University of Michigan and is currently a Research Associate at the Center for Gender in Organisations at the Simmons Graduate School of Management.

Molly den Heyer completed the TLM research as part of the MSc in Rural Planning and Development at the University of Guelph, Ontario. She is currently a Research Associate working in IDRC's Evaluation Unit.

Thomas S. Dierolf is Country Co-Representative for the Heifer International-Indonesia (Heifer Indonesia) Country Programme.

Sarah Earl is a Programme Evaluation Officer with the Evaluation Unit and has been with IDRC since 1998. Her current work includes the conceptual development of outcome mapping and its application for planning, monitoring, and evaluating at the programme and organisational levels.

David Ellerman is recently retired from being Economic Advisor to the Chief Economist at the World Bank, where he focused on issues of labour, capacity building, transition economies, and private-sector development. He was also adviser and speech-writer to the previous Chief Economist Joseph Stiglitz and is the author of numerous books and papers on economic democracy. He is currently writing a book on development assistance and the World Bank.

Alan Fowler is an independent adviser, analyst, and writer on NGOs, civil society, and development, based in South Africa, and has recently completed studies on NGO leadership and governance. He is vice-president of the International Society for Third Sector Research and a director of CIVICUS, the World Alliance for Citizen Participation.

Kent Glenzer is a consultant on non-profit and public-sector strategy, currently leading an 18-month research project in Mali looking at the intersection of development discourse, democratisation, decentralisation, and the strengthening of civil society.

John Hailey is Professor of International Management at Oxford Brookes University with a special interest in the management of NGOs. He was also one of the founders of the Oxford-based International NGO Training and Research Centre (INTRAC).

Dorothea Hilhorst is a development sociologist specialising in disasters, conflict, and humanitarian aid. She lectures in Disaster Studies at the University of Wageningen.

Rick James is a Senior Training and Consultancy Manager at the Oxford-based International NGO Training and Research Centre (INTRAC), and a specialist in organisational change in NGOs. His recent books include *Demystifying Organisation Development* and *People and Change.*

David Kelleher is an organisational consultant and coordinator, with Aruna Rao, of the Gender at Work Collaborative (www.genderatwork.org).

Rienzzie Kern is Director of Planning and Evaluation at Heifer International.

Matthew Maury is the Director of Community Development for American Leprosy Missions, an INGO supporting work in 20 countries worldwide. From 1991 to 1999 he worked in several African countries with Habitat for Humanity International.

Susan Maury works for Habitat for Humanity International as Director of Organizational Development in the Africa and Middle East Region. Over the past ten years she has worked at the community, national, and regional levels, helping development NGOs transform into learning organisations.

Esther Mebrahtu is currently Planning, Monitoring and Evaluation Officer at Christian Aid. She recently completed her PhD at the Institute for Development Studies at the University of Sussex. Her most recent work is *INGOs and the Burden of Proof* (1999), published by ESCOR at the Department for International Development (DfID).

Samuel Musyoki is in the Participation Group at the Institute of Development Studies (IDS) at the University of Sussex, where he works with IDS partners and networks to deepen understanding of participatory approaches and to strengthen the quality of participatory practice. He is involved in promoting South-South exchanges, critical reflection and learning, and documentation and communication. He has extensive experience in the use of participatory approaches and has worked with bilateral development programmes and with international and local

NGOs in various parts of Africa. He holds an MA in Development Studies from the Institute of Social Studies (ISS) in The Netherlands, and a degree in anthropology from the University of Nairobi.

Tim Ogborn is Vice President of Organizational Development at Heifer International.

Charles Ogoye-Ndegwa is a social scientist with an MA in Anthropology from the University of Nairobi. He is currently conducting fieldwork for his PhD on food security in western Kenya.

Vijay Padaki has been a management researcher, trainer, and consultant in various institutional settings for over 35 years. His specialised interests are in organisation and institutional development, and in partnership management.

Jethro Pettit is a member of the Participation Group at the Institute of Development Studies (IDS) at the University of Sussex in the UK. Before joining IDS, he worked for many years in the US NGO sector, most recently at World Neighbors in Oklahoma City, but also at Oxfam America and Unitarian Universalist Service Committee, both in Boston.

Grant Power has ten years' experience of working in non-profit organisations involved in inner-city community development in the USA and recently completed a two-year term of service with the Mennonite Central Committee (MCC) in the Philippines. He now works as an organisational consultant for international NGOs, and domestic NGOs with a local focus, involved in community-based, sustainable development.

Mark Protti is Director of Training at Heifer International.

Laura Roper is Director of Planning and Learning at Oxfam America, where she has worked since 1989. Prior to that, she was a research manager at the Leonard Davis Institute of Health Economics at the University of Pennsylvania, where she also received her PhD in Political Science.

Nadja Schmiemann has worked as a development agronomist in several projects in Central America. She is currently coordinating the NGO OtherWise.

Marvin Schwartz is Director of Grants at Heifer International.

Patta Scott-Villiers is a member of the Participation Group at the Institute of Development Studies (IDS), where she convenes the organisational learning and change cluster. Before coming to IDS, she worked with NGOs and in the UN system for 13 years, mainly in Africa.

Marla J. Solomon is Associate Dean and Programme Director, Programmes in Intercultural, Service, Leadership, and Management at the School for International Training.

Diane Steiner was an independent researcher on the study discussed in her paper and is now Manager of the Centre for Intergenerational Practice at the Beth Johnson Foundation, Stoke-on-Trent.

Pauline Tiffen works in mainstream and alternative business, cooperative and community development, North and South, and has over 15 years of experience in the alternative sector, in both traditional and non-traditional commodities, across three continents. Her work shows that new institutions and mechanisms for cross-cultural exchange and business collaboration of scale are feasible and have considerable social impact. She is currently Operations Adviser to the International Task Force on Commodity Risk Management Secretariat based at the World Bank, and her non-executive trustee/directorships include the New Economics Foundation, Gateway Trust, the Moscow School of Social and Economic Sciences, and the Day Chocolate Company.

John Twigg is a Research Fellow at University College London specialising in organisational aspects of sustainable development, especially in non-profit organisations.

Marshall Wallace is Project Director of the Local Capacities for Peace Project at The Collaborative for Development Action.

Preface

Deborah Eade

This *Reader* is based on a special issue of *Development in Practice* (Volume 12/3&4, published in August 2002) by guest editors **Jethro Pettit** and **Laura Roper**, both of whom have been dedicated to fostering a learning approach to development within the various NGOs and academic institutions in which they have worked.

Why should learning be so important to development agencies? One obvious answer is that we should not be wasting our resources on re-inventing the wheel. Of course, every situation is unique, but not to the extent that we cannot draw on our own and others' experience to inform what we do. To pretend otherwise, in what a former colleague referred to as 'the fingerprint syndrome',[1] is also to imply both that development agencies live only in the present, and that they are conceited enough to imagine that they can do it all themselves.

Second, we know that once a person loses the willingness or ability to learn, then senility is probably not far around the corner. Similarly, a development NGO that rests on its laurels or is stuck in its ways is likely to die on its feet, possibly continuing to limp on, but bereft of the energy and originality of its youth. On the other hand, an agency that repeatedly restructures itself in a desperate attempt to keep ahead of the Joneses is more than likely to lose contact with its past, and to end up suffering a form of institutional Alzheimer's, reliant on others to be the guardian of its memory. To pursue the same metaphor from another direction, while all creatures are born with the *capacity* to learn, our early years are very much about learning *how* to learn. This is not so much in the obvious sense of acquiring the building blocks of knowledge and the skills to use them, but how to tune in to what is relevant, what truly *matters* to us, while maintaining a sufficiently open mind to question received opinions and assumptions. A development agency also needs to learn how to learn, and to be willing to learn from many different sources, while also having a sure sense of its own values and *raison d'être*. Undirected change is the organisational equivalent of adolescent experimentation and mood swings, responding to the trivial and the profound with equal intensity. By contrast, learning makes it possible for us to make conscious change as opposed to spouting the latest development discourse, or falling for yet another management fad. The need for change is often recognised in some parts of an organisation, but is also often resisted – hence, presumably, the new breed of 'change management' consultants to help guide the process and keep it moving.

Where change that is based on learning takes place, then new knowledge and energy are created, which in turn make deeper transformation and learning possible. And this learning is most likely to happen, as many of the contributors show, in the intersections between different layers or sets of actors right across the development spectrum. It is where diverse communities come together and find ways to interrelate, whether learning new skills or deferring to the other's greater competence. It is about developing hybrid forms of knowledge and communication, rather than believing that any one player or discipline or culture has a monopoly over the truth, or, in the development context, that 'development professionals' necessarily have a deep or sensitive understanding of the complex issues with which they are grappling. International development agencies *par excellence* ought to be in a privileged position as learning organisations, precisely because they work across different cultural divides and operate in ambiguous multi-stakeholder environments. And since this kind of inter-sectionality is precisely what characterises *Development in Practice*, our guest editors found it an ideal forum in which to explore the theoretical and practical questions this poses.

Note

1   Bridget Walker used this metaphor in her role as a Gender Adviser in Oxfam GB.

About the guest editors

Jethro Pettit works at the Institute of Development Studies (IDS) at the University of Sussex as a member of the Participation Group. Before joining IDS, he served for seven years with World Neighbors in Oklahoma City, as director of international programmes and then as head of communication. Prior to this, Jethro was senior associate for Asia and Latin America at the Unitarian Universalist Service Committee, a human rights NGO, and was for five years Oxfam America's representative for Central America, Mexico, and the Caribbean, based in Boston, MA. Experienced in urban community development, social justice, environment, and peace movements in the USA and UK, Jethro studied Social Anthropology at Harvard, and also holds a BA in International Studies from the School for International Training in Vermont, and an MPhil in Development Studies from IDS.

Laura Roper has worked at Oxfam America since 1989, where she has held a range of senior posts, from being a key member of the team dealing with major foundation and corporate donors to heading the programme planning and learning unit, to serving as acting director of the global programme department. Laura's work and publications have been characterised by her deep involvement in research and evaluation, and her experience in managing inter-institutional and multi-stakeholder projects of various kinds. Her recent focus has been on developing skills in participatory planning methodologies, facilitation, and mediation – all with the end of creating group settings in which to draw out and explore tacit knowledge, generate new ideas, and bring underlying assumptions and conflicts to the surface. Prior to joining Oxfam America, Laura worked for several years at the Leonard Davis Institute of Health Economics. She holds a degree in History from the University of Arizona, and a PhD in Political Science from the University of Pennsylvania, where she also taught Latin American Politics.

Development and the Learning Organisation:
an introduction

Laura Roper and Jethro Pettit

---

*If we had a keen vision and feeling of all ordinary human life, it would be
like hearing the grass grow and the squirrel's heart beat, and we should die
of that roar which lies on the other side of silence. As it is, the best of us walk
about well-wadded with stupidity.*
(George Eliot, *Middlemarch*)

Why development and the Learning Organisation?

Why a *Development in Practice Reader* on development and the
learning organisation? We were aware that an increasing number of
NGOs, particularly some of the large international ones, as well as
some bilateral and multilateral actors, were embracing the idea of
'becoming a learning organisation'. Over the past decade, as NGOs
have either rushed into the mainstream in their claims of innovative
and effective practice, or have tried to transform themselves to fit new
realities, organisational learning has emerged as one way to live up to
expectations and needs. Certainly, it is difficult to find organisations
that are not touting the importance of knowledge generation and
organisational learning in one form or another. We were curious to
know how practitioners were approaching the issue of learning in
organisations and whether their approaches were yielding positive
results. We were especially interested because much of the writing
and thinking on learning organisations has come out of the private
sector, and we wondered how applicable and how useful development
practitioners were finding it in their own field.

This Reader is based on a special issue of *Development in Practice*,
which we were invited to guest edit. As readers will see, our call for
papers for this issue generated an interesting mix of responses and
cases, ranging from major organisational transformation efforts
significantly informed by learning organisation theory to micro-level

case studies of individual and group-learning practice in very specific circumstances. The responses were varied as the literature itself, although the primary focus was on NGO experiences. To help orient the reader, it may be helpful to make some distinctions among terms that are often used interchangeably: the learning organisation, organisational learning, and monitoring and evaluation (learning) systems. Most importantly, there is a need to distinguish between the body of thought that focuses on the 'learning organisation', and that dealing with 'organisational learning.'

The Learning Organisation

Mark Easterby-Smith (1997), in a very useful review article, makes a distinction between writers on the learning organisation and those who focus on organisational learning, and among several strains of thought in the latter category, as well. He notes that the learning organisation, most closely associated with the writing of Peter Senge (1990), is 'pragmatic, normative and inspirational'. The literature is pragmatic in that it focuses on how organisations successfully acquire, share, and use knowledge to achieve organisational goals. There is a strong emphasis for creating 'knowledge for action', not knowledge for its own sake (Agyris 1993). Further, it recognises that organisations are a part of complex social systems, systems over which it is unlikely they can exert control. Rather than trying to isolate or protect an organisation from its environment, an organisation ought to be closely attuned to it, embrace the opportunities that changing circumstances can offer, and, as more recent theorists have urged, 'ride the wave' (Duesterberg and London 2001, Merron 1997). Another aspect of the pragmatic orientation is that learning organisation theorists, unlike many of their academic counterparts, have also developed an array of techniques and tools for doing diagnostics, examining patterns of behaviour in organisations, and engaging in 'transformative thinking' (Wycoff 1995).

This approach is normative in the sense that there is a strong set of underlying values that inform practice within a learning organisation, which include a commitment to:

- valuing different kinds of knowledge and learning styles and creating a 'learning environment' so each organisational member can realise his/her full potential;
- encouraging dialogue and the exploration of different perspectives and experiences to generate creative thinking;

- working collectively and breaking down traditional barriers or blinders within organisations so as to release creative potential;
- fostering leadership potential throughout the organisation and reducing distinctions, such as those between management and staff, between strategists and implementers, between support and professional staff, and so on.

There is also a strong element of 'self-improvement' found in the literature, whereby individuals in a learning organisation are not only in an ongoing quest for work-related knowledge, but also for self knowledge. One aspect of this is the need to understand their own 'mental models' – deeply ingrained assumptions about how the world works, what motivates people, cause-and-effect relationships – and to be open to challenges regarding these assumptions.

The writing on learning organisations is also normative in the sense that it encourages organisations to go beyond 'single-loop learning', which often focuses on finding efficiencies and dealing with first order problems (symptoms), to double- and even triple-loop learning. In double-loop learning, organisations consistently test assumptions, identify the roots of problems, and are open to fundamental rethinking of strategy. Organisations practising double-loop learning are open to examining how organisational practice diverges from 'espoused theory' and addressing these inconsistencies (for example, an organisation that espouses gender equality would be willing to examine the extent to which it lives its own values and make the necessary changes). In triple-loop learning, the highest form of organisational self-examination, people are open to questioning the very *raison d'être* of the organisation.

The learning organisation literature is aspirational in the sense that the models are presented as something of 'ideal types' which no real organisation can realise in full. Individuals as well as the organisation are engaged in an ongoing quest for knowledge, their struggle to 'unlearn' dysfunctional behaviours is continuous, and because change is a constant, they must constantly change.

Organisational Learning

The 'organisational learning' literature is much more extensive and diverse. Entering 'organisational learning' in a web search generated over 92,000 entries. Just to mention of few of the streams in this literature, we have:

- A management science stream that focuses on the processes of knowledge acquisition and information management. This literature covers a range of topics, from effective management information systems (MIS) design, to more challenging issues, such as the relationship between explicit knowledge (such as that captured by MIS) to tacit knowledge (the know-how in people's heads). It is under this broad stream that the thinking related to monitoring and evaluation systems would fall.

- A sociological perspective that focuses on organisations as social systems with structures and a culture that either enhance or, more often, inhibit learning. As social structures, organisations are characterised by internal politics, conflict, and power differentials – aspects of organisational life that are generally downplayed or ignored by leading proponents of organisation theory – but which have a huge impact on the capacity of individuals and organisations to learn and act on that learning. (It is noticeable that even in this stream of the literature, gender issues are very rarely directly identified or addressed.)

- A third stream relates to how learning contributes to increases in productive output, market share, and/or profitability. It sees organisations as embedded in competitive environments and the effectiveness of its learning systems are judged on the basis of the extent to which an organisation keeps its competitive edge. This stream examines such topics as innovation and adoption of new technologies and practices, behaviour of organisations within a given sector and determinants of decisions to expand or diversify, and the efficacy of joint-venturing.

- Other streams in organisational learning literature include psychological and behavioural aspects of individual learning and cross-cultural comparisons of organisational learning (principally in the USA and Japan, and a few European countries), but these have not been much developed in the mainstream literature.

It should be noted that works cited in the Easterby-Smith (1997) review, from which these categories are largely drawn, as well as other literature reviews, deal almost exclusively with private-sector experience and organisations (although there is a growing literature on the health and education sectors, in which some of the actors are non-profit). In addition, the orientation towards learning in organisations is a modern Western one, with a bias towards dynamism and disequilibrium, rapid response and high performance, and embracing change in part because it is impossible to exert control.

As we mentioned earlier, we were curious as to how this literature has informed thinking and practice in the development field. We also wondered if thinking and experience from the latter might make useful contributions to the theoretical literature. The material fell into five thematic areas, giving us a convenient structure for this volume. The first set of articles deals with the broader dynamics of organisational learning and change, including issues of power, culture, and gender. The second set looks more specifically at 'learning in partnership' – organisational learning involving more than one institution or sector, such as academic–practitioner collaboration, bilateral programmes, and those involving the private sector. The third is a set of case studies that reveals the diverse 'levels of learning' within organisations, identifying a variety of effective leverage points for innovation and change. A fourth set of articles looks at learning within the humanitarian relief sector, where a context of conflict, high staff turnover and operational pressures can yield challenging organisational cultures. The fifth and final set deals more specifically with 'ways and means': tools, methods, and approaches that can either inhibit or enable effective learning.

While each of the papers in this collection can be read on its own, when viewed as a whole a number of powerful ideas and questions emerge. We shall comment on three aspects of these papers that drew our attention. The first is the paradox of origins, the second relates to the challenge of complexity, and the third is about the nature of incremental approaches to transformative process.

The paradox of origins

Where and why have development organisations taken up the idea of becoming learning organisations? The diverse views on this are worth untangling. David Kelleher *et al.* see learning organisation theory as a 'borrowed toolbox', while Vijay Padaki suggests that the learning organisation is simply the latest management fad. Grant Power *et al.* argue that '[a]lthough many businesses are modelling learning practices, neither the for-profit environment nor corporate structures fit well with the environmental and organisational forms needed for grassroots development'. The absence of shareholders and profit as priorities for NGOs, as noted by Didier Bloch and Nora Borges, means that values that are related to principles and mission tend to dominate. Yet the concept of 'being a learning organisation' and the transformative promise of effective organisational learning clearly resonate deeply in a great range of organisations represented here, as they do in many others besides. Why should this be so?

First of all, there is a long tradition in the development field of recognising untapped human potential in all human beings as well as the transformative power of learning. Even in the earliest years of international development, significant support was given to literacy and adult education, primary and secondary schools, and to some extent higher education. Beyond valuing education simply as a ticket to a better standard of living, there were thinkers who saw education as more than an investment in skills and capacities; non-formal learning in particular was recognised as a process of sparking critical awareness and consciousness, leading to both individual and social change. Paulo Friere's *The Pedagogy of the Oppressed* (1970) is among the most brilliant and influential expressions of this tradition, showing that critical analysis of one's reality can be a powerful tool for empowerment and collective action. In the African context, the idea that development should be a 'mutual learning experience' was powerfully expressed by Julius Nyerere as early as 1968 (Oakley *et al.* 1991, cited in Cornwall 2001). Both thinkers were inspired by Christian thought as well as socialism, and their work – rather than viewing learning in a strictly instrumental way – shared a redemptive vision, as well as a commitment to liberation from oppression in the here and now as the right of all people.

Indeed, these early concepts of learning as a process of personal and structural transformation have nurtured much of today's continued interest in participatory action research, action-learning, and participatory monitoring and evaluation. Broadly, these traditions place value on diverse sources of knowledge, respecting different learning styles and trusting that the inclusion of many players, acting together, will be more likely to generate creative and meaningful change. A key principle emerging from this tradition is that learning and change are mutual processes, affecting both the participants and the agents of change – and by extension the structures and organisations involved. Much of the writing on participatory development focuses on the need to foster creative processes – including more flexible and enabling structures, behaviours, and attitudes – that will enhance participation and integrate different realities (Chambers 1997). The approaches developed by practitioners in these participatory traditions anticipate language and methods that are used in the corporate sector today.

A second aspect of learning organisation theory with which development practitioners should feel comfortable is the emphasis on embracing change. Most people join the development field because they want to change the status quo – whether in a relatively restricted way such as improving nutrition, housing, or educational opportunities, or in a more profound way, such as addressing the root causes of poverty, and challenging those economic and political structures that perpetuate it (see, for example, Hope and Timmel 1984). For the development practitioner, change is both desirable and necessary. Consequently, how to generate 'knowledge for action' and be constantly monitoring a dynamic environment in order to identify opportunities and anticipate challenges have strong appeal. Development organisations themselves are also seeking to embrace change, to become more flexible and adaptive in a rapidly changing global context, and to become more strategic in addressing deeper structural inequalities and policy issues (Edwards and Hulme 1996). For some, organisational learning approaches hold the promise of helping to introduce urgently needed shifts in culture, vision, and purpose.

Another aspect with which many development professionals will identify relates to the focus on changing internal structures and practices that inhibit learning and, in turn, fulfilment of an organisation's mission. An enormous area of work in the development field has to do with 'institution building' or organisational capacity building. The learning organisation literature has the merit of going beyond much of the mainstream capacity-building guides put out by organisational development consultants and technical intermediaries, which often have a prescriptive feel and are not characterised by their sensitivity to different economic, social, and cultural contexts. (For notable exceptions see Eade (1997) and Kaplan (1996).) The limitations of the conventional capacity-building guides are a function, in part, of the influence of neo-liberal thinking on (and funding for) management and governance. This has become more pronounced as NGOs have come under pressure to live up to their idealised role of 'providing models of good practice for others to follow' (Cornwall 2001), and to do so efficiently. Learning organisation approaches – with their emphasis on flatter organisational structure, nurturing the leadership potential in all staff, closer connection with and greater accountability to clients, better internal communication, the efficacy of teamwork – may be seen by some as a potential antidote to more traditional organisational practices of many NGOs, which can often be hierarchical, narrowly construed, and non-participatory.

In short, a lot of the thinking that has been done by development practitioners in fact anticipates significant aspects of learning organisation theory. That said, we would encourage you to read the articles by Kelleher *et al.*, Powers *et al.*, and Padaki, who suggest that the theory does not go far enough. As a normative theory, it does not argue explicitly for internal democracy and because it does not examine 'deep structures' and power inequities within organisations, is unlikely to have the transformative impact it aspires to (Kelleher). Related to this, because learning organisation theory emerges from the private sector and consequently is not concerned about development, much less development that is firmly grounded in a grassroots approach, the scope of its interest in transformation is in fact quite limited (Powers *et al.*). Regarding the degree to which it is pragmatic, Padaki argues that it actually detracts attention from management fundamentals, and may generate more heat than light. Bloch and Borges, on the other hand, find potential in those strands of organisational learning theory that focus on critical reflection, transforming values and personal behaviour (Agyris and Schön 1974).

The challenge of complexity

In reading these papers, one point emerges particularly strongly: learning is hard to do, both for individuals, and particularly for organisations and groups of organisations. When we do learn, we often learn the wrong things. Huge gaps often remain between our learning and our behaviour or practice. It is important to keep in mind the characteristics of the development and humanitarian work that may present particular learning challenges. We might summarise these as the complexity of the development process; the complexity of accountability demands and duties, the complexity of measurement; and self-inflicted complexity. We will comment briefly on each of these.

The complexity of the development process

David Ellerman notes that '[t]he questions that face development agencies about inducing economic and social development are perhaps the most complex and ill-defined questions facing human kind'. As practitioners know, development is non-linear, unpredictable, and what is needed for sustaining development on a non-trivial scale is poorly understood. In this process, there is only a small range of things organisations actually have any control over, and a great many over which they don't. It is not clear which aspects are most important, when and how they interact, and what downstream effects will be if 'success' or anticipated change is achieved in any one area. This presents a significant challenge to any organisation committed to learning, because it is not always clear what it should be learning or how to make sense out of what it learns. This is a problem that can be particularly pronounced in humanitarian work, particularly in situations of complex emergencies or very high degrees of vulnerability (see John Twigg and Diana Steiner; Dorothea Hilhorst and Najda Schiemann).

Ellerman further argues that this learning challenge is greatly compounded when development organisations, including some with enormous influence and resources, embrace 'dogma', try to identify the 'One Best Way', and become deeply wedded to these beliefs. This creates significant obstacles to learning, as people focus on explaining away failures (bad single-loop learning) rather than question the dogma or dominant paradigm (double- and triple-loop learning). Bloch and Borges suggest that NGOs tend to get stuck in single-loop learning because their planning and evaluation tools focus on the operational level, and fail to engage people in critical reflection on underlying issues of behaviour, values, and agency. They agree with Michael Edwards that the complexity and diversity of the development process 'means that to develop capacity for learning and to make the connections is even more important than accumulating information' (Edwards 1997).

The development effort is also made much more complex because it is not a solo enterprise. Nor is business, of course, and there is a considerable literature on joint enterprise. However, the private sector literature focuses on developing characteristics of a learning organisation in order to maintain an edge over competitors. The competitive lens is not the most useful for analysing actors in the development sector, particularly as collaboration has become increasingly important for achieving development and humanitarian goals. Development and humanitarian organisations in different countries, of different sizes, with different missions, mandates, and accountability structures have to collaborate with each other in the hope of having an impact. Even within a given organisation, there can often be many hierarchical levels and a variety of sectors or units, as well as remote offices, each with their own cultural contexts, each of which may have very different worldviews. The challenge in the development field is to instil learning capabilities, including the learning challenge of consistently and effectively working with others, in a range of very diverse organisations, which operate at different and/or multiple levels and in profoundly different contexts.

Several papers tackle aspects of the challenge that collaboration poses for both individuals and organisations. Laura Roper examines academic–NGO learning collaborations and argues that different organisational cultures can undermine partnerships that would seem to have enormous potential. To be successful, there needs to be a clear negotiated agreement about both the ends of the collaboration and the means of reaching those ends, with both parties being aware of the nature of their differences. This message is reinforced by Gelaye Debebe in her paper on a collaboration between a Navajo service and capacity-building organisation and the 'anglo' technical intermediary. Marla Solomon and A. Mushtaque R. Chowdhury examine the challenges and benefits of a learning collaboration between the School of International Training, a US-based academic institution, and BRAC, a Bangladeshi NGO.

Samuel Musyoki asks whether organisational learning principles are relevant or useful in complex bilateral programmes, looking at a joint rural development effort of the Dutch and Kenyan governments in Keiyo and Marakwet districts. He examines how participation was institutionalised at different stages of the programme, as both a learning and a conflict-generating process. In the politicised context of bilateral programmes, Musyoki finds that the ability to carry forward any learning from one phase to the next is hindered by high staff turnover, national politics, diplomatic considerations, and shifts in the international development agenda. Learning organisation theory tends to assume some degree of consensus or shared vision, both of which can be elusive in development programmes that involve multiple actors, competing interests, and conflicting goals.

Pauline Tiffen, writing about producing and marketing fair-trade chocolate, documents a fairly complex multi-institutional collaboration and highlights how each participant – from a rural Ghanaian producers' cooperative, to two international technical support organisations, to the UK-based Day Chocolate Company – engaged in strong learning practice. Learning occurred on many dimensions. The cocoa producers learned from past experiences and mistakes in trying to establish a strong, responsive farmers' cooperative. Twin, a specialist

NGO based in the UK, used research and its experience of working with Latin American coffee, sesame, and honey producers, to support the development of a fair-trade marketing strategy for cocoa. Day Chocolate, among other strategies to promote fair-trade chocolates, set out to break down the distance between the faceless producer and the faceless consumer, through a number of interesting innovations.

The complexity of accountability

It became common 'wisdom' in the private sector during the 'go-go 90s' that a company's primary responsibility was to maximise shareholder value. This implied accountability and responsiveness to customers, and to a more limited extent to employees, to the extent that doing so served to maximise profits and return on investment. Compared with the NGO sector, private sector accountability is quite straightforward, particularly since there is an arguable congruence of interests among its immediate stakeholders. This apparent congruence can, of course, be disrupted if a company develops a monopoly over the market, if influential shareholders are exclusively focused on short-term profit, or (increasingly rarely) if labour is highly organised in a tight labour market. Today, there is growing awareness in the corporate boardrooms of the need not only to satisfy the shareholders, but also to protect the company's reputation (and deflect public criticism), and to minimise practices that are environmentally unsustainable – the so-called 'triple bottom line' (Elkington 1997).

Accountability is not necessarily so straightforward for NGOs, whether local or international. Powers *et al.* are most explicit in identifying the conflict of interest between two primary stakeholders of an NGO: its donor institutions and the 'clients' of the NGO's services or actions. Because donors control the purse strings, they often exert undue influence on how the NGO views accountability. Consequently, monitoring and evaluation systems, how reports are developed and used, and criteria for success are determined not by those the NGO sets out to serve, but by the donors. This obviously has consequences for how learning processes are structured and whose interests they serve. Esther Mebrahtu illustrates how this plays out across a number of organisations, while the case histories of CARE (Colin Beckwith *et al.*), ActionAid (Patta Scott-Villiers), Heifer International (Thomas S. Dierolf *et al.*), and Médicins sans Frontières (Hilhorst and Schmiemann) deal with the challenges faced by individual international NGOs. These experiences highlight the extent to which the 'development project' remains the currency of most agencies, driven by the transfer of resources from donors to recipients. Reporting systems and procedures are geared towards the control over resource flows, rather than towards learning and innovation.

The accountability challenge is still more complex when NGOs belong to confederations (such as Care International, Oxfam International, or Save the Children Fund Federation); have diverse and segmented publics (different types of donors, volunteers, activists, etc.); as well as having, in some cases, relationships with policy makers, the media, and a range of allies. An NGO often needs engagement from these other stakeholders (free labour from volunteers, the placement of stories by colleagues in the media, favourable decisions or policy positions from policy makers, and so on). These stakeholders are also frequently physically closer and may also be more similar to headquarter staff (for instance in terms of class, ethnic background, education) than are partners or beneficiaries in the South. As a result, the former set of stakeholders are quite likely to be better organised and be more able to exercise voice than are the poor communities on whose behalf we work. As international NGOs, in particular, increasingly take on advocacy and campaigning roles, very close relations may develop with media, sympathetic policy makers, and other like-minded agencies, and opportunities in relation to the domestic public can become more pronounced in driving the organisation, albeit for good strategic reasons. Finding the right balance and methods for handling accountability relationships becomes a major challenge. Neither the literature on learning organisations nor that on organisational learning deals extensively with questions of accountability to multiple stakeholders, although as the scope of NGO work broadens, this is becoming a more pressing issue. (See Lindenberg and Bryant 2001; Moore *et al.* 2001; Coates and David in this volume.)

The challenge of finding the right metrics and methods

Development organisations are not producing and selling widgets. They are interested in both process and outcome. Outcomes are multi-dimensional and often not easily measurable. How do you measure organisational capacity? How do you measure empowerment? If a coalition does not achieve its articulated policy-change goal, are there other achievements that lay the groundwork for a more successful effort in the future? How do you evaluate a process and even define what a good process is? The things you can most easily count are often things that don't tell you very much. There are fundamental questions to consider about who does the measuring, who benefits from monitoring and evaluation procedures, and whose learning and knowledge is valued (Estrella *et al.* 2000).

The challenge of metrics and methods runs up smack against the accountability issue. Numerous papers note that their monitoring and evaluation (M&E) systems are designed to conform to donor demands (Esther Mebrahtu; Sarah Earl and Fred Carden). There is also the organisational imperative, particularly in large, sprawling, multi-million dollar agencies, to try to make coherent sense out of diversity of experience (Scott-Villiers). There is, however, a good deal of creative work being done in both the development and humanitarian arenas. Marshall Wallace describes the inductive process carried out over several years by the Local Capacities for Peace Project (LCPP) to tackle the difficult challenge of humanitarian intervention in the context of complex emergencies. Mebrahtu also highlights innovations by field staff, outside the formal demands of the system.

Bloch and Borges, in their work with a reproductive health rights NGO in Brazil, describe efforts to engage staff in deeper reflection on their own values and behaviour, and to build skills for more effective listening, dialogue, and relationships. They link this effort to the NGO's M&E, so that qualitative changes in organisational response and performance can be measured over time, and so that staff can reflect on its own behaviour in the process of defining indicators, documenting progress, and learning from the evaluation process, and so break with 'defensive routines'.

The rapid growth of advocacy work is challenging many development organisations to develop effective ways to monitor, measure, and learn from programmes. Barry Coates and Rosalind David explore the complex and changing nature of advocacy, drawing on the experiences from ActionAid and the World Development Movement. They suggest that conventional M&E and impact-assessment methods are likely to be inappropriate or even counter-productive. A focus on measuring short-term advocacy impacts, for example, may undermine longer-term aims such as strengthening the capacity and voice of partner groups to effect deeper change. Similarly, causality can be hard to pin down. Efforts to assess the impact of one organisation may create perverse incentives that undermine joint action. Coates and David argue that an analysis of power and power structures should guide advocacy strategy and inform the ways in which advocacy is evaluated. Their review adds to a growing body of work on the challenges of doing and assessing advocacy and policy-change work (Chapman 2002; VeneKlasen and Miller 2002; Cohen *et al.* 2001; Roche 1999; Brown and Fox 1998). To contribute to organisational learning, those applying conventional M&E approaches to advocacy work are advised to join the search for alternative tools and methods.

Self-inflicted complexity

Development and humanitarian organisations are notorious for the imbalance that is almost inevitably found between aspirations, capabilities, and resources (human, financial, and temporal). As Twigg and Steiner note, '[o]ne of the most significant, and emphatic, findings of our research is that overwork and pressures of work are not minor factors in NGO operations and performance, but systemic weaknesses [which] in our view ... [are] a major obstacle to the uptake of new approaches'. Mebrahtu, Scott-Villiers, and Hilhorst and Schiemann also identify time as a major constraint. Another challenge is staff turnover, especially within organisations, such as Médicins sans Frontières and Peace Corps, which embrace voluntarism. Various authors highlight the importance of simply creating a 'space for learning.' It is interesting to note that in the case of the LCPP described by Wallace, space had to be created outside the individual humanitarian organisations and that often it was the field staff rather than headquarters who drove the learning effort.

Despite emphasis on learning and knowledge creation, many practitioners feel themselves to be in a vicious cycle. How many of us work in organisations where we are rewarded for reflecting on our work, for reading and listening to what others have to say, for systematising and sharing our experiences so others can critique our work, both within our institutions and in the broader development community? We are working with ever more ambitious NGO agendas, increasing numbers of relevant actors and stakeholders, and more complex change processes. As we learn by doing, real learning becomes even more important. Yet increased complexity increases demands on staff and strains existing infrastructure, meaning there is even *less* time for reflection and learning. When and how can this vicious cycle be transformed into a virtuous one of reflective practice?

Transformation through incrementalism? Sustaining learning practice

We are all humiliated by the sudden discovery of a fact which has existed very comfortably and perhaps been staring at us in private, while we have been making up our world entirely without it.

George Eliot, *Middlemarch*

The gulf between the ideal type of a learning organisation and the organisations many of us work in is often huge, although there certainly are exceptions. John Hailey and Rick James identify a number of successful South Asian NGOs, characterised by good learning practices, and emphasise the importance of top leaders' commitment to learning and critical inquiry for creating a learning culture. Patta Scott-Villiers deals with ActionAid's attempt to undergo a major strategic transformation through its Accountability, Learning and Planning System (ALPS). A driving force behind this transformation is the decision taken by ActionAid that it owes the highest level of accountability to its primary stakeholders: the communities it serves. There are interesting examples of how ActionAid is putting its guiding institutional principles into practice, such as sharing detailed financial information with communities. Although less explicit than in the Hailey and James article, the role of top leadership for moving change through the system is clearly significant.

More often than not, one finds pockets of good learning practice in organisations whose leadership may either simply allow (as Mebrahtu illustrates in some of her case examples) or may nurture with varying degrees of intentionality. Dierolf *et al.* describe how Heifer International has created an enabling environment for learning experimentation at the country level, as well as establishing mechanisms at headquarters to foster cross-regional and cross-functional learning and planning. In the case of CARE (Beckwith *et al.*), the decentralised nature of the system, as well as a mandate coming out of a participatory planning process that, in effect, changes the business model of CARE from a service-delivery agency to being part of a movement for development, has allowed the Latin American Regional Unit to innovate in planning, programming, and learning. The question the paper leaves us with is how an organisation can handle the tensions generated by innovative leadership from the middle that is considerably ahead of the rest of the organisation.

There are also examples where organisations try to undertake an evaluation process and ensure that it creates a genuine learning moment. The joint evaluation carried out by the School for International Training (SIT) and the Bangladesh Rural Advancement Committee (BRAC) of its Global Partnership's NGO Leadership and Management Programme, is such an example (Solomon and Chowdhury). The International Development Research Centre (IDRC) is focusing considerable energy on developing methods that allow for more effective planning and learning, and we include two examples of the tools they are developing (Earl and Carden; Molly den Heyer).

While the focus of this Reader is on whether and how organisations learn, clearly a key aspect for successful organisational learning is to structure learning processes in such a way as to enhance individuals' agency and learning capabilities. The paper by Charles Ogoye-Ndegwa, Domnic Abudho, and Jens Aagard-Hansen looks at how learning and participation in a nutrition programme was structured in such a way that students, usually the passive recipients of information dispensed by teachers in an authoritarian schooling tradition, became researchers, active learners, teachers of their peers and parents, and contributors to community good through identification and cultivation of nutritious traditional foodstuffs.

Wallace illustrates a process where individuals were brought together outside their organisations to share their individual learning regarding delivery of humanitarian aid in complex emergencies. Through an inductive, iterative process, a framework for assessing interventions in complex emergencies was developed, and it was later adopted and tested, often by interested individuals or small groups with a given relief agency. The challenge that many participants were left with was how to institutionalise that learning within their respective organisations, particularly when headquarters staff had not been much involved. An interesting follow-up will be to see which organisations mainstream the model and how they go about doing it.

Debebe details the challenges inherent within a bicultural collaboration that includes participants with very different worldviews and value systems, from the perspective of one of the actors who is trying to get a long-stalled project moving forward. It demonstrates a point made by several other authors (e.g. Hilhorst and Schmiemann; Mebrahtu), which is that each of us negotiates our place within systems, often seeking simply to cope. It also illustrates that the extent to which individuals can learn is limited by the extent to which they have insights into underlying issues of values, power, and culture. The importance of this cannot be overstated. Very often, organisational evolution or transformation is derailed by the limitations of key individuals to learn deeply and genuinely.

This is forcefully highlighted in the papers by David Kelleher *et al.* and Sara Ahmed, both of which deal with gender relations within organisations and efforts to make organisations more gendered in their policies and practices. To many people, it is, in fact, very threatening to examine the 'deep structure' within organisations, including the position of privileges that men hold and which are reinforced by institutional policy and practice. Those holding positions of privilege in a society (or organisation) may be totally oblivious to its many manifestations. While they can gain insights and are willing to address the more obvious and obviously unfair examples, they may be completely unaware of other aspects, and cannot recognise them even when they are pointed out. Very often, leaders will embark upon organisational change processes with real commitment to transform the organisation, until they realise how genuine transformation will challenge their own authority and prerogatives. Even when top leadership remains committed, it is often middle-management or upper-level professionals who feel threatened by the constant challenge to basic premises and by the more egalitarian values embodied in learning organisation theory. As Kelleher observes, '[a]s change agents we may recognise that gender equality requires a very different set of power relations in an organisation, but we are seldom, if ever, asked by organisations to lead a cultural revolution'.

Where leadership structures are highly politicised, as in the case analysed by Musyoki, learning and change may be very threatening to the status quo. Commitment to a shared vision may not exist, even nominally, and it may be necessary to create alternative, community-based structures that can build trust and hold officials accountable. Musyoki argues for more rigorous attention to the political and power dynamics at play within and among organisations, and observes that this is missing from much of the writing on organisational learning. He also cautions that even alternative structures and processes of participation can then be formalised in ways that fold them back into the existing power structure, where in the end it is 'political dynamics that determine what is to be learned, by whom, how, and for what purpose'. By understanding these political dynamics, we can engage in more critically reflective and open processes where people can develop their own learning agendas and manage the outcomes.

Conclusions

Obviously, a key challenge, and one with which many development workers are familiar, is how to get those transformative breakthroughs that get us closer to our goals. In the context of organisations, learning organisation theory has been effective in articulating a set of values and practices that has galvanised a lot of creative thinking and basically changed the nature of the discourse on organisational development. It seems appropriate, however, for us in the development sector to push both the discourse and practice even further.

As Kelleher *et al.* note, given the values that underlie our work, we should also be committed to achieving organisations that are '[s]ufficiently democratic that those ideas with merit can be enunciated with power from all levels of the organisation and evolve into practice', and 'possessing teams capable of functioning democratically and effectively'. We should use whatever tools help us achieve the aspirations of mission-driven organisations, some of which may come from the management literature, while many others have roots in other disciplines and in development practice itself. These traditions, identified earlier in the paper, focus on individual reflection and empowerment for collective action, and on transforming oppressive structures and power dynamics.

As Power *et al.* argue, if we are truly committed to poor communities and the potential of the grassroots to move a development agenda forward, we have to make the investments in time, resources, and experimentation with innovative learning methodologies to ensure bottom-up learning, mutual accountability, and a people-driven, rather than donor-dominated, development practice. They warn that this can have profound implications for organisations in terms of their size, their mission, and their organisational drivers. To take their argument a step further, and perhaps return to the thinking of Freiere and Nyerere, should we not be finding ways in which the poor and marginalised are able not simply to *influence* NGO practice, but actually to *define* the development paradigm, drawing on the richness and diversity of philosophical, religious, and cultural traditions? At the very least, organisations should be searching for ways to create space for innovative development and learning practice, sometimes referred to as learning laboratories or communities of learning, with the explicit intention of challenging standard practice and/or dominant paradigms. This includes negotiating with official donor agencies (bilateral and multilateral) so that they in turn could, at a minimum, negotiate with their funders (legislatures and governments, respectively) to allow more flexible application and reporting requirements on at least some of their funds.

A third area in which development practitioners can potentially contribute a great deal to debates on organisational effectiveness and change concerns cultural aspects of organisational learning. The business literature is extremely weak in this domain, although Bloch and Borges find promise in the values-based approaches to learning and change that promote reflection on personal behaviour (Senge 1990; Argyris 1993; Argyris and Schön 1974). In this era of accelerated globalisation, where multi-institutional collaborations, such as that described by Tiffen, are increasingly becoming the norm, understanding the ways individuals and institutions collaborate and learn in their own settings, as well as how they learn to collaborate across great cultural and economic divides, will become essential for achieving the development breakthroughs needed for significant numbers of people to overcome poverty. International NGOs have a special role to play in this effort because they have feet in more than one environment, and are particularly positioned to bring non-Western understandings of development, management, and cultural practices from a variety of settings that could serve to not only reduce dependence on the overwhelming influence of Western, business-sector theorising, but actually create more hybrid forms of knowledge and theory.

Finally, the papers provide practical insights into what needs to be in place for the generation of knowledge for action, and offer the beginning of an empirical base upon which to refine both organisational learning and learning organisation practice in the development field. Time is essential (and one of the most scarce commodities for development practitioners) and neutral space is extremely important, as Wallace's paper attests. The skill and the patience to value contributions from people whose knowledge may have been devalued or ignored for years, as both Tiffen and Ogoye-Ndegwa *et al.* illustrate, is enormously empowering. There are numerous examples of how development organisations – usually operating in more dynamic, more complex, and more ambiguous contexts than most private sector organisations – identify the need for change and operationalise it (Scott-Villiers, Beckwith *et al.*, Dierolf *et al.*)

Many of the examples offered in this Reader are documenting early stages of institutional processes. These are worth following over the coming years to gather more empirical evidence about how these processes unfold, how they affect culture and practice within organisations, how both internal and external stakeholders experience these processes, and finally, whether these organisations become more effective actors.

We therefore close by inviting readers to send us more cases, so that the debates, networking, and the sharing of experience that underpin learning can continue beyond the contribution we trust this volume has made.

References

Agyris, Chris (1993) *Knowledge for Action: Guide to Overcoming Barriers to Organizational Change*, San Francisco, CA: Jossey-Bass.

Agyris, Chris and Donald Schön (1974) *Theory and practice: increasing professional effectiveness*, San Francisco, CA: Jossey-Bass.

Brown, L.D. and J. Fox, (1998) *The Struggle for Accountability: The World Bank, NGOs, and Grassroots Movements*, Cambridge, MA: MIT Press.

Chambers, Robert 1997, *Whose Reality Counts? Putting the first last*, London: ITDG.

Chapman, Jennifer (2002) *Monitoring and Evaluating Advocacy*, PLA Notes No. 43, London: IIED.

Cohen, David, Rosa de la Vega and Gabrielle Watson (2001) *Advocacy for Social Justice: a global action and reflection guide*, Bloomfield, CT: Kumarian Press.

Cornwall, Andrea (2001) *Beneficiary, consumer, citizen: perspectives on participation for poverty reduction*, SidaStudies No. 2, Stockholm: SIDA.

Duesterberg, Thomas and I. Herbert (eds.) (2001) *Riding the Next Wave: Why this Century Will Be a Golden Age for Workers, the Environment and Developing Countries*, Indianapolis, IN: Hudson Institute.

Eade, Deborah (1997) *Capacity Building: An Approach to People Centred Development*, Oxford: Oxfam.

Easterby-Smith, Mark. (1997) 'Disciplines of organizational learning: contributions and critiques,' Human Relations 50(9)1085-2013.

Edwards, Michael (1997) *Organizational Learning in Non-Governmental Organizations: What have we learned?*, Washington DC: World Bank.

Edwards, Michael and David Hulme (eds.) (1996) *Beyond the Magic Bullet: NGO Performance and Accountability in the Post-Cold War World*, West Hartford, CT: Kumarian Press.

Elkington, John (1997) *Cannibals with Forks: The Triple Bottom Line of 21st Century Business*, Oxford: Capstone.

Estrella, Marisol, with Jutta Blauert, Dindo Campilan, John Gaventa, Julian Gonsalves, Irene Guijt, Deb Johnson, and Roger Ricafort (2000) *Learning from Change: Issues and experiences in participatory monitoring and evaluation*, London: IT Publications.

Freire, Paulo (1970) *The Pedagogy of the Oppressed*, New York, NY: Continuum.

Hope, A. and S. Timmel (1984) *Training for Transformation*, Gweru: Mambo Press

Kaplan, Allan (1996) *The Development Practitioner's Handbook*, London: Pluto Press.

Lindenberg, Marc and Coralie Bryant (2001) *Going Global: Transforming Relief and Development NGOs*, Bloomfield, CT: Kumarian Press.

Merron, Keith (1997) Riding the Wave: Designing Your Organization's Architecture for Enduring Success, New York, NY: John Wiley.

Moore, Mark, L. D. Brown, and J. Honan (2001), 'Toward a Public Value Framework for Accountability and Performance Management for International Non-Governmental Organizations', Discussion paper for the Hauser Center/Keio University Workshop on Accountability for International NGOs, Cambridge, MA: Harvard University, November 2-11.

Oakley, Peter, *et al.* (1991) *Projects with People: the practice of participation in rural development*, Geneva: ILO.

Roche, Chris (1999) 'Impact assessment and advocacy' in *Impact Assessment for Development Agencies: Learning to Value Change*, Oxford: Oxfam.

Senge, Peter (1990) *The Fifth Discipline: The Art and Practice of the Learning Organisation*, New York: Currency Doubleday.

VeneKlasen, Lisa with Valerie Miller (2002) *A New Weave of People, Power and Politics: The Action Guide for Advocacy and Citizen Participation*, Oklahoma City, OK: World Neighbors.

Wycoff, Joyce *et al.* (1995) *Transformation Thinking: Tools and Techniques that Open the Door to Powerful New Thinking for Every Member of Your Organization*, Berkeley, CA: Berkeley Publishing Group.

This paper was first published in Development in Practice *(12/3&4:258-271) in 2002.*

Operationalising bottom-up learning in international NGOs:
barriers and alternatives

Grant Power, Matthew Maury, and Susan Maury

What's wrong with this picture?

In 1995, a leading international NGO (INGO) fielded two community organisers in Harare, Zimbabwe, to live and work with residents of two different urban poor areas.[1] In the ensuing months, the organisers unhurriedly tried to encourage 'bottom-up' development: understand the local situation, build on the local people's material resources, creativity, knowledge, and views, strengthen local collective action, and facilitate a process in which the communities propose and pursue ideas that are organic to them. The workers did not put any funding into the communities for over a year. However, funds for the projects had been raised from private sources under the banner of community-based, sustainable development.

In 1996, the organisers were told by their regional programme manager that they were behind schedule in producing results. The programme director stressed that INGO performance criteria required that communities show progress on specific material improvements within one year. Further delays could result in a cut-off of funds, as donors might think the projects were going nowhere.

The organisers, hoping their bosses would come to understand the communities' perspectives and adjust their expectations, resisted pressure from headquarters to spend money. They believed their work would be undermined if the communities realigned their activities to receive outside funds, rather than rallying around a shared vision of a preferred future relying primarily on their own resources. In the end, under pressure to spend the funds and in danger of losing their jobs, the organisers finally relented. The funding tap was turned on, and the INGO reported to donors in 1997 that the projects were reaching their targeted benchmarks.

Do INGOs have a learning disorder?

The Harare case reflects a tendency in INGO operations to resist allowing communities to lead the development process. Given the choice, many of us in the INGO world still are opting for fast results on the ground while only rhetorically embracing community-based self-development. Producing visible results validates the INGO's activities and secures ongoing funding. Facing uncertainty and rapid change, we tend to make decisions that privilege our organisations' self-preservation. However, the emphasis on achieving rapid, visible results often backfires. While we can 'see' development happening, the less photogenic, but ultimately longer lasting aspects of development, such as local initiative, community cohesion, resilience, self-reliance, and resourcefulness – leading ultimately to self-determination – take a back seat. In other words, INGOs tend to set up internal but largely unrecognised barriers to their own values-driven goals. Observers in the early 1990s attributed this problem to a state of confusion among INGOs regarding their purpose, direction, and identity. However, we believe this incongruity of behaviour to be rooted in a failure to translate new knowledge gained from development experience into changed organisational behaviour. As Edwards (1997) notes, INGOs tend to have difficulty with organisational learning because it requires humility, honesty, openness, and the ability to welcome error. Development institutions, like other organisations, have a natural propensity not to dwell on the past (that is, on mistakes) and to move forward without the painful self-scrutiny necessary to learn from experience.

On the other hand, many INGOs have eagerly embraced organisational learning in principle, following the lead of commercial businesses. This appears to be a step in the right direction, but can in fact be problematic. Although many businesses are developing models of learning practice, neither the for-profit environment nor its corporate structures fit well with the environment and organisational forms needed for grassroots development. Have INGOs mimicked a for-profit model of organisation too closely?

INGOs differ from their for-profit counterparts in important ways. One is the values-driven approach to attaining justice, equity, and empowerment for the poor that most international non-profits share (Hailey 2000). Often these goals are accompanied by the promotion of full stakeholder participation, mutual learning, accountability and transparency, local self-governance, long-term sustainability, and, perhaps above all, a people-centred approach (Korten 1990; Hailey 2000). Much development theory focuses on the benefits of building on these values, and many practitioners develop, test, and share various processes that can be used to promote and further their use.

An alien-hand syndrome

This leads to a second key difference between for-profit and non-profit organisations. From a values-based paradigm, the notion of 'organisation', as borrowed from the for-profit world, can be argued to work against responsiveness to the poor.[2] In a traditional for-profit organisation, there is a direct link between the customer and the success of the business. In general, the business must be responsive to customer needs, or sales will decline and the company will be in danger of liquidation. INGOs and other non-profits, on the other hand, are usually set up to serve marginalised communities that are generally without voice. Whether or not an INGO adequately understands and responds to their needs seldom has an impact on the solvency of the organisation.

In order to remain solvent, the INGO must be responsive to its *donor base* – a group that is neither receiving the organisation's primary services, nor is generally capable of monitoring and ensuring that the INGO is adequately responding to the needs of the poor. While the for-profit world has built-in accountability structures between customer and company, there is a 'disconnect' between the 'customer' and organisation for most non-profits which is inadequately bridged by the donor community. This is a symptom of the *alien-hand syndrome*, an organisational learning disorder which ' ... involves a disconnection between organisation intentions and actions ... Organisations may have clear goals and well-defined routines, yet lack adequate incentives to ensure that actions are consistent with intentions' (Snyder and Cummings 1998). An alien-hand syndrome afflicting INGOs has its origins in a model of organisation and learning borrowed from the for-profit world that is inappropriate to the goals and outcomes of development initiatives, but that is nonetheless beneficial to the INGOs' survivability.

What are the practical implications? An INGO may provide inadequate and at times appalling 'service' to marginalised individuals and communities without any repercussions. As long as the donors are satisfied, the organisation can continue not only to operate but also to grow, thrive, and expand. 'Success' in a developmental sense – that is, empowering poor communities, giving them voice, and developing self-governance skills – may in fact be detrimental to the success of the organisation for two reasons. First, it creates a direct accountability link, which may threaten the organisation's method of operations, focus, mission, and vision. Once the community has voice, it can question or reject the organisation's operational choices. In other words, the INGO faces a conflict of interests – succeeding at its mission could threaten its existence. Therefore, most INGOs, from a self-preservation perspective, prefer to keep accountability links solely with donors and perpetuate the status quo, even though this may fail to empower targeted communities.

Second, donors are generally unenthusiastic about supporting a long, iterative, people-centred process because it may not produce an immediately measurable impact, or may not accomplish the original intention of the intervention. Funding agencies tend to prefer short-term, measurable outputs, which demand a high level of control over decisions and the conditions in which projects are implemented.

This is not to imply that INGOs are conspiring to subvert their own values. But they have significant, unrecognised barriers to aligning behaviour with those values, particularly through learning that comes from communities. Perhaps this is because 'members may see only what the strong culture of the organisation permits them to see' (Snyder and Cummings 1998). Perhaps there has been no push to look for more appropriate models because the sense of self-preservation is strong in any human system. Few have dared to question the system because those who have the ability to do so benefit from the current structure, and those who suffer most from failures in the system do not have a voice adequate to challenge it. To the degree that a conflict persists between an INGO's mission and self-preservation, the former is often, unconsciously, sacrificed. The INGO may not recognise negative consequences because it lacks an effective feedback mechanism and accountability link to communities where the effects are felt.

We are not advocating that INGOs close down or that one type of unidirectional accountability replace another. But we believe INGOs can do better in bringing their practices in line with their core values. For this, INGOs must recognise and correct the power asymmetries embedded within them so that both sustainable development *and* organisational sustainability are possible.

Some INGOs, seeking a solution, are institutionalising a corrective kind of organisational practice – bottom-up learning (BUL). This is a process of comprehensively (re)orienting their operations to the concrete realities of people living in poverty and injustice in vastly diverse local contexts worldwide, and allowing those realities to form the basis for programme designs, fundraising targets and methods, and management policies, plans, and budgets. In a 'bottom-up' approach to learning, organisations strive sensitively to understand people's needs and conditions in each area where they are working, and to allow each community's priorities to determine (not just inform) organisational objectives, methods, timetables, benchmarks, and funding.

Bottom-up organisational learning

Bottom-up organisational learning is a sub-discipline of organisational learning (OL). OL has been defined as a process of developing new knowledge that changes an organisation's behaviour to improve future performance (Garvin 1993).

Such learning is not simply about making better decisions but also about making sense of our perceptions and interpretations of our environment. Organisational learning may be either adaptive (questioning the basic assumptions an organisation holds about itself and the environment) or generative (questioning an organisation's perceptions of both its internal and external relationships) (Barker and Camarata 1998).

The agenda of the 'learning organisation' has likewise been described as a challenge 'to explore ... how we can create organisational structures which are meaningful to people so they can assist, participate and more meaningfully control their own destiny in an unhampered way' (Jones and Hendry 1994:160). In practising bottom-up learning, an organisation makes a moral choice to draw insights and feedback from people at the low end of a socially constructed hierarchy (that is, from those who are most vulnerable in the system). It then refocuses and redefines itself, its operational choices, and its performance measures in light of its accountability to the poor. This is not the only type of learning in which an organisation can, and should, engage, but it provides a counterbalance to other types of learning that may fall short of addressing the alien-hand syndrome. BUL assumes that an organisation sees the most vulnerable part of its constituency as its primary source of legitimacy. A BUL organisation commits itself to work for the liberation of those at the bottom by drawing its own sense of direction and priorities from this group, rather than 'developing' them. As those at the bottom are given a voice and enabled to develop themselves on their own terms, most other stakeholders (including donors, managers, and staff) may also find greater freedom, as they no longer need to control development outcomes in an effort to sustain the life of their organisation. They are instead incorporating the massive resource represented in the partner community.

BUL asks organisations to adapt their internal *structure, systems,* and *culture* to the complex and evolving struggles of those in poverty, including even the choice not to be 'developed'. INGO operations following BUL are comprehensively recalibrated to let go of the controls in community development. They recognise that they need to adapt themselves to environments that are chaotic, uncertain, fraught with risk, unpredictable, not conducive to being standardised, often hard to fund, and which defy linear, quantifiable models for project planning and evaluation. While BUL organisations' roles become pliable and versatile, their mission of strengthening the poor and increasing social justice remains at the forefront. They situate their work inside a broader context of serving and advancing the agendas of organised grassroots social movements, and thus work as often as possible in situations where they can work alongside partners. This partnership helps further the struggle of an established, indigenous, local organisation (or network of organisations) that is embarking on social change, based on the wishes of the local people. Over time, new initiatives may be carved out through mutual agreement and increasing trust.

BUL is contrasted with *organisational pragmatism* in which the primary agenda is to 'adjust' the poor to fit in (and thus benefit from) standardised INGO programmes, usually through the promise or provision of material assistance. Making constituents adjust to an existing programme suggests that the INGO may not acknowledge the uniqueness of the needs and conditions in each new community, preferring (even with the best intentions) to find an 'easier fix', based on time and budget constraints. This is often driven by an overarching premium in INGOs on utilitarian thinking and practice, which states that *'what is useful is true, and what works is good'*. It is based on the false objectivity of a cost-benefit calculation that, while claiming to benefit the poor, in the end works more to protect the interests of employees who benefit most from maintaining the status quo (Murphy 2000). A decision by the newly selected president of a major INGO in 1997 to retain child sponsorship as the organisation's primary (and lucrative) funding vehicle for the sake of financial stability, despite emerging evidence that development outcomes implemented under the sponsorship system were not self-sustaining, is a clear example of such pragmatism.

BUL does not romanticise the poor or suggest that their interests can be easily defined or treated as an unfragmented whole. On the contrary, a core strength of BUL is precisely that it is grounded and realistic in approaching the complexities of poverty and development 'from below'. In short, BUL rejects top-down development programmes, and promotes the interests and priorities of marginalised individuals and groups, so that their voices are not only heard, but can exercise a discrete and overriding influence not only on the actions of INGOs on the ground, but in their internal operations as well.

Theoretical underpinnings

BUL is grounded in a convergence of theories within the disciplines of development studies and organisational psychology. From development theory, we draw from the framework of alternative development, or *democratic development*, depicted by Friedmann (1992), among others. Poverty here is understood mainly as *disempowerment*. Development is a process of vision-driven organising, initially at the local level, which 'focuses explicitly on the moral relations of persons and households, and it draws its values from that sphere rather than from any desire to satisfy material wants, important as these may be' (Friedmann 1992:33).

People's active participation in identifying and addressing forces that marginalise them leads to respect for the diversity and complexity of local communities, and is the most effective and lasting way to remove structural constraints on their development at national and global levels.

This perspective moves development out of the realm of charity and into a moral framework of justice and rights. For development workers, an alternative development commends a position of *solidarity* with the poor. Advocacy with the poor in defence of their rights (to land, capital, and other productive assets) can go hand in hand with sensitive, tailored support for local people's self-development, self-reliance, and increased ability to sustain their own desired improvements. The fundamental questions to be answered in any initiative are 'In whose interest? In whose voice?' (Murphy 2000).

Even when we embrace an alternative, democratic development paradigm, we still need further conceptual tools to undertake BUL. In this regard, the theoretical literature on organisational learning in the NGO sector is thin, but initial inroads have been made. Korten (1990), building on people-centred development theory, offers an organisational typology in which young NGOs tend to focus on charity but mature (fourth-generation) NGOs on solidarity. Coopey (1995) and Snell and Chak (1998) build an argument for 'learning empowerment' in organisations through constitutionally protected democratic rights and obligations for all members, coupled with a culture of developmental leadership. In this connection, Srivastva *et al.* (1995:44) look to INGOs to initiate 'the discovery and mobilisation of innovative social/organisational architectures that make possible human cooperation across previously polarising or arbitrary constraining boundaries'. Presumably, organisations advocating such broad participation by societies' members in the face of the 'stark legislative pressure of governments' would themselves be bottom-up learners. Elliott (1999) begins to address this issue by arguing that NGOs themselves are most likely to become effective learners through a broadly authentically participative process of appreciative inquiry, similar to the process now being used to facilitate change in some 'flat' corporations.

The ambitious changes implied by BUL may seem utopian to seasoned INGO workers. However, a movement among some INGOs in this direction (described below) suggests there is interest and the possibility of making real and lasting change. We believe that by recognising and directly addressing the built-in barriers many INGOs have to utilising BUL principles fully, great strides can be made in increasing INGO impact. To this end, we now look at some hopeful alternatives and discuss how barriers can be minimised or eliminated, leading to successful community empowerment.

Signs of mission-centred thinking – and practice

Development practice has come a long way since the 1940s, when many INGOs were first formed. From an initial focus on providing immediate needs, development theory and practice have matured to include such considerations as community empowerment and self-governance, gender equality and opportunity, solidarity and voice, advocacy issues, economic advancement, and political recognition and participation. Most development practitioners express an understanding of and commitment to the importance of helping communities to self-develop, and they recognise the danger of providing goods and services without some sort of community input or response (note the proliferation of food-for-work or labour-for-development models in the past decade or so). The principles are known and understood, and attempts have been made to put them into practice.

Specifically, research and practice in the sub-fields of community research and evaluation have tended to reflect progressive thinking. The development and wide dissemination of tools used in Participatory Rural Appraisal and Participatory Learning and Action (PRA and PLA) methods show a hunger for appropriate tools and methodologies for engaging local communities in the development process. Programme evaluation increasingly draws on participatory techniques and processes as well, with many organisations reporting positive results. Additionally, new breakthroughs in organisational theory are helping development organisations rethink their internal processes and external delivery systems from top to bottom.

The evolution of theory and practice has been rapid, and many organisations report positive results in using these methods. Yet, despite the practical application of BUL principles, many of the same problems stemming from values conflicts continue to afflict INGOs. Why is this? We argue that good practice at the field level is not sufficient where organisational practice inhibits or retards learning from field outcomes. Organisational structure and practice is seldom in alignment with development principles, but rather adheres to principles which ensure self-preservation and perpetuation, as reflected in policies and procedures, reporting practices, and relationships with communities of need as well as donors and the general public. Development practice is compartmentalised to *field* practice, and is not allowed to permeate the organisation as a whole. Assumptions about what is good for the organisation as an institution lead to stability and self-perpetuation, but also shut out the potential learning and change that adopting BUL principles offers as reward. Not only do these operating principles restrict institutional development, organisational practice at times reaches down and inhibits the implementation of good field practice (as the Harare case illustrates). Often, tools such as PRA or participatory evaluation methods may be employed but are not allowed to inform fully what occurs in the community, or else community members are given the promise of self-determination, only to have it pulled away when their outcomes conflict with organisational priorities. The following section will briefly outline areas where barriers tend to exist, and some suggestions for removing or minimising them.

Barriers and alternatives

Community interaction

Barrier: most INGO interactions with community groups can be defined by a single input: money. While there are often attempts to build a more holistic partnership, once funds are introduced the relationship becomes one of power held by the INGO with the community often forced to respond 'appropriately' to INGO's real or perceived wishes in order to secure the elusive funds. Some INGOs have sought to mitigate this effect by working through local community organisations or local NGOs. However, the unequal power relationship generally is transferred to this relationship as well. Ashman (2000) observes that formal agreements as written by INGOs (a) almost always ensure upward (rather than mutual) accountability; (b) are bounded by timelines too short for effective development (usually three years); and (c) suffer from a lack of mutual agreement on the terms for ending funding (tending to be INGO driven).

Potential alternatives: it is difficult to separate the link between funding and power. One radical but seriously proposed solution is to redirect the attention currently placed on funding towards organisational autonomy. For example, in working directly with communities, more INGOs are providing training in the skills required for self-governance. The aim is to enable communities to use appropriate methods to self-assess their current situation, develop a vision for their desired future, develop a plan *for themselves* (and not reliant on an external agency) and move towards that vision, self-monitor progress, and finally evaluate the results and adjust future plans as necessary. In this scenario, the power lies not in the funds but in the skills and self-knowledge that are developed *and remain* in the community, including appropriate methods for guiding and directing action and reflection.

If an INGO's primary input to communities is the ability to govern the process of self-development, an implication is that the INGO also changes *as an organisation*, including administration, fundraising, and management. In practice, INGOs might still introduce funding, but mainly to promote communities' self-development plans by linking them to other organisations or perhaps offering small grants or low-interest loans to finance planned activities. Other concepts that have been tried and have met with success include teaching small business and budgeting skills for locally based enterprises, or providing scholarships for specialised schooling that result in stronger local leadership. These approaches de-emphasise the receipt of a large cheque and instead look at building skills that lead to autonomy and independence.

Because such intensive, hands-on activities often demand a deep sensitivity and familiarity with local needs and conditions, we believe it may be most effective if INGOs go beyond decentralising their operations and *cease being operational* in the field. This can be done by forging ties with autonomous local NGOs that have a proven commitment and track record in handing over controls in the development process to the communities where they are working. To the degree that terms for partnership can be negotiated equitably, the imperative for standardised and impersonal mass reproduction of one strategy, which ironically is often only magnified (rather than adapted) in the process of decentralisation, can be significantly curtailed.

Systems and procedures

Barrier: organisational systems and procedures are too often excused as a 'necessary evil' in meeting bureaucratic requirements. We contend that many systems and procedures are inappropriate for attaining the goals of most INGOs and may work to limit their effectiveness and impact. For example, standard INGO accounting and management information systems (MIS) are complex and require individuals in the field who have specialised training to operate them effectively. It can be difficult to find accountants who are adequately trained in computer skills (much less a specific accounting or MIS package), and INGOs often find they spend excessive resources recruiting, training, and then losing these individuals (who once trained are valuable to other INGOs). Additionally, the reporting required for these systems often forces accommodation at all levels of the organisation, reaching to the community level. At times this may require field staff to be hired and trained simply to fill and submit reports to the INGO national office on behalf of the community.

Programme planning and reporting are another key barrier. Instruments now widely used by INGOs, such as the logical framework approach (LogFrame), were originally developed by and for engineers and planners in heavy industry. LogFrame models fit with the way that INGOs and donors typically budget and package projects, but they are alien to community processes and understanding, and can prevent communities from driving the development process. A few years ago, a staff member from one large INGO sat down with community representatives from a historically nomadic tribe in Botswana to discuss the annual INGO planning and budgeting forms. When she posed the question, 'What would you like to see accomplished and funded by the end of next year?' she was met with silence. After several minutes of dialogue in the local dialect, someone responded, 'How can we plan for the next year when we do not know if we will be alive tomorrow?'. INGO planning and reporting procedures usually cannot accommodate people with such vastly different worldviews, even though these procedures are sometimes claimed to be necessary to empower communities.

Potential alternatives: the goal here is not to require the *programme* to accommodate the systems, but rather the other way around. It is important to build systems and procedures starting from the community's needs and abilities, rather than expecting communities to conform to organisational or donor requirements. Appropriate methods of accounting, planning, and reporting would allow community groups to self-report back to the INGO. This not only frees valuable staff time, it also puts the responsibility for action where it should be – on the community. As long as staff members are responsible for reporting on the 'INGO's projects', they will remain the INGO's projects in the eyes of the community. This means that reporting systems and procedures need to be appropriate for community use – ideally that community groups actually use the information and processes for their self-development, and not merely to meet reporting requirements. By developing systems in response to community needs, it probably means that INGOs would need to abandon their high dependency on computer-based reports, graphs, and charts, and replace them with methods and processes that are meaningful to local people in vastly diverse settings. Examples include plans, accounts, and reports developed using pictures, graphics, or narrative stories which are appropriate to communities and to BUL.

Donor and public relations

Barriers: in the late 1970s, as he was about to retire, the founder and president of one large INGO looked back over the organisation's history. In considering its past and present difficulties, he reflected in a moment of unusual candour that the organisation had erred when it began to believe what it was telling donors about itself. Today, we might add that

INGOs err to the degree they believe what they are telling donors about poverty and development. Educating constituents and donors about the complexity of international development seems largely out of fashion among INGOs. What passes for public education tends to be slanted towards child sponsorship and emergency appeals. Public relations systems rely on a continuous stream of uncomplicated success stories (Edwards 1997) that not only obscure community realities but skip over problems in the performance of the organisations themselves. While there are notable exceptions, the central tendency, with scale, is for INGOs to increase gloss and decrease substance in donor communications. The reason, INGO resource-development personnel argue, is that donors will not fund complexity, process, and ambiguity. Like business investors, they want clear results, now. INGOs give donors what donors are saying they want. As discussed earlier, this creates barriers to development by the poor: first, it unduly restricts the focus of accountability to donor expectations, which do not adequately address the aspirations of marginalised people in distant lands. Second, it may create long-term barriers to complex, messy, but potentially much more long-lasting and far-reaching development efforts.

Potential alternatives: admittedly, it can be difficult for large INGOs to make the time and effort necessary to educate a populace on the complexities of international development. However, some organisations have taken on the task as part of their call to advocacy. One Australian development organisation, for example, employs staff to work with their base of church supporters to provide seminars and workshops to explore difficult development issues, thus providing individuals and the church as an institution with a deeper understanding of and commitment to international work. Fundraising is an opportunity to advocate for people's rights with a particular audience. INGOs using a rights-based framework are able to facilitate a process of mutual transformation (involving both donors and communities) as donors (both institutional and individual) respect communities' discretion over their own future and learn from them as partners on a common journey, rather than 'helping' them meet externally imposed criteria. Ultimately, a donor who is involved in this deeper way will prove more beneficial to communities, and may in turn be more enriched personally, than one who is fed success stories and quantitative data showing community improvement.

In our experience, INGOs' failure to restrain the level of controls on development in order to 'protect' their funds has the effect of further crippling the poor. Because accountability for genuine self-policing in INGO funding policies is almost totally lacking right now, one alternative is to establish a global funding 'watchdog' organisation modelled on the National Committee for Responsive Philanthropy (NCRP) in the USA. The NCRP educates US donor publics on the practices of various funding organisations and related government policies, rating them on the basis of their degree of respect for community self-determination and commitment to empowerment.

Feedback loops

Barriers: perhaps the most challenging aspect of organisational learning is to develop the feedback loops that allow for bottom-up transformation and mutual accountability. Some of the barriers to establishing effective feedback loops have already been mentioned, such as reporting systems. Elsewhere, INGOs will conduct extensive evaluations and collect information from their beneficiaries, only to have the report sit on a shelf with no realistic way to act on the findings. The beneficiaries themselves are sometimes blamed for their unhappiness with the programme, often linked to their 'unwillingness' to conform to programme requirements. Field staff are generally the best conduit of information and impressions from the beneficiaries to upper management levels – but they may carry biases of their own, selectively hearing and interpreting what is communicated from the communities. This information may or may not be passed back up the chain, or it may be misrepresented in some way. Without a direct link to the beneficiaries, impressions and informal reports of this kind are seldom triangulated and verified but often have a powerful impact on organisational attitude and practice. Even where field staff have excellent relations with communities, field positions are often considered 'entry level', and good fieldworkers are quickly promoted up the ladder and away from direct contact with the local population. The ultimate barrier is the lack of direct contact or practical formal feedback flows from the communities to the INGO (although, interestingly, communication is often solid in the other direction). This barrier is just as serious for non-operational INGOs, who may not bother to investigate directly the realities they are seeking to address and are wary of offending their local NGO partners if they appear to be 'going around' them.

Potential alternatives: if an organisation truly is embracing BUL as a critical foundation of good development practice, it must find viable ways *as an organisation* to listen and respond to the concerns and perceptions of its host communities. Recent breakthroughs in organisational theory are helping INGOs rethink their internal processes and external delivery systems from top to bottom. A key example may be the tools of appreciative inquiry, which in some cases can lead INGOs to make radical, organisation-wide changes based on a participatory process. All stakeholder groups are invited to consider the possibilities of strategic change based on both a desired future and a 'positive present'.

Some INGOs are experimenting with governance structures that include formal feedback loops. For example, representatives of the INGO's target population are elected to a General Assembly which meets once yearly at the Annual General Meeting. During this time, they confirm and retire board members, hear a report on the organisation's activities over the past year, review budget-to-actual information, and confirm the coming year's plan and budget. This builds a direct accountability structure between the beneficiaries and the organisation's activities and expenditures, while also modelling and providing experience in genuine self-governance. Does a model of this nature complicate things for the organisation? Most certainly! But it also seeks to model principles of development *throughout the entire organisation* which are more consistent with its mission than a more pragmatic approach.

The way forward

The alien-hand syndrome in INGOs raises uncomfortable questions. Whose needs (and interests) have we privileged in the past, and why? How can those at the bottom of society gain a decisive voice in INGO planning and operations? How do strategies for re-tooling operations for downward accountability become adopted by an entire organisation, rather than a small group of thoughtful individuals within it – especially in an organisation as departmentally fragmented as most INGOs are? How can we find courage to face our collective and unconscious resistance to change? What is blocking us from respectfully engaging the community in a partnership of negotiation that leads to *mutual* use of pertinent information – collection, analysis, and interpretation – and to decisions that are made jointly, implemented jointly, and evaluated and adjusted jointly?

We have proposed BUL as a normative framework for INGOs as they confront an alien-hand syndrome in their operations, replacing systems of control with tools for facilitating mutual learning and community-based sustainable development that can have an impact throughout the entire organisation. Our discussion of INGO barriers to learning, and of current experiments in institutionalising BUL, presupposes the existence of a *process of learning* in organisations that is understood, accepted, and accessible. In reality, our understanding of how organisations learn is still in its infancy. Recent studies on this subject in the government and business sectors may be helpful to INGOs, as they work through the questions posed above. In addition, we believe two process-related steps may be helpful as INGOs begin to put BUL into practice.

First, INGOs might begin by engaging in *second-order learning*, or *learning how they learn*. Here, INGOs focus on their inward process of developing and spreading new understandings across their departments and programme sites. They also might consider ways in which they may be resisting change that is needed in order to align their practices with their core values. Is it possible that INGOs do not want to know about some hidden dimension of themselves, or might have to un-learn something, or change what they are doing even to the point of reducing budgets or losing employment? Is it possible that communities we have tried to help have in fact been harmed because we chose not to assess critically the outcomes of our actions? Will we have to redirect ourselves radically? Are we allowing our fear of the implications of such learning to make us block needed change?

Second, INGOs in this process will need to face up to the political implications of becoming downwardly accountable. This could mean opening more space for equal exchange with local partner organisations and grassroots communities in their operations. Internal champions of such steps may not be enough. BUL may only come about if INGOs move towards adopting flatter, more democratic structures and dramatically revamping administrative, fundraising, and staffing systems and policies to let communities take control of their own development. In addition, BUL promotes partnerships with local NGOs that are autonomous, or without any dependent linkages to an INGO. In short, INGOs will need to move towards truly participatory management in an open system, tying sustainability of their operations to authentic sustainable development on the ground (Johnson and Wilson 1999). In this regard, the meanings, processes, and output of development become a matter to be negotiated between equals, with no predetermined outcomes, and involving INGOs, local partner organisations, and their constituent communities.

In the short term, BUL organisations may find it necessary to make some painful changes, and possibly shrink their operations as they redirect and retool themselves for less controlling and fewer hands-on roles in development. However, it is noteworthy that those INGOs already putting the interests of poor communities ahead of other interests, with a clear commitment to downward accountability, are increasingly able to operate with moral and structural integrity, gain deeper respect and trust with the communities where they work, and see those communities empowered. *These* invisible assets are the surest indicators of their viability and effectiveness, whatever their other stakeholders' interests may be.

Notes

1   We define international NGO (INGO) as a non-profit development agency with global operations whose mission is (among other things) to assist the poor through community development. Examples include CARE, Oxfam, Save the Children, World Vision, and other similar groups. The names of INGOs have been omitted from our examples to avoid unfairly singling out specific organisations that are facing problems or challenges endemic to the INGO sector as a whole.

2   It is difficult to find a phrase that adequately captures the intended target population of most INGOs without sounding over-simplistic. We use the term 'poverty' to indicate disempowerment, and the term 'poor' to indicate lack of choice and marginalisation from formal political and social institutions. Many within this population also fall within the lower fortieth percentile of the GNP within their respective countries. Having said this, we realise the terms used here do not adequately to reflect the diversity in terms of gender, urban versus rural settings, working

poor versus the unemployed, issues of stigma, and vast socio-cultural differences found throughout the world.

References

Ashman, Darcy (2000) 'Strengthening north-south partnerships: addressing structural barriers to mutual influence', IDR Reports 16(4).

Barker, Randolph T. and Martin R. Camarata (1998) 'The role of communication in creating and maintaining a learning organisation: preconditions, indicators, and disciplines', *Journal of Business Communication* 35(4):443-467.

Coopey, John (1995) 'The learning organisation, power, politics, and ideology', *Management Learning* 26(2):193-213.

Edwards, Michael (1997) 'Organisational learning in non-governmental organisations: what have we learned?', *Public Administration and Development* 17:235-250.

Elliott, Charles (1999) *Locating the Energy for Change: An Introduction to Appreciative Inquiry*, Winnipeg: International Institute for Sustainable Development.

Friedmann, John (1992) *Empowerment: The Politics of Alternative Development*, Cambridge, MA: Blackwell.

Garvin, David A. (1993) 'Building a learning organization', *Harvard Business Review* July-August:78-91.

Hailey, John (2000) 'Indicators of identity: NGOs and the strategic imperative of assessing core values', *Development in Practice* 10(3&4):402-407.

Johnson, Hazel and Gordon Wilson (1999) 'Institutional sustainability as learning', *Development in Practice* 9(1&2):43-55.

Jones, Alan M. and Chris Hendry (1994) 'The learning organisation: adult learning and organisational transformation', *British Journal of Management* 5:153-162.

Korten, David (1990) *Getting to the Twenty-first Century: Voluntary Action and the Global Agenda*, West Hartford, CT: Kumarian.

Murphy, Brian K. (2000) 'International NGOs and the challenge of modernity', *Development in Practice* 10(3&4):330-347.

Snell, Robin and Almaz Man-Kuen Chak (1998) 'The Learning Organisation: learning and empowerment for whom?', *Management Learning* 29(3):337-364.

Snyder, William and Thomas Cummings (1998) 'Organisation learning disorders: conceptual model and intervention hypotheses', *Human Relations* 51(7):873-895.

Srivastva, Suresh, Diana Bilimoria and David Cooperrider (1995) 'Management and organisation learning for positive global change', *Management Learning* 26(1):37-54.

This paper was first published in Development in Practice (*12/3&4:272-284*) *in 2002.*

Should development agencies have Official Views?

David Ellerman

Introduction: a 'Church' or 'party' organisation versus a 'learning organisation'

In the world today, most organisations want to be seen as 'learning organisations' that emphasise the importance of the accumulation of 'intellectual capital' and 'knowledge management'. Yet many old habits persist that are in direct contradiction to learning and to the advancement of knowledge. Church- or political party-like organisations proselytising their own dogmas apply the new rhetoric of 'learning' as a veneer. (Throughout this article, I use both the 'Church' and 'Communist Party' metaphors to indicate unitary organisations espousing certain 'truths' or messages instead of being engaged in an open-ended search for knowledge.)

Focusing on an organisation or agency involved in knowledge-based development assistance (such as the World Bank) operating as a 'knowledge bank', the main question I seek to address is: how can such an agency function as a learning organisation? I approach this question by first considering some of the major roadblocks in the way of organisational learning, before launching into a discussion of the open learning model and how development agencies can become learning organisations.

Roadblock to learning No. 1: branded knowledge as dogma

To put it simply, the basic problem is that in spite of the espoused model of a 'learning organisation', the theory-in-use of a development agency is often a model of a 'development church' giving definitive *ex cathedra* 'views' on the substantive and controversial questions of development. As with the dogmas of a Church, the brand name of the organisation is invested with its views. Once an 'Official View' has been adopted, then to question it is to attack the agency itself and the value of its franchise. As a result, new learning at the expense of established Official Views is not encouraged. Thus when licensing an Official View, the authorities need to have what Milton called the 'grace of infallibility and incorruptibleness' (see Morley 1928:218), since any subsequent 'learning' is tantamount to disloyalty.

When an agency adopts Official Views, then discussions between the agency staff and its clients is a pseudo-dialogue, given that the former are not free unilaterally to change Official Views (just as missionaries are not free to approve local variations in Church dogmas) or to approve of a project that departs substantially from those views. The slogan is something like: 'Give the clients an inch of nuance, and they'll take a mile of status quo' (Kanbur and Vines 2000:101). Clients are like Henry Ford's Model T customers who were free to choose any colour car so long as it was black. The clients who wish to receive assistance are free to 'learn' and to 'make up their own minds' so long as they do so in conformity with Official Views.

There is little motivation for the staff actively to appropriate or understand any deeper rationale for the views since they must espouse the Official Views *vis-à-vis* the clients in any case. The views are generally not those that individual staff members have decided upon personally based on evidence or argumentation. In project design, the herd instinct takes over. If a manager designs a project in conformity with Official Views and the project fails, then those involved in the project can hardly be blamed for the outcome of their team efforts.

Publicly airing ambivalence or discontent about the Official Views outside the confines of the agency is frowned upon. The reasoning is standard: parents should not argue in front of the children; doctors should not debate in front of the patients. There can be debate inside the party but once a decision is made, then the members must publicly adhere to the party line. The Church or party model fits perfectly with the standard 'dissemination' or transmission-belt methodology of knowledge-based development assistance. The agency believes it holds the best 'knowledge for development' and is to transmit it to the recipients in the developing world through various forms of aid-baited proselytisation.

What is the alternative? The organisation of science provides the paradigm example of an 'ecology of knowledge' where the open and public contestation of ideas and criticism of conjectures is essential and actively encouraged:

Criticism of our conjectures is of decisive importance: by bringing out our mistakes it makes us understand the difficulties of the problem which we are trying to solve. This is how we become better acquainted with our problems, and able to propose more mature solutions: the very refutation of a theory – that is, of any serious tentative solution to our problem – is always a step forward that takes us nearer to the truth ... Since none of [the theories] can be positively justified, it is essentially their critical and progressive character – the fact that we can argue about their claim to solve our problems better than their competitors – which constitutes the rationality of science.
(Popper 1965:vii)

Another example of the 'ecology of knowledge' is provided by the modern Western university. The university does not set itself up as an arbiter of truth, but as an arena within which contrary theories can be examined and can collide in open debate. As Barrington Moore Jr has noted, 'among contemporary social arrangements the modern western university is the main one that has endeavoured to make intellectual criticism and innovation a legitimate and regular aspect of the prevailing social order' (Moore 1972:91). The organisation does not itself have Official Views or 'messages' on the questions of the day – and thus it does not need a public relations department to monitor and control the propagating of Official Views to the press.

When an agency takes Official Views on complex questions of development and considers its views as branded knowledge, then the genuine collision of adverse opinions and the rule of critical reasoning tend to give way to the rule of authority and bureaucratic reasoning within the hierarchy of the organisation (The 'Soviet Theory of Genetics' based on Trofim Denisovich Lysenko's work is a good example of this). While a sort-of-debate may be 'encouraged' within the agency, the perimeter of that discussion is framed, not coincidentally, by the jurisdiction of organisational authority. Debate should not stray beyond its pale into the public domain where the authorities have no writ. The authorities in the organisation determine 'the Official Views' and tend to shut off or 'embargo' any feedback loops that may call into question those views, thereby diminishing the 'franchise value' of the 'brand name' – not to mention reflecting poorly on the wisdom of the authorities who sanctioned the views in the first place. Learning from errors, which involves changing 'Official Views' and modifying 'branded knowledge', is minimised, so that the organisation tends to function more as a Church- or party-type organisation than as an open learning one – regardless of the espoused theory.

The Church/party model of proselytising directly contradicts autonomous or self-directed learning in the client countries (see below for more on the Socratic rationale for not having Official Views). The standard dissemination or transmission-belt methodology inhibits learning in a similar manner. The project manager from the agency wants the clients to 'learn' as long as they learn 'the right thing'. Any genuinely self-directed learning process in the client country may veer off in the 'wrong direction', which the project manager cannot withstand. The project manager would return to headquarters as a failure without a project. Therefore, the flow of knowledge must be carefully managed to prevent the clients from being distracted by alternative views.

Roadblock to learning No. 2: funded assumptions as dogma

Why is it so necessary for a development agency to take an Official View on the 'One Best Way' to solve a development problem? One common answer is that a development agency is not a university; the agency puts money as loans or grants behind projects based on various assumptions. Since university professors do not 'put their money where their mouth is', they are free to debate questions for ever. Once an agency has committed significant resources to certain assumptions, then it becomes necessary to 'fall in line' and support the funded assumption.

But while there may be obvious bureaucratic reasons why individual project managers and their superiors would like a funded project assumption to be treated as 'gospel', that does not explain why the whole institution should take such a stand. The commitment of funds and prestige even seems to alter perceptions.[1] For instance, subjective assessments of winning probabilities tend to increase after the bets have been placed at a race track, but horses do not run faster when bets are riding on them. Theories are corroborated by evidence, not by funding commitments. Many businesses have come to grief because managers would not revisit strategies after initial costs were sunk. In view of the record of international development aid (see, for example, Easterly 2001), there is little support for the similar practice of hardening project assumptions into gospel simply because funds have been committed.

Roadblock to learning No. 3: 'social science' as dogma

Today, 'science' has long since replaced religious authority as the source of dogmas that one can appeal to without further reasoning or corroboration, even though that line of argumentation completely misrepresents the scientific method, not to mention the role of critical thinking. But the all-too-human factors that previously made Church dogma appealing have not suddenly disappeared in today's scientific age, so one should expect the appeal to 'science' to be thoroughly abused. This is nowhere truer than in the social sciences (see Andreski 1972). Economics is the 'rooster who rules the roost' in the social sciences, so one should expect much to be passed off in the name of 'economics'. Yet many of the theses imposed by bureaucratic power as the 'Truths of Economics' would not pass without serious challenge in any open scientific forum – particularly when one goes beyond academic model building to policy applications. One example that springs to mind is the role in the Russian reform debacle played by Harvard economic geniuses and the Western agencies who tried to 'install' the institutions of a market economy (see Ellerman 2001).

It is particularly unfortunate when a Tayloristic 'One Best Way' (OBW) mentality creeps into development policy making in the name of 'science' (see Kanigel 1997). The problems of developing and transition countries are far too complex to yield to formulaic 'best practices' and 'magic bullets'. Many different approaches need to be tried on an experimental basis, so when a major development agency forsakes experimentalism to stake its reputation on the 'One Best Way', then the development effort as a whole is impoverished.

The idea that a development agency always has to have an Official View (rather than house competing views) is about as scientific as the 'scientific' socialism of the communist parties of the past. John Dewey quotes the English Communist John Strachey's statement that the communist parties' 'refusal to tolerate the existence of incompatible opinions ... [is] simply asserting the claim that Socialism is scientific'. Dewey goes on to comment that it 'would be difficult, probably impossible, to find a more direct and elegantly finished denial of all the qualities that make ideas and theories either scientific or democratic than is contained in this statement' (Dewey 1939:96). Critical reasoning and scientific methodology go in quite the opposite direction of fostering the

willingness to hold belief in suspense, ability to doubt until evidence is
obtained; willingness to go where evidence points instead of putting first a
personally preferred conclusion; [and the] ability to hold ideas in solution and
use them as hypotheses to be tested instead of as dogmas to be asserted ...
(Dewey 1939:145)

This part of the scientific attitude is translated into the policy domain with such suggestions as multiple advocacy (Haas 1990:210) and double visioning (see Schön 1983:281). But it is not some wanton perversity that prevents this scientific attitude from being implemented in a large organisation such as a major development agency. There are quiet human impulses that push for conformity and rigidity:

To hold theories and principles in solution, awaiting confirmation, goes
contrary to the grain. Even today questioning a statement made by a person
is often taken by him as a reflection upon his integrity, and is resented. For
many millennia opposition to views widely held in a community was
intolerable. It called down the wrath of the deities who are in charge of the
group ... Baconian idols of the tribe, the cave, the theater, and den have
caused men to rush to conclusions, and then to use all their powers to defend
from criticism and change the conclusions arrived at.
(Dewey 1939:146)

Roadblock to learning No. 4: the rage to conclude

Albert O. Hirschman has often noted the problems created in developing countries by the tendency that Flaubert ridiculed as *la rage de vouloir conclure*, or the rage to conclude (see Hirschman 1973:238-240). The same attitude is rampant in development agencies. Indeed, this is another self-reinforcing lock-in between development agencies and their client countries.

[Policy makers] will be supplied with a great many ideas, suggestions, plans,
and ideologies, frequently of foreign origin or based on foreign experience ...
Genuine learning about the problem will sometimes be prevented not only
by the local policy makers' eagerness to jump to a ready-made solution but
also by the insistent offer of help and advice on the part of powerful outsiders
... [S]uch practices [will] tend to cut short that 'long confrontation between
man and a situation' (Camus) so fruitful for the achievement of genuine
progress in problem-solving.
(Hirschman 1973:239-240)

The puzzles that development agencies face about inducing economic and social development are perhaps the most complex and ill-defined questions confronting humankind. Donald Schön (1971, 1983) noted the novel complexity, genuine uncertainty, conflict of values, unique circumstances, and structural instabilities that plague problems of social transformation and preclude definitive blueprint solutions. Yet one must marvel at the tendency of the major development agencies to rush forward with universal 'best practices'[2] – a tendency based not on any methods resembling social science but on a bureaucratic need to maintain élite prestige by 'having an answer' for the client. In contrast, every field of science is populated by competing theories, and scientists do not feel the need to artificially rush to closure just to 'have an answer'.

Consider, for example, the complex problem of fighting corruption. Economists might approach the topic by trying to minimise government-imposed discretionary regulations which present rent-seeking opportunities to officials who might offer to relax a restriction for appropriate compensation. Accountants might emphasise transparency and uniformity of data and the independence of auditing. Civil servants might emphasise codes of ethics, organisational morale, and disclosure requirements. Lawyers might encourage civil discovery procedures and criminal sanctions. Others will promote a free and independent press, a high standard of public ethics, and a vigorous civil society. There are clearly many ways to approach the topic and so a multi-pronged approach rather than a 'One Best Way' seems advisable. Yet the dogmatic mentality might express alarm and dismay when different groups from the same international development agency take different approaches to fighting corruption and these different views are aired openly. Why can't the international agency 'get its act together' and tell the client the One Best Way to address the problem?

When journalists try to 'build a story' by pointing out differences within a development agency, then agency bureaucrats should point out the necessity of the open clash of adverse opinions to intellectual progress (perhaps with references to Mill's *On Liberty* or the history of science). They should point out that the real story is the intellectual honesty and integrity of an agency willing to have such open discussions, which are the lifeblood of intellectual and scientific progress. Instead, PR-oriented bureaucrats are more typically alarmed at the lack of 'coordination of messages' and re-dedicate themselves to better 'vetting' the public statements of agency officials and researchers, a tragi-comic effort usually carried out in the name of 'quality control'.

The Church/party approach has implications for the question of client-centred versus paternalistic approaches to client learning. What would be 'wrong' with an international development organisation acknowledging, and listeners or readers realising, that reasonable people within the same agency may differ on the remarkably complex questions of development? Indeed, such a realisation might have the rather positive effect of encouraging listeners or readers to reflect upon the matter more seriously and thereby take some responsibility in forming their own opinions.[3] In short, it would foster active learning rather than promoting passive acceptance of the 'truth' promulgated by a Church- or party-like organisation.

Often the argument is that 'Yes, there are doubts and differences within the agency, but the agency must show a united front in order to steel the resolve of the clients trying to implement a difficult programme of social and economic change.' Perhaps the clear resolve of the agency's Official View and the possibility of conditioning aid on the acceptance of that reform package will tip the domestic balance between reform and anti-reform coalitions in a developing country in favour of the former and bring the internal advocates of that view to power. But there are several problems with this line of argument. First, it implicitly assumes a Jacobinic (or market-Bolshevik) rather than an adaptive and experimentalist strategy of change. Indeed, a Jacobin-Bolshevik strategy does assume a fanatical resolve that cannot publicly entertain doubts, but that is one of the many problems with such a philosophy of social change. An adaptive, experimental, or pragmatic approach requires no such certitude and in fact welcomes a variety of parallel experiments in multiple regions or sectors to see what works (the social and economic reforms undertaken in China over the past two decades are a good example of this). Second, this argument assumes that the client is deriving its reform motivation from the agency, and not from within its ranks. Third, while Hirschman notes that this imagined sequence is not impossible, 'it is our conviction that this picture of program aid as a catalyst for virtuous policies belongs to the realm of rhapsodic phantasy' (1971:205).

The open learning model and autonomy-compatible assistance

Surely much has been learned about economic development. What is wrong, one might ask, with espousing the best practices from successful development efforts as well as promoting underlying guiding principles? Should international development organisations just be agnostic on the questions of development and treat all opinions as having equal weight? To approach these questions, it is useful to consider the methodology of science. Science as a loosely structured international open learning organisation is hardly agnostic in any given area. All opinions are not given equal weight. Certain theories have so far run the gauntlet of criticism better than others, so they are accepted as the 'received' or current theories in a field. The difference from a more dogmatic Church- or party-type approach lies in the methodology used to sustain or overturn the hypotheses. In mathematics, it is inter-subjectively verifiable proof, not authority, that is the basis for theorems. In the empirical sciences, hypotheses are developed on the basis of intellectual coherence and factual cues, and are then openly subjected to experiments that can be inter-subjectively verified and reproduced (for example, as in the 'cold fusion' controversy). As long as inter-subjective verification remains the touchstone of any scientific theory, then no theory needs, in principle, to be accepted on the basis of authority. Science does not operate on the basis of brand names. Adding the brand name of an agency to a thesis in order to make it an Official View *adds nothing of scientific value* to the thesis. Indeed, the association of bureaucratic power with the thesis tends to corrupt the operation of critical thinking.

This methodology of science shows, at least in general terms, how an open learning model of a knowledge-based development agency might translate into assistance that is compatible with the autonomy of the client. The important thing is not to teach a client country the 'truth' but first to ensure that all major positions on a controversial question are presented, and second (and of greater long-term importance), to foster the active learning methodology within the country in order to find and corroborate or disprove the hypotheses and theories. That means capacity building in the knowledge institutions of the country.

When theories clash then experiments should be encouraged to 'see what works'. Indeed, there are usually different decentralised experiments going on in a country (sometimes called 'moving trains') often unbeknownst to government officials. As Hirschman has noted, 'the hidden rationalities I was after were precisely and principally *processes of growth and change already under way* in the societies I studied, processes that were often unnoticed by the actors immediately involved, as well as by foreign experts and advisors' (Hirschman 1984:91-93). Where the train of reform is already moving on its own, then reformers can jump on board to attempt to help it run more smoothly. The 'moving trains' can be held up as models and benchmarks for other reform efforts in the country. Everett Rogers (1983:Chapter 9) describes decentralised diffusion systems for social innovations with the primary example being the Chinese system of 'models' (e.g. model communes or enterprises) dating from the beginning of the modern reform period in the 1970s and forming an important part of the most remarkable growth episode in history (the 'Chinese economic miracle' of the 1980s and 1990s).

For instance, if a knowledge-based development agency wants to promote the OBW of reforming or changing certain institutions (e.g. the 'best' model for fighting corruption or the 'best' form of privatisation), then it should be willing to share the source of that 'knowledge', to promote experiments to corroborate hypotheses or to validate a local adaptation, and to encourage horizontal cross-learning from similar experiments documented in the organisation's knowledge management system – all before the reform is accepted as a 'blueprint' for any country as a whole. In short, the inter-subjectivity and reproducibility that are key to scientific knowledge translate into *local* experimentation and verification in the case of development knowledge. The message to policy makers should run along these lines:

> To the best of our accumulated experience (which we deem to call 'knowledge'), here is what works best in countries like yours. Why don't you study these principles together with their corroboration to date (best practice success stories), take a look at these case studies, contact the people who designed those reforms, set up horizontal learning programmes with those best practice cases, and try some experiments to see what works in various parts of your own country? After carrying out this learning process on your own, you might call us back if you feel we could help by partially but not wholly funding the reform programme you have decided upon.

The most important thing is to get away from a paternalistic model of 'teaching' as the transmission of knowledge from the development agency to the developing country. Using the slogan, 'Stop the teaching so that the learning can begin!', Ortegay Gasset suggested: 'He who wants to teach a truth should place us in the position to discover it ourselves' (1961:67). To impose a model without this local learning process would be to short-circuit and bypass the active learning capability of local policy makers, to substitute authority in its place, and thus to perpetuate the passivity of tutelage.[4]

If the development agency can move beyond the Church or party model to an open learning model, then it can also move from standard knowledge dissemination or transmission-belt methodology towards knowledge-based capacity building:

> The aim of teaching is not only to transmit information, but also to transform students from passive recipients of other people's knowledge into active constructors of their own and others' knowledge. The teacher cannot transform without the student's active participation, of course. Teaching is fundamentally about creating the pedagogical, social, and ethical conditions under which students agree to take charge of their own learning, individually and collectively.
> (Elmore 1991:xvi)

This form of activist pedagogy adapted to developing countries (as active learners) would constitute autonomy-enhancing knowledge-based development assistance.

Competition and devil's advocacy in the open learning model

How can a large bureaucratic agency itself advance from the Church or party model towards an open learning model? One way is for the agency to foster competition in a market-place for ideas internally – something which requires an open ecology of knowledge and criticism, not the closed system of Official Views. This is expressed in the 'market-place of ideas concept – the proposition that truth naturally overcomes falsehood when they are allowed to compete ... The belief that competing voices produce superior conclusions [is] ... implicit in scientific reasoning, the practice of trial by jury, and the process of legislative debate' (Smith 1988:31). For instance, the defendant's right to an attorney in a US courtroom takes away from the prosecutor the monopoly right to present evidence and arguments. A judge may not go to the jury before both sides of the arguments have been heard, and a patient should not go to surgery before getting a second opinion. Even the Roman Catholic Church, when considering someone for sainthood, has a 'devil's advocate' (*Advocatus Diaboli*) to state the other side of the story. A development agency should not pretend to greater authority or infallibility when it canonises a good practice success story as the OBW.

This idea of the constructive role of public criticism goes back at least to the time of Socrates in Athens:

For if you kill me you will not easily find a successor to me, who, if I may use
such a ludicrous figure of speech, am a sort of gadfly, attached to the state by
God; and the state is a great and noble horse who is rather sluggish owing to
his very size, and requires to be stirred into life. I am that gadfly which God
has attached to the state, and all day long and in all places am always
fastening upon you, arousing and persuading and reproaching you.
(Plato 1997:30-31)

The penchant for competition seems to be one of the key features of
Athenian Greece that distinguished it from other societies of antiquity,
and Socrates represented the use of dialogue and contestation as the
road to improving knowledge. 'The form Socrates' teaching took –
intellectual duelling before a sportive audience – looks much odder to
us than it did to Athenians, whose whole culture was based on the
contest (*agon*), formal and informal, physical, intellectual, and legal'
(Wills 1994:163). Immanuel Kant recognised that the 'means which
nature employs to bring about the development of innate capacities is
that of antagonism within society', and he portrayed the insight with
the analogy of trees competing in a forest:

In the same way, trees in a forest, by seeking to deprive each other of air and
sunlight, compel each other to find these by upward growth, so that they
grow beautiful and straight – whereas those which put out branches at will,
in freedom and in isolation from others, grow stunted, bent and twisted. All
the culture and art which adorn mankind and the finest social order man
creates are fruits of his unsociability.
(Kant 1991:46)

Of course, not all antagonism or unsociability is helpful, and
Hirschman (1995) has investigated which forms of social conflict are
more beneficial than others (see also Coser 1956), a question that also
goes back to the contrast between Socrates' use of provocative
dialogues to improve knowledge and the Sophists' eristic methods
employed simply to defeat an opponent.

For our purposes, however, the focus is on the difference between an
organisation that incorporates (one hopes, beneficial) antagonism and
one that aims at a non-antagonistic idea of agreement, cooperation, and
'team play' – a small society like that dryly satirised by Kant as the
Arcadian ideal where men would be 'as good-natured as the sheep they
tended' (Kant 1991). Some modern research (Lloyd 1996) has used this
contrast to address the question of why, after such promising beginnings
in ancient China, science developed so strongly in ancient Greece did not

develop further in China. The key feature in ancient China was the intermix of power with the desire to answer questions of empirical truth – a feature shared by the Church during the Middle Ages or by Lysenkoism (and the role of the party in general) in the Soviet Union. In ancient China, the emperor's Mandate of Heaven was based on a view of the world that pictured the emperor in the central role of maintaining harmony between heaven and earth, and the views of philosophers and scientists needed to accommodate that basic scheme. By contrast, Greek intellectual life exhibited 'radical revisability' (Lloyd 1996:216) where thinkers would offer theories completely at odds with those of their rivals. Chinese intellectual life emphasised accommodation and harmony while the Greeks thrived on antagonism and adversarial clashes. The differences extended throughout social and legal affairs:

> *Differences between individuals or groups that might well have been the subject of appeal to litigation in Greece were generally settled [in China] by discussion, by arbitration, or by the decision of the responsible officials. The Chinese had, to be sure, no experience that remotely resembled that of the Greek dicasts [large public juries], nor, come to that, that of Greek public participation in open debate of political issues in the Assemblies.*
> (Lloyd 1996:109)

Given the rather clear historical verdict of the mixing of power and knowledge in ancient China, the medieval Church, and more recently the Communist Party, there seems to be little basis for a development agency dedicated to promoting development knowledge to adopt 'Official Views' on some of the most complex and subtle questions facing humankind.

Aside from not licensing Official Views, how might an agency promote internal adversarial engagement? Devil's advocacy is one practice that might be fostered in a development agency functioning as an open learning organisation.[5] The political scientist Alfred De Grazia recommends such a countervailing system as a part of any large bureaucracy: 'The countervailors would be a corps of professional critics of all aspects of bureaucracy who would be assigned by the representative council of an institution to specialise as critic of all the subinstitutions' (De Grazia 1975). Devil's advocacy might provide a constructive alternative in addition to negative criticism of the proposed policy. In economics, the opportunity-cost doctrine evaluates an option by comparing its value to the value of a best alternative. If plan B is the best alternative to plan A (and the plans are mutually exclusive), then the opportunity cost of choosing plan A is the value foregone by not choosing plan B. Plan A is preferable if its value exceeds its opportunity cost (assuming both can be quantitatively measured). The application of the opportunity-cost doctrine requires the analysis and evaluation of the best alternative – and that is the more general role of devil's advocacy even when quantitative values are not available. By eliciting plan B, devil's advocacy generalises the opportunity cost doctrine from cost-benefit analysis to general policy analysis. Just as in an open market competition provides the B plans, organisational devil's advocacy could be seen as an attempt to provide benchmark competition within an organisation.

The general case for a more systematic devil's advocate or countervailing role in an organisation is much the same as the case for genuine debate and open discussion. One classic statement of that argument can be found in John Stuart Mill's 1859 essay *On Liberty*. If little is known on a question, then real debate and the 'clash of adverse opinions' are some of the best engines of discovery. If 'partial truths' are known, then the same is necessary to ferret out a clearer picture and to better adapt theories to new and different contexts. Mill argued that even in cases of settled opinions, debate and discussion serve to disturb the 'deep slumber of a decided opinion' so that it might be held more as a rational conviction than as an article of faith:

> So essential is this discipline to a real understanding of moral and human subjects, that if opponents of all important truths do not exist, it is indispensable to imagine them, and supply them with the strongest arguments which the most skilful devil's advocate can conjure up.
> (Mill 1972:105)

Non-dogmatism and Socratic ignorance in organisations

I have argued that organisational learning can best take place if open competition, devil's advocacy, and the collision of ideas are fostered instead of being suppressed in favour of an outward show of allegiance to Official Views. This openness is now taken for granted in the institutions of higher learning as well as in the informal communities of the sciences, but many development agencies still operate on the basis of the Church or party model, regardless of the espoused theory.

I now turn from these competition- or rivalry-based arguments to a different type of argument against having Official Views in an organisation that aspires to be a learning organisation and to foster learning in its clients. How can the development agency help the client 'own' the knowledge being acquired? The helper needs to refrain from trying to teach or impose a certain representation or view on the doers.[6] That will call for the helper to display non-assertiveness, non-dogmatism, cognitive humility,[7] tolerance, 'egolessness' (Davenport and Prusak 1998:113), or Socratic ignorance.[8] This Socratic humility or ignorance is the cognitive counterpart to the forbearance of the type of material assistance that would create dependency and undercut the volition of self-help on the part of the doers. As George Bernard Shaw put it: 'if you teach a man anything he will never learn it' (Winsten 1962:174).

Thus even if an agency has the 'answer' (and that is a big 'if'), it should still refrain from 'teaching' it (not to mention enforce its 'learning' through aid conditionalities). It should engage in capacity building and facilitating the doers' own learning process, and not in trying to 'teach' or 'disseminate' what it takes to be the answers. Paulo Freire made this point about development professionals working with people in a community:

> Whatever the specialty that brings [the professionals] into contact with the people, they are almost unshakably convinced that it is their mission to 'give' the latter their knowledge and techniques. They see themselves as 'promoters' of the people. Their programs of action ... include their own objectives, their own convictions, and their own preoccupations. They do not listen to the people, but instead plan to teach them how to 'cast off the laziness which creates underdevelopment' ... They feel that the ignorance of the people is so complete that they are unfit for anything except to receive the teachings of the professionals.
> (Freire 1970:153-154)

For an example closer to home, upon seeing a child struggling with a homework problem parents may feel the urge to just supply what they think is the answer, but parents also presumably know they should resist that urge as it would undercut the learning process. Why do development agencies find it so difficult to apply the same principle?

Disclaimer

Notes

1   When predictions fail, then skewed perceptions and rationalisations are a likely outcome. See Festinger (1957) and Elster (1983). See Akerlof and Dickens (1982) for an economic treatment of cognitive dissonance.

2   The universal suggestion that everyone should wear a three-piece suit still requires local tailoring or adaptation to each person's size and shape. This illustrates the fallacy in the argument that an agency does not recommend a 'universal recipe' simply because it explicitly recognises the need for local adaptation.

3   Some of the best computer-based training programmes have 'experts' popping up on the screen giving contradictory advice. 'In other words, the program communicates that there's not always one right answer. It invites trainees to learn to use their own judgement rather than rely on someone else's – especially when the someone else isn't as close to the situation as you are. Organisations today are facing increasingly complex situations where there are many possible answers. Traditional training that insists on right and wrong answers disempowers the individual – it robs people of their decision-making ability' (Schank 1997:24).

4   In 1784, Immanuel Kant wrote a short but influential pamphlet *What is Enlightenment?* Enlightenment, he wrote, 'is man's release from his self-incurred tutelage. Tutelage is man's inability to make use of his understanding without direction from another. Self-incurred is this tutelage when its cause lies not in lack of reason but in lack of resolution and courage to use it without direction from another. *Sapere aude!* "Have the courage to use your own reason!" –

that is the motto of enlightenment' (see Schmidt 1996; see also Ellerman 1999 on these issues).

5   Devil's advocacy (see Schwenk 1984) is interpreted broadly to include a number of related techniques to better elicit the main policy alternatives. A *Cassandra's advocate* (Janis 1972:217) is a person who emphasises alternative interpretations of data and focuses on all the things that can go wrong ('Murphy's Law-yer'). The *Rashomon effect* (see Schön 1971:210) illustrates that the same set of circumstances and events can be interpreted very differently by different people.

6   The Socratic-Kantian Leonard Nelson emphasises this aspect of the Socratic process of instruction: 'Philosophical instruction fulfills its task when it systematically weakens the influences that obstruct the growth of philosophical comprehension and reinforces those that promote it. Without going into the question of other relevant influences, let us keep firmly in mind the one that must be excluded unconditionally: the influence that may emanate from the instructor's assertions. If this influence is not eliminated, all labor is vain. The instructor will have done everything possible to forestall the pupil's own judgement by offering him a ready-made judgement' (Nelson 1949:19).

7   'But all true effort to help begins with self-humiliation: the helper must first humble himself under him he would help, and therewith must understand that to help does not mean to be a sovereign but to be a servant, that to help does not mean to be ambitious but to be patient, that to help means to endure for the time being the imputation that one is in the wrong and does not understand what the other understands' (Kierkegaard, quoted in Bretall 1946:334).

8 'True Socraticism represents first and foremost an attitude of mind, an intellectual humility easily mistaken for arrogance, since the true Socratic is convinced of the ignorance not only of himself but of all mankind. This rather than any body of positive doctrine is the contribution of Socrates' (Guthrie 1960:75).

References

Akerlof, George and William Dickens (1982) 'The economic consequences of cognitive dissonance', *American Economic Review* 72 (June):307-319.

Andreski, Stanislav (1972) *Social Sciences as Sorcery*, New York, NY: St. Martin's Press.

Bretall, Robert (ed.) (1946) *A Kierkegaard Anthology*, Princeton, NJ: Princeton University Press.

Coser, Lewis (1956) *The Functions of Social Conflict*, New York, NY: Free Press.

Davenport, Thomas and Laurence Prusak (1998) *Working Knowledge*, Boston, MA: Harvard Business School Press.

De Grazia, Alfred (1975) *Eight Bads – Eight Goods: The American Contradictions*, Garden City, NY: Anchor Books.

Dewey, John (1939) *Freedom and Culture*, New York, NY: Capricorn.

Easterly, William (2001) *The Elusive Quest for Growth: Economists' Adventures and Misadventures in the Tropics*, Cambridge, MA: MIT Press.

Ellerman, David (1999) 'Global institutions: transforming international development agencies into learning organisations', *Academy of Management Executives* 13(1):25-35.

Ellerman, David (2001) 'Lessons from East Europe's voucher privatisation', *Challenge: The Magazine of Economic Affairs* 44(4):14-37.

Elmore, R. (1991) Foreword, in C. R. Christensen, D. A. Garvin and A. Sweet (eds.) *Education for Judgement*, Boston, MA: Harvard Business School Press.

Elster, Jon (1983) *Sour Grapes: Studies in the Subversion of Rationality*, Cambridge: CUP.

Festinger, L. (1957) *A Theory of Cognitive Dissonance*, Stanford, CA: Stanford University Press.

Freire, Paulo (1970) *Pedagogy of the Oppressed*, New York, NY: Continuum.

Guthrie, W. K. C. (1960) *The Greek Philosophers: From Thales to Aristotle*, New York, NY: Harper & Row.

Haas, E. B. (1990) *When Knowledge is Power: Three Models of Change in International Organisations*, Berkeley, CA: University of California.

Hirschman, Albert O. (1971) *A Bias for Hope: Essays on Development and Latin America*, New Haven, CT: Yale University Press.

Hirschman, Albert O. (1973) *Journeys Toward Progress*, New York, NY: Norton.

Hirschman, Albert O. (1984) 'A dissenter's confession: "The Strategy of Economic Development" revisited', in G. Meier and D. Seers (eds.) *Pioneers in Development*, New York, NY: OUP.

Hirschman, Albert O. (1995) *Development Projects Observed*, Washington, DC: The Brookings Institution.

Janis, I. L. (1972) *Victims of Groupthink*, Boston, MA: Houghton Mifflin.

Kanbur, Ravi and David Vines (2000) 'The World Bank and poverty reduction: past, present and future', in C. Gilbert and D. Vines (eds.) *The World Bank: Structure and Policies*, Cambridge: CUP.

Kanigel, Robert (1997) *The One Best Way: Frederick Winslow Taylor and the Enigma of Efficiency*, New York, NY: Viking.

Kant, Immanuel (1991, orig. 1784) 'Idea for a Universal History with a Cosmopolitan Purpose', in H. Reiss, *Kant: Political Writings*, New York, NY: CUP.

Lloyd, Geoffrey Ernest Richard (1996) *Adversaries and Authorities: Investigations into Ancient Greek and Chinese Science*, Cambridge: CUP.

Mill, John Stuart (1972, orig. 1859) *On Liberty*, in H. B. Acton (ed.) *J.S. Mill: Utilitarianism, On Liberty and Considerations on Representative Government*, London: Dent.

Moore Jr, Barrington (1972) *Reflections on the Causes of Human Misery and upon Certain Proposals to Eliminate Them*, Boston, MA: Beacon Press.

Morley, John (1928) *On Compromise*, London: Macmillan.

Nelson, Leonard (1949) *Socratic Method and Critical Philosophy*, New York, NY: Dover.

Ortega y Gasset, Jos, (1961) *Meditations on Quixote*, New York, NY: Norton.

Plato (1997) *Apology of Socrates*, Warminster: Arias & Phillips.

Popper, Karl (1965) *Conjectures and Refutations: The Growth of Scientific Knowledge*, New York: Harper & Row.

Rogers, Everett (1983) *Diffusion of Innovations*, 3rd edn, New York, NY: Free Press.

Schank, Roger (1997) *Virtual Learning: A Revolutionary Approach to Building a Highly Skilled Workforce*, New York, NY: McGraw-Hill.

Schmidt, J. (ed.) (1996) *What is Enlightenment? Eighteenth-century Answers and Twentieth-century Questions*, Berkeley, CA: University of California Press.

Schön, Donald (1971) *Beyond the Stable State*, New York, NY: Norton.

Schön, Donald (1983) *The Reflective Practitioner: How Professionals Think in Action*, New York, NY: Basic Books.

Schwenk, C. R. (1984) 'Devil's Advocacy in Managerial Decision Making', *Journal of Management Studies* 21 (April):153-168.

Smith, Jeffery A. (1988) *Printers and Press Freedom: The Ideology of Early American Journalism*, New York, NY: OUP.

Wills, Garry (1994) *Certain Trumpets: The Call of Leaders*, New York, NY: Simon & Schuster.

Winsten, Stephen (ed.) (1962) *The Wit and Wisdom of Bernard Shaw*, New York, NY: Collier.

This paper was first published in Development in Practice (12/3&4:285-297) *in 2002.*

Engendering organisational practice in NGOs: the case of Utthan

Sara Ahmed

Introduction

Although gender issues have been on the development agenda since the early 1970s, it is only in the last decade that development organisations, including NGOs, which have traditionally been other-centred, have begun to address the question of gender within their organisational boundaries. The concern for organisations as 'engendering mechanisms' grew out of the debate on mainstreaming women/gender in development and the need to look critically at gender-inequitable structures, procedures, and policy outcomes, which both determine and are the result of gendered organisational practice.[1] 'Mainstreaming' is the term used to describe strategies aimed at integrating a gender perspective into all decision-making aspects of an organisation, i.e. policies, strategies, programmes, and administrative and financial activities, thereby contributing to organisational transformation.

This paper begins with a conceptual overview of the gendered hierarchy of organisations before looking at how Utthan, as a development organisation, is 'gendered'. With its headquarters in Ahmedabad, in the Indian state of Gujarat, Utthan is a registered NGO working on natural-resource management through community participation in three districts of the state. Underlying its participatory approach to development, Utthan seeks to strengthen gender equity in natural-resource management by facilitating rural women's participation in decision making at the household and community levels. Drawing on in-depth interviews with one district team and with Utthan's senior management in Ahmedabad, this paper examines Utthan's willingness and capacity *as an organisation* to address gender equity in development practice. The research for this paper was undertaken as part of a larger study on rural change, gender relations, and development organisations which looks at the role of NGOs in negotiating spaces for addressing gender equity in water-management policies and practice.[2]

Understanding the gendered hierarchy of development organisations

> *To say that an organisation, or any other analytical unit, is gendered means that advantage and disadvantage, exploitation and control, action and emotion, meaning and identity are patterned through and in terms of a distinction between male and female, masculine and feminine. Gender is not an addition to ongoing processes, conceived as gender neutral. Rather, it is an integral part of those processes, which cannot be properly understood without an analysis of gender.*
> (Acker 1990:146)

Feminist concern about gendered organisational practice originated from bringing ideas about sexuality, authority, and power out of the private sphere of 'intimate relations' into the 'domain of the public organisation of control' (Acker 1992:249). Drawing on economics, sociology, and organisational theory, social scientists have looked at gender, work, and the division of labour in organisations as well as the relationship between organisational structures, authority, and power. They have analysed how the different positions of men and women within organisational hierarchies affect the nature and valuation of their work (tasks, segmented opportunity structure) and their access to resources and decision making. In addition, the growing debate on sexual harassment in the workplace has highlighted how reproduction and sexuality, particularly in relation to women's bodies, are often objects of, and resources for, control. If the feminist vision is to make organisations more democratic and supportive of humane goals, then it is important to understand the social construction of gender by organisations in order to challenge gender inequalities.

It is in this context that development practitioners have begun to look at the 'archaeology of gender' (Goetz 1995) within development organisations, including donor agencies, bureaucracies, and NGOs (Plowman 2000). Not only do these organisations reflect and are structured by the values articulated within the larger institutional arenas in which they are embedded, they produce gendered outcomes and personnel who, whatever their sex, reproduce gender discriminatory outcomes (Goetz 1995:3). However, since NGOs have some degree of autonomy from patriarchal structures and play an important role in renegotiating gender relations through struggles for social justice and gender equity, they can also be seen as 'en-gendering' organisations (Murthy 1998:204).

Organisations can be gendered in a number of ways, and recently organisational change-agents have developed several tools for analysing gender and organisational practice (Lingen *et al.* 1997). One such analytical framework is constructed around three interdependent levels or elements within an organisation (Sweetman 1997:3) namely: the substantive (organisational mission, ideology, and policies); the structural (procedures and mechanisms for enforcing its goals and objectives, its strategy); and the cultural (shared beliefs, values, and attitudes). While we look at these levels separately in the context of Utthan, it is important to understand the linkages between them. Before doing so, the next section sketches out a brief organisational profile of Utthan.

Utthan: a background note

Utthan, which means 'upliftment' in Hindi, was founded in 1981 with the purpose of facilitating development action in Dhandhuka *taluka* (block), part of the coastal, semi-arid Bhal region of Gujarat. Under its aegis the grassroots project 'Mahiti' (literally meaning 'information') was initiated to develop information linkages between communities and the state. According to Utthan's founders, knowledge leads to awareness, which in turn leads to self-sustained development action. Utthan provided the support structure and was the 'outsider group', consisting mainly of dedicated development professionals, while Mahiti, the primary 'insider group', comprised local individuals, especially women, who had actively participated in earlier development initiatives. In 1994, as part of Utthan's withdrawal strategy, Mahiti became an independent community-based organisation (CBO) continuing to maintain strong links with Utthan.

One of the critical problems in the Bhal region was the availability of potable water, particularly during the dry season. Conflicts over water were common and women became the major victims, largely because of the gender division of labour whereby women and girls are mostly responsible for domestic water collection. Utthan-Mahiti did not begin with a specific focus on women only, as they did not want to isolate other members of the community, nor did they want to have a 'compartmentalised' approach to meeting developmental needs. However, as the mobilisation process proceeded, they realised that they needed to create spaces for people with different needs and that there were different views emerging from men and women:

Men were saying – look at all this unproductive land, we need to generate employment through reinvesting in the land, while women were saying – there is a drinking water problem in the village which leads to migration. Men saw it as a seasonal problem but not the women, who were able to link it to other aspects of development.

(Interview with Nafisa Barot, Utthan Executive Trustee, January 1999)

Another problem mentioned by the women was the exploitative money-lending system, run by the *Darbars*, the most powerful upper castes in the area, and so Utthan-Mahiti began working on both these issues simultaneously. Through interaction with local communities, alternatives were sought for making saline land productive, for providing women with income-earning opportunities through the formation of self-help groups, and, most importantly, for finding sustainable solutions for the water crisis. Building on traditional knowledge and community management systems, Utthan-Mahiti facilitated the construction of lined village ponds in 20 'no-source' villages to store water, primarily for drinking purposes.[3] These ponds were lined with polyethylene sheets to prevent seepage of saline water and the water was tapped through a hand pump after passing through a slow sand filter.

Although community institutions, with both women and men as members, were formed to manage and maintain these ponds, the degree to which they are sustainable varies from village to village for a number of contextual reasons, which cannot be elaborated here (Barot 1997). However, two aspects or outcomes of Utthan-Mahiti's efforts need to be highlighted. The first concerns the participation of women in the management of community assets in an area where traditionally women's participation in the public domain was limited. The second concerns the growing recognition by the state, policy makers, and donor agencies of the need for decentralised water management with community participation. Utthan continues to work on both these aspects while Mahiti extends its development work in Dhandhuka *taluka*, strengthening local networking and capacity building.

Utthan: organisational structure

Since 1995–96, Utthan has been working in three districts of Gujarat, namely, Dahod, Bhavnagar, and Amreli. Each district has its own field office and there are currently 31 projects spread over 81 villages broadly covering natural resources management, community organisation and mobilisation, and women's participation and empowerment. Utthan's annual budget is about Rs25 million (approximately US$600,000) and it receives funding from a number of sources including central- and state-level government agencies and donors such as HIVOS, Swiss Aid, the Royal Netherlands Embassy, and the Ford Foundation (Utthan 2000a).

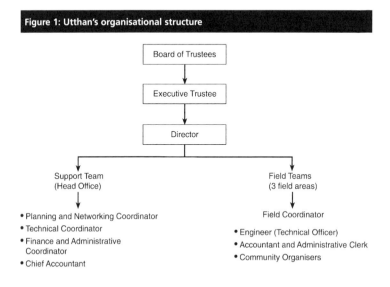

Figure 1: Utthan's organisational structure

As Figure 1 illustrates, Utthan has three field teams and one programme support core unit based in Ahmedabad which plans and monitors programme activities with the field teams and provides them with training, technical, administrative, and financial guidance. In addition, the core team is also involved in networking with a number of development organisations as well as policy advocacy on drinking water initiatives and the legitimisation of women's role as community natural resource managers.

The Board of Trustees consists of seven members, including Barot, prominent NGO leaders, academics, and development practitioners. Earlier, the Board used to meet annually, but now it meets two or three times a year, partly to enable members to come for at least one of these meetings. Although the Board does not intervene in Utthan's day-to-day activities, the recent expansion in Utthan's work and staff means that it needs more specific guidance in certain areas (e.g. strategic planning). Sometimes this is provided by Board members who are based in Ahmedabad or by Utthan's funding partners.

The remainder of this paper looks at how Utthan is gendered at three interdependent levels – the substantive, the structural, and the cultural. The discussion is based on in-depth interviews with all pre-expansion phase staff at Ahmedabad (core team) and the Bhavnagar field team (Centre for Drinking Water Resources Management). For reasons of confidentiality, all individuals quoted are referred to by their sex and broad designation within the organisation and not by name.

The substantive level: reaching a shared vision for gender equity

The substantive level of an NGO, as defined in its vision or mission statement, reflects its perspective on gender relations and social change. In this respect, Naila Kabeer's typology of gender policies (1994) is a useful tool for distinguishing between different organisational policy approaches. *Gender-blind policies* (e.g. those which claim that 'this is a household programme') reinforce or perpetuate gender hierarchies in society. This is typically the case in the design of community institutions in relation to natural-resource management interventions, where the predominant membership norm is one adult from each user household. Inevitably, this is the male head of the household, and women who are the principal users of natural resources for household subsistence are left with token representation on the management committees.

Gender-neutral policies believe that targeting resources to the 'right' gender (e.g. health and hygiene education to women) will enhance the effectiveness of such interventions and bring more sustainable benefits. In other words, this 'instrumentalist' use of women for delivering community health services, or other welfare needs such as clean water and sanitation, is not only meant to be more efficient, but it further perpetuates the social construction of women as 'natural carers'.

Other development organisations have begun working on gender as a result of their focus on poverty alleviation, wherein women are seen as the 'poorest of the poor'. *Gender-ameliorative policies* favour the targeting of specific resources to women (e.g. microcredit interventions), but, without a transformatory potential built into them, such approaches do not necessarily question the existing distribution of resources and responsibilities. In contrast, *gender-transformative or redistributive policies* seek to move beyond the provision of practical gender needs (water, fuelwood, credit, etc.) to provide spaces for women to articulate and organise around their strategic gender interests. This may require men to give up certain privileges and take on new or additional responsibilities in order to achieve gender-equitable development outcomes.

In this framework, let us look at Utthan's mission:

> *To initiate sustainable processes of socio-economic and political*
> *development in the communities, which have been exploited and oppressed,*
> *through issues pertaining to drinking water, environmental sanitation,*
> *natural resource management, community and women's health, economic*
> *status that leads to empowerment, and social justice, that leads to gender*
> *justice and community empowerment.*
> (Utthan 2000a)

The statement describes a process of rural transformation beginning with the provision of a critical livelihood resource, such as drinking water to the communities in Utthan's project areas. In meeting a practical gender need, Utthan's approach at one level could be described as gender ameliorative since it is focused on reducing the drudgery of water collection faced by poor women. And in making potable water more easily available throughout the year, Utthan's interventions also have an impact on the health and economic status of households and communities. However, in its organisation of women in self-help groups for access to credit, Utthan has moved beyond a gender-ameliorative intervention to look at other aspects of social change (e.g. challenging the dominance of the traditional money-lender). Furthermore, in involving women in decision making on water (and other resources) through facilitating and strengthening their participation in community-level institutions, such as *pani samitis* (water-management committees), and providing assets (e.g. roof-water collection tanks) in their name, Utthan is initiating a gradual process of empowerment. In so doing, it is trying to address strategic gender interests (e.g. women's access to, and control over, resources such as water and credit). The question remains as to whether Utthan has the capacity to sustain and strengthen this process of transformatory change in the long term.

The structural level: translating gender equity concerns into action

> *Social transformation in organisations can be de-railed at the structural*
> *level – verbal and paper commitments to a vision of gender have a tendency*
> *to 'evaporate' when there is resistance to putting policy into practice through*
> *the procedures, mechanisms, and rules of the organisation.*
> (Sweetman 1997:5)

Looking at gendered structures and practices necessitates an analysis of time and space within organisations, as well as recruitment procedures, promotion policies, the allocation of tasks and responsibilities, the distribution of resources, and patterns of decision making. As Acker argues (1992:255):

> The gendered substructure lies in the spatial and temporal arrangements of work, in the rules prescribing workplace behaviour and in the relations linking workplace to living place. These practices and relations, encoded in arrangements and rules, are supported by assumptions that work is separate from the rest of life and that it has first claim on the worker. Many people, particularly women, have difficulty making their daily lives fit these expectations and assumptions.

Practical arrangements of space (office space, approaches to fieldwork) and time (flexibility of the working day, life cycles, and career management) are essentially expressions of power as they 'reflect the physical and social capabilities of those who dominate organisations' (Goetz 1997:17). Where organisations are dominated by men, a response to legitimate demands raised by women staff are usually seen as 'concessions' rather than as opportunities to promote capacity building of all staff.

Moreover, the presence of more women in an organisation does not necessarily mean that it is going to reflect a greater degree of gender awareness, though it certainly affects its capacity to work on gender issues. This is particularly important in socio-cultural environments where male fieldworkers do not find it easy to approach rural women. But questions need to be asked about where women staff are located in the organisation, and equally, what tasks are allocated to them. Gender parity is also important in drawing attention to a number of practical gender needs of women staff (e.g. childcare provision or flexible working hours). Although this does not imply any structural change in terms of the gender division of roles and responsibilities, it has the potential to stimulate the examination of more strategic aspects of gender inequalities within the organisation (Macdonald *et al.* 1997:88).

Another issue is the structure or 'shape' of the organisation – it is usually assumed that flatter, decentralised organisations are more open to participatory decision making and are therefore more gender sensitive. But research has shown that collective or consensual management does not eradicate problems of dominance – it simply makes them invisible or 'latent' while other ways are found to establish dominance. Linked to the debate on hierarchy is the issue of management style, that is, is there a distinctively masculine or feminine style of management? Some organisational analysts feel that women leaders and managers are inherently more nurturing, flexible, and sensitive, while men are driven by targets, tasks, and authority. But bringing personal gender attributes into the public domain is highly debatable, and it has thus been argued that these should be seen as preferred styles of working because of the multiplicity of roles and responsibilities that women and men have to manage.

Gender-sensitive leadership

Translating the organisational commitment to gender equity into practice requires gender-sensitive leadership, which is not necessarily vested in one individual, but more broadly includes the head of the organisation as well as those involved in senior management positions who are able to influence the direction, style, and values of an organisation. Barot, as one of the founder-leaders of Utthan, has played a critical role in creating gender-sensitive understanding among the staff members, but she does not link this to her gender:

> What is important is the sensitivity of a person – whenever I talk to one of my employees, whether they are men or women, I always try to put myself in their place, to feel the way they feel about a particular problem so that I can understand them better. But I am sure that other staff members would try to do the same.

(Interview, Ahmedabad, 1999)

However, she admits that women probably respond to and confide in other women more so than they would do with men, a fact that is corroborated by some of the women staff members who still feel more comfortable talking to her about their problems. Most of the staff, particularly the older ones who have been with Utthan for at least ten years, agree that having a woman as leader meant that they could have a clear focus on gender-equity issues right from the beginning. But now that gender equity is beginning to be institutionalised within the organisation, some staff contend that it does not make a difference if, as is the case currently, the executive director is a man.

As the founder-leader of Utthan, Barot articulated a vision motivating other professionals and local people to work with the organisation. Although she may not be able to travel to the field as extensively as she used to, Barot continues to provide the critical interface with the external environment. Today she is involved in policy advocacy on decentralised alternatives for water management, networking with other organisations working on gender issues in Gujarat, and mobilising funds, despite having to use a wheelchair as the result of a car accident in 1998.

Staff recruitment: the question of numbers

In the patriarchal context where Utthan works, the practice of *purdah* (seclusion) makes it difficult for male staff to reach out to women beneficiaries. The process of social mobilisation requires considerable time and interaction, often in the privacy of women's homes, which male outsiders cannot access easily:

> *In the beginning, women [in the village] did not trust us because they had had a very bad experience with another organisation. So they told us to talk to the men only. But now they talk and discuss things with us – for example, they have suggested a place for the standposts.*
> (Male community organiser, interview, Bhavnagar, 1999)

Over the years, Utthan has tried to make a conscious effort to hire more women, especially because in the areas where the Darbar community is strong, interaction with women is constrained by cultural barriers. In September 1999, as a result of its growing activities, Utthan went through a major expansion from 14 to 44 full-time staff with various roles and responsibilities as indicated in Table 1. Presently, 36 per cent of the staff are female, which is one of the highest female:male ratios enjoyed by the organisation and certainly compares well with other mixed NGOs working on similar issues in the country. As Table 1 shows, the number of women in management positions is equivalent to the number of men, but interestingly there are no women in any technical positions. Women staff tend to dominate in process-oriented roles such as community organising, even if they come from technical backgrounds and/or are exposed to technical training at Utthan.

Apart from gender parity, Utthan is also sensitive to the ethnic diversity of its staff and encourages representation from disadvantaged groups, including minorities, scheduled castes and tribes, and the physically challenged. Currently, just under a quarter of the staff are from these groups, though they tend to predominate as community organisers, partly because of their educational background, skills, and experience.

Table 1: Full-time staff at Utthan in March 2000			
Category	Women	Men	Total
Managerial	2	2	4
Technical	0	4	4
Prog. Coordinator	1	2	3
Administrative	1	4	5
Accounts	2	3	5
Computers	0	1	1
Comm. Organiser	10	12	22
Total	16	28	44

Source: Utthan (2000b:11)

An effort is being made to hire more local staff, in the hope that they would be retained and that women in particular would be able to be closer to their families. All new staff go through an induction period of six months in which they learn about the organisation's work and approach as well as attend workshops to develop skills and knowledge in specific areas related to their proposed work (e.g. gender awareness). Staff performance review is an annual process, which determines salary increments. It involves self-assessment as well as peer-group review by the director, programme coordinator, and monitoring-in-charge.

Gender and space: women, mobility, and life-cycles

As is typical of many other NGOs, it is difficult for Utthan to retain women staff, particularly at the field level. Not only are there societal pressures (e.g. from their families) which prevent young, single women from doing extensive fieldwork, but marriage (patri-local) and motherhood also restrict women's mobility. Apart from restrictions because of their place in the lifecycle, women face added physical constraints in terms of doing fieldwork. Public transport is minimal in the areas where Utthan works and not all women feel comfortable about using a motorbike. One of the women staff members in Bhavnagar recounted how in the early days they often walked 2 to 3km to reach villages, or hitched rides on local trucks and jeeps, but now that they have access to office motorbikes, albeit via their male colleagues, it has saved time. As it is not safe for women staff to go to villages at night when most community meetings are held, the Bhavnagar field office has asked male and female members to travel together in pairs.

Childcare and child-support facilities

The issue of childcare and child support is emerging as critical, particularly as the number of women in the organisation has increased and older women are having their first children. As women struggle to cope with their home responsibilities and work commitments, support from male colleagues is mixed. Sometimes, women bring their small children (especially nursing infants) to the office if there is no home caretaker. But interviewed male colleagues said that they often find this practice disturbing: small infants crying or older children running around and shouting – this is not what 'office space' is meant for in their opinion. One of the female programme coordinators discussed the difficulties she was facing while working with Utthan after her first child was born:

> Earlier I had no problems with the management as such and I enjoyed being in the field, but after my son's birth I have been facing a lot of difficulties. It is not easy for me to commute daily, 30kms each way in a public bus with a small child. There is no creche facility here [referring to the place she currently lives in and where her husband works] so where can I leave him? Sometimes I reach the office late, but I usually compensate for this by bringing work home. However, the organisation, particularly my male colleagues, does not seem to understand this and they have begun to cut (my time) from my annual leave. We may shift to Ahmedabad so that he can go to school there and I will have the support of my parents too. Then I could visit the field for 1 or 2 days and he could stay with them.
> (Interview, Dahod, 2000)

Utthan is in the process of developing a gender policy for the organisation, and one of the factors under consideration is a creche facility in each office. Although there is no explicit flexi-time arrangement, women are given 'time off' to attend to sick children or other family members and if they are not feeling well themselves, or have their monthly period, they are not compelled to go to the field.

Roles and responsibilities: gendered tasks?

Utthan encourages all its staff members, whether male or female, to be involved in both technical ('hardware') aspects, such as water-related infrastructure, and social ('software') aspects of its programmes, such as the process of forming community groups. However, while some women staff have been trained in the technical aspects of watershed and water-resources development by Utthan, their participation is not always forthcoming for a number of reasons. Male staff members feel that women lack the self-confidence to deal with technical matters ('they are self-doubting') and given the choice they would prefer to stay in the office and do deskwork. In this respect, they cite the example of the last receptionist at Utthan who was a highly qualified civil engineer: but she preferred to take up an office job, rather than go to the field, though this was more due to family compulsion than to personal choice. Similarly, Utthan had a part-time woman accountant for a short period, but in 1997, based on arguments raised by senior staff, they decided to hire a full-time male accountant who would be able to help the field offices with their accounting processes.

Men maintain that while women are competent in administrative work, they are hesitant to carry out certain tasks in the field by themselves. For example, in the neighbouring project area of Amreli, women staff were reluctant to be involved in the purchase of materials for watershed programmes, while in Bhavnagar women are part of the materials management committee. In contrast, male staff members readily join in the process of community institution building, attending meetings of the *pani samitis* and *mahila mandals* along with their women colleagues. As a result, they have an understanding of the problems faced by rural women in the project area and the factors affecting their participation in community meetings.

Resources for sustaining a focus on gender

Perhaps the most critical factor, before the staff expansion, was the sheer shortage of human resources, particularly women staff, to cope with the growing amount of work, both geographically and in terms of Utthan's focus on gender equity. Although the recent addition of staff will meet this need to some extent, they will need to be trained and sensitised to the organisational perspective. Moreover, Utthan still requires a full-time trainer to handle organisational training and human resource development as well as another person to look after research, documentation, and dissemination.

In terms of financial resources to sustain its focus on gender equity, Utthan is fortunate that most of its funding partners share a similar perspective and are supportive of capacity building for community institutions. One of the problems which Utthan, like many other NGOs, faces is the late approval of funds and the time-lag between the sanctioning of a grant and the actual flow of money. These two factors affect the smooth functioning of the organisation and it is compelled to arrange funds for the buffer period, borrowing from other commercial agencies with a high rate of interest, or to fall back on its own reserves.

In 1996, budgeting, which until then was a centralised process, was decentralised to involve the three field teams in the development of project or programme proposals with the finance committee at the head office. Non-financial expenditure earmarked for each project is now deposited directly into the respective account and those involved with the project have the power to take certain financial and administrative decisions.

The cultural level: changing attitudes, changing minds

This is perhaps the most fundamental level at which transformation needs to take place, as it touches on the beliefs and value systems of individuals and is thus the point at which the personal really does become the political in organisations. 'No matter how radically structures and systems may be reformed, if organisational culture is unchanged, the changes will remain superficial, cosmetic and ultimately without effect' (Macdonald *et al.* 1997:20). People do not leave their culturally defined gender perspectives and attitudes at the gates of organisations – they enter with them and this has a significant bearing on the organisation's own gender perspective.

In this respect, the leadership of an organisation, as well as strong, articulate gender-sensitive women and men, play an important role in developing an appropriate value system for the organisation. Such a value system is not necessarily imposed from the top, but needs to evolve gradually in response to organisational processes of sharing and learning. Gender-sensitisation training for all staff is one method increasingly being used by a number of NGOs to facilitate such institutional change, empower women staff, and redefine the power of men within the organisation (Murthy 1998:203). However, training cannot be seen as an end in itself, but needs to be part of a wider process which includes the creation of space within NGOs for staff to share experiences and reinforce their learning as well as network with other organisations that have similar concerns.

It is also important to recognise that organisations do not have a monolithic culture, although they may appear to in terms of their public face. Rather, organisations are made up of a number of 'sub-cultures' and 'counter-cultures' which will either facilitate or resist efforts to integrate a gender perspective in the organisation (Sweetman 1997:7). In the final analysis, the development of a gender perspective, policies, and culture in an NGO is reflected not only at the level of organisational change, but equally in its accountability to its programme partners, particularly the poor and vulnerable, and in its advocacy efforts towards more gender-sensitive policies. Mayoux (1998) defines this as the 'gender accountability' of development organisations, and she maintains that it is one of the more contentious aspects of accountability, partly because of the complexity of gender subordination, and partly because of the unwillingness and, to some extent, the inability to take it on board fully.

Gender-sensitisation training: assessing organisational impact

Most of Utthan's staff have attended gender-sensitisation workshops and have begun to 'own' the concept of gender equity, though the understanding of gender varies across the organisation. This is partly due to an individual's social background, educational and work experience, length of time with the organisation, and his or her expectations from gender-training workshops.

For one senior male staff member, these workshops did not provide any significant new or interesting insights: 'Women are human beings just like us [men]. If we treat animals with great care why can't we behave nicely with women as they play an important role in life. As a child I was raised to respect women' (interview, Ahmedabad, 1999). Given his years of experience with Utthan, this kind of welfarist attitude towards women is surprising as it equates gender with women, rather than understanding the social construction of gender relations.

Sometimes the content of gender workshops can be too radical and men don't feel comfortable about translating concepts into practice. As one male staff member explained: 'A few days back I had gone for a gender awareness workshop, but the steps they were proposing for achieving gender equity were not practically possible in my opinion' (interview, Ahmedabad, 1999).

It is difficult to assess the impact of gender training on the organisation and its work because of the lack of documentation and analysis in this respect. Qualitative insights suggest some changes in people's attitudes and their behaviour. A number of women employees agree that there has been a change in the organisation as far as understanding the constraints that women staff encounter, both as a result of their biology and social pressures: 'Earlier men never understood women's [health] problems, but now if a woman says she cannot go to the field, they understand that she may not be feeling well', claimed one of the senior female coordinators (interview, Dahod, 2000).

Another senior female employee who has been with Utthan for 14 years explained that when she got married, her in-laws, who are quite wealthy, did not like her working: 'They did not mind me doing an office job, though personally I prefer going to the field, but they did not approve of it. So after my marriage, I made it very clear to the management that I could not continue with a field placement and they understood' (interview, Ahmedabad, 1999). She added:

> My family members are very conservative. As the daughter-in-law of a joint family there is so much work at home, but I do everything without complaining. Sometimes the situation at home depresses me, but I really want to work [with Utthan] so I struggle hard, usually with little encouragement or support from either my husband or other family members. I did not take any leave during my pregnancy, just the three months of maternity leave which was due to me, and then I immediately re-joined work.

It is this growing perception of the problems that women staff members face that has helped men and women within Utthan gradually support each other more in their work. This bonding, almost as a family, is very visible in the Bhavnagar office, where men and women, often coming from conservative families, share common social spaces and are learning to respect each other's capabilities.

Towards gender-sensitive organisational practice

The analysis of gender within Utthan reveals that as an organisation it is committed to gender equity at the substantive level, that is, in terms of its mission and its overall policy goals. However, at the structural level this process of social transformation has shown mixed results. On the one hand, strong leadership has played a critical role in engendering change, while on the other hand, resource constraints, a target-driven project approach, and social barriers underlying gender discrimination have made it difficult to translate gender equity concerns into sustainable initiatives. At the cultural level, however, it is clear that the understanding of gender varies across Utthan, with more experienced and older staff members acknowledging that it is an integral part of their work and organisational environment.

Male staff members tend to accept a gender perspective both because of their political commitment to social justice as development workers and perhaps more importantly, because they have seen the potential role that rural women can play as change agents. To a large extent this perspective is rooted in the WID (women in development) discourse. Men interpret gender as being exclusively concerned with meeting (rural) women's needs and expect gender workshops to provide them with 'technical' solutions (tools and techniques) for enhancing project output based on strengthening women's participation. They fail to see themselves as 'part of' gendered structures and 'inside' gender relations (Macdonald *et al.* 1997:42). For example, the presence of small children in the office was often termed a 'nuisance' and seen as a 'woman's problem', rather than working towards an organisational response to provide women (and men) employees with a convenient and practical alternative.

Women staff members, on the other hand, are able to draw parallels between the patriarchal structures which govern their ability to work (the family) and those which restrict rural women's participation in the public domain. One employee described how she had broken out of the *purdah* system and was now convincing village women to speak out at meetings, even in the presence of other male family members. But women staff members have not yet collectively organised to demand any specific attention from Utthan, partly because most of them are quite new to the organisation and do not occupy significant decision-making positions. They would prefer to be accepted by their male colleagues first, and whatever gender concerns they share as women they do so privately and not necessarily in the public space of the organisation.

On the whole, it is the management and leadership within Utthan which is more visibly concerned about engendering the organisation and about the *Realpolitik* aspects of promoting this from the point of view of the organisation's image. Staff members tend to focus on gender as an issue which affects the practical running of programmes and projects they are responsible for, as they have little space to manoeuvre around organisational policy. In the final analysis, looking at gender within an organisation raises questions about 'the self', the gendered nature of power, and the willingness to change or at least challenge this. As a development organisation, Utthan has shown that it is committed to putting its own house in order. But it realises that this agenda cannot be pushed from the top, and that staff need the time, the exposure to knowledge, tools and techniques, and, more importantly, collective support to promote gender awareness in relation to their roles and responsibilities. However, the frequent urgency of development work makes it difficult for small NGOs like Utthan that face resource constraints to provide the space for self- or collective reflection. In this respect, the role of donor agencies which are committed to gender, as well as strong and sustained leadership to translate learning into organisational practice, are critical.

Notes

1 'Gendered', in the context of an organisation, refers to the social construction of power within an organisation, while 'engendering' defines a process of changing or challenging this to support women staff and project partners towards gender-just and sustainable development.

2 'Rural Change, Gender Relations and Development Organisations', a study undertaken by IRMA and Dalhousie University, Halifax, through the CIDA-funded Shastri Indo-Canadian Partnership Programme (1999-2000).

3 'No-source' villages essentially do not have an accessible and potable source of water within a radius of 0.5–1km.

References

Acker, J. (1990) 'Hierarchies, jobs, bodies: a theory of gendered organisations', *Gender and Society* 4(2):39-158.

Acker, J. (1992) 'Gendering organizational theory', in A. J. Mills and P. Tancred (eds.) *Gendering Organizational Analysis*, London and New Delhi: Sage.

Barot, N. (1997) 'A people's movement towards creating sustainable drinking water systems in rural Gujarat', in N. Rao and L. Rurup (eds.) *A Just Right: Women's Ownership of Natural Resources and Livelihood Security*, New Delhi: Friedrich Ebert Stiftung.

Goetz, A. M. (1995) 'Institutionalising women's interests and accountability to women in development', *IDS Bulletin* 26(3):1-10.

Goetz, A. M. (1997) 'Managing organisational change: the gendered organisation of space and time', *Gender and Development* 5(1):17-27.

Kabeer, N. (1994) *Reversed Realities: Gender Hierarchies in Development Thought*, London: Verso.

Lingen, A. *et al.* (1997) *Gender Assessment Studies: A Manual for Gender Consultants*, The Hague: Netherlands Ministry of Foreign Affairs.

Macdonald, M., E. Sprenger and I. Dubel (1997) *Gender and Organisational Change: Bridging the Gap between Policy and Practice*, Amsterdam: Royal Tropical Institute.

Mayoux, L. (1998) 'Gender accountability and NGOs: avoiding the black hole', in C. Miller and S. Razavi (eds.) *Missionaries and Mandarins: Feminist Engagement with Development Institutions*, London and Geneva: ITDG and UNRISD.

Murthy, R. K. (1998) 'Power, institutions and gender relations: can gender training alter the equations?', *Development in Practice* 8(2):203-211.

Plowman, P. (2000) 'Organisational change from two perspectives: gender and organisational development', *Development in Practice* 10(2):189-203.

Sweetman, C. (1997) 'Editorial: gender and organisational change', *Gender and Development* 5(1):2-9.

Utthan (2000a) 'Organisation at a Glance', unpublished report, Ahmedabad: Utthan.

Utthan (2000b) 'Understanding Gender Equity in Water Resource Management: An Agenda for Research and Programme Activities', research proposal, Ahmedabad: Utthan.

This paper was first published in Development in Practice *(12/3&4: 298-311) in 2002.*

Organisational learning:
a borrowed toolbox?

David Kelleher and the Gender at Work Collaborative

Background

In a field such as gender and development, which has suffered from an excess of stated intentions over actual change, ideas like that of the learning organisation are more than welcome. Organisational learning was originally intended to help organisations respond better to the demands of their environment. It also envisaged changes to how the organisation itself functioned. This 'double-loop learning' was seen as a way in which the organisation could change fundamental beliefs (Argyris and Schön 1978). The promise of change in fundamental beliefs makes learning organisations attractive to advocates for gender equality.

This paper grows out of an e-conference hosted by the Gender at Work Collaborative. The Collaborative is a recently established knowledge-building network dedicated to institutional change for gender equality. It was founded by four organisations: the United Nations Development Fund for Women (UNIFEM), the Women's Learning Partnership (WLP), the World Alliance for Citizen Participation (CIVICUS), and the Association for Women's Rights in Development (AWID). The paper itself is a collaborative project led by David Kelleher arising from an ongoing international discussion about gender equality and institutional change and focused in an e-conference among the following participants: Hala Ghosheh, Evangelino Holvino, David Kelleher, Kate McLaren, Sarah Murison, Penny Plowman, and Ingrid Richter. Many of the key ideas have been developed over a long collaboration with Aruna Rao.

What is a learning organisation?

The concept of the learning organisation as defined in the call for papers for the special issue of *Development in Practice* on which this Reader is based, arises from the following tenets:

- Organisations are mission-driven and their organisational form evolves to best meet that mission within their own particular dynamic context.

- Staff should be empowered to maximise their potential and contribute at both the operational and strategic levels.

- Teamwork and the need to break down functional barriers within an organisation are central tenets.

- The organisational culture is one that values experimentation, risk-taking, and learning in order to breed innovation (i.e. knowledge for action).

- Organisations are sensitive to, and have strategic linkages with, the external context, combined with in-built flexibility, which allow them to thrive in a changing environment.

My understanding is similar in many respects but it is worth commenting on some differences. In earlier writing about organisational learning, Abbey-Livingston and Kelleher (1988) and Kelleher and McLaren (1996) have also highlighted the importance of power, the nature of knowledge, and paradoxical action.

Many have written about the importance of empowerment, participation, and team relationships as key factors in organisational change. These are crucial, but I think that experience has shown that participation within existing power relations confines the dialogue to the box of permissible conversation. For learning to happen, this set of power-related understandings must be challenged – generally from outside the organisation. In the e-conference, McLaren reminded us of the importance of well-organised and well-connected women's organisations in pushing key government departments to launch equity efforts. Therefore, permeability to influence and to ideas from outside becomes an important part of the equation. Of course, 'bad' ideas from outside are also part of permeability. This highlights the importance of political analysis and action within the organisation in order to amplify ideas that further equality and translate them into policies, programmes, and practices.

The last two factors, the nature of knowledge and paradox, require some explication. Traditionally, organisations behaved as if knowledge was objective and true absolutely. Knowledge was held by experts and the senior people in the organisation. But Paulo Freire's work (1981) challenged that, and showed that knowledge is created (and accompanied by a series of explicit and implicit political messages).

Recent thinking (Von Krogh *et al.* 2000) sees knowledge as an individual construction of reality that involves feelings, beliefs, and experience (some of which are not even conscious). This is a much more fluid and democratic understanding of knowledge which, as Murison pointed out in the e-conference, permits the sharing of information and its translation into knowledge through practice – a crucial aspect of learning organisations.

The other aspect of organisational learning is non-rational or paradoxical decision making and action. Huberman and Miles (1984) first wrote about this in their analysis of innovative schools. They found that innovation depended on both freedom and control. In other words, schools which were most innovative existed in a situation where there was some magical mixture of freedom and control. This was not news to experienced managers but the literature had always emphasised the importance of support and freedom and lessening control. Later work (Quinn 1988) extended this idea to a theory of non-rational leadership.

In summary, we understand a learning organisation as:

- permeable to outside ideas and pressures;
- sufficiently democratic that those ideas with merit can flourish from all levels of the organisation and evolve into practice;
- possessing teams capable of functioning democratically and effectively;
- capable of resolving apparent contradictions between such issues as stability and change, and support and pressure;
- capable of using processes and tools for organisational learning.

Before leaving this section it is important to temper any apparent clarity as to the nature of learning organisations. In our conference, Holvino first pointed out that much of the writing about organisational learning reifies 'organisation' and 'learning'. I agree; a learning organisation is not a 'thing' that can be described in any complete way that would allow us to say, 'this is a learning organisation, this isn't, this one scores 7', or the like. As McLaren highlighted, many of the organisations we work in would not meet the definition of learning organisations and yet much learning is happening. Richter said: 'I no longer use the phrase "learning organisation" because it has become ... whatever you imagine it to be. Saying that there is such a thing or animal as a learning organisation is like saying there is a "doing" organisation.'

Increasingly, we are coming to believe that the idea of learning organisations is like a myth: a collection of ideas, woven into a story that helps us make sense of experience and forms one of many ideals to which to aspire. The story is compelling and useful in many situations, so it is a story that is often told (although with many variations).

The last point is that it is important to ask what it is that a learning organisation is learning. Is the learning happening within a set of cultural and organisational norms, or is it challenging those norms both internally and in its work in the society?

This leads us to the question of the usefulness of these ideas for institutional change for gender equality. Is this toolbox, developed largely within the private sector, helpful to those working for gender equality? Our first clue that we might be using a borrowed toolbox comes when we look for the word 'gender' in the index of leading (and even lesser) texts on organisational learning. It is, of course, conspicuously absent for (at least) three reasons. First, organisational learning, while concerning itself with change (even at a deep level) has never claimed to be about transforming power or gender relations. Learning organisations have been advanced as a more effective response to the problem of change. The measure of success is whether the firm does better within existing understandings of the idea of 'better'. Its purpose is not social transformation or change in gender-biased institutional norms that shape families, markets, or the State. Second, although organisational learning believes in participation and a certain democracy, it doesn't admit to politics: constituencies, pressure, or accountability. In other words, it represents a strong advocate for wide participation and involvement of staff at all levels, but it leaves the authority structure intact. For those of us who have been managers in NGOs, this is not necessarily a bad thing on a day-to-day basis, but changing gender relations demands that we think differently about organisations and hierarchies and consider organisational forms with more accountability to clients, staff, and beneficiaries. (Some NGOs have made considerable progress with this – but not by reading organisational learning texts.) Third, organisational learning doesn't focus on key elements of importance to gender equality. There is a growing body of work that describes organisations as gendered in very fundamental but invisible ways and requiring a kind of anthropological dig to understand their gendered aspects (see Acker 1990; Goetz 1997; Rao et al. 1999).

In order to understand this gender bias in the very fabric of organisations and the effect this has on development and human rights work, we turn to the question of institutional change.

Gender equality and institutional change

The founding meeting of the Gender at Work Collaborative agreed that significant progress towards gender equality could be made only by changing institutions and gender-biased institutional norms. The meeting also clarified the difference between institutions and organisations. We understood institutions as the frameworks of rules for achieving social or economic ends (Kabeer and Subrahmanian 1996). These rules specify how resources are allocated, and how tasks, responsibilities, and value are assigned – in other words, who gets what, who does what, and who gets to decide. Institutions, then, are *societal* rules of the game, and are different from organisations, although they affect organisations (and can be affected in turn).

Although institutions vary within and across cultures and are constantly evolving and changing:

> ... *each major institutional arena is gendered in its male bias – its failure to value or recognise reproductive work, defining it as 'unproductive' or basing effective participation on a capacity to attain freedom from the reproductive sphere ... [this bias] is then deeply reinforced – institutionalised through the formation of social networks, or shared understandings and conventions of inclusion or exclusion, justified ideologically, which privilege the participation of a particular social group.*
>
> (Goetz 1997:13)

There are various ongoing efforts to change gender-biased institutions. Examples include legislative reform, women's budgets, and judicial reform. These macro-level changes, however, are dependent upon the organisations that plan and implement them. One would not expect a patriarchal, misogynist organisation to lead an effort to change gender-biased institutions (although many organisations are far from monolithic and not all behaviour conforms to a particular orientation).

The task of changing organisations so that their work can be more effective in changing institutions is a primary interest of the Collaborative. Briefly, how do we understand this?

If institutions are the frameworks of rules, organisations are the social structures that operate within these frameworks and act either to reinforce the rules or to challenge them. These institutional norms often operate below the level of awareness but are knitted into the hierarchies, work practices, and beliefs of organisational life, and thereby constrain organisational efforts to challenge gender-biased norms. This includes not only how the organisation functions internally (the number of women managers, for example) but how it conceives of its mission and whether it delivers services and programmes in a way that challenges gender norms.

Acker (1990) outlines at least five 'gendering processes' in organisations. Formal practices may be apparently neutral but in fact discriminate against women. Informal practices, such as expectations that committed staff work nights and weekends even though women are more likely to have family responsibilities, also discriminate against women. Symbols and images in the organisation, such as the unspoken idea in one case that supervisors need to be men who can make the hard decisions, exclude women from even considering their own possible promotion. Everyday social interactions such as the 'teasing' practised in one development organisation reinforces women's 'place' within it. All of this is internalised by both women and men, making it all seem reasonable and 'normal'. This results in a set of assumptions not only about internal organisational dynamics but also about the work itself. Gendered organisations condition what is seen as possible, reasonable, or appropriate. For example, one peace-building organisation had a very difficult time seeing any role for women in the peace-building process. The men in the organisation genuinely felt that including women in any significant role would not be an effective way to work. Other aspects of this organisation that were not necessarily or obviously gender biased, such as hierarchical power and control over information, simply blocked efforts to see the work differently. Describing a meta-difficulty facing organisational change for gender equity, Acker (2000:630) writes:

> Another dilemma ... arises from the pervasive cultural representation of organisations as instrumental, goal-oriented, no-nonsense arrangements for getting things done ... this belief in gender-neutral organising is comfortable for those with privilege. Indeed one of the privileges of those with power is the privilege to not see the systemic sources of privilege.

This writing would lead us to say that work must focus (at least) on changing what Rao et al. (1999) call the deep structure: power relations, work-family relations, and the valuing of individual effort and heroism.

Application of organisational learning to gender equality in development and human rights organisations: an example

Gender equality advocates have been involved with ideas associated with organisational learning in a number of organisational settings and have found them to be helpful. Over the past ten years there have been a growing number of efforts to change institutions for gender equality based on an organisational approach.[1]

Perhaps my most intensive use of organisational learning technology was with BRAC, a large NGO in Bangladesh. The Gender Team was charged with leading a long-term effort to improve gender equality both within BRAC and in the provision of services to poor rural women in Bangladesh. From the beginning, we identified the need to change organisational norms, systems, and relationships as critical to our efforts to promote gender equality. Briefly, the process can be seen as having the following stages:

1 *Start-up:* clarifying management interest, finding resources, negotiating the essential elements of the process and establishing the Gender Team.

2 *Needs assessment and knowledge building:* a participatory process that involved over 400 staff at all levels in two-day workshops to assess gender issues in BRAC and in BRAC's programme.

3 *Strategic planning:* working with the results of the needs assessment, the Gender Team met for two days with the senior management team and then followed up in a series of one-to-one meetings. This discussion led to a proposed design for the process, which evolved through more management discussions. Ultimately the management group met again to approve the programme design and the idea of an action-learning approach that would involve local area staff in a collaborative analysis of the gender dimensions of their work and then plan action to strengthen gender equality.

4 *Training of trainers and micro-design of the programme:* the training built a core group of 25 facilitators (which has since grown to nearly 50) who would work with area office staff to facilitate the action-learning process. We first used the training of trainers to test and refine the programme design and then launched a pilot in which new facilitators worked with Gender Team members to begin to deliver the programme in area offices.

5 *Implementation:* the trainers worked in area offices to lead staff through a cycle of learning, analysis, and action planning. Area office teams developed analyses of gender issues in their setting and in the programmes they worked in, and developed local solutions. Meetings of area managers considered issues that seemed beyond the capacity of local staff. After two years, the most

important outcomes were a democratisation of BRAC and a changing of relationships between women and men and between levels of the hierarchy. The programme continues some six years later. Approximately 20,000 staff have been involved in the programme. (For a more complete description, see Rao *et al.* 1999.)

In the BRAC case, a number of the ideas related to organisational learning were central to the work:

Permeability to outside ideas and pressures: in the early 1990s BRAC was a restless, constantly growing, constantly changing organisation. Its Executive Director was a visionary who would often bring a discussion of potential action to a close by saying 'why not?' Some of BRAC's senior managers were more open to the idea of women's empowerment and gender equality than others, but they were all in touch with currents in development thinking and had received some suggestions that they consider gender more carefully. As they considered these ideas, they brought in a number of people from outside BRAC and outside Bangladesh to help them think through different approaches. BRAC's permeability was critical to getting started on the project.

Internal democracy: it is fair to say that BRAC was ambivalent about organisational democracy. It was a value espoused in the organisation but many middle managers adopted an authoritative, even harsh, management style. However, the Gender Quality Action Learning (GQAL) programme took the organisation at its word and structured a democratic analysis of gender issues (and more) in area offices and in programmes. These analyses often challenged the manager's right to have the final (or only) word on a number of issues and resulted in a real democratisation of relations within BRAC. Much one-to-one 'political knitting' was needed on the part of the Gender Team leader and members to help managers see how this democratisation was also in their interests. Ultimately, this democratisation was only possible through the intercession of senior managers who rode out the concern of a number of managers as the project began to result in critiques of ways of working at BRAC.

Effective teamwork: for many theorists in the subject, teamwork is at the heart of organisational learning. This was also true at BRAC. Many successes could be traced to good teamwork, which made it possible to analyse problems and develop good solutions that avoided the pitfalls of blame, conflict, and organisational politics. Similarly, some of our greatest difficulties could be blamed on poor teamwork.

Tools and processes for organisational learning: central to the success of the project was the use of tools such as needs assessment, strategic planning meetings, residential retreats, training of trainers, and the action-learning process used in the area offices. All of these tools were designed to allow people at all levels of the organisation to bring issues to the surface and develop solutions. At the same time we were trying to build up skills in these methods and acceptance of their use. We started from a strong position. For years BRAC had had a very strong training ethic and had invested heavily in staff training. The transition was from learning as individuals (training and adult education) to learning as systems (organisational learning).

Resolving contradictions: this is more difficult to analyse. There were some obvious contradictions that BRAC resolved well. One was the democratisation and opening up of the organisation, coupled with the need to manage a disciplined workforce of 15,000 people spread over 30 regions in 750 area offices. Another was in the management of the GQAL programme itself – the use of management power to democratise relations between staff and managers. A more difficult contradiction was the need to marry ideas of increased women's empowerment with the need for 'repayment discipline' in a microcredit programme. Although the tension between these two ends was discussed, BRAC hadn't made significant movement on the issue while we were involved.

In retrospect, then, the ideas associated with organisational learning were of considerable help in the project aimed at gender equality. In particular, there were three important ways in which the project was shaped by the use of organisational learning tools and understandings:

1   The change process was seen by both the Gender Team and the management of BRAC as being 'managed'. This meant that the ultimate judges of the effectiveness and viability of the project were the managers of BRAC. These people were remarkably open to a wide range of changes but it meant that, to stay on the agenda, change had to be seen as responding to the issues and priorities of BRAC managers. There was no broader group of clients or staff to which the programme reported. This not only may have constrained the agenda, it also reinforced the power relations in the organisation. While the project opened up opportunities for democratic decision making, there was no thought of changing the right of managers to make whatever final decision made sense to

them. At the same time, were it not for the interest and power of some senior managers, the programme would not have happened.

2 We didn't think in terms of constituencies that could exert pressure on BRAC for particular kinds of changes. The process was seen as organisational, not political. This also reinforced management power and limited the agenda.

3 We did not focus on societal change and then state what needed to change at BRAC to further that agenda. Instead, we focused on organisational change and capacity building. Our assumption was that efforts at societal change for gender equality would follow. By starting with the organisation we risked getting mired in organisational dynamics and losing sight of the ultimate aim of societal change for gender equality.

Of course, it is impossible to say whether the project at BRAC would have been more effective had we used any of these alternative paths. BRAC has since pursued a variety of gender-related interventions that have taken the organisation much further than was evident when I was last involved. However, these alternative paths imply a process that would go beyond the practice of much organisational learning to focus on power relations and the capacity of the organisation to challenge gender-biased institutional norms.

Conclusion: an expanded toolbox – and 'isn't it a little more complex?'

This section is necessarily speculative because, to our knowledge, these practices have not been used in an integrated way, though a number of ideas stand as hopeful experiments. Tentatively, then, organisational learning for transformation would:

- *Deal with deep structure:* particularly the question of work–family balance and the deep-down aversion to allowing the reproductive sphere to intrude on organisational life. This is difficult for NGOs – which of us wants to risk being 'less productive' in order to accommodate dimly understood ideas about institutional change? (Although Rapoport and Bailyn's (1996) work at Xerox demonstrated that movement can be made on work–family issues while also increasing productivity.)

- *Deepen democracy:* particularly the question of accountability to women and men served by the organisation, but also coming to grips with the question of internal constituencies and their use of power to press for change towards equality.

- *Develop tools for consensus and learning:* particularly those which can bridge the real differences in interest between organisational stakeholders. The development of dialogue and interest-based bargaining hold some promise in this regard.

- *Lead to recognition of the spiritual:* although most organisational thinking is silent on the place of the spiritual, personal conversations with people who are working in this area testify to the importance of this deeper level. The physicist David Bohm, in his book on wholism (1995), reminds us of the importance of being open to the fundamental shift of mind from seeing the world as being made up of things that are separate, fixed, and resistant to change, to a world that's open, full of possibilities, and primarily made up of relationships.

The above critique of organisational learning is not intended to mean that those ideas are of little use in furthering a gender-equality agenda. On the contrary, as Ghosheh pointed out in the e-conference, these tools and ideas have been important in getting started in a variety of organisations. Further, the idea that nothing will happen by using existing understandings of organisational learning and that something big will happen if we enhance our toolbox is just too simple. As McLaren wrote:

> Such profound change is far more complex, politicised, chaotic, and much less instrumental … there is lots of important learning going on as a result of sustained efforts using these traditional tools. Some of it is a direct result of planned activities. There will inevitably be individuals whose understanding and practice will change as a result, and this will have an organisational or collective impact in some way, over time. But just as important, there is also learning and change that is piggy-backing on the formal activities. There are lots of other organisational processes at work at the same time. Some of these are deliberate, but others are not. I am thinking here of the incredible importance of human interaction, the interpersonal connections and relationship building that go on around 'learning' and 'change' initiatives: trust building, influence peddling, gentle persuasion, exchange of favours, getting on the band-wagon, power plays etc. – the full range of human behaviour in all its bounty.

Such comments should also remind us that we are far from the only game in town when we are working with an organisation. Even with the best tools and skills, we are only a part of a complex soup of organisational evolution.

The last point is that there are always differences between our goals as change agents, what is possible in a given situation, and what organisations want when they ask us to help them become more gender equitable. As change agents we may recognise that gender equality requires a very different set of power relations in the organisation, but we are seldom, if ever, asked by organisations to lead a cultural revolution. Our work is generally an effort to move the organisation towards being somewhat more equitable, perhaps more democratic, and more accountable. We may also be working to get the organisation to pay more attention to work–family and other equity issues, knowing that the overwhelming bulk of organisational change work is incremental. This doesn't mean that we are content with these incremental changes. We do this believing that our work is contributing to a larger change that is taking place over time.

As we work in these complex places, settling for a series of incremental changes, the questions are: are we on the right path, do we have the right tools, is our work adding up to significant change, and are we working in a way that will live up to our ideals and justify our effort and the trust of those we are working with?

Note

1   See Rao *et al.* (1999), Goetz (1997), Porter *et al.* (1999), Van Dam *et al.* (2000), and Plowman (2000). See also the work of KIT Gender (www.kit.nl/gender), The Novib Gender Route Programme, and the Center for Gender in Organizations (www.simmons.edu/gsm/)

References

Abbey-Livingston, Diane and David Kelleher (1988) *Managing for Learning: The Fundamentals*, Toronto: Government of Ontario.

Acker, Joan (1990) 'Hierarchies, jobs and bodies: a theory of gendered organisations', *Gender and Society* 4(2):139-158.

Acker, Joan (2000) 'Gendered contradictions in organisational equity projects', *Organisation* 7(4):625-632.

Argyris, Chris and Donald Schön (1978) *Organizational Learning*, Reading, MA: Addison-Wesley.

Bohm, David (1995) *Wholeness and the Implicate Order*, London: Routledge.

Freire, Paulo (1981) *Pedagogy of the Oppressed*, New York, NY: Continuum.

Goetz, Anne Marie (1997) *Getting Institutions Right for Women in Development*, London: Zed Press.

Huberman, A. Michael and Matthew Miles (1984) *Innovation Up Close: How School Improvement Works*, New York, NY: Plenum.

Kabeer, Naila and Ramya Subrahmanian (1996) 'Institutions, Relations, and Outcomes: Frameworks, Tools, and Gender-aware Planning', IDS Discussion Paper, Brighton: IDS.

Kelleher, David and Kate McLaren with Ronald Bisson (1996) *Grabbing the Tiger by the Tail: NGOs Learning for Organizational Change*, Ottawa: CCIC.

Plowman, Penny (2000) 'Organisational change from two perspectives: gender and organisational development', *Development in Practice* 10(2):189-203.

Porter, Fenella, Ines Smyth, and Caroline Sweetman (eds.) (1999) *Gender Works: Oxfam Experience in Policy and Practice*, Oxford: Oxfam GB.

Quinn, Robert (1988) *Beyond Rational Management: Mastering the Paradoxes and Competing Demands of High Performance*, San Francisco, CA: Jossey-Bass.

Rao, Aruna, Rieky Stuart, and David Kelleher (1999) *Gender at Work: Organizational Change for Equality*, West Hartford, CT: Kumarian.

Rapoport, Rhona and Lotte Bailyn (1996) 'Relinking Life and Work: Toward a Better Future', unpublished report, New York, NY: Ford Foundation.

Van Dam, Henk, Angela Khadar, and Minke Valk (eds.) (2000) *Institutionalising Gender Equality: Commitment, Policy and Practice – A Global Source Book*, Amsterdam: Royal Tropical Institute (KIT).

Von Krogh, Georg, Kazuo Ichijo, and Ikujiro Nonaka (2000) *Enabling Knowledge Creation*, New York, NY: OUP.

This paper was first published in Development in Practice (*12/3&4:312-320*) *in 2002.*

Making the organisation learn:
demystification and management action

Vijay Padaki

A tribute

This article has been written as a tribute to Russell L. Ackoff, one of the foremost thinkers in management science and one of its greatest teachers. He has persevered for over 30 years to refine organisational theory from the perspective of systems science and, more importantly, to make it reliably applicable to management tasks. Many of the twentieth-century's greatest systems scientists have collaborated with him, from the field of cybernetics to that of the learning organisation. The origins of many enduring management ideas can be traced back to Ackoff's original work, although this is not always recognised. He has demonstrated in his long and distinguished career the wisdom of Kurt Lewin's famous dictum: 'There is nothing so practical as good theory.'

Always impatient with the fads, panaceas, and quick fixes that abound in management literature, Ackoff has devoted his time and energy to building the foundations for valid constructs. In the rush to find a place on the bandwagon, we must not forget that the concept of the learning organisation originated in the application of systems science to understanding organisational effectiveness. The relevance of Ackoff's work to the world of development can be readily seen in his insistence on dealing with social justice as a core parameter in system purposefulness. Indeed, his systems science definition of development merits serious attention.

Models and metaphors in management

The assumptions underlying any management practice may be viewed in both a cross-sectional and a longitudinal timeframe. Preoccupation with the former leads us to a 'flavour of the month' orientation. The longitudinal view helps us appreciate the evolution of thought and to regard ideas as products of their time, rather than the quantum leaps they are often portrayed to be. Indeed, if all the management mantras that make such claims were put together into a single organisational entity for everyday practice, the organisation would probably shudder to a stop. Management is the only 'science' that produces 'theories' at a rate that can only be called cheaper by the dozen. It must be obvious that this facility (a 'core competency'?) comes from the department of bandwagon marketing. 'New formula' products in management literature have grown impressively in the last 25 years. Alas, growth cannot be equated with development.

The learning organisation (LO) is a brand. It has, undoubtedly, a huge brand equity value. It has replaced total quality management (TQM) at the top of the top-ten charts worldwide. The downfall of TQM was accompanied by reluctant revelations of its failure rate, which has been estimated to be as high as 65–70 per cent. In other words, for every one showcase 'success', there were two failures not mentioned. Should we be surprised if the backlash from LO brings in similar unpleasant statistics? Even as the issue of *Development in Practice* on which this Reader is based is being read, the counting of burnt fingers has begun. The pattern is remarkably similar for all management 'revolutions'. TQM and LO are merely the two most recent illustrations. The pattern seems to conform exceedingly well to the brand lifecycle model in marketing!

What makes a management system succeed?

How do we explain the failure rates (as well as the successes) of TQM and LO? The usual polarisation of views – faulting the product or faulting its usage – does not help. Here is another way of explaining failure and, in the process, ensuring a higher probability of success. We will consider a *three-way compatibility test*, proposing that the test be applied to any management system being brought into an organisation. Figure 1 depicts the framework.

Management structure refers to the critical mass of decision makers who influence the organisation's strategic perspective and policies. There may be more than one 'level' of critical decision makers and, therefore, of decisions. The extent of congruence in the thinking across two or more centres of decision making appears important.

Management system refers to the formal, codified set of procedures that determine the processes of decision making. There may be more than one formal system at work in the organisation. The extent of congruence across key areas of decision making by two or more systems appears important.

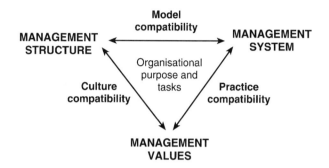

Management values refers to deep, enduring convictions about what is right or wrong, good or bad, and acceptable or unacceptable conduct in management practice. There may be more than one area of management practice with a recognisable value basis (e.g. a 'caring' value in staffing and an 'efficiency' value in project management). What appears to be important are (a) the extent of consensus on the value among the majority of managers, and (b) the congruence across two or more areas of management practice in the value 'system'.

The three types of compatibility may now be examined.

1 *Model compatibility* begins with the (often unstated) model of the organisation, i.e. assumptions of what an organisation is, how it functions, and, therefore, how to make it work. Ackoff (1994, 1999) refers to three main types of assumptions about the organisation: the mechanistic-deterministic, the animate-organismic, and the social-systemic, and there might be other ways of classifying our notions of the organisation. 'Models' of organisation are often reflected in the metaphors we employ in management communications – keeping the wheels turning, the warp and weft of operations, the house, the tree, the body, the family, and so on.

It is important to note that assumptions about the nature of the organisation exist both in the minds of the managers and in the construct of a management system. Every management system has (often unstated) assumptions of what an organisation is and how it functions. For instance, the production-management system which employs operations-research techniques appears to take a mechanistic view of the organisation, as does the discipline of job analysis. In contrast, the systems of management by participation (MbP) or management by objectives (MbO) would seem to be closer to an animate view of the organisation. Interestingly, a system to enhance the engineering process in an organisation may also invoke an animate-organismic model. For instance, a software development organisation may monitor its engineering processes by a system called the capability maturity model in which the underlying assumptions of 'maturation' are certainly organic.

Is it possible for those in the *management structure* within an organisation to have one model of the organisation in their minds, and for the *management system* to have another model as an underlying premise? It most certainly is. And it can happen in the non-profit NGO setting as much as in the corporate context. The most common discrepancy in the former is between an animate-organismic viewpoint in the management structure and the mechanistic-deterministic assumptions in methods employed in project management, for instance in PERT/CPM, ZOPP, LogFrame, etc.

The problem is compounded when two or more management systems in the organisation have conflicting models of the organisation – for instance, between the mechanistic assumptions in job analysis and the synergistic assumptions in team-based project management.

2 *Culture compatibility* begins with the concept of culture as *perpetration* of patterns of behaviour – making them characteristic, predictable, and enduring.

By definition, a value represents a 'central' belief in our cognitive organisation, ensuring a strong internal consistency across thinking, emotions, and conduct. When an organisation articulates its value positions (e.g. in vision and mission statements), it is saying what it would *like to believe* its character to be. On the other hand, the management structure determines the decision-making process that results in the actual behaviours of people in the organisation (Padaki 2000a). It is a common observation (even in our own lives) that the same person may display two quite contrasting orientations in the roles played in two different management structures in two different organisations (e.g. empathetic in one, impersonal in the other, or risk-taking and collaborative in one, playing safe and non-cooperative in the other, and so on).

Is it possible for the stated management values in the organisation to profess one pattern of conduct, and for the predispositions in the management structure to be at variance with it? It most certainly is. For instance, in an NGO with a project-based management structure (determined, in turn, by the funding pattern), there may be a natural predisposition to empire building by project staff. This is a negation of the values of resource conservation, putting the community before oneself, collaborative efforts to overcome poverty, and so on.

3 *Practice compatibility* begins with recognition of the fact that every management system – made up of methods, tools, and techniques – has underlying assumptions of what *ought to be* the way to do things in the organisation. Many of these assumptions are about how people *ought* to relate to others in carrying out their roles. A management system is invariably a product of its time and, therefore, a carrier of a value system. The emergence of 'participative style' as a leadership prescription, the stress on delegation and joint goal setting in MbO, and the importance given to 'internal customer focus' for continuous improvement in organisational processes have all had certain value premises embedded in them.

On the other hand, there exists in every organisation an established (perpetrated) culture. The culture includes values that determine orientations, norms of conduct, and ways of relating with others. Is it possible for the value premises in a management system to be in conflict with the prevailing orientations and norms of conduct? It most certainly is. For instance, the MbO system for monitoring performance stresses bilateral accountability and a coaching leadership process, calling for democratic values and managerial responsibility for developing others. If the prevailing values in the group are strongly authoritarian, accompanied by low transparency in decision making, there are likely to be two parallel systems at work – the formal, 'paper' system of MbO, and the informal, 'real' system of managing the group. The dysfunctional outcomes of such parallel systems must be noted.

Problems of incompatibility can also occur with two or more management systems making demands on people with underlying value conflicts – for instance, seeking collective effort through team-based project management structures, and reinforcing individualistic effort through the reward mechanisms.

Finally, it must be recognised that the compatibility we seek in the three-way framework is with reference to the given organisational purpose – the particular tasks in its mission – in a given operational context. Marked uniqueness in the nature of the task or the operational environment may certainly influence one or more of the three points in the framework. However, the internal consistency within the framework will still be a necessity.

Locating the learning organisation

Three questions arise from the three-way compatibility framework. First, is there an organisational model that is inherently superior – more valid, closer to the 'truth' – than other models? Second, is there an ideal 'mix' in the three-way framework that is good for all organisations? And finally, how can the learning organisation be located within the framework? We may begin with the first, but it will be seen that after we start that it is not necessary to address the questions separately.

The simple answer to the first question appears to be: yes, there is indeed a one best model of organisation. But which is the model that has stood the test of time and proved its validity, rising quietly and firmly above the fads, panaceas, and quick fixes in the management supermarket? There is clearly one candidate for this distinctive position. It is the perspective of general systems theory which makes us view the organisation *as an open system* with all the accompanying features: interactivity among the parts, the need for purposefulness to define its fit in the environment, the extent of robustness in its functioning, the need for system intelligence, and so on (Ackoff 1974; Ackoff and Emery 1981). Indeed, the concept of *proactive orientation* defines an organisational state of continuous learning that is the same as a learning organisation.

The contribution of general systems theory to our understanding of organisational effectiveness and, therefore, to management methodology has increased steadily. Looking back over 50 years of management theorising, it can be seen that the small number of concepts and practices that have stood the test of time – while dozens of fads have fallen by the wayside – have all been consistent with the basic tenets of systems thinking. Here is not the place to dwell on the basics of systems theory – there is an abundance of introductory literature on the subject. Padaki (2001) has shown the relevance of 'a system of system concepts' in development programmes and NGO management.

The central ideas in the open system view of the organisation are often missed, even if there is a general inclination towards systems thinking. It is often not recognised, for instance, that the entire discipline of *organisational development* (OD) has developed steadily over 50 years because of the solid theoretical foundations in systems science. Contrary to popular (and unhelpful) notions of OD being a set of esoteric training techniques to 'change people's mindsets', the methodology of OD begins with the acceptance of organisational variables as powerful determinants of the typicalities of attitudes and behaviours (Padaki 2000b). The classic S-P-A model, derived from Kurt Lewin's Field Theory, may be depicted as:

Structures
(The mechanisms that determine the nature of interactivity among the parts of a system)

Processes
(The psychological orientation or 'climate')

Acts
(The behavioural predisposition or 'the done thing')

The 'process sensitivity' that OD attempts to create in a group is to get people to understand how the behavioural predispositions in the organisation are of their own making, i.e. the consequences of structures and systems set up by themselves. However, it must also be appreciated that the entire discipline of OD rests on certain value premises – in particular, the cluster comprising democratic, egalitarian, and humanistic values. Even if not fully observed in practice, a critical mass of decision makers in the organisational system must at least find these values acceptable before any OD-like process is undertaken there (Padaki 1997, 2000b). All of this is in contrast to the application of systems science with a mechanistic model of the organisation. (Even the terms employed are a reflection of this, e.g. 'business process re-engineering', 'industrial dynamics', etc.)

Next, it must be clear that certain management systems are naturally compatible with systems thinking and the accompanying value premises of OD. Others simply will not work. Too many of the available tools and techniques are mechanistic in nature, assuming that different parts of the organisational whole can be 'improved' in isolation, without recognising that the system's performance is the product of the *interactivity among its parts*. Treating the parts in isolation leads predictably to *sub-optimisation* in the system – the performance of one part at the expense of some other parts. It is not easily appreciated that it is quite possible simultaneously to improve the performance of each part of a system separately and still reduce the performance of the whole.

> *Nowhere is the fallacy of the mechanistic model more evident than in the*
> *performance appraisal system. Techniques and incentives to stimulate*
> *individual effort are based on the underlying (and unquestioned)*
> *assumption that the output of the team is additive in nature, i.e. the sum of*
> *the outputs of individuals. If there is a universal distrust of performance*
> *appraisal it is because of the intuitive understanding among the people*
> *concerned that the performance of the system is really quite systemic.*

Since the concept of a learning organisation is essentially a derivation from systems thinking and, further, a specialised extension of theory and methodology in OD, it must be clear that its location in the three-way compatibility framework is likely to be as shown in Figure 2.

The social-systemic model of the organisation appears best suited for the OD process and for building the learning organisation. Locating OD and LO in this way clearly calls for the recognition of a *paradigm* position.

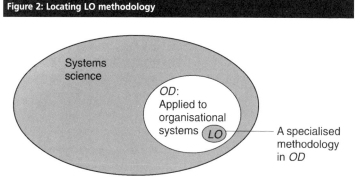

Figure 2: Locating LO methodology

Systems science

OD: Applied to organisational systems *LO*

A specialised methodology in *OD*

The specialised methodology in *LO* may include specialised tools and techniques, e.g. all of 'knowledge management' may be viewed as a natural subset of *LO*.

Indeed, many organisations 'trying out' LO practices might not be aware of the paradigm shifts needed to make them work. If the three points of compatibility in the triangle in Figure 3 are rooted in two (or three) different paradigms, we can expect dissonances. These dissonances can be dealt with either by processes of healthy confrontation or by self-deceptive reactions, worsening dysfunctional states in the organisation. The contrasting features between the most commonly held paradigm and the required OD/LO paradigm are discussed below.

The relevance in development organisations and programmes

The relevance of the above concepts to management tasks in voluntary organisations or development NGOs is best examined around the three-way compatibility framework, outlined in the recommended model contained in Figure 3. The 'model' has been implemented successfully in several NGOs – international donor agencies, operational NGOs, and support or resource NGOs. The elaboration that follows is a generic case, drawn from the experiences in several organisations.

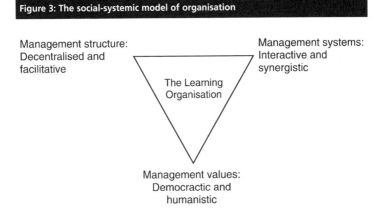

Figure 3: The social-systemic model of organisation

Management structure:
Decentralised and
facilitative

Management systems:
Interactive and
synergistic

The Learning
Organisation

Management values:
Democractic and
humanistic

Management structure

We begin by recalling a dictum in organisation theory that has stood the test of time: *form follows function*. How work is *organised* or *structured* must be decided by the circumstances in which the work is performed. Four main factors represent the variety of circumstances possible:

- the nature of the task (e.g. making bricks or making movies);
- the range of competencies required (e.g. physical, intellectual, social skills);
- the technology deployed (e.g. the extent of automation);
- the scale of operations (e.g. in volume and geographic reach).

These four factors must be viewed as being interdependent. For instance, a larger scale may need a different technology, which in turn may call for a different mix of competencies.

What are the characteristics of development work that may determine the optimum structures for an organisation? The most important features seem to be the following:

- work is project-based, carried out in designated project groups and subgroups;
- there is an emphasis on 'services' rather than on 'products';
- work patterns or schedules cannot be routinised ('no two days are the same');
- tasks are interdisciplinary (with strong within-group interdependencies in roles, representing specialist competencies);
- there are strong cross-group interdependencies from specialist functions (e.g. across projects);
- there are frequent and continuing transactions with the 'customer', i.e. the community and its groups or organisations; and, most importantly,
- *not everything is known about the development process. It is important to be learning while doing all the time.* This is the classic action-research condition, which is also a premise in OD.

> *These features demand work structures that are unique and fundamentally different from those prevailing in most other types of work organisation. Among other things, development work calls for genuinely team-based work structures.*

The term *team* is used here in the technical and not in the popular sense. The sentiment of 'teamwork' and the good intentions of 'team building' come to nought without the structural features that distinguish the team from any other grouping of people. Some critical differences between teams and groups are shown in Figure 4.

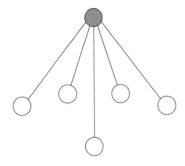 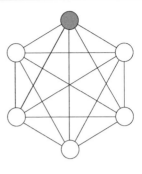

Groups	**Teams**
1 Emphasis on personal leadership: – single-point decision making – expert leadership	Emphasis on leadership process: – multiple-point decision making – facilitative leadership
2 Individual/vertical accountability	Multi-lateral accountability
3 Group performance/output: additive – sum of individual work contributions	Group performance/output: Synergistic – the product of inter-activity among the roles
4 Interdependence medium-low	Interdependence high-critical
5 Emphasis on individual or personal skills	Emphasis on complementarity of skills

It is seen that team-based structures and project-based work tend to go together. This is especially so in development work, where teams are formed and disbanded over project cycles. A person may belong to more than one team in varying capacities, with varying extents of involvement. A team may also have members coming in and going out throughout its life. In sum, while all teams are groups, not all groups are teams! Development work appears to require – and benefit from – team-based structures.

Management system

Of all the formal procedural systems that an organisation adopts, none is closer to its purpose than a sound performance-management system. The greater the concern for *accountability* in the organisation, the stronger the need to define organisational performance more correctly, with the desire to do something about enhancing it. Performance management, of course, is not to be equated with performance appraisal or project management, although helpful elements from both of these procedures may be incorporated into a comprehensive performance management system.

A performance-management system that stresses organisational learning for continuous improvement must have at least three sub-systems integrated within it, as three 'arms' of the system:

- *Arm 1:* a procedural system that views performance outputs in *interactive terms*, aimed at *systemic* corrections and improvements – resembling the project management PIME process, but going far beyond it to collective responsibility and action in bringing about the systemic changes.

- *Arm 2:* a procedural system that aids individual adaptations to the systemic demands – resembling performance appraisal, but going beyond the regulatory orientation in most appraisal systems to a distinctive developmental orientation.

- *Arm 3:* a procedural system that aids the reinforcement of attitudes and practices deemed helpful, and the correction and control of those deemed unhelpful – resembling reward (and punishment) systems, but going beyond them.

The primacy of the systemically oriented procedures in the first arm must be evident. If the larger organisational system is not facilitating improved performance, any amount of emphasis on individual 'appraisal' and 'rewards' can only be increasingly frustrating. On the other hand, the learning orientation created by Arm 1 of the system helps in making individuals *want to* attempt changes in orientation and practice.

Management values

Following the three-way compatibility framework, we will see that the combination of team-based structures and a systemically oriented performance-management system calls for an alternative value system in the people concerned. For the social-systemic model to work, the conventional notions of 'leadership' need to be replaced. For instance:

- from authoritative to facilitative leadership;

- from vertical, unilateral accountability within a work group to multilateral accountability, including the downward accountability of the formal leader to members of the group;

- from a manipulative orientation to a collaborative orientation towards people in the group, and so on. 'Management by participation' takes on a different meaning. It is appreciated as a desirable human process in itself, a value, rather than a management technique for better control.

In OD consulting work with NGOs we often come across a dilemma within the organisation, which reflects a deeper conflict in the realm of values that has not been addressed, i.e. the need to be people-oriented (valuing participation, empathy, caring, etc.) versus the need to be task oriented (emphasising efficiency, achievement, targets, etc.).

Management often experiences considerable difficulty in dealing with this dilemma and may be divided sharply, polarised around the two positions. In almost every case it has been shown, first, that neither position is either correct or complete in itself and, second, that conflict occurs because of inconsistencies in the three-way framework.

In reality the two 'poles' are complementary, rather than opposed. Most important, *the complementarity can come only out of the internal consistency in the social-systemic model.*

> *The relevance of the social-systemic model is not only for the NGO itself; it is equally significant in its work with communities. It is too easy to persuade a community to set up organisations with notions of 'ideal structure' and 'ideal systems' that may actually be completely unhelpful to the mission.*

The learning organisation aids the complementarity, and vice versa. This should not come as a surprise, as both concepts have arisen out of the open systems view of the organisation. According to this view, the *purposefulness* and *robustness* of an organisational system can be related to a *vital organic balance* to be struck between two seemingly opposed processes:

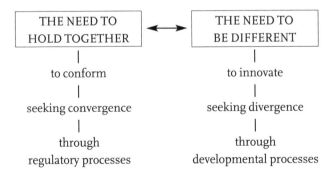

| THE NEED TO HOLD TOGETHER | ⟷ | THE NEED TO BE DIFFERENT |

to conform

to innovate

seeking convergence

seeking divergence

through
regulatory processes

through
developmental processes

The two complementary forces need to be brought under control and to be balanced in *all* management, in all types of endeavours. However, the task appears as a special challenge in the management of NGOs because of the newness of the experience. Too much conformity at the expense of innovation can be just as dysfunctional as too much innovation without conformity.

Making it work

The proof of the learning organisation, it can be said, is in the acts of learning – not in the wishing. One of the most common complaints about LO is that it appears elegant and attractive in the introductory seminar, but then what? Methods to translate the ideas into actual practice appear vague or are not mentioned at all. As one chief executive put it: ' ... when I went home and was in my shower thinking about it, there was a feeling of disempowerment. It came from not seeing a path in a forest, beautiful as the forest might be, and the increasing anxiety that the elusiveness might be the nature of the beast.'

Some starting principles

The author has been part of the OD 'movement' since the 1960s. Because of its all-embracing nature, OD has welcomed many different models and methods into its fold over the years, even redefining the field of OD occasionally as needed. But the following represent some of the central *principles* in the practice of OD:

1   Satisfy yourself about the soundness of theoretical premises in any 'new' prescription. Methodology is best understood as*: theory + methods + tools + operating skills.* Remember, 'There is nothing so practical as good theory.'

2   Go for the substance rather than the brand. It is possible to build a truly *learning organisation* without ever using the term, just as it is possible to have global feedback for a performance orientation without calling it '360 degrees'. The assigning of labels often makes the effort cultist, falsely exclusive, and deprived of eclectic enrichment.

3   Demystify the system. It is extremely important for the client system to relate easily to the concepts and, therefore, the implications for action. Explorations in simple language must precede the adoption of any 'model' or 'framework'.

4   Empower the client system. The people themselves must conceive, design, plan, implement, and manage the operating system involved in the change process. All knowledge and 'expertise' must be transferred to the client system. It should be noted that the empowerment principle includes within it the complete transparency of the change agent and her or his agenda – an important point that could be developed into an essay in itself.

5 Find the 'gateway' most suited for the client system to initiate the change process, around which other interventions may be viewed systemically. There is no 'one best way' to get an organisation moving towards a more proactive state.

6 Constantly urge everybody to view the woods rather than the trees, the organisation's state of effectiveness as a whole, rather than a single function or one organisational unit. Organisational *performance* and organisational *purposefulness* must be the shared backdrop for all players in the entire change process.

A model programme of change

While no two organisations can ever be the same in their operational contexts and the gateways they need for a change process, a generic 'model' seems nevertheless possible for initiating such a process. First and foremost, it must be recognised that creating a learning organisation is a task which requires a process of organisational transformation. The flow chart in Figure 5 suggests four stages in the process.

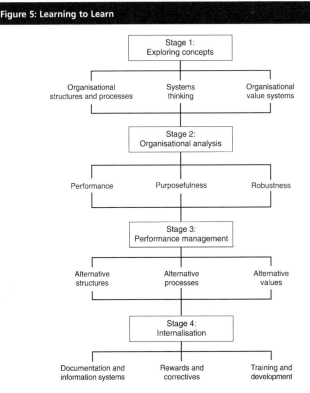

Figure 5: Learning to Learn

Stage 1: Exploring concepts
- Organisational structures and processes
- Systems thinking
- Organisational value systems

Stage 2: Organisational analysis
- Performance
- Purposefulness
- Robustness

Stage 3: Performance management
- Alternative structures
- Alternative processes
- Alternative values

Stage 4: Internalisation
- Documentation and information systems
- Rewards and correctives
- Training and development

The sequence of tasks in each of the four stages appears important. The completion of each stage prepares the ground for the next one. In actual practice, some elements of a later stage may be undertaken towards the end of the previous stage. Brief descriptions of the task ingredients in the four stages follow.

Stage 1: exploration The main purpose of this stage (as its name suggests) is for the critical mass of managers or decision makers in the organisation to explore ideas and concepts about human organisations. This is best done in a non-invasive, non-intrusive manner, for instance in seminars in which there is ample opportunity for all to express opinions and experiences without having to defend any particular position. It is useful to spread this exploration over a few sessions, spaced conveniently, rather than to compress too much in one sitting. It is also useful to provide as much time for discussion as for the seminar inputs. *Exploring* ideas and concepts also means employing a vocabulary and syntax that is simple, jargon-free, and that refers to people's common experiences. Some examples are given in Table 1.

The general theme for the seminar series in Stage 1 can be called *exploring organisational effectiveness*. Any reflection on conditions back home must come naturally, from the participants themselves, and not from the seminar leader. The minimum coverage in the seminar series would be:

- systems thinking, applied to organisations;
- understanding structures and processes in organisational systems;
- organisational value systems.

Stage 2: organisational analysis It is only at this stage that the group is encouraged to examine its own organisation along the lines covered in Stage 1. The methodology in Stage 2 will change from seminars to workshop exercises, relying largely on experiential methods. The theme might well be *purpose and performance*. As seen in the flow chart (see Figure 5), the objective in this stage would be to achieve a firm understanding of organisational health and dysfunction and, therefore, the options available to management to sustain long-term performance.

Stage 3: managing performance Here the group takes on the responsibility of conceiving, designing, and introducing helpful structures and systems for the transformational process. At this stage, rather than at the start, the group will readily see the interconnections across structures, processes, and values in the alternative set-up. For instance, overcoming sub-optimisation in the system will call for

Table 1: User-friendly approaches to exploring ideas

Concept	Unhelpful approaches	Helpful approaches
Structures– Processes– Acts	Every individual functions in a behavioural field. The structural properties of the field determine transactional processes which, in turn, determine the behavioural predispositions of the individual. Structures may be defined as …	How many of us here have worked in more than one organisation? You can reflect on your own experiences working in two or more organisations … Did you find yourself behaving differently in the two jobs? In efficiency? Problem solving? Cooperating with others? Risk taking? Why do you think that happened? The same person, but two different 'personalities' …
Group dynamics	Individuals display certain response tendencies when they operate by themselves. These predispositions change at different system levels of functioning – in the interpersonal, small group, large group, and organisational settings …	In fieldwork, have you noticed that a person expressed an opinion to you when you met privately … but another opinion when the group met? Or the other way … the group expressed a 'consensus' opinion … and later, you found individuals expressing disagreement … Why does this happen?
System intelligence	All living systems need a boundary function that helps in arriving at a realistic match between realities in the external environment and realities in the internal environment. The ability to assess these two sets of realities in valid and reliable ways, including the positive and negative features of the external and internal environments …	How do we define the word intelligence? Let's have some ideas … Is there something common in all the ideas from the group? The ability to learn – how does that sound? Can organisations differ in their ability to learn? Where is the intelligence of the organisation located?

stronger interfaces across functions or units which, in turn, will require team-based structures rather than conventional pyramidal structures; the team-based structures will promote multilateral accountabilities and even a downward accountability from the formal leader to members of the group; obviously, the leadership process will also change – from expert leadership to a facilitative leadership. The theme for work in Stage 3 may be called *learning to change*.

> *Creating the conditions for a learning orientation through an alternative performance-management system has the advantage of working on 'deliverables' that matter to all, which can also be observed as actually improving. It is seen that the most reliable source of motivation for human achievement is …* the experience of achievement. *A team-based performance-management system not only produces the learning orientation more reliably, it is also genuinely empowering.*

Depending on the size of the organisation and the complexity of operations, Stage 3 may be completed easily in a short time, or extended over a considerable period. Since the reality of any organisation is systemic interactivity, this is the stage in which participants will discover several interconnected organisational processes to be dealt with that had not been foreseen. 'Dry runs' certainly help. Patience and sensitivity to internal strains in the process of change are major requirements of the external facilitator. The hand-holding needs to be firm, but not inadvertently directive.

Several 'models' of comprehensive performance management exist. Again, it is not the 'brand' that matters, but we do need to ensure the essentials:

- alternative structures (team-based) for identifying and controlling system sub-optimisation;
- alternative processes for enhancing 'system intelligence' and the learning orientation, along with the operating systems;
- alternative values (and the soft skills) to accompany the processes.

The critical requirement in the operating system is the procedure for constantly examining performance *systemically*, reinforcing systemic conditions for achievements, and addressing systemic conditions for shortfalls.

Stage 4: internalisation Even through the dry runs in Stage 3 the organisation will recognise the back-up systems needed to function in the chosen, alternative manner, of which the three most important are likely to be:

- documentation and information systems to aid the synergies sought, whether or not termed 'knowledge management system';
- systems for reinforcing the value premises underlying the new practices, both rewarding and corrective mechanisms;
- training and development measures, including both the technical skills and the soft skills to help people adopt the new practices more effectively. It will be seen that training *follows* changes in structures and processes.

The paradigm shift

The above path leading towards a widespread learning orientation in an organisation calls for a fundamentally different way of viewing the organisation itself. If 'resistance to change' is viewed as 'human nature', we are likely to rely too heavily (and too unrealistically) on trying to change people through incentives, exhortations, appeals, training, rewards, punishment and so on. The greater the preoccupation with change in people, the greater the likelihood of neglecting the reality of organisational variables that have perpetrated the resistance to change. With a reasonably good recruitment and selection process, it can be said that the capacity to learn and to aid organisational performance exists in all members of the organisation. We must then accept that the principal responsibility of management is to create the conditions within the organisation through which the same people will first *want to learn*, then *learn to learn*, and finally internalise the habit of *continuous learning*. On another front, the management systems developed (such as the performance-management system) will need to ensure that such learning takes a direction that is moving away from system sub-optimisation towards system synergy.

All this requires considerable preparation of the ground before any off-the-shelf tools are inflicted on groups of people marshalled into 'learning organisation workshops'. Every management group in every organisation can be expected to be functioning with a prevailing paradigm. If that paradigm contrasts markedly from the paradigm required for an OD process and, especially, for the methodology of a learning organisation, the change agent – whether internal or external – has the professional responsibility of taking a critical starting decision: either to ensure a paradigm compatibility for the intervention process or not to initiate the process. Should the change agent choose to work towards a shift in paradigm in the management group, then that, too, needs to be accomplished by the value premises that are part of the OD paradigm.

Table 2 juxtaposes two contrasting paradigms, the conventional approach to managing organisational performance and the approach of the learning organisation. The manifestations of the two paradigms in the specifics of management practice are too real to be wished away.

Table 2: Two contrasting paradigms in managing peformance

Paradigm 1	Paradigm 2
• Core assumption: Organisation performance is the sum of unit performances ... Hence the efforts to maximise performance – down the line to the individual unit or person	• Core assumption: Organisational performance is the outcome of interactivity among units ... Hence efforts to optimise performance – up the line from individual units or persons
• Mechanistic/additive logic: units as closed systems	• Organic/synergistic logic: units as open systems
• Group structures: separated reporting relationships with formal leader	• Team structures: interactive reporting relationships across all, including formal leader
• Expert leadership: focus on work content	• Facilitative leadership: significance of work process recognised
• Emphasis on individual performance or contribution: primacy of 'job description' ... rigidity in viewing individual roles	• Emphasis on team performance or contribution: primacy of team-level key tasks ... flexibility in viewing individual roles
• Heavy reliance on individual attributes ... emphasis on task-related skills	• Sensitivity to interactive and systemic realities ... significance of process-related skills recognised
• HRM orientation, stress on individual performance ... translated into procedural systems in recruitment, induction, appraisal, training, etc.	• OD orientation, stress on systemic performance ... translated into work review, interface building and systemic goal-setting practices
• Heavy reliance on 'Performance Appraisal' – Resented/resisted/suspected – Periodic 'revisions' and 'refinements' through 'up-to-date' tools – Driven by HRM – Informal system prevails and finds ways to beat the formal system	• Priority given to creating conditions for high performance – Individual appraisal acceptable with fair playing field – Objective basis for individual review more important than tools – Driven by line management – Transparency: no gap between the formal and informal process
• Performance management equated with appraisal, i.e. individual performance review, but with extended features	• Performance management multi-dimensional and comprehensive: individual review and development as one sub-system
• Assumptions of pyramidal career-growth paths: appraisal and reward systems most critical HRM procedures	• Multiple career paths, delinked from 'management' connotations: induction, training and development, assessment centres become important
• Reward system reinforces individualistic orientation/values: negates interfaces, interactivity, teamwork	• Multi-tier reward system provides recognition to both team effort and individual effort: reinforces collaborative values
• Tendency for orientation to short-term gains: target perspective	• Facilitates long-term orientation: strategic perspective
• Elements interconnected: tendency for internal consistency	• Elements interconnected: tendency for internal consistency
Overall: organisation predisposed to unit maximisation, with consequent *sub-optimisation* at several levels	**Overall:** organisation predisposed to strengthening interfaces, with consequent *synergistic* performance at several levels

References

Ackoff, R. L. (1974) *Redesigning the Future*, New York, NY: John Wiley.

Ackoff, R. L. (1994) *The Democratic Corporation*, New York, NY: OUP.

Ackoff, R. L. (1999) *Re-creating the Corporation*, New York, NY: OUP.

Ackoff, R. L. and Fred E. Emery (1981) *On Purposeful Systems*, Seaside, CA: Intersystems Publications.

Padaki, Vijay (1997) 'Organisational development: yesterday, today, tomorrow', *Search Bulletin* XII(1): 20-25.

Padaki, Vijay (2000a) 'Coming to grips with organisational values', *Development in Practice* 10(3&4):420-435.

Padaki, Vijay (2000b) 'Organisational development revisited', *Management Review* 12(2):45-56.

Padaki, Vijay (forthcoming) 'Thinking systems', in Vijay Padaki and Manjulika Vaz (eds.), *Institutional Development: Beyond Organization Development*, New Delhi: Sage.

This paper was first published in Development in Practice *(12/3&4:321-337) in 2002.*

Achieving successful academic–practitioner research collaborations

Laura Roper

Introduction

Academic collaboration with NGOs occurs frequently and seems to offer a win-win situation for all participants. For the NGO, caught up in the daily demands of its work with limited staffing and financial resources, the academic can provide perspective and analytical capacities that often are not available in-house. For the academic, working with NGOs enables the use of expertise in an applied manner, while at the same time providing an opportunity to test ideas and theories or gather case material for larger intellectual projects. There are certainly numerous cases of NGOs having established long-term relationships with individual academics or research centres, enriching the experience of both and contributing to more effective development interventions.[1]

However, such an outcome may be the exception rather than the rule. The potential for academic–NGO collaboration is enormous, but such collaboration is far more difficult than it appears on the surface, even when collaborators share a commitment to, and values that support, a particular cause or issue. There have been many instances where such collaborations begin with high hopes and the best of intentions, only to go wrong, often gradually, but sometimes suddenly. This is a source of puzzlement and confusion to those who have been caught up in an unproductive collaboration, which may in turn have long-term adverse consequences for NGOs that are struggling to find ways to learn more effectively from experience.

Reflecting on Oxfam America's experience of academic collaboration (both successful and unsuccessful), discussions with colleagues from both the academic and NGO communities, and readings on organisational learning, it seems that the roots of the problem are both intellectual and cultural. Different intellectual approaches in the NGO and academic communities, combined with their own characteristic styles of discourse and engagement that are unfamiliar to the other, can lead to misunderstandings and missed opportunities for learning on both sides.

Looking at learning through different lenses

Developing theory versus solving problems

In *Organizational Learning II*, Chris Argyris and Donald Schön (1996) discuss the problematic aspects of practitioner–academic collaboration in a chapter entitled 'Turning the Researcher–Practitioner Relationship on its Head'. They start by noting that academic research and practitioner inquiry operate from two different logics. While both are concerned with causal inference, the academic researcher wants to identify generalisable rules that lead to probabilistic predictions. The development of such rules requires experimental or quasi-experimental design. Sophisticated, multivariate analytical techniques are often used in an attempt to isolate key variables that influence outcomes. In addition, in an academic context, where inquiry is valued in and of itself, research is often open ended, iterative, and ongoing.

The practitioner, on the other hand, is more often than not trying to solve a particular problem in a particular setting. General rules or laws rarely provide a useful guide to action. On occasion, an NGO may compare different sites or communities to determine whether an intervention is having an impact, but generally experimentation takes the form of testing a 'theory of change' or 'model of causality' within a programme context, and making adjustments when outcomes do not meet expectations. Finally, inquiry is time-bound and specific and valued only to the extent that it produces results that can be acted upon or put into practice.

Status and terms of engagement

Given these two distinct approaches, it is not surprising that academic–practitioner collaborations can be problematic. There are other factors that can act as obstacles to realising the full potential of a collaborative effort. The practitioner may tend to view the academic as an expert – immersed in the theoretical literature and bringing a toolkit of rigorous methodologies – who will solve an organisation's problems. In such circumstances, the practitioner may take a deferential posture towards the academic researcher and see her or himself more as an observer than as a participant in a research process. In the case where the academic does 'solve' the problem to the practitioner's satisfaction, an unfortunate dependency can develop, even if the academic seeks to share resources and transfer skills.

Conversely, practitioners may be sceptical of (or threatened by) the credentials and expertise of academics, and dismiss their contributions as 'book learning'. This tends to play itself out in particularly pronounced ways if the academic, in turn, feels that s/he has to prove her or himself in the collaborative context. It may be that the academic is fairly young (and consequently has had limited work or field experience), or feels that s/he has to offset status disadvantages (gender, ethnicity, religious differences) by demonstrating superior command of the field of inquiry, whether or not it directly pertains to the matter at hand.

A related obstacle can be the difference in the way in which discourse and debate are carried out in the two settings. An academic is accustomed to pressing an opinion in the challenging arena of academic discourse where breadth and depth of knowledge of 'the literature' is valued and a certain degree of competitiveness (not always constructive) fuels debate. NGOs often have a very different style of discourse, ranging from very participatory and consensual to more hierarchical, with high deference to leadership authority. In either case, an academic who engages with NGO staff in the same way that s/he might engage with fellow scholars is likely to generate cultural clashes with NGO staff and leadership.

Too complicated to understand

This gap becomes particularly wide if the research methodology is complicated or sophisticated and not easily understood by the practitioner. Anyone who is not trained in quantitative analysis and is presented with the results of a multivariate regression or a cost–benefit analysis, undergirded by a series of assumptions and generated by processing large quantities of data, has to take the results on faith to some extent. Many researchers are extremely comfortable with quantitative methods and may not even realise that they are failing to present their methods and results to the layperson in a comprehensible way. This becomes even more of an issue if the results of the research are not consistent with the practitioner's own experience and analysis. The practitioner (perhaps recalling the famous joke: 'There are three kinds of lies: lies, damned lies, and statistics') may end up feeling at worst manipulated or misled by the academic, and at best bewildered and unconfident of the results (see Barnett 1994:38-45).

Any one of these factors – competing logics, incompatible styles of discourse and attitudes towards authority, or inaccessibility of methods and results – can undermine collaboration. These difficulties tend to appear in conjunction with each other, leaving even extremely well-disposed and open collaborators with unsatisfactory results. In the worst cases, where a vicious cycle of misunderstanding develops, the end result can be low opinions of the other's commitment to learning and collaboration and a breakdown in the relationship.

That said, it is quite possible to construct useful and productive academic–practitioner collaborations. To do so requires that collaborators approach the relationship with open eyes, being aware both of their counterpart's agendas, preferences, and dispositions, as well as of their own perspectives (which are often so ingrained that they are not readily accessible for critical scrutiny).

Constructing productive collaborations

All parties in a learning collaboration are responsible for making it work. Several factors are essential for achieving success in the academic–practitioner context. These are:

- being clear about the goals of the collaboration;
- understanding what is at stake for each of the participants regarding the outcomes of the collaboration; and
- calibrating the engagement to match the needs, capacities, and interests of the NGO partner.

In other words, learning is not simply a technical exercise, but a process that occurs in a particular context, with a range of stakeholders, and is shaped by the resources, motivation, and capacities of the participants.

Being clear on the goals of a collaboration

A collaboration may begin with the shared goal of conducting research to improve the effectiveness of an NGO's intervention. However, an important first step is to 'unpack' what both parties mean by this. There are several possible approaches that are distinguished by their scope and by the way in which each party defines the terms of the collaboration:

1 *The expert-consultant model:* in which the academic expert comes in and analyses a problem and makes recommendations, and the organisation is a consumer of the product.

2   *The expert-trainer model:* in which the academic helps the NGO develop organisational skills to deal with a particular set of problems.

3   *The joint-learning model:* in which research regarding a particular problem is used as a platform for developing skills in conscious or critical inquiry (discussed below).

4   *The 'best practice' model:* in which the researcher is documenting organisational practice for the purpose of sharing that experience more broadly in order to improve development practice.

5   *The theory-development model:* in which the research is meant to contribute to the development of theoretical literature and may be part of a broader intellectual undertaking.

In the first two instances the NGO is often the initiator and is, in a sense, contracting the services of the academic researcher to focus on specific areas of organisational performance. In the last two instances the academic is usually the initiator and may be working with a range of NGOs, or may be building on his or her previous work or the previous work of other researchers. Any individual collaboration is indirectly helping the NGO by contributing to the overall level of knowledge in the field (although depending on the design, the NGO can derive direct benefits through action-research).

In the joint-learning model, the starting point of the collaboration may be to answer a research question or solve a particular problem. However, the long-term interest is to develop capacity and an organisational culture that promotes and rewards inquiry that tests basic assumptions, practices, and beliefs on an ongoing basis. The participants approach their work in a spirit of humility (no one has a corner on the knowledge market) and with the recognition that each brings expertise, experience, and insights that, when fully deployed, create new knowledge and improved practice. In this model, there is no end product as such; rather, there are processes, a series of products, and various configurations of relationships that are ongoing, fluid, and adaptable to the needs of the moment.

Each of the five models has particular implications for the resources, timing, and types of expertise needed, and for creating or relieving stress within an organisation. However, the complications increase exponentially if there is a misunderstanding concerning the approach being adopted. If an NGO thinks an academic expert is coming in to develop strategies for enhancing security in a refugee camp where the delivery of services is being adversely affected by violence, when s/he is in fact gathering data as part of a larger study on determinants of violence in refugee settings, there are obviously going to be problems. Another not uncommon scenario is that the headquarters agrees on a broader research agenda (e.g. documenting best practices in the customising of education kits), while the interest in the field may be narrower (e.g. simple delivery of those kits and identification of teachers within the camps). Because of poor communication (and understanding) between the headquarters and the field, the field staff may have no idea why a researcher is there, what they are supposed to do with him or her, and they may be suspicious about the stated agenda.

Knowing what is at stake

Knowing what is at stake raises another important point about research in an organisational context. Sometimes research is directed at acquiring information about the context or environment in order to provide a better basis for NGO action. Often, however, such research involves analysing the NGO's capacity and behaviour and its ability to intervene constructively in its environment in order to achieve its goals, with a view to improving the organisation's effectiveness. While, rationally, organisational inquiry should be a high priority, in fact organisational learning, and beyond that, change based on that learning, is very difficult to achieve.

There are time and resource constraints, but in addition:

Organizational inquiry is almost inevitably a political process in which individuals consider ... how the inquiry may affect their standing or their reference group's standing, within an organizational world of competition and contention. The attempt to uncover the causes of systems failure is inevitably a perceived test of loyalty to one's subgroup and an opportunity to allocate blame or credit. [Inquiry may lead to] strategies of deception, preemptive blame, stone-walling, fogging, camouflage ... [which] frequently inhibit inquiry into the causes of organizational events and the reasoning of the actors involved in them.

(Argyris and Schön 1996:49)

While this is written about the business sector (and most research and writing on organisational learning focuses on this sector), an NGO can be just as political a place as any competitive business and engage in the same dysfunctional behaviours described above.

The point here is that research is not necessarily viewed as a benign intervention. Who initiated the activity? Who are the key contact people within the agency? Is research taking place at a time of expansion or contraction in the agency's programmes? Is there a culture of learning in the organisation or is this a departure from normal practice? The answers to all of these questions affect the practitioner–academic relationship.

Another complicating factor, touched on above, is that it is not unusual, particularly in activist or community-based NGOs, to find an anti-academic bias. This may not be something that is explicitly held or stated, but it is important for the academic collaborator to determine if such bias exists and, if so, what its roots are. Is it because academics are in an 'ivory tower' talking 'theory', when the NGO staff members are out there 'making a difference'? Does it come from latent class conflict or intellectual insecurity in the face of the 'expert' with the PhD? Does it come from the belief that the academic may have a lot of knowledge but not much wisdom? Or are strains coming from other sources – such as who has mandated the research (e.g. an external funder), an institutional crisis that some are hoping the research will resolve, real ambivalence about the usefulness of spending scarce resources on research as opposed to direct service, and so on?

It may not necessarily occur to academics, particularly those new to collaborative relationships, to concern themselves with these questions; they are not organisational development specialists, after all. Likewise, an NGO's leadership may not be fully aware of these internal issues or, conversely, may be all too aware of internal dysfunctions and be turning to academic researchers to break log-jams within the organisation through their rigorous, objective, and 'value-free' methods. Whatever the situation, all these factors will shape the nature and the likelihood of success of a collaborative relationship, and sensitivity and insight on the part of all parties is necessary.

Calibrating engagement to the characteristics and needs of the practitioner

There are many different types of NGOs – small, grassroots activist organisations, multi-million dollar international organisations that rely on government funding, technical organisations that provide services to community groups or other NGOs, and so on. Aside from size and sources of funding, NGOs are distinguished by their ideology, their state of organisational evolution, the extent to which their capacity is matched to the goals they have set themselves, and so on. Finally, as touched on above, there are the internal dynamics within an organisation – which may be cohesive or conflictual, consensual or hierarchical, proactive or reactive, reflective or non-reflective.

The academic designs a course based on the overall quality of training of the students, previous work done on similar topics, and level of the course. The good teacher also recognises that students have different learning styles. (Some learn through reading, others through lecture, some learn through research or hands-on experience while others need the incentive of exams and grades. Some learn through some combination of these approaches, and others apparently not at all.) Likewise, the effective academic collaborator knows the NGO and engages with it in ways that match its interests, its capacity to provide data, its learning culture, and so on. The practitioner's responsibilities include identifying the right academic collaborator(s), being aware of how the research is perceived by key stakeholders, and helping to structure and manage the institutional relationship appropriately.

A final point in this section is to note that different research interventions may be appropriate at different times, and an implicit goal among those who try to promote academic–practitioner collaborations is that *ongoing* relationships will be established. Given the different worldviews of academics and practitioners, an initial engagement may be one of building trust by doing some very preliminary work. In keeping with a commitment to developing a capacity for ongoing critical inquiry, the first phase may be just to demystify the process of research by using participatory, inductive methods that allow people to systematise what they already know and identify what they do not know. Over time it is possible to develop a relationship in which the practitioner becomes an eager partner in contributing to theory development, sets aside the necessary resources for research, is proactive in coming up with research ideas, and actually recruits colleague institutions to participate.

Learning to learn together

All five approaches to research that have been mentioned above are valid. Furthermore, they are not necessarily mutually exclusive. Of the five models, practitioners are perhaps most inclined to view that of joint learning as being most likely to contribute to organisational effectiveness. However, organisations often come to this model only after having gone through a number of 'problem-solving' exercises and finding that old problems keep re-emerging. Likewise, the academic researcher who is really committed to NGO–academic collaboration comes to see the limitations of his or her approach and, through exposure to the day-to-day workings and challenges of practitioners, begins to combine, adapt, and create new methods.

A necessary condition for good academic–practitioner collaboration is for both to recognise that they need to learn how to learn together. For the academic this might mean acknowledging that NGOs are often looking for the minimum amount of information necessary to make a somewhat better decision (95 per cent confidence levels, and the investment it takes to achieve them, are way beyond the pale). It might also mean recognising that better information is not enough, and that who is consulted, and how information is collected, presented, and reviewed will strongly influence whether learning leads to any change.

For the NGO, good collaboration requires a genuine commitment to questioning underlying assumptions, the willingness to make the investment in time and funds to move beyond anecdotal evidence to more systematised information, and a recognition that NGOs occasionally become victims of their own rhetoric. In other words, because so much NGO funding depends on convincing others of how well they do, they may begin to believe the content of their direct-mail appeals, foundation proposals, and reports as the sum of their experience when, in fact, failure, setbacks, and slow, very incremental progress more accurately reflect reality.

Criteria for success

Taking this approach, the success of the academic–NGO collaboration is not measured solely by the 'quality' of the final report in terms of methodological rigour and the robustness and comprehensiveness of results, although this is important. An alternative view is to look at the research activity as a platform for helping an organisation develop the capacity for critical inquiry and a learning orientation:

- Did the NGO find the process of inquiry and the results useful and did the NGO use the research (results, recommendations, areas for further study)?

- Did more people within the NGO become interested in or directly engaged with the research effort? Did they want to continue the collaboration?

- Was the researcher skilful at affirming the intuitive or experiential knowledge of the practitioner(s), helping them to gain confidence in their analytic capacity? Were participants motivated to read some of the 'literature' to help them gain a more substantial theoretical grounding?

- Was the researcher skilful in facilitating discovery by the practitioner of areas of weakness and strategies for improvement, rather than simply saying what the results were, and creating synergy between their different foundations of knowledge and experience?
- Did the engagement lead to a constructive questioning of basic assumptions and strategies and a strengthened learning orientation of both practitioner and academic?
- Was an environment created where difficult issues could be raised and dealt with in a systematic and professional manner?
- Did those who participated in the experience want to share that learning outside the agency with clients, peer organisations, or others?

For the academic, measures of success might include:

- Did the collaboration open the door for other collaborative efforts in the future either with that particular NGO or others s/he might be referred to?
- Did the academic improve his or her capacity for eliciting information and creating actionable knowledge?
- Did the experience generate learning that contributes to the broader development discourse both within academia and within the NGO community?

Conclusion

One of the most distressing things about a failed academic–practitioner collaboration is that those involved feel that it *should* have worked and recognise that a promising opportunity slipped from their hands. When they do work, there is something almost magical about such collaborative exercises – ideas are flying, connections are made, people feel validated and empowered, and distant ambitions can be transformed into achievable goals. In the best cases, this experience can take root at an organisational level and an organisation can go through a significant developmental leap. While the gains ultimately may be great, experience seems to indicate that it is often more effective to start small, with one unit or aspect of a programme participating in a collaboration (being low key and low visibility also helps remove pressure). A successful outcome will create advocates within the agency and an internal momentum for constructing similar experiences, which then gradually expand (either in number or in scale). Eventually, the role of the academic specialist should diminish significantly, if not disappear entirely.

There are a number of positive trends in recent years that are helping to diminish the academic–practitioner divide. One has been the growing number of Master's-level programmes that are geared towards practitioners, primarily in Europe and the USA, but also elsewhere, which people attend for a year or two, and then return to development practice. Likewise, there are now more opportunities within the UN system, bilateral aid agencies, and some NGOs (generally the larger, well-established ones) for individuals with higher degrees to contribute to these agencies in a staff capacity. In addition, an increasing number of institutions seek to serve as a bridge between NGOs and academics, such as INTRAC in Oxford, the Hauser Center for Non-Profit Management at Harvard, and others reflected in this special issue such as the School for International Training. Self-awareness, mutual understanding, and enabling institutional settings all contribute to a learning culture in a world where knowledge is an extremely valuable development currency.

Note

1 This paper was inspired by a collaborative experience that Oxfam America and Oxfam Québec enjoyed with Winifred Fitzgerald, then Executive Director of the Harvard Center for Population and Development. The collaborative review of peace building and reconciliation in post-genocide Rwanda was supported by Mellon Foundation funding through the Mellon–MIT Inter-University Program on Non-Governmental Organizations and Forced Migration. For a detailed discussion of that experience see Fitzgerald and Roper (2000).

References

Argyris, Chris and Donald A. Schön (1996) *Organizational Learning II*, Reading, MA: Addison-Wesley.

Barnett, Arnold (1994) 'How numbers can trick you', *Technology Review* (October):38-45.

Fitzgerald, Winifred and Laura Roper (2000) *Designing Processes that Promote Reconciliation: The Results of an NGO–Academic Collaboration Researching the Role of an International NGO Funding for Reconciliation in Rwanda*, a report of the Mellon–MIT Inter-University Program on Non-Governmental Organizations and Forced Migration, Cambridge, MA: MIT Center for International Studies.

This paper was first published in Development in Practice *(12/3&4:338-345) in 2002.*

Knowledge to action:
evaluation for learning in a multi-organisational global partnership

Marla J. Solomon and
A. Mushtaque R. Chowdhury

'Partnership' is a dominant approach to international development cooperation today. But the challenges of multi-institutional collaboration are vast, even more so when they aspire to collaborative learning. At the same time, partnerships have access to a potential tool for organisational learning in a process they must undertake anyway: evaluation. Increasingly, evaluation is seen through the lens of learning, shaping (e.g. a 'learning-based approach to institutional assessment', Carden 2000:175), and revitalising forms of participatory monitoring and evaluation as 'learning from experience' and 'shared learning' (Estrella 2000:6). However, evaluation, in spite of its obvious potential as a learning exercise, is seldom used for this purpose. Perhaps organisations do not know how to shape their evaluation activities towards this end. 'There are many NGOs that claim to be "learning organisations", but how they promote shared learning and engage their staff in new learning is still unclear' (Hailey 2000:63). Or perhaps they do not know how to view and articulate evaluations as such. Taylor tells us that the learning organisation concept 'is most effectively used as a reminder that the process of learning is inherent in everyone and in all organisations. The first challenge is not to start learning, but to become more conscious of how learning already takes place, in order to use and further develop this innate ability' (Taylor 1998:1).

This paper attempts to examine our own practice of evaluation, showing how evaluation processes have been used in the Global Partnership's NGO Leadership and Management (NLM) Post-graduate Diploma Programme in Bangladesh to support learning and change. From this experience, we draw out lessons that may be helpful to other organisations striving to create or maintain thriving partnerships, foster learning, and enhance their organisational capacity to use evaluation for learning and development.

Global Partnership's NGO Leadership and Management Programme: background and methodology of the evaluation

The Global Partnership for NGO Studies, Education and Training (GP) is a consortium of educational centres established by BRAC in Bangladesh, the Organisation of Rural Associations for Progress (ORAP) in Zimbabwe, and the School for International Training (SIT) in the USA. The Global Partnership offers the postgraduate diploma in NGO Leadership and Management (NLM) leading to a master's degree programme, providing middle- and top-level managers of Southern development NGOs and those who liaise or support such NGOs (trainers, consultants, government officials, donors, etc.) with an opportunity for international higher education specifically relevant to their organisations and career development. From 1997 to 2000, 79 NGO managers from Africa, Asia, Europe, the Americas, and Australia and New Zealand came together to develop skills, exchange perspectives, and complete the diploma programme.

In the fifth year of the programme's operation (2000/01), the Global Partnership undertook a systematic evaluation of the NLM programme to inform decisions about continuous improvement and about expansion of the programme to other sites and in alternative configurations.[1] The specific objectives of the evaluation were:

- to understand the results for participants and the impact once participants return to the NGO workforce;
- to identify the strengths and weaknesses of the course in relation to its objectives, in light of the impact desired and impact achieved, and in relation to other similar international courses;
- to determine what we needed to do to maintain the strengths of the programme, to improve areas where weaknesses exist, and to plan for increasing participant numbers and outreach (Chowdhury *et al.* 2001:2).

The evaluation methodology consisted of a self-study entailing surveys, interviews, and a reflection workshop with graduates, supervisors of graduates, and faculty. Following this self-study, an external review by experts in the field of NGO management and development took place.

The approach to the evaluation process was based on the idea of evaluation as learning, involving deep self-study to lay recurring issues on the table for careful collective examination, in combination with an outside perspective for healthy critique and infusion of new ideas. Evaluation for learning

... is a means for fostering individual and team learning about complex organizational issues. Evaluative inquiry for organizational learning and change is more than a means to an end; it is more than developing skills that result in increased competence or improved profits. A significant consequence of evaluative inquiry is the fostering of relationships among organization members and the diffusion of their learning throughout the organization; it serves as a transfer-of-knowledge process. To that end, evaluative inquiry provides an avenue for individuals' as well as the organization's ongoing growth and development.
(Preskill and Torres 1999:18)

We viewed this approach as more than appropriate; in fact it was essential to this stage of development of the programme and the Partnership. Though we evaluated a specific programme of the Partnership, the growth of that programme and others depend on the vitality of the Partnership itself. This evaluation provided an opportunity not only to learn about the programme's impact, strengths, and weaknesses, but also to strengthen the programme's learning culture and capacity for self-critique and change, and to build stronger capacity for doing and using evaluation effectively within the Partnership.

Many evaluations, however, begin with this well-meaning intent but are challenged to fulfil it. What in this particular case contributed to actually fulfilling that intent? This article begins to answer this question. How did this process and its results contribute to learning within the Global Partnership, the NLM programme, and the two primary partner institutions involved in the evaluation, BRAC and SIT? Why did this evaluation work as a learning exercise as opposed to a 'policing' exercise?[2] What specific elements of the evaluation process contributed to creating knowledge used for action? And last, but equally important, what challenges blocked further potential learning or could prevent translating knowledge into action?

Six factors that made learning work

Orientation towards learning and change

Of the Global Partnership's main members, BRAC and SIT are primarily responsible for the planning and implementation of this programme. Both institutions are oriented towards learning and change within their organisations. The success of the exercise had its roots in the two organisations' past receptiveness to learning from their own experiences. 'BRAC has been characterised as a learning organisation, and its extraordinary success in rural development has been attributed to this basic feature of its operational mode (Korten 1980)' (Lovell 1992:4). BRAC also has a long tradition of examining its programmes with a research lens and of acting on the basis of the outcome of such studies. BRAC's Research and Evaluation Division (RED) produces research that helps 'achieve programme objectives by modifying and improving the programme strategies and identifying new programmatic issues' (BRAC RED 2001:10). SIT's orientation towards organisational learning is founded on its pedagogical approach – experiential learning, which it uses in its academic and non-credit training programmes alike and is often also infused into the operations of its programmes.

These commitments to learning, made concrete through an effort to use careful planning and evaluation, have been evident in the Global Partnership from the outset. For example, the three member institutions of the Global Partnership designed the NLM programme over more than a year with concentrated efforts carried out through three planning forums, one held at each of the three partners' home locations. External advisers were invited to contribute their views to the programme design, and an external evaluation was commissioned early on in the NLM programme. Though, in hindsight, this evaluation was done too early to provide in-depth assessment, it became a useful advisory exercise; the Global Partnership used several of the recommendations and built extensive formative evaluation processes into the programme itself.

Although the Global Partnership's orientation to learning from experience is not always problem-free in practice, it helped set the stage for the use of evaluation for learning in this case. Without this orientation, bringing about learning through evaluation might be an arduous paradigm-shifting effort. Because of this orientation, framing this evaluation as a learning exercise was, although not a seamless process, something that made sense.

Planning and resources

A second factor that made learning work in this evaluation involved adequate planning and resources. Once the idea of carrying out a systematic evaluation emerged, we sought substantial funding to 'do it right'. We also committed Global Partnership's own funds to start the planning process well. The SIT evaluation team leader travelled to Bangladesh to meet with the BRAC evaluation team leader and to build a team and work on an evaluation process that all could agree upon. Both organisations were willing and able to commit the time and talents of personnel with appropriate skills. The individuals involved had good process-facilitation skills as well as technical skills in evaluation, essential to creating a collective approach to evaluation for learning. The use of these resources in this way renewed the organisational commitment to learning for this specific evaluation exercise.

Trust

Trust between SIT and BRAC was the third key factor. This trust has been built up over the years, even pre-dating the formalisation of the Global Partnership. In fact, the Global Partnership emerged in part because of positive collaborative experiences and relations of mutual respect between staff members of the two organisations. Through working together on the NLM programme since 1995, this trust has developed further. Building on these institutional and individual relationships, the evaluation team leaders took time and effort to develop trust within the evaluation team as well.

Building a shared paradigm of learning

Following from these three factors, we were able to build a shared paradigm of evaluation for learning. The evaluation used a team approach involving cross-departmental collaboration within BRAC (RED and GP/Training Division) and with SIT. The view of evaluation as learning was discussed by the team and used to shape the evaluation design. It was fortunate that the outside reviewers also held this view and so helped push learning from the external exercise. (More on the contributions of the 'outside' view appears below.)

But there were tensions here that proved to be stumbling blocks to further learning. Adjusting to the view of evaluation for learning was challenging for some team members, as their research backgrounds gave them a very different perspective. This impeded the presentation and analysis process of questionnaire data and the preparation for its use at the reflection workshop more difficult. Thus, there was little exploration and interpretation of questionnaire data at the reflection workshop, a great loss to learning. Also, the need for collective analysis was difficult to reinforce and even harder to implement given long-distance relationships. Data analysis was carried out largely by the individual writer of each section, and rigorous group analysis was done in only a few of the sections. In addition, completing the analysis and final self-study report with a long distance between SIT and BRAC was challenging. Deadlines were invariably extended, and in the end the evaluation team leaders did more of the final analysis than was originally desired. Even with our history of trust and the time and resources to create a shared team paradigm and approach, these obstacles were considerable. Perhaps this shared paradigm was part of what allowed us to work through these obstacles and still emerge with a learning result.

Learning became action

What in particular contributed to using knowledge for action? The fifth factor helps answer this question: Global Partnership decision makers were involved in the evaluation process. This made it possible to take action as we proceeded, even before there was a final report. For example, the evaluation activity dovetailed with an opportunity to act immediately to solve some of the problems raised by the evaluation. SIT gained an opportunity for programme development through a FIPSE[3] grant for curriculum enhancement through educational technology and because the NLM programme evaluation chose to use this grant to develop the Global Partnership through electronically enhanced learning. The learning from the evaluation shaped this new direction and opportunity; the findings from the reflection workshop were used to shape the FIPSE grant request (in fact, the grant request was written just following the workshop), and the opportunity to apply for the FIPSE grant shaped the writing of implications and recommendations from the findings, especially those pertaining to expansion of the programme in the self-study. This kind of 'incremental' use of evaluation results (Hailey 2001) was possible because the General Secretary of the Global Partnership Board and the academic director of NLM were closely involved with the evaluation, and were present at the reflection workshop. In addition, supplementary funding became available to enable us to address some of the needs emerging from the evaluation findings.

Of course, the goals that have been achieved in this way address only a portion of the recommendations from the evaluation. Many still remain to be acted upon. The will to translate these into action exists, but obstacles include time, resources, and the difficulty of shifting focus from implementing a programme in its current form to putting energy into changing it. It is perhaps too early to say to what extent we will be able to achieve what we have agreed upon as a result of this learning evaluation. This will depend largely on our ability to harness additional resources, both human and financial, to work towards our goals.

Internal–external views working together

The sixth factor was the use of an internal–external study combination in the evaluation design. Because of a shared paradigm and the agenda for deep self-understanding, recognising and naming problems, and accountability, the internal–external combination was especially effective in this case. CDRA makes the point that two functions of evaluation – learning and accountability – are necessarily intertwined. 'It so happens, if we were learning from our actions, we would be in a position to fulfil, in a meaningful way, the accountability demands made of us. We would also be enormously strengthened to manage external evaluations in a productive and collaborative manner, and to learn from them too' (CDRA 2001:8). This happened in this case. The external report gave new insights, examined the programme's blind spots, and contributed to further learning and action; at the same time the external review was richer because it built on an internal study. The external reviewers used the self-study extensively and we were able to determine what we needed from them because we had already done the self-study. We knew the gaps that we needed to fill and what their perspective could help us do. Further, because of a commitment on the part of the external reviewers and ourselves to using evaluation, one reviewer made a follow-up visit to the Global Partnership Secretariat to give further input for future planning on the basis of the evaluation (Rahman Khan and Hailey 2001).

What we learned from the evaluation results

Much was learned *about* the NLM programme through the evaluation. All those involved in the self-study felt they had learned a great deal about the uniqueness and value of the programme, especially its importance for individual graduates at a personal level. In particular, the reflection workshop showed testimonial evidence of the important effect of the programme on graduates' lives, thinking, and careers. These testimonies – and Global Partnership managers' direct witnessing of them – had a far greater impact on what was learned than any of the questionnaire data. (See more on limitations of the questionnaire data below.)

At the same time, the evaluation brought to the fore certain issues and concerns in such a way that action could be taken. Many of these issues had been named in ongoing formative evaluation during each programme cycle, but laying them out for all to see and making clear recommendations (both those of the self-study and of the external reviewers) allowed the NLM management to move forward and think of solutions to continuing problems. Again, qualitative data strongly influenced learning about, and creating a commitment to, taking action on these issues.

Finally, the results of the evaluation shaped the October 2001 planning session of the Global Partnership Board. The recommendations from the internal and external reports pointed out ways to approach marketing, fundraising, and networking to ensure future programme sustainability and expanded impact. At the same time, the generally very favourable internal and external evaluation results justified asking potential funders for resources to strengthen the programme. This will be one of the key tasks for the Global Partnership over the next year.

What we learned from the evaluation process

The evaluation process itself contributed greatly to learning with the Global Partnership, highlighting organisational challenges and bringing about organisational benefits.

Linkages and relationships

Through the evaluation, relationships were both enhanced and challenged, reinforcing in our minds the importance of linkages in global-scale efforts. On the challenge side, the evaluation process raised important questions about the composition of the Global Partnership membership, including how many and what kinds of partners are needed to grow and vitalise the Global Partnership's programmes. It became clear that without some serious attention to broader external networking, we would be unlikely to achieve our goal of increasing the quality and impact of the programme. On the enhancement side, the evaluation process led to the first visit by the SIT president to BRAC and the NLM programme on the occasion of the external review visit. Further, the process enhanced cross-departmental cooperation and understanding (RED and GP/NLM) within BRAC. The process also raised the interest and support of key experts through their involvement as external reviewers.

Credibility and accountability within the partner organisations

The combination of wide participation internally and an outside expert perspective led to enhanced credibility and accountability of the NLM programme. The credibility of the programme was enhanced within BRAC and SIT, both for those directly involved in NLM management and for those at other levels of the organisations. Donor money for the evaluation elevated the status of the programme. Key decision makers understood the programme better. A sense of accountability and credibility grew within the programme, among the partners, and externally.

Models and modes of learning

What were the benefits of the process for the Global Partnership's orientation towards learning? And what did we learn about evaluation for learning that we might use in future learning efforts within Global Partnership? First, the sense that self-study (internal evaluation) is valuable, which was doubted at some levels of the Partnership at the beginning, grew enormously. The evaluation laid the issues on the table for everyone to see and own – stakeholders could recognise the issues together and didn't have to convince each other of what they were – and this was the result of doing the evaluation collectively rather than being evaluated only from the outside. Second, evaluation served as a training ground for BRAC personnel within RED and NLM; the involvement of staff with little evaluation expertise gave them skills to use in future evaluation studies and broadened the commitment to evaluation for learning. The process also led to increased desire on the part of the NLM programme director to carry out enhanced ongoing evaluation and study of the programme; he saw the benefits of systematic study, of finding out and documenting lessons learned.

Difficulties of assessing impact and the importance of qualitative data

As for how we might do evaluation in future, we learned that the organisational and field-level impact of this training programme (or any training programme) is difficult to measure. We learned that this type of data collection has to be context rich. The quantitative data themselves could not provide the whole picture; the qualitative data generated at the reflection workshop provided more sense of the programme's meaning and led the data analysis. Some problems in the quantitative data contributed to this situation. The response rate on self-study questionnaires was limited, making the statistical analysis of the data not particularly meaningful. We were also unable to take the quantitative analysis beyond its first limited iteration, owing to time and communication constraints.

However, even if we had had deeper quantitative data – and certainly because we did not have them – the richness of the qualitative data, especially those collected at the reflection workshop, probably would have overshadowed it. At that event, graduates almost spontaneously took the workshop in the direction of recounting their experiences following the programme, how they had applied their learning, and the benefits they had derived from it both personally and organisationally. Those testimonies led to a thorough exposure of problems in the programme and ways they could be solved. This qualitative data became an important part of learning because Global Partnership managers and Board members were present to hear it first hand. The reflection workshop could have been more meaningful had more faculty, supervisors, and donors attended; but this kind of evaluation is very time consuming and it was difficult to obtain their time or participation. Participation of local supervisors and donors was also restricted because a national strike was called by the opposition parties in Bangladesh at the time of the reflection workshop.

What it takes to take knowledge to action

Perhaps the most important lesson – not new, but reinforced by this experience – was that you need resources to solve problems. The resources gathered to do a systematic evaluation and the new resources available to help solve some of the programme problems that had been raised bear witness to this. The human, financial, and knowledge and networking resources are equally important. This lesson has reinforced our commitment to building a strategic and effective marketing, networking, and fundraising approach to Global Partnership programmes in order to ensure their impact on the future of the development NGO sector. Along with helping us achieve impact, this approach will help us assess impact.

> As we begin to articulate what we see and know, so another contribution takes shape – a picture of what is being measured, how we measure it and what it looks like. When we manage to express this, then we will have something to say, something engaging, interesting and persuasive to put on the table in response to those questions, 'How do you know that your work makes a difference? How do you know that it does any good?'
> (CDRA 2001:19)

We hope to continue to build our capacity to learn from our experience, to link knowledge to action, and to understand if and how it 'makes a difference'.

Notes

1 This evaluation was funded by the Ford Foundation, which had previously supported the development of the Global Partnership and the design of the NLM curriculum. Salehuddin Ahmed, G. Samdani Fakir, and Jeff Unsicker, all Global Partnership officials as well as participants in this evaluation, generously agreed to be interviewed for this article.

2 Thanks to John Hailey and Paul Ventura for this and other stimulating ideas in early discussions about this article.

3 The Fund for the Improvement of Post-Secondary Education (FIPSE) is a foundation-like arm of the US Department of Education.

References

BRAC Research and Evaluation Division (RED) (2001) *BRAC Research 2000*, Dhaka: BRAC.

Carden, F. (2000) 'Giving evaluation away: challenges in a learning-based approach to institutional assessment', in M. Estrella *et al.* (eds.) *Learning from Change: Issues and Experiences in Participatory Monitoring and Evaluation*, London: IT Publications.

Chowdhury, A. M. R., G. S. Fakir, A. Hadi, H. Rahman, S. Sarkar, M. Solomon, and J. Unsicker (2001) 'Self-Study Report: Evaluation of the Global Partnership for NGO Studies, Education and Training's Postgraduate Diploma Programme in NGO Leadership and Management', unpublished report, Brattleboro, VT and Dhaka: Global Partnership.

Community Development Resource Association (CDRA) (2001) 'Measuring Development: Holding Infinity', from the Community Development Resource Association's Annual Report 2000/01, available at www.cdra.org.za/Publications/Annual_Rep_00-01.htm (accessed 1 October 2001).

Estrella, M. with J. Blauert, D. Campilan, J. Gaventa, J. Gonsalves, L. Guijt, D. Johnson, and R. Ricafort (eds.) (2000) *Learning from Change: Issues and Experiences in Participatory Monitoring and Evaluation*, London: IT Publications.

Hailey, J. (2000) 'Learning for growth: organizational learning in South Asian NGOs', in D. Lewis and T. Wallace (eds.) *New Roles and Relevance: Development NGOs and the Challenge of Change*, West Hartford, CT: Kumarian.

Hailey, J. (2001) Personal conversations with John Hailey, 1-2 October 2001, Brattleboro, VT, USA.

Korten, D. (1980) 'Community organisation and rural development: a learning process approach', *Public Administration Review* 40(5):480-511.

Lovell, Catherine H. (1992) *Breaking the Cycle of Poverty: The BRAC Strategy*, West Hartford, CT: Kumarian.

Preskill, H. and R. T. Torres (1999) *Evaluative Inquiry for Learning in Organizations*, London: Sage.

Rahman Khan, Z. and J. Hailey (2001) 'Global Partnership: Postgraduate Programme in NGO Leadership and Management: Evaluation by External Review Team', unpublished report, Dhaka: Global Partnership.

Taylor, J. (1998) 'NGOs as learning organisations', available at www.cdra.org.za (accessed 1 October 2001).

This paper was first published in Development in Practice *(12/3&4:346-354) in 2002.*

Guest learning and adaptation in the field: a Navajo case study

Gelaye Debebe

Introduction

Inter-organisational relationships (IORs) are one of the common mechanisms used in implementing economic development projects, and are often formed for the purpose of technical assistance. In addition, many IORs in the development context are formed between organisations representing populations that are culturally dissimilar and have a history of conflict that has resulted in inequality.[1] Individuals from one organisation, usually representing a more powerful group, are assigned and relocated to another in order to bring specialised skills to deal with development problems faced by the host organisation. Because these individuals are new to the organisation, I refer to them as *guests*. Often, guests work closely with members of the host organisation, whom I refer to as *hosts*, to achieve project goals. This article explores a particular problem encountered by guests when they try to draw on knowledge from their home culture to address problems in a host context. In particular, guests bring expectations and values to a project that may or may not be appropriate in the new milieu. The paper explores how guests contribute effectively to the achievement of development goals through a process of learning.

The central argument is that the ability of guests to provide effective technical assistance in a development project requires them to learn about local realities and to adapt in consonance with this understanding (Dyck *et al.* 2000). A guest's contribution is effective if his/her task-related activities result in the accomplishment of project goals as defined by the host. By definition, learning refers to a change in understanding regarding a problematic situation which then leads to a change in behaviour. Adaptation refers to the kind of change that a guest undergoes as a result of the learning process, and involves the revision of *a priori* assumptions and the acquisition of new ideas and constructs that allow the individual to understand previously confusing behaviours and points of view of people within the new cultural milieu. Such an understanding enables the guest to appreciate the constraints and opportunities in the new cultural context, and provides a basis for exercising judgement about what issues need to be addressed and how their own technical knowledge and skill can best be brought to bear.

Successful adaptation is a difficult and impressive accomplishment. It is difficult because learning from hosts requires that guests confront, manage, and explore the discomfort and ambiguity resulting from the disruption of expectations. It is impressive because learning in a new cultural context involves working through disorientation and confusion to make 'sense' of a situation that is not 'sensible' from one's prior frame of reference (Carroll 1990). Furthermore, when there are historical power differences, the outsider's approach to the confusing situations s/he encounters has an impact on his or her ability to cultivate helpful relationships with hosts. Thus, skills and practices that enable guests to learn involve managing power and cultural differences.

Adaptation involves what I call *cross-cultural communicative competence*,[2] a term I use to refer to the skill involved in managing expectations based in prior acculturation experiences so as to learn in intercultural relationships. The presence or absence of these competencies is manifested in a guest's learning practices. Cross-cultural communicative competence can be said to be present when the guest behaves in a way that makes possible the generation of relevant information and explanations, thereby rendering previously confusing cues sensible, and facilitating the identification of issues that need attention. This article focuses on one aspect of such practices, which I refer to as *acts*.[3] Acts are the things said and done in a given interaction that encourage or inhibit the surfacing and exploration of issues relevant to a task-related problem. Drawing on a Navajo case study, this article explores guest acts that enabled a guest to learn and adapt to a new cultural and organisational milieu. This article seeks to describe what is involved in the competent employment of such acts.

The learning process is triggered by a problem (Dewey 1938). For the guests, the confusion that arises from their inability to give meaning to a task-relevant cue is a problem that needs to be resolved. In this situation, individuals seek others who may be able to help them do this, and learning takes place in these interactions (Brown and

Duguid 2000; Lave and Wenger 1991). As a newcomer to a cultural milieu, the guest initially experiences confusion and disorientation, and this makes taking action problematic (Hall 1981). This confusion stems from the fact that the ways things are done in the new setting differ significantly from the other organisational contexts in which the guest has participated. Consequently, s/he lacks the frame of reference for interpreting what s/he encounters in the new milieu, and for devising an effective plan of action (Hall 1981). Without an understanding of the local milieu, ideas emanating from the guest's untested assumptions may be misplaced, inappropriate, resisted, and consequently lead to actions that prove ineffectual in achieving project goals. Learning about the host organisational context needs to take place before outside knowledge can be brought to bear on local problems. This involves managing prior expectations in a manner that facilitates learning and adaptation.

The notion of participation has an important place in both the development and learning literatures. Development scholars have argued that participation of the right actors is critical for democracy and practical from the perspective of achieving sustainable solutions to development problems (e.g. White 1996). Learning theorists have argued that the resolution of problems requires consultation with those people who understand the breadth of relevant issues (Brown and Duguid 2000). Participation of the right people facilitates learning by enabling such issues to be identified, promoting an accurate interpretation of the problem, and generating appropriate solutions. This article argues that learning and adaptation are optimised when guests seek information and guidance from hosts and when they are skilled in doing so. By suggesting that it is not only *who* participates, but *how*, the paper adds another dimension to the problem of participation.

I will illustrate the use of *acts*, one aspect of guest learning practices, through a description of the activities of Tom, an 'Anglo' guest involved in an economic development project on the Navajo nation.[4] Specifically, it shows how Tom uses acts, and analyses what made them effective in his learning. Tom is a member of an organisation involved in an IOR. This IOR was between the Navajo Membership Organisation (NMO), and an Anglo organisation, Development Training Associates (DTA).[5] This article discusses the Canyon Inn project, in which Tom was successful in learning about the local milieu and making an effective contribution.

My analysis of Tom's acts suggests that part of the skill involved in guest learning is one of maintaining a delicate balance between prior expectations and confusing 'cues' encountered in the new cultural milieu. Engaging in two complementary categories of acts – calibrating and progressing – creates this balance. Calibrating allows the guest to assess the appropriateness of his or her assumptions in the new context. Progressing allows the guest to elicit information and explanations that would help in developing an understanding of the context. Thus, calibration involves managing *a priori* expectations in such a way that these do not block information-seeking behaviour, accomplished through progressing acts.

The case and project

Below, I describe the inter-organisational relationship, the roles of IOR members and their activities, the host organisation, the project, and the guest organisational member.

The inter-organisational relationship

The relationship between NMO and DTA has been in existence for approximately ten years. The idea for this IOR emerged in conversations between members of the two organisations in a chance meeting at a conference of US federal grant recipients. In this conversation, the NMO representatives learned of DTA's provision of technical assistance in small business development to organisations in transitional economies. The DTA organisational member learned of NMO's training activities in a wide variety of areas, integrating Western and Navajo knowledge. At this meeting, a mutual interest in forming an IOR was expressed. The NMO members indicated that there was a need for small business development on the Navajo Nation and that there might be interest at NMO in developing training programmes in the area. The DTA representative expressed an interest in expanding DTA's technical assistance work to organisations within the USA in communities facing difficult economic circumstances. The IOR evolved from the efforts of these and other individuals within DTA and NMO.

Roles and activities

Within DTA, the IOR is part of an existing programme called the Collaborative Economic Development Initiative (CEDI), and it is administered by the president's office. The work of the IOR proceeds with activities involving members of both organisations in two phases. The first phase stretches approximately from autumn to spring, and the second phase is during the summer. The project described in this article occurred during the summer of 1998.

The NMO and DTA organisational members play one of three roles during the summer phase: administrators, facilitators, and implementers. While administrators and facilitators are on the permanent staff, implementers are temporary employees. A fourth role is that of client, an NMO staff member with ultimate administrative responsibility for the project.

In the summer, DTA hires implementers to provide NMO with short-term technical assistance in projects selected by NMO organisational members. Their chief activity is to carry out tasks aimed at achieving NMO project goals. Hence, the DTA implementers leave their organisational and cultural milieu and are transplanted to NMO for approximately four months. There, they are expected to work closely with a counterpart implementer as well as with NMO facilitators and a project client. Figure 1 depicts the actors from both DTA and NMO who served in these roles in the Canyon Inn project.

The host organisation

Arriving at NMO, one is immediately struck by the circular design of the compound and buildings, the circle being a crucial element in Navajo cosmology. An asphalt road runs around buildings that house a variety of offices. Almost all of the buildings are designed in the

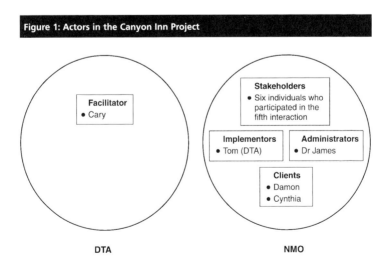

Figure 1: Actors in the Canyon Inn Project

circular form of a traditional Navajo home called a *hogan*. This architectural environment is the first message a guest receives about a core organisational value: the maintenance of Navajo culture. Indeed, NMO is a membership organisation whose mission is to provide training in a number of areas in keeping with Navajo cultural practices. As I will discuss later, addressing this issue was critical to the legitimation of any project undertaken at NMO.

Canyon Inn

Tourism is a major growth industry on Native American reservations and a potential arena of job creation and income generation for many Navajo families (Cornell and Kalt 1995). However, there is a general view on Navajoland and in NMO that, because of very limited infrastructure (e.g. outlets for Navajo arts and crafts, restaurants, and hotels), tourists tend to pass through Navajoland without staying long enough to spend their money. With the exception of a community called Kayenta, either the tribal government or non-Navajos own the few existing businesses on the Navajo Nation. Furthermore, these outlets capture only a fraction of tourist spending.

Consequently, there was a desire at NMO to promote jobs in the tourism sector by providing training to would-be micro-entrepreneurs. Many NMO members are skilled craftspeople producing goods such as rugs and jewellery. Others have *hogans*, which they could upgrade for use as inns. In order to promote the involvement of their members in the tourism business, the business division of NMO had developed a hospitality programme.

NMO organisational members hoped that Canyon Inn, a bed and breakfast establishment owned and managed by NMO, would be a training tool in the hospitality programme and more generally a means of addressing the unemployment problem. While they recognised that this enterprise might also generate profit, they distinguished this from their primary purpose of using Canyon Inn as a training tool for how to manage a bed and breakfast enterprise. Canyon Inn is a round red-brick building encircled by a concrete walkway leading to two separate entrances on the north and south side of the *hogan*-like structure. The interior is also circular and wide open, with very high ceilings. A huge fireplace raised on a stone base is located in the centre. The smokestack, enclosed in a black tube, extends through the roof. The Inn is very bright during the day from the light shining into the central core.

The guest member

Tom is an energetic Anglo-American. He is a man with a keen sense of responsibility and described himself as 'an intense and passionate person' who, when faced with a task, likes to 'give it his all'. Having grown up in a family of small businesspeople, he had been entrusted with significant responsibilities from a very young age. He explained that if you want a small business to survive, you have to be a 'self-motivated' and a 'self-directed' person. You have to make sure that you have done everything in your power to meet the needs of current or prospective customers, and this may mean going above and beyond the call of duty. He told me that he was a 'practical person' and that he 'hated bureaucracy'. The qualities he valued – self-motivation and self-direction – were particularly important to understanding his point of view in this project.

By the time Tom undertook the project, he had spent a couple of months at NMO. During this time, he learned that his Navajo counterparts might not wish to move into action as quickly as he would like. He also learned that, unless an activity was clearly linked to NMO's mission, it would not enjoy the support of its members.

The evolution of the project

Below, I describe five interactions between Tom and NMO organisational members in an attempt to resolve a core problem of NMO's commitment to the Canyon Inn project, focusing on Tom's changing understanding of the commitment issue.

First interaction

Tom began his involvement with the project by talking to several individuals regarding the operation of Canyon Inn. From his conversations and observations, he concluded that a major problem with the inn was the lack of an 'active' manager.

He first approached Cynthia McDermott, a trainer in the business division. Cynthia did not show any interest in the managerial issue. Instead, she asked Tom to write a business plan. However, she left for an extended period of time shortly thereafter. Upon her departure, no one at NMO expressed interest in working on the project. Thus, Tom concluded that there was no interest in or commitment to it, and he decided to invest his time elsewhere.

However, the hesitation on the part of NMO members was not due to a lack of interest but to a concern about the ambiguity of Canyon

Inn's purpose. Several individuals said that NMO's mission was training, not managing a business, and therefore there would be support for Canyon Inn only if it were framed as a training tool, and not as a profit-making enterprise. However, since these concerns were not raised at this time, no progress was made, and Tom did not learn what was required to pursue the project.

The project was reinitiated during the mid-point evaluation, when all IOR members pause to assess their progress on summer projects and decide how to address any problems. Cary, the DTA administrator, became aware that no progress had been made on the project, and in consultation with Cary, Tom decided to assess NMO's commitment to this project before expending further time and resources.

Second interaction

Tom's first meeting after the mid-point evaluation was with NMO clients Damon Wright and Cynthia, who by now had returned to NMO. Damon was in charge of the Office of Community Development (OCD), responsible for connecting NMO to the community through economic development activities. His office was involved because there were questions about the role it might play in managing Canyon Inn. Cynthia's primary goal was to use the inn for training NMO members in small business development.

The main topic was NMO's commitment to the Canyon Inn project. Several facets of the commitment issue were identified. The first was support from top management. Damon and Cynthia told Tom to talk with the Vice President, Dr George James, and assess his commitment to the project. A second facet concerned who would manage Canyon Inn. Both Damon and Cynthia were hesitant about assuming day-to-day managerial responsibilities: Cynthia said that, at present, the business division did not have the capacity, and Damon was concerned about assuming this responsibility without unambiguous and explicit support from top management. This issue was resolved up to a point in that Damon and Cynthia developed a proposal that Tom was to present to Dr James. The proposal was that an individual solely responsible for management of the inn should be hired. For the first three years, this person would report to Damon's office. After that time, the business division would assume responsibility for day-to-day management of the inn.

Tom raised his concern about the lack of an 'active manager', whom he described in terms of interpersonal traits and behaviour as being 'forthcoming', 'active', and 'greeting customers'. Furthermore, he envisaged the active manager as someone who would organise a variety of interesting activities in the inn, such as cultural presentations. Cynthia responded by saying that these types of activities would be carried out by trainers. In response to this suggestion, Tom dropped the topic.

Tom's concern was deeper than was apparent in this exchange. Although Cynthia's response suggested that the active manager could be understood in terms of a person who performs certain activities, Tom was describing what in his mind constituted an ideal type. He was describing subtle interpersonal skills and attitudes that had particular meanings regarding service work in his own cultural setting. However, Cynthia's response and Tom's reaction left unexplored several questions regarding the applicability and meaning of these cues in the Navajo context.

An additional issue concerned the purpose of Canyon Inn. Tom asked whether Canyon Inn was envisaged as a 'training tool' or a 'profit centre'. Both Damon and Cynthia told him that the inn would only receive support if it was framed as a training activity. From Tom's perspective, however, the inn could serve both purposes. If it were to generate a profit, it would ease the financial burden on NMO to keep it running. Given the apparent reluctance of NMO members to envisage the inn as a profit-generating entity, he did not push the matter further at the time. However, the host's insistence that Canyon Inn be framed solely as a training tool did not fully make sense to him.

From interviews with NMO members, I learned what might explain their reluctance to view Canyon Inn as a profit-generating entity. They explained that there was considerable concern about the loss of Navajo culture at NMO. The organisation itself had been formed in an attempt to maintain Navajo culture. Thus, any initiative perceived as potentially threatening to this mission was resisted. Some individuals argued that profit seeking went counter to Navajo values. For them, the motivation for fostering entrepreneurial activity was to enable community members to earn a living on the Navajo Nation so that they would not have to leave the reservation to seek jobs elsewhere. Other NMO organisational members were concerned that if Navajos did not find a way of marketing their resources, outsiders would capture the tourist market. They argued that it was possible to maintain traditional values while responding to external forces.

Another concern with defining Canyon Inn as a profit-generating entity had to do with the institutional environment of the Navajo economy. Some argued that the business environment on the Navajo Nation made it difficult to engage in micro-entrepreneurial activity. This was a thorny issue that raised a fundamental question about the efficacy of training in small business. Yet many argued that this was the only way to address the severe unemployment problem. There were, however, no easy answers or ways to resolve the complex problem of maintaining cultural values while at the same time fostering entrepreneurial activity on Navajoland.

If Canyon Inn were to be used as a training tool, it needed to be linked to the business division's hospitality programme. Thus, a final facet of NMO's commitment was the status of the proposed programme. In the course of its discussion, the group realised that there was uncertainty regarding the business division's readiness to implement this programme. Cynthia offered to clarify this matter. In the meantime, Tom was to meet with the senior administrator, Dr James, to assess whether there was top management support for the project, and whether there was support for the management proposal.

Tom entered this interaction with the idea that the active manager was a key issue for successfully achieving the goals of the Canyon Inn project. During the course of the conversation, however, this issue fell to the bottom of the list of priorities, and other issues which the clients felt were crucial came to the fore, i.e. day-to-day management, the hospitality programme, and support from top management. Thus, Tom's awareness of the relevant issues expanded considerably.

Third interaction

Dr James strongly reiterated what Tom had already heard with respect to purpose – that there was support for Canyon Inn as long as it was intended for training. He indicated his support but told Tom that it was necessary to secure the backing of Dr Jason Alexander, the president of NMO, who oversaw all administrative activities. Dr James also noted that without clear commitment from the business division, Canyon Inn's purpose would not be realised and inaction would reinforce the perception that nothing was happening on the project. Dr James recommended that Tom meet with both Dr Alexander and Barbara Clemens, the head of the business division, to ascertain that unit's commitment, to which Tom agreed.

Interestingly, in his exchange with Dr James, Tom did not raise the issue of Canyon Inn's profit-generating capacity. His understanding of the issues involved was expanded and deepened in this meeting. It was expanded by obtaining new information concerning the need for Dr Alexander's support, and by securing Dr James' backing for both the project and the managerial proposal. It was deepened because some issues, such as the purpose of Canyon Inn and the importance of the hospitality programme, were reiterated. However, Tom's concerns regarding the active manager and the profit-generating potential of Canyon Inn lingered on.

Fourth interaction

As planned, Tom spoke with Barbara about the business division's vote on the hospitality programme and its plans for using Canyon Inn as a training facility within it. The business division had voted to move forward on the hospitality programme, but Barbara told Tom that the division could not manage Canyon Inn. She was willing, however, to talk further about how Canyon Inn could be used as a training tool within the context of the hospitality programme. Tom did not speak with Dr Alexander regarding his support for the programme.

Fifth interaction

At this juncture, a decision was made to convene all the relevant stakeholders and discuss the remaining issues and their implications for NMO, as well as for Tom's workplan. Present at the meeting were the IOR members involved up to this point (Cynthia, Damon, Barbara, Dr James, and Tom), along with four new individuals.

The group revisited the key aspects of the commitment issue, most of which were resolved. However, for Tom, there were still problems with the purpose and management issues. These concerns were raised one last time in this meeting. Tom argued that while the focus of the meeting was to discuss how to use Canyon Inn, the enterprise could also be a viable profit-generating entity. This elicited two strong statements. The first person indicated that NMO would not support the project unless it was aligned with NMO's mission. The second told Tom that that NMO was not interested in making 'millions of dollars':

> We are not a money-making institution, we are a non-profit training institution. Even in the business division they are not managers. No one in this institution is a manager. This project can be a unique opportunity for our Navajo members to learn what it takes to be a successful business person on the Navajo Nation. So as a training programme I support it since it is consistent with our mission.

This was the clearest and strongest statement underscoring what Tom had learned regarding this issue and put unequivocal closure to the purpose question. It was not contested further.

Tom also raised the issue of the active manager. He explained that Canyon Inn needed 'a single accountable person' who could handle everything. This issue was redefined as a problem of hiring a manager for the inn, a concern that had been expressed by the clients. The qualities this individual should exhibit, an issue of concern to Tom, did not seem to register. The group agreed that a manager should be hired.

With most of the commitment-related issues resolved, the meeting focused on implementation. Rather than going into this next phase, I will instead turn to an analysis of the interaction and in particular of how Tom's evolving understanding of the commitment issue was accomplished through learning acts.

Learning practices in a new cultural context

I have described Tom's evolving understanding of the commitment issue in five interactions. Tom began this project with the intention of working on the problem of the active manager. Before doing so, however, he wanted to be sure of NMO's commitment to Canyon Inn. The commitment problem turned out to be multi-faceted and complex. Furthermore, the aspects and issues that were explicitly discussed and resolved were the organisational dimensions of the commitment problem, not its underlying *value dimensions*. Differences in perspective between Tom and NMO organisational members arose around the issue of the active manager and the purpose of Canyon Inn. As suggested above, underlying these differences were deeper issues rooted in cultural and historical experiences. The cross-cultural literature suggests that such value differences can be a major stumbling block to learning (Hall 1981). Yet the results show that some degree of learning can be achieved even when underlying differences remain unresolved. This is possible when guests are skilful in managing differences. We now take a closer look at how such differences were managed and how this facilitated guest adaptation, through an analysis of Tom's acts. I will begin with conceptual ideas that will assist in this analysis.

Types of difference and resolution

I would suggest that the resolution of the value aspects of a complex problem requires going beyond 'level-one issues' to explore 'level-two issues'. Level-one issues are those where actors have differences in perspectives that can be resolved by implicitly drawing on shared premises or frames of reference. Although actors do not explicitly cite their shared assumptions, they render their differing perspectives mutually sensible with reference to these assumptions (Heritage 1984). In contrast, at level two, actors' differences in perspective are based on differing cultural values and historical experiences, and they lack a shared frame of reference for recognising one another's concerns as relevant or meaningful.

Thus, one problem with the resolution of such differences is whether the nature of the practices matches that of the differences. The two levels of the triangle in Figure 2 match the types of differences and types of exploration appropriate to resolving the differences in question. Task-focused conversations are sufficient to resolve level-one differences in perspective, while level-two issues are those whose meaning can only be established by considering the second level of the triangle – underlying value and historical differences. Part of engaging in practices that match the difference requires that actors recognise the nature of the difference when it is encountered. Mistaking a level-two for a level-one difference is a common problem in cross-cultural interactions, including those in development projects. Based on a mis-recognition, an actor may think that by appealing to what s/he assumes to be shared or universal values, or by trying to explain better, the other can understand and ideally accept a particular view. The question then is: what are the consequences of the mis-recognition of the type of difference and subsequent mismatch of practice?

Tom conveyed an awareness that things on the Navajo Nation and NMO in particular were very different from his home culture. He also expressed a strong interest in learning about Navajo culture and read a great deal about it. Ironically, he did not seem to recognise that the differences in perspective between himself and his counterparts with regard to the purpose of Canyon Inn and the active manager reflected such cultural differences and presented opportunities for learning about lived Navajo culture. Such mis-recognition has consequences for guest learning. One could conceivably deal with differences by imposing one's own perspectives. Tom did not do this. Although he did not show any awareness that the issues that he was confronting were potentially due to different cultural and historical experiences, he held his assumptions at bay and engaged with his partners on issues whose rationale he could understand. This suggests that, barring the ability to

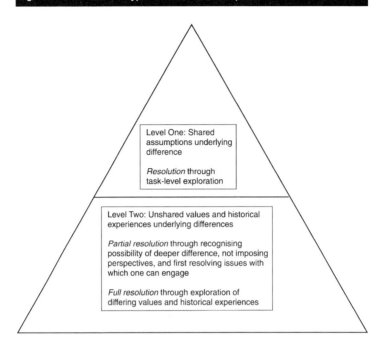

Figure 2: Match between type of difference and exploration

Level One: Shared assumptions underlying difference

Resolution through task-level exploration

Level Two: Unshared values and historical experiences underlying differences

Partial resolution through recognising possibility of deeper difference, not imposing perspectives, and first resolving issues with which one can engage

Full resolution through exploration of differing values and historical experiences

engage in value exploration, there may be an intermediate level of dealing with level-two issues: not directly engaging with the hosts, not trampling over them, but first exploring common ground. Although Tom's acts did not allow for an exploration and resolution of deeper differences, they did facilitate the articulation of level-one issues.

Newcomer learning practices

The analysis of Tom's learning practices suggests that there are at least two broad categories of acts involved in guest learning: calibrating and progressing. Calibrating involves assessing the relevance of one's perspectives in a new setting in such a way that these are not imposed on partners. Progressing involves eliciting information and explanations to build one's understanding of the issues relevant to one's task.

Two specific acts fell within the calibrating category: probing and suppressing. These were used to manage level-two differences in perspectives. *Probing* involves stating one's perspectives 'lightly', while calibrating others' receptivity, and making adjustments based on the observed response. Probing can vary in its 'lightness' or subtlety. An important aspect of probing is that the guest does not insist on his or her perspective but gently attempts to generate a discussion around the differing perspectives. In the first meeting, after Damon and Cynthia came up with a management proposal, Tom elaborated on the role he envisaged for the active manager. When Cynthia indicated that a trainer could handle this, Tom did not offer further explanations, but turned to another issue. We saw a more insistent probe by Tom in the fifth meeting, where he tried to pursue the issues of profit and the active manager for one last time. This type of probing was risky because, as happened in this instance, the suggestion that the inn might be used for profit elicited a strongly negative reaction from one of the hosts.

A second calibrating act is *suppressing* one's views. Tom did this in all three meetings. Although he felt strongly about the active manager and profit issues, recognising his hosts' lack of readiness to deal with them, he repeatedly changed the topic to elicit their views. Although this expanded his understanding in other areas, their responses to the active manager and profit issues left him not fully convinced.

These two acts enabled Tom to manage level-two issues in such a way that the articulation of level-one issues was not blocked. Tom's practices in the category of progressing acts were used to surface level-one issues. Four observed acts in this category were: stating his point of departure, focusing attention, asking questions, and summarising.

Stating one's point of departure involves defining a problem that is inhibiting one's progress on a task. Tom did this at the outset of the first meeting by stating DTA's concern that Canyon Inn was not a priority for NMO. Before undertaking the project, he wanted to assess NMO's commitment to it. Stating a position in this manner is not advocating for any substantive solution to a problem. That is, it is not a statement of what the commitment issue should entail or how it should be resolved. Instead, it sets up a problem that requires joint resolution. This practice was intended to generate a discussion, and it was received in this spirit.

Focusing attention on the problem of commitment was a second act that facilitated progress. This was accomplished by returning to an unresolved issue when an intervention had shifted the conversation in a new direction. This occurred early in meeting one. Tom began by stating that he had called the meeting in order to resolve the issue of commitment. Cynthia responded by raising fairly detailed issues regarding the hospitality programme. However, Tom reframed her comments and directed the conversation back to the issue of commitment. The following excerpt illustrates this dynamic:

Tom: I would like to work on the Canyon Inn project, but I am concerned about the commitment from NMO. I want to clarify two things. Can you use me for the Canyon Inn project? And what is the commitment to the hospitality programme?

Cynthia: We want to have the hospitality programme in place by Fall, but we don't know if it will actually fall into place by then. These are the people you need to talk to: Barbara Clemens who is the head of the Business Division and Dr James. He's interested in the spin-off from business. You need to talk to the chapter people because if we do anything with Canyon Inn, we need to involve the chapter people because tourism has been discussed at the chapter level.[6] Also, Abbot, who is someone in the community who has 19 dirt-floor hogans, needs to be consulted. He has talked to us about Canyon Inn. Also there is James Kirk and Angela Parks. We are planning to collaborate with them both on the programme.

Tom: Contacts are very useful, but I'm interested in whether it will be something that NMO is committed to and is useful for training purposes. Last year I understand the reports were written but they were not read, or no-one did anything with them.

Asking questions that open up a deeper exploration of a particular issue was another act. One type of question involved clarifying the meaning of an event. For instance, in the first meeting, Cynthia explained that the business division had 'voted unanimously in favour of the hospitality programme'. Tom responded by asking: 'What does it mean that the division has voted?' It turned out that Cynthia did not know whether this meant that the business division was ready to implement this programme in the near future. Another type of question that moved the conversation towards deeper exploration involved dissolving momentary confrontation between competing desires. For instance, Cynthia stated that she felt that Damon's office should take responsibility for managing Canyon Inn because the business division did not have the managerial capacity. Damon posed a rebuttal: 'Who is going to manage it? That is a huge problem.' At this point, Tom responded 'How should I find an answer?' This elicited a response from Damon about what his office could do and the conditions under which it could take on responsibility for Canyon Inn. This allowed the group to go into a discussion about what each party could do and what was needed. Finally, Tom posed questions to try to predict the future. For instance, he wanted to know the likely scenario regarding how the management issue would be addressed in the following year if the proposal was not accepted or implemented.

Summarising the main issues being discussed and the steps that were agreed to by the group was a last progressing act observed in the first and second meetings. This provided an opportunity for others to add, elaborate, or raise different understandings if the summary had not captured the concerns of all involved parties.

Implications

This article began with the claim that a guest's ability to be effective in providing technical assistance in a development project evolves through a process of learning and adaptation. By the fifth meeting, Tom had a few weeks left at NMO, and it was decided that the best use of his remaining time was to write a business plan. In fact the client, Cynthia, had asked him to do this in the very first interaction. The reader may reasonably contend that carrying out this task did not require the four subsequent interactions between Tom and NMO members. In addition, the knowledge he acquired in these interactions was not necessary in order to write a business plan. However, I would argue that Tom's main contribution came from facilitating the resolution of the commitment problem through the process of learning that he generated.

Although the Canyon Inn project had started several years ago, no progress had been made in using it for its intended purpose: training. Hence, there was a widely shared perception at NMO that there was no commitment to Canyon Inn. By initiating a process of assessing the commitment issue, Tom helped NMO organisational members articulate what was needed to resolve this problem. We saw how the multi-faceted nature of this problem emerged in the five interactions. Specifically, resolving the commitment issue involved securing moral, programme, and human resource support from a variety of actors. By the fifth meeting, these issues had been resolved and NMO organisational members were moving towards considering implementation.

We have also argued that a guest's ability to learn in a new cultural context is a skilled accomplishment, which involves managing assumptions developed in prior acculturation experiences. Although Tom was not able fully to resolve level-two differences, he was able to manage these in such a way that they did not block the articulation of level-one issues. This allowed him to prevent any culture-based conflict. Further, by not imposing his own views, Tom successfully managed the sensitivity of Navajos to the long history of cultural devaluation and external imposition by Anglos. This prevented what NMO organisational members report has been the common fate of outsiders who are referred to as a 'typical Anglo', namely, being ignored. If Tom had been unable to manage such dynamics, which are rooted in inter-group political history, he would not have been able to learn anything.

Despite this impressive accomplishment on Tom's part, an important aspect of the commitment issue, the cultural maintenance dimension, remained unresolved by a failure to explore issues that brought this dimension into relief. Both guests and hosts were concerned with the current efficiency and effectiveness of the management of Canyon Inn. How might Tom's ideas have been modified and applied to address these problems? Also, some at NMO were concerned with external actors taking over the tourism market. How could NMO provide training in small business management in accordance with Navajo values? How does this address the long-term problems in penetrating the business environment on the Navajo Nation?

Is the failure to resolve the underlying problem a reason for despair? I would argue that one has to understand what can be learned within such a project in the context of its short-term timeframe. By focusing on the issues that could be jointly understood, common ground was established, and further exploration could build on this in the future. It was the presence of a degree of cross-cultural communicative competence that facilitated what learning did occur. That is, Tom's practices involved a competent management of differences in a context of political inequality.

In light of these observations, a practical issue for development organisations concerns how guest workers may develop these types of skills. Anecdotal evidence suggests that while classroom training in cross-cultural communications skills provides useful information, it may not be easily transferable. Tom's acts were performed 'in-the-moment' without a chance for detached reflection. How can development organisations address the need for cross-cultural effectiveness in this type of situation? Although part of Tom's flexibility may have been due to personal characteristics, he also consulted various individuals about the differences he encountered and about how he should deal with these. Specific information on these exchanges is not available, but certainly some of these individuals had extensive experience working in similar environments. This suggests that development organisations may be able to reinforce classroom training by providing ongoing consultation for development workers once they are in the field.

Finally, although it is evident that the hosts also played a role in the learning process described here, this aspect of the issue is beyond the scope of this article (but is discussed further in Debebe 2002). Suffice it to say here that hosts played a major role by focusing the conversations on the key issues that needed resolution without dismissing Tom's ideas, and by advising him on how to proceed at each stage of the process.

Acknowledgements

I would like to thank Richard Bagozzi, Jane Dutton, Martha Feldman, Joyce Fletcher, Kenneth Reinert, and Mayer Zald for helpful discussions related to this topic. I am especially grateful to Kenneth Reinert for kindly reading and commenting on an earlier draft of this article. Finally, I offer my thanks to the organisations that provided access, and the individuals who participated in the fieldwork described here.

Notes

1 There are many possible dimensions of inequality (e.g. financial, historical) that could be used to characterise the relationship between organisations. Here I focus on political inequality based on historical conflict between the groups that these organisations represent.

2 The term 'communicative competence' was coined by Dell Hymes (1972). This idea brings our attention to the interactive competencies involved in communication in particular cultural contexts. Similar ideas have been cited in cross-cultural research. Redmond (2000) used the term 'intercultural communication competence' and suggested that it included six dimen-

sions. Jacobson *et al.* (1999) used the term 'intercultural competence' to refer to the development of new strategies for managing interactions effectively in a new cultural context. In the organisational literature, ideas related to communicative competence have also emerged (Putnam and Kolb 2000; Fletcher 1999). For the interested reader, my use of this idea is described in Debebe (2002).

3 The other two aspects of learning practice are *interpretation* and *strategy formulation*. These aspects are explored elsewhere (Debebe 2002).

4 I use the term 'Anglo' to refer to the broad European-American culture rather than to British culture. In using the term in this way, my intention is not to deny the rich ethnic and cultural diversity within this group. I use this term because this diversity is not central to this analysis, but the dominant culture of which sub-groups are a part *is* relevant, and many scholars have referred to this dominant culture as 'Anglo' culture. Hereafter, it will appear without quotation marks.

5 To protect the anonymity of those concerned, all names of organisations, people, programmes, and project have been changed.

6 A chapter is the local government unit on the Navajo reservation.

References

Brown, John S. and Paul Duguid (2000) *The Social Life of Information*, Boston, MA: Harvard Business School Press.

Carroll, Raymonde (1990) *Cultural Misunderstandings*, Chicago, IL: University of Chicago Press.

Cornell, Stephen and Joseph P. Kalt (1995) *What Can Tribes Do? Strategies and Institutions in American Indian Economic Development*, Los Angeles, CA: American Indian Studies Center.

Debebe, Gelaye (2002) 'Power-over and power-with modes of interaction: intercultural coordination as joint learning', unpublished doctoral dissertation, University of Michigan.

Dewey, John (1938) *Experience and Education*, New York, NY: Simon & Schuster.

Dyck, Bruno, Jerry Buckland, Harold Harder and Dan Wiens (2000) 'Community development as organisational learning: the importance of agent-participant reciprocity', *Canadian Journal of Development Studies* 21:605-620.

Fletcher, Joyce (1999) *Disappearing Acts: Gender, Power, and Relational Practice at Work*, Cambridge, MA: MIT Press.

Hall, Edward (1981) *Beyond Culture*, New York, NY: Doubleday.

Heritage, John (1984) *Garfinkel and Ethno Methodology*, Massachusetts: Polity.

Hymes, Dell (1972) 'On communicative competence', in J. B. Pride and Janet Holmes (eds.) *Sociolinguistics*, Harmondsworth: Penguin.

Jacobson, Wayne, Dana Sleicher and Maureen Burke (1999) 'Portfolio assessment of intercultural competence', *International Journal of Intercultural Relations* 23(3):467-492.

Lave, Jean and Etienne Wenger (1991) *Situated Learning: Legitimate Peripheral Participation*, New York, NY: CUP.

Putnam, Linda L. and Deborah M. Kolb (2000) 'Rethinking Negotiation: Feminist Views of Communication and Exchange', Working Paper 7, Michigan, Center for Gender in Organizations.

Redmond, Mark V. (2000) 'Cultural distance as a mediating factor between stress and intercultural communication competence', *International Journal of Intercultural Relations* 24:151-159.

White, Sarah C. (1996) 'Depoliticising development: the uses and abuses of participation', *Development in Practice* 6(2):6-15.

This paper was first published in Development in Practice *(12/3&4:355-369) in 2002.*

Can bilateral programmes become learning organisations?
Experiences from institutionalising participation in Keiyo Marakwet in Kenya

Samuel Musyoki

Introduction

Bilateral programmes are inherently politicised. Any analysis of bilateral programmes as learning organisations will be incomplete and skewed if it fails to treat the political dynamics as central. These dynamics determine what is to be learned by whom, for what purpose, when, and how. In discussing the case study drawn from Keiyo Marakwet, Kenya,[1] I use two metaphors (following Morgan 1986): organisations *as machines* and organisations *as political systems*. The image we start out with (acknowledged or not) frames our thinking about organisations and their capacity to learn and change.

The case compares three major programme phases between 1983 and 2000, and analyses how different actors engaged in the process of institutionalising participation and managing its intended and unintended lessons and consequences. While the concept of the learning organisation presumes an interest in institutional memory as a basis for future learning, the Keiyo Marakwet case study shows that every transition from one phase to the next appears to have been a missed learning opportunity. The case illustrates that if one views organisations as political systems, the process of institutionalising participation emerges as one that will inevitably generate conflict, and any learning from it is therefore bound to be selective and contingent on the perspectives of specific actors.

Key concepts and context

In Kenya, participation has become increasingly crucial in decision making with the introduction of decentralisation policies and strategies such as the District Focus for Rural Development Strategy (DFRDS) in 1983 and the emergence of Participatory Rural Appraisal (PRA) a few years later. Connell (1997) describes people's participation as both a methodology and a strategic goal of development. Participation is a model that proposes to improve people's standards of living and also to give them a measure of control of these standards. Participation in development projects should therefore be seen as an entry point to enable the poor to challenge and transform existing power structures. In Kenya, although many bilateral programmes are moving away from their traditional 'top-down' styles and adopting 'bottom-up' approaches to development, they have tended to limit participation and the use of participatory methods to a means of generating projects.

While institutionalising participation demands that organisations create an environment that is conducive to it, the way we go about changing organisations in order to do this is shaped by our assumptions about them (Pimbert *et al.* 2000). Morgan (1986) argues that there is a tendency to think of organisations as machines and thus expect them to operate in a conditioned and predictable manner. This view tends to assume that managerial control and procedures are what makes an organisation function well. The focus is on organisational performance in terms of outputs. Viewed from this perspective, institutionalising participation would simply be a means for improving an organisation's efficiency rather than a learning process with the goal of empowering weaker actors to transform it.

Morgan (1986) also presents a contrasting view of organisations as *political systems* in which different interests are represented, conflicts occur, and actors use space provided by the organisations to promote or inhibit the process of change. This metaphor enables us to dig beneath the 'common goal', the organisational map, rules, and procedures, and begin to understand the politics behind the 'machines'. This in turn enables us to engage with the process of institutionalising participation as a critical learning process that could lead to organisational transformation.

Background to the case study

Keiyo and Marakwet Districts are named after two ethnic groups who were traditionally herders but also practised some subsistence agriculture. The area is characterised by three major agro-ecological zones: the highland plateau, the intermediate escarpment, and the valley. Most of the poorer people live in the valley, which is hot, receives low rainfall, and is considered an arid or semi-arid (ASAL) zone. The ASAL programme[2] was established in 1983 as the vehicle for development in this area with the goal 'to improve the living standards of the ASAL population by integrating ASALs into the mainstream of the national economy and social development, in an environmentally sustainable manner' (Republic of Kenya 1992:6). The policy identifies three reasons why the government should make such an investment. First, ASALs have substantial potential for development, although its realisation might entail higher costs than in other areas. Second, since most of Kenya's poorest people live in ASALs, there is a need to improve their livelihoods through increased productivity and the creation of employment opportunities so that they may share equitably in the benefits of development. Third, the increasing problems of soil erosion and environmental degradation could lead to desertification, which would result in severe hunger and malnutrition and in turn lead to the unplanned expenditure of public resources on famine-relief operations. The policy underscores the importance of participation by grassroots communities for the development programmes in ASALs to be successful. This emphasis on community participation and the multi-sectoral programme approach are among the features of the policy that attracted the Dutch government (GON) and other donors to support ASAL programmes in the early 1980s. Since its inception in 1983, the Keiyo Marakwet programme has tried to promote the participation of grassroots communities in decision making, but it has done so with very little success.

ASAL Phase I: 1983–1987

The bilateral agreement between the Dutch and Kenyan governments gave the Kenyan government (GOK) line ministries exclusive mandate to provide technical expertise in planning, implementation, monitoring, and evaluation of the Keiyo Marakwet programme.

The first phase (ASAL I) invested mainly in major infrastructure projects such as water, irrigation, roads, health, and education. Despite the stated ideals of decentralisation and grassroots participation, the reality was one of standardised procedures or blueprints. Government officials were in a position to assert their power over both the decision-making process and programme resources. The 1983 decentralisation policy (DFRDS) required that all ASAL programmes be implemented through it. Ironically, the Dutch government saw this policy as complementing the programme's efforts, little realising that it gave the government officials too much power. Grassroots communities were perceived as passive recipients and their participation was viewed in terms of cost sharing through their contribution of local materials and unskilled labour.

The GON seems to have applied the *machines* view of organisations as it failed to dig beneath the DFRDS structure to question the level of power that it gave to district-level bureaucrats. It had assumed that the GOK policy statements, as well as the elaborate management and control systems put in place, would enable the programme to deliver development to the poor.

By the second year, serious conflicts erupted between GOK officials in the district and the Dutch Programme Adviser. The former wanted the programme's budget quadrupled but the adviser disagreed. This conflict forced the adviser to leave, and his successor did not take up post for another five months. When he arrived, he found that extensive leakage and embezzlement had taken place in the intervening period, on account of which the programme was temporarily shut down (ASAL 1999a). Both governments avoided talking about the episode publicly, as this would hurt diplomatic relations. When Dutch support was resumed in 1990, the Netherlands Development Organisation (SNV) was contracted to run the programme primarily as a way of avoiding direct conflict between the two governments. Rather than deal with the causes of the problem, diplomatic considerations dictated only a minor change in managerial structure.

ASAL Phase II: 1991–1994

In its second phase, the programme adopted Community-Oriented Project Planning (COPP), an adaptation of ZOPP (Goal-Oriented Project Planning, a tool developed by the German government agency, GTZ). COPP's major objective was to sensitise the rural population about its role in identifying, planning, and implementing development projects (Mbagathi 1991). However, the COPP pioneers did not have a free hand in initiating a genuinely participatory process. Rather, their role was to train the District Development Committees (DDCs) to write and forward proposals within the government's framework. Despite the intention of promoting community participation through COPP, the government bureaucracy remained the greatest obstacle to the processes of institutionalising participation in ASAL Phase II. GOK officials and provincial administrators dominated the planning and implementation of projects. Efforts to create a shared vision through COPP bore little fruit, as these key people had personal visions that ran counter to what the programme sought to achieve. The COPP moderators took a 'neutral position' by avoiding conflict-generating processes and thus became merely an instrument for producing project proposals. Participants were always assisted to reach consensus or compromise and bury their differences. Instead of empowering the communities to engage in questioning the management of the programme, COPP reinforced the interests of the official bodies. Thus, COPP did not create reflective learning spaces in which conflicting interests would have been brought to the surface and openly debated. Had it done so, this would have provided an opportunity for sharing experiences, which would have forced government officials to come face to face with the fact that their interests were overriding those of the grassroots communities.

ASAL Phase II did not appear to have learned from the previous phase. There was no analysis of the political dynamics underlying the formal structure, nor was participation viewed as offering learning opportunities that could help transform the government bureaucracy. The latter had become a tool for enhancing state efficiency in controlling the ASAL programmes and the rural poor, exploiting the latter's potential and excluding them rather than addressing their needs.

The following section describes how a team of participatory methods practitioners engaged in the politics of the ASAL programme and facilitated a process of institutionalising participation that created opportunities for learning and for the transformation of the management of the programme and the GOK bureaucracy.

ASAL Phase III: 1995–1999

During the five-month lapse before the new full-time Dutch Programme Adviser assumed his post, the programme was managed by a GOK officer and a part-time Programme Adviser (PA), leaving the doors wide open for the local counterpart and his associates to control the project's resources.

The GOK officials seemed to be uncomfortable with two *Mzungus* (white persons) in the programme. The Programme Officer (PO) objected to the Dutch advisers visiting project sites unless accompanied, while the accounts showed that there had been misappropriation (ASAL 1999b:38). The PO tried to avoid conflict, hoping that the advisers would forget the past and move on to ASAL III. The advisers used their first encounters to learn about the programme's organisational set-up, culture, and the behaviour of individual actors. Some GOK officers also volunteered information to them.

The two advisers had attended a pilot exercise on the use of Participatory Educational Theatre (PET) organised by a programme that I was facilitating. They invited me to present the approach, and a proposal on how this could be used in their programme was accepted.

Few of the officers present in the consultative meeting realised the implications of using PET as an entry point to ASAL Phase III.

Steps in the process of institutionalising participation

Team formation

Not all GOK officers had a genuine interest in the process of institutionalising participation in the programme. The management therefore decided that it was going to work with a taskforce of only ten officers. The heads of department (HOD) attempted to influence the selection process but the advisers rejected some of the names they proposed.

It inevitably became important to build alliances within and outside the programme, lobby for support from the two governments, and build coalitions among line-ministry officers and the local communities. Informal methods of establishing allies were used, such as chatting, meetings in local bars, and eliciting information from support staff.

The strategy

The taskforce became a think-tank on land-use planning for the new strategy through which an organisational framework called the 'Transect Area Approach' (TAA) was developed. Unlike the earlier phases, where the activities were restricted to the valley zone, ASAL III would also include the escarpment and the highlands.

The strategy sought to apply the programme's resources more efficiently in the concentrated Transect Areas (TAs) rather than spreading them too thinly in the whole district. A wider section of local communities would also be organised to participate in these selected areas. In order to neutralise any tensions, the new approach was presented as a strategy that would strengthen district planning, in keeping with the government policy. However, unlike the DFRDS, the new strategy would promote community participation through a 'mixed grill' of approaches, namely PET, COPP, and PRA.

The strategy had political implications for the DDC. The decision to work in concentrated TAs implied that the administrative units, i.e. the districts, divisions, locations, and sub-locations, also had to change. The TAA strategy meant that the DDC would become redundant, hence creating the need for alternative decision-making structures and new actors. In a nutshell, the TAA strategy laid the foundations for weakening and transforming the government bureaucracy and creating space for the communities in the TAs to participate in managing the programme.

The programme introduced a new funding policy that created tension and division among government officers, further weakening the bureaucratic structures. This policy meant that 70 per cent of the programme's budget would be spent in the productive sector (agriculture, environment, water, and veterinary services) and 30 per cent in the service sector (health, education, and roads). It was in the service sector that most of the misappropriation and other financial irregularities had occurred in earlier phases. While the programme management capitalised on the tension and found allies in the productive sector to support the new strategy, some of the senior personnel sought to frustrate the initiatives intended to institutionalise participation. The Keiyo Marakwet community, who had witnessed how the programme had been managed in the past, saw this process as an opportunity for transforming it and making it more accountable to the people, and therefore supported the programme's management.

Selection of concentration areas

Initially, the taskforce divided the programme area into 14 potential concentration areas (ASAL 1999b), but eventually only four were selected, two in each district. The leaders, communities, and government offices whose ongoing projects were outside these TAs complained bitterly, and negotiated with the programme management to ensure that their projects would be supported until completion.

The local politicians also voiced their interest and the programme ensured that each of the four constituencies got a TA, which served to neutralise any basis that the politicians might have used to discredit the programme. In fact, they became strong allies and played a supportive role in the process of institutionalising participation. Upon realising that the politicians were in favour of the programme's new strategy, some of the government officers also crossed over.

People's stories

The process began with Awareness Raising Campaigns (ARC),[3] using PET as the entry point. The ARC provided a space for stakeholders to reflect, analyse, and learn from the experiences of ASAL Phases I and II. The presentations articulated problems such as inadequate water supply, poor hygiene, environmental degradation, loss of soil fertility and low crop yield, inadequate community participation in projects, politicians' interference in development projects, and corruption by government personnel. The communities called for the management's assurance that the programme would be managed better and that they would be involved in decision making and have control over the projects and resources in ASAL Phase III.

The DDC was publicly questioned for the first time by the Keiyo Marakwet communities about embezzling the programme's resources. Using the image of a 'big rat', local people accused the DDC of destroying project proposals that had been forwarded to them by the communities. The ARC provided transformative learning opportunities, and the campaigns were a major step towards institutionalising participation beyond projects. Interests surfaced, conflicts arose, and resolutions were reached. It was like washing dirty linen in public as wrongs done in earlier phases of the ASAL programme were brought out into the open for discussion. The ARC was a critical entry point in that it not only enabled all the actors to learn from past mistakes but also helped to build rapport and lay the foundation for trust between the programme's management, the government, and the Keiyo Marakwet communities.

Participatory planning

ASAL engaged a team of PRA trainers to train GOK officers and the core facilitation team, which I headed. The training aimed to develop participants' skills in using PRA for designing land-use and natural resource management (NRM) projects. The trainers presented PRA as an instrument that would enhance the efficient operation of the programme, rather than as a political process for learning and empowering the communities in order to transform the government bureaucracy. The PRA training contradicted the political process we had begun during the ARCs.

PRA did not seem very different from the COPP approach that had been used in ASAL Phase II. However, the visual aids and tools it offers enabled us to involve non-literate members of the community in gathering and analysing data as well as drawing up Community Action Plans (CAPs). We introduced a budgeting component with the communities, and this boosted their trust in the programme. Their knowledge of, and access to, budget information gave the communities a tool for mobilising local resources and also laid a basis for holding all parties accountable.

The outcomes of the first PRA exercises were not very impressive. The CAPs were just shopping lists of projects not unlike those generated through the COPP approach, and they did not seem to have been informed by the data generated by the PRA teams. This was in part due to the fact that the three-day PRA training had not been sufficiently thorough. Trainers emphasised the application of tools to generate NRM projects, ignoring the critical reflection and analytical aspects necessary for facilitating sharing and learning during the PRA process. Also, some officers were not committed to the process and saw their duty as being simply to produce CAPs. They argued that the process was lengthy and tedious and not commensurate with their daily stipends. We dropped them and retained those who had demonstrated good facilitation and analytical skills and interest. Through a reflection session we learnt that we needed to be open minded and to accept failures, conflicts, and mistakes as part of the learning process, and there was marked improvement in the following PRA exercises. Although PRA had been presented to us as a very mechanistic approach, through reflecting critically on its application we managed to move beyond the 'sticks' and the 'maps' and to integrate other tools into it.

Transect Area Action Plans (TAAPs)

The PRA exercises produced 19 CAPs that were synthesised into four TAAPs. These were in turn consolidated into the 1996 Annual Work Plan (AWP), which was approved by the ASAL steering committee. For the first time, the programme had involved the communities in developing the Work Plan.

An alternative grassroots organisation, the Transect Area Committee (TAC), emerged from this process.[4] TACs gained more popularity and legitimacy at the grassroots level than the DDC, and they became the yardstick for the communities to assess the government body. This revealed further weaknesses, and as the bureaucratic structure began to disintegrate at the bottom, it enabled alternative community-based structures to evolve.

Feedback and training

Following approval of the AWP by the Dutch government, the TAAPs were presented back to the communities through forums similar to those held during the ARC. The communities renegotiated some priorities and budgets with the management team and these were amended accordingly. The government officers in charge of the approved projects were invited to declare their commitment publicly as though they were being sworn into an oath of transparency and accountability. Some found this exercise intimidating and embarrassing and declined to attend.

The TAAPs led to the birth of Project Management Committees (PMCs), which numbered 319 by the end of 1997, with a total membership of 4147. Capacity building became a very important step for preparing the PMCs to take up new responsibilities in the programme. An important outcome of each training event was a detailed implementation schedule, which provided a description of the project, objectives, activities, indicators, timeframe, responsibilities, inputs, and budget. This in turn became a management tool for ensuring accountability among the stakeholders.

Outcomes of the process

Through the ARC a space for dialogue was created, communities' voices were heard, and verbal agreements were made to the effect that these would be involved in planning and management of project resources and benefits accruing from them. The communities took over the role of planning from the line ministries and the Programme Management Unit (PMU). They had gained the power of knowledge and information about resources. More importantly, they discovered the power they already had within themselves – potential that had not been realised in ASAL Phases I and II.

Another community-based structure also emerged out of this process, with two major units: the PMC and the TAC. The PMC is the smallest unit within the structure and is made up of 13 members elected by the beneficiary communities. It created an opportunity for more people from the grassroots to participate in decision making and managing development projects that affect their lives.

The TACs play an important role in mobilising the communities, thus phasing out the role of GOK officers in coordinating grassroots development. Since 1997 the TAA structure has become the main decision-making and management body for ASAL programmes in Keiyo Marakwet. These radical changes caused considerable tension in the programme, shifting the power base that had been established by the government in earlier phases. While the process of institutionalising participation in the programme had empowering outcomes for the groups who had been marginalised, those who had been in power suffered disempowering consequences.

Managing the outcomes

Government officials had not anticipated that institutionalising participation in the programme would threaten their positions of power. The PMU, comprising the two Dutch PAs, a GOK representative, and a gender adviser, was a relatively small but powerful body whose main role was to coordinate the implementation of ASAL operations by supervising the PMCs. With all the implementation plans coming from the PMCs, the PMU faced an increasing workload, and the PAs feared that there might be fraud within the PMU and in the line ministries. One adviser computerised the accounts system and networked it with his office computer, enabling him to track all transactions. With his laptop set like a trap, he was like a hunter waiting to catch the big 'rats'. As implementation began, the trap started catching out minor instances of misappropriation, such as drivers cheating on use of fuel and officers using fake receipts for expense claims.

Tension began to build between the adviser and his local counterpart, and cliques formed around them. While the former had the support of the junior staff, core facilitation teams, and the community, support for the PO came from the accounts department, top district officials, and the ministry headquarters. Under the slogan 'all the *Mzugus* out', the PO and his team seemed determined to get the Dutch PAs out of the district, blaming them for initiating the new strategy. As the battle high-toned, some community leaders camped near the programme offices to monitor the situation closely. They feared that the programme would be closed down, as had happened with ASAL I, while the PAs received threats on several occasions. The conflict served to widen the gap between government officers and the local people as the communities lost confidence in the government system when they learned that the PO had the support of the ministry headquarters. Subsequently, the GON revoked the joint venture and one PA became the sole signatory for the donor's funds while the PO became the sole signatory for the GOK money (ASAL 1999a:38). The PO eventually left the programme, and the embezzlement proved so extensive that the entire accounts office staff was later replaced (ASAL 1999a:38).

The GOK officials also underwent a painful experience. They learned that by relinquishing their responsibilities during the participatory planning phase they had let go of the power over, and access to, the programme's resources. Under the new structure, departmental workplans were no longer used as the basis for project design and implementation. The HODs complained of being ignored and sidelined as the programme shifted planning and implementation to the communities (ETC 1997). The PMCs opened bank accounts and became signatories for all expenditure related to their projects, including vouchers for the line ministry officers' allowances. While senior officers opted out of the programme activities, their juniors, who had been involved in the process from the beginning, became the Transect Coordinators, with the full support of the PAs.[5]

The DDC was also affected by the new structure. An ASAL programme steering committee used to coordinate the departments during planning, appraisal, implementation, and approval of annual budgets. Within the new framework, these roles had been shifted to the communities, who now had their representatives in the steering committee. This had never happened before and government representatives felt that the PMU was taking its power for granted. Instead of drawing lessons from the outcomes of the new strategy, they accused it of being responsible for creating parallel and illegal structures, which they claimed were usurping the powers of the government structure.

A 1997 external evaluation confirmed that the programme's performance had improved. There was improved sector coordination, less bureaucracy, prompt disbursement of funds to the communities, and flexibility in shifting budget lines from one sector to another in response to local needs. There were reduced opportunities for corruption and marked improvements in supervision, monitoring, and evaluation. The communities and local politicians began trusting the ASAL programme, and the politicians and local élites began to understand the programme and the real meaning of participation in development. The entire reorganisation of the operating structure that took place had effectively empowered the communities and represented real progress towards decentralisation (ETC 1997). Although institutionalising participation had succeeded in developing an effective 'alternative structure' for involving the communities in decision making and management of the programme, the government side did not want to draw lessons from it. Government officials did not recognise it as a legitimate body that could replace or complement the DDC, but rather saw it as a threat.

Back full circle: changes from above

Recent restructuring of ASAL by the GON includes name change to Semi-Arid Rural Development Programme (SARDEP), and its attention has shifted from the political process that was initiated during ASAL III towards a more mechanistic use of participation and participatory approaches in order to realise short-term programme goals. This experience highlights the risks embedded within these shifts and raises further debate on how lessons from ASAL phase III could be used to engage in a political process of transforming GOK bureaucracy rather than solely focusing on SARDEP's immediate goals.

The changes in the ASAL programme have been associated with two major exercises, both commissioned by the Royal Netherlands Embassy: a review carried out by ETC East Africa (1997) and a Value for Money Audit (VFMA) undertaken by the auditors PriceWaterhouse, also in 1997. The review noted problems of corruption, unmotivated civil servants, political interference, and non-enforcement of existing procedures. The VFMA also revealed misappropriation of funds and weak procedures and financial control systems, and recommended overhauling the institutional structure to improve efficiency and effectiveness. It also suggested that the programme should build on the strengths of the participatory approach used in ASAL phase III and promote community ownership of the projects. The review mission, however, favoured more controlled and centralised management units at the national and district levels. These would give the management units the power to control resources as an instrument of increasing output and efficiency.

Both sets of recommendations seem to have been based on the view of organisations as machines. They focused on getting systems, rules, and procedures right as the means for improving the programme's efficiency and performance. They assumed that, by putting in place managerial control and procedures, the programme would function better. SARDEP was contracted out to the Dutch organisation SNV, and then major decisions were made by the Embassy without the involvement of the GOK or the grassroots communities.

Since SNV took over SARDEP in July 1999, the process of institutionalising participation as a political process is slowly shifting to the 'machine mode' of generating projects. Although an essential feature of the programme's vision is the development of viable institutional vehicles that can stimulate, facilitate, and sustain the change process (SNV 1999), there seems to be more emphasis on building 'legitimate' grassroots organisations for attracting support from other donors after the planned phase-out of Dutch funding in 2002. Sustainability in this sense is perceived in terms of operation and maintenance of the physical projects – not the political empowerment of community organisations to engage in terms of the process of transforming the structures of power.

Although SARDEP's basis for community capacity building is the experience of ASAL III, it places more emphasis on the structure and the projects than on the political process of institutionalising participation that the programme went through before such structures evolved. Efforts to replicate and adapt the experience of ASAL III in other Dutch-funded programmes have been rushed, compromising community empowerment in favour of achieving short-term goals.

The Keiyo Marakwet programme seems to be learning and responding to the current direction as dictated from the central management unit. Lessons from the ASAL III strategy of institution-alising participation as a political process have been shelved. The current team seems to have begun a new chapter, erasing the recent history that had shaped the programme. They seem to avoid any confrontation with the government that could derail the implementation of projects within the short timeframe of the programme.

Conclusions

This article reveals the real difficulty of learning from participatory processes in a highly politicised context. The case study of ASAL Keiyo Marakwet exposes certain gaps and assumptions in the theory of learning organisations in the context of bilateral programmes that have multiple actors, competing interests, and conflicting goals. While most theorists imply that there is a kind of consensus or shared vision within organisations about which learning should occur, experience reveals that learning depends on where individuals are situated within a programme or organisation. This argument does not automatically lead to the conclusion that such organisations cannot learn. Rather, it raises the question as to whether what individuals choose to learn or not to learn contributes to a shared vision. In the ASAL case, for instance, some people were forced by circumstances to learn while others chose to resist learning because their own interests were at stake. In fact, they learned how best to defend their interests in changing circumstances.

While individuals and teams may learn from the process of institutionalising participation, in the programmes we have seen in the case study these lessons may not necessarily translate into action towards a common goal. While the learning led to changes in ASAL III, it was not easy to predict what was going to be learned by whom and the effects the learning would have in the programme.

The concept of the learning organisation also seems to presume that there is an interest in keeping institutional memory as a basis upon which learning can occur. But as we have seen, every phase of the ASAL programme marked the beginning of new history. The staff turnover in bilateral programmes is very high and there is a tendency of the new management to erase history and create a new knowledge base.

We have also seen that bilateral programmes learn and respond more to macro-level factors such as policy directives and diplomatic considerations than to what is happening locally. While the SARDEP programme could have used the case of Keiyo Marakwet to bring about changes in the government bureaucracy and to influence Dutch international development policy, it yielded to pressure and the GON decision to withdraw funding. Other donors were also pulling out of the country, with the IMF and the World Bank withholding their funding on the grounds of bad governance.

In order to make the concept of the learning organisation effective in bilateral programmes, we must view organisations as political systems and begin to recognise that it is these dynamics that determine what is to be learned, by whom, how, and for what purpose. This way we will be able to design participatory processes as critically reflective and open forums that allow more stakeholders to participate and develop the learning agenda as well as to manage the learning and its intended and unintended outcomes.

Acknowledgement

The author thanks Celestine Nyamu-Musembi for detailed comments.

Notes

1 The case study is based on my experience as lead facilitator and consultant. My tasks and interests were to advise and facilitate the process of institutionalising participation in the programme. For a more detailed account, see Musyoki (2000).
2 The ASAL programme and the subsequent Semi-Arid Rural Development Programme (SARDEP) were funded by the Dutch government, implemented through the Kenyan government line ministries, and managed through the DFRDS decentralisation policy and the government District Development Committees (DDCs).
3 For detailed steps see KEPNET (1996). KEPNET is the consultancy firm under which the author was contracted for this assignment.
4 Unlike the DDC, whose members were exclusively from the government, TAC membership was diverse in scope and representation.
5 Interviews with the former PAs, July 2000.

References and background documents

ASAL (1994) 'Plan of Operations 1994–1998 Arid and Semi Arid Lands Development Programme Elgeyo Marakwet District', unpublished report, Iten, Kenya: ASAL.

ASAL Development Programme Keiyo-Marakwet (1998) 'End of Phase Report', unpublished report, Iten, Kenya: ASAL.

ASAL Development Programme Keiyo-Marakwet (1999a) *Bringing Development Closer to the People: The Keiyo and Marakwet Experience*, Iten, Kenya: ASAL.

ASAL Development Programme Keiyo-Marakwet (1999b) 'Semestrial Report First Semester', unpublished report, Iten, Kenya: ASAL.

Connell, D. (1997) 'Participatory development: an approach sensitive to class and gender', *Development in Practice* 7(3): 248–259.

Cornwall, A., S. Musyoki and G. Pratt (2001) 'In Search of New Impetus: Practitioners' Reflections on PRA and Participation in Kenya', IDS Working Paper 131, Brighton: IDS.

ETC East Africa (1997) 'Review of the ASAL Programmes Keiyo Marakwet Districts Report: Part One and Two', unpublished report, Nairobi: ETC.

Kenya Environmental Promotions Network (KEPNET) (1996) 'Awareness Raising Campaigns Report: Keiyo and Marakwet Districts', unpublished report, Nairobi: KEPNET.

Mbagathi, S. (1991) 'Kitany Location Elgeyo Marakwet ASAL Development Project Planning Workshop', unpublished report, Nairobi: GS Consults.

Mezirow, J. (1990) 'How critical reflection triggers transformative learning in fostering critical reflection', in J. Mezirow (ed.) *Fostering Critical Reflection in Adulthood: A Guide to Transformative and Emancipatory Learning*, San Francisco and Oxford: Jossey-Bass.

Ministry of Land Reclamation Regional and Water Development (1993) 'Joint Kenyan Netherlands Review District Integrated Development Programme in ASAL Districts', unpublished report, Nairobi: MLRRWD.

Morgan, G. (1986) *Images of Organizations*, Beverly Hills: Sage.

Musyoki, S. (2000) 'Participation and organisational change: the political dynamics of institutionalising participation in bilateral programmes in Kenya', unpublished MA thesis, The Hague: Institute of Social Studies.

Pimbert, M., V. Bainbridge *et al.* (2000) *Transforming Bureaucracies, Institutionalising Participation and People Centred Processes in Natural Resource Management*, Nottingham: Russell.

Republic of Kenya (1984) *District Focus for Rural Development*, Nairobi: Government Printers.

Republic of Kenya (1992) *Development Policy for Arid and Semi Arid Lands*, Nairobi: Government Printers.

Republic of Kenya (1995) *District Focus for Rural Development*, Nairobi: Government Printers.

Republic of Kenya (1997) 'National Development Plan 1997–2001', unpublished report, Nairobi: Government Printers.

Republic of Kenya (1999) *National Poverty Eradication Plan* 1999–2015, Nairobi: Government Printers.

Royal Netherlands Embassy (1998) 'Position Paper: The Future of ASAL Programmes in Kenya', unpublished report, Nairobi: RNE.

SARDEP (1999a) 'SARDEP Keiyo & Marakwet Annual Work Plan 2000', unpublished report, Iten, Kenya: SARDEP.

SARDEP (1999b) 'SARDEP Keiyo and Marakwet Plan of Operations 2000–2001', unpublished report, Iten, Kenya: SARDEP.

SARDEP (2000) 'SARDEP Keiyo and Marakwet Districts Half-Yearly Report', unpublished report, Iten, Kenya: SARDEP.

Senge, P. (1990) *The Fifth Discipline: The Art and Practice of the Learning Organisation*, London: Random House.

SNV (1999) 'Semi-Arid Rural Development Programme Project Proposal', unpublished report, Nairobi: SNV.

SNV (2000) 'SARDEP Position Paper on Decentralised Planning and Local Governance', unpublished report, Nairobi: SNV.

World Bank (2000) *Participation Source Book*, available at www.worldbank.org.participation (accessed February 2002).

This article was first published in Development in Practice *(12/3&4:370–382) in 2002.*

A chocolate-coated case for alternative international business models

Pauline Tiffen

Introduction

Work to ensure minimum standards and conditions for salaried workers in industries like clothing, shoes, information, and technology is advancing. Many large companies are playing their part, prodded by NGOs and consumer lobbying. Codes of conduct and social auditing, while not 'solving' all problems, do provide a point of entry for continuous improvement and dialogue.

By contrast, since structural adjustment programmes (SAPs) were implemented in the 1980s, small farmers in developing countries have not received much support through state agricultural policies, unlike farmers in the USA, Japan, and Europe, even though 70 per cent of the world's poorest people live in rural areas. As 'self-employed', non-salaried, and not organised workers, most farmers are still beyond the reach of these new, voluntary corporate codes. Yet they are irrevocably if unaccountably connected to a few very large companies that broker raw materials, or brand and distribute the finished products, companies that operate far away from them. Chocolate companies, for instance, are still deemed to be not directly responsible for the impact of their commodity purchases on the farms of the developing world.

This article seeks to show the commercial and developmental importance to the long-term prospects of cash-crop farmers, and rural areas generally, of questioning and changing the status quo. The problems of this 'irrevocable but unaccountable connection' will be illustrated through the case of West African cocoa farmers, while the commercial chain developed over the past ten years from Ghanaian farmers to chocolate consumers in the USA and UK will be analysed as a living example of the opportunities and rationale for the large companies to amend their ways of working. In order to do this, the article aims to:

- review the context and set-up of a new cocoa farmers' organisation and trading company in Ghana upon partial liberalisation of the sector in 1993, and its growth and trajectory from 2,000 to 35,000 farmers by 2001;
- describe the simultaneous initiative to set up a new or alternative global chocolate company with the aim of breaking into a mature and concentrated market and addressing consumers with a new farmer-oriented voice;
- consider some of the lessons learned from this experience and the market challenges to poverty reduction among smallholders who rely on cash income from coffee and cocoa, as well as in countries where this income still constitutes the backbone of the economy;
- offer some concluding thoughts and ways for development practitioners and promoters of social justice to have wider impact in small- and medium-enterprise (SME) development or consumer education work.

The cocoa growers

The changing relationships between primary production, processing, and marketing

Much attention has been paid to the relationship between technological advances and the redundancy or devaluation of manual labour (e.g. Rifkind 1995). Agricultural labour has not escaped this. Yet for the most part, technological advances have impinged only indirectly on the lives of African cash-crop smallholders. For example, the boom in production of low-cost cocoa in Malaysia, which reached 10 per cent of world production in the 1980s, was largely due to the introduction of 'special', fast-growing cocoa trees. The timing was significant: cocoa prices reached new lows from 1989 to 1993 as Malaysia entered the free market.[1] Most producing countries, struggling to service their debts, promote traditional exports as a means to do so. When many countries did this all at once – sometimes called the 'composition effect' – they experienced falling prices, not the 'export-led growth' promised by the proponents of SAPs (Barratt Brown and Tiffen 1990). Increasing supply and stockholdings of beans relative to requirements for the raw materials at the processing or 'grinding' stages have continued to affect cocoa prices in the 1990s, driving these down – but so did market sentiment, as instability influences the differentials paid above or below the prevailing price.

The impact of structural adjustment and the response of the growers

Farmers in Ghana, like other West African smallholder-dominated systems, were operating without recognition of their strengths in the market. Farmers were protected from the market and prohibited access to information by monopolistic state marketing boards, but equally, and more surprisingly perhaps, the market was also detached from farmers and the mixed farming systems which favoured peasant farmers over plantation-style intensive systems and delivered good-quality cocoa beans.

Looking back from the vantage point of 2001, we see, by marked contrast, a new focus on the desirability of 'sustainable production' of key commodities like coffee and cocoa, the need for quality beans, and 'respect' for mixed farming systems (Giovanucci 2001).

In the 1980s farmers were on their own. Even development NGOs seldom opted to support small farmers: they were often not the 'poorest of the poor' or the 'lowest decile', or they required forms of assistance that bordered too closely on investment, and needed commercial know-how, which at that time was not recognised as a form of legitimate development assistance. And while many farmers wanted to 'act' because they held deep-seated grievances against the state monopolies and the officials who behaved in unaccountable and exploitative ways, practical responses were difficult to formulate – so strong was the push for free-market reforms. Further features of most SAPs were significant barriers to the development of pro-poor commercial institutions within the liberalised commodity sectors, for example:

- the speed of their implementation;
- the totality of the reforms;
- the lack of rural credit;
- the end of legitimate support for farmers;
- poor roads and infrastructure.

Above all, there was an almost total lack of preparation and process of awareness raising about the marketplace among farmers whose lives were being so altered. Lack of information about the workings of the market beyond the farm gate, and how these might affect farmers, produced significant apprehension and many mixed reactions.

Liberalisation programmes produced a social development paradox, here expressed by *The Economist* in relation to structural adjustment in Zambia:

In the past, a monopoly board bought up the crop, from all farmers, at a fixed nation-wide price. This, plus a subsidy, helped keep food prices low in the swelling cities. Peasant farmers did not do very well but at least they sold all they wanted at a guaranteed price. Now the market rules. Big farmers and those near the cities have prospered, as merchants compete to buy, paying better prices than before. But in remote parts, away from the roads, small farmers find that, as before, only one buyer turns up, but now a middleman, offering a pittance.
(*The Economist* 23 November 1996)

In Ghana, the state Cocoa Marketing Board was omnipresent and the cocoa farmers' will to organise had been sapped first by nationalisation and the deliberate destruction of local groups, and then by continued harassment of any farmers attempting to 'bargain' with the Cocoa Board officials (e.g. by owning independently calibrated scales). The Cocoa Board took the lion's share of the market price and operated a zealous and commercially valuable, but ultimately dehumanising, quality control system, earning premiums (to the nation) for better quality than cocoa from other origins. For example, extension workers would frequently arrive and spray the farm without first talking to the owners, the farmers. In the words of one farmer interviewed by the author in 1993, whose conversation and opinions were sought *before* a walk to see his farm: 'No one comes to visit us. We are not even farmers. We are just tree minders.'

Independent-minded Ghanaian cocoa farmers began to discuss the reforms and consider their options in 1992. Profit was part of the motive. The new pricing and extra 'buyer's margin' offered by the Cocoa Marketing Board appeared to give farmers an opportunity to increase their earnings and be 'sellers', not just growers, and to enter the market now as new licensed 'buyers'. But farmers had deeper motives. Setting up to do cocoa business appeared a way for them to:

- overcome their pent-up frustrations with cheating and delays in payments;
- find new options for credit;
- end the endless 'protocol' payments (i.e. bribes), often extracted with menace, even when entering the bank to deposit a cheque for sales of cocoa or to Cocoa Board officials;
- gain a better sense of identity and political status as farmers;
- prove themselves by setting up their own company, as this was now 'permitted'.

The 'switch' from being 'tree minders' to 'buyers and sellers' of their cocoa was a leap of thinking for farmers after many years of disempowerment, and this aspiration is reflected even in the name they eventually chose: Kuapa Kokoo, which in Twi means 'good cocoa farmer'. As momentum grew around the idea in early 1993, through discussions in many villages, and business-planning work supported by two NGOs (UK-based TWIN and the Dutch development organisation SNV), there was an interesting convergence of the generations in the villages. As farmers – men and women – prepared for registration of the first, and to date still the only, farmer-owned and cooperatively run company in Ghana, older farmers had much to contribute: they had 'been there before', running their own organisations, supplying the colonial traders up to independence. The organisational process consciously attempted to recapture the 'best elements' of the remembered past. The prior nationalisation experience was an impediment to mobilisation, however. In the words of one pioneer Kuapa Kokoo farmer in 1993: 'If we ever amount to anything, they'll nationalise us and steal everything ... again.'

Who supports farmers?

Small-scale farmers appear to have been invisible to the designers and implementers of SAPs in Ghana and elsewhere. Efforts to trigger a new private-sector presence in commodity marketing to replace parastatal bodies did not see farmers as potential 'entrepreneurial' players in the chain. No allowances – e.g. technical assistance or targeted financial facilities – were made for this. But farmers themselves, and a number of alternative traders and NGOs, were asking an awkward question: why should farmers not set up and run their own companies? Farmers are often prey to 'cut and thrust' and predatory merchants, urban-based companies or their agents who show only contempt for rural life and 'uneducated' rural people. Product quality, farmers' earnings, and 'confidence' are all threatened by this kind of result. The story of the formation and extraordinary results of the Kuapa Kokoo group is a tale of constructing a farmer-rooted response to liberalisation.

In retrospect, since Kuapa Kokoo has achieved such a significant level of recognition and attracted so much attention in print and in international development circles (ICCO, the World Bank, etc.), it is difficult to explain how rare and challenging the start-up was. Yet the need to build *a small farmers' response* to liberalisation looked so crucial that it gained much support and interest along the way. Debt and prejudice meant that farmers were viewed as high risks by formal institutions using traditional criteria. And sometimes for good reason: nobody could or would lend, prices were low, and small-scale farmers in Ghana were in a weak position to prepare for a period of significant transition to a new commercial régime. TWIN broke this schema by offering the new farmers' company operational and financial advice, a start-up loan, and a loan guarantee. This covered working capital and funds for the first 22 village groups to purchase their 'tools of the trade' (sacks, scales, tarpaulins, and wooden pallets). SNV offered village-level development and participatory training of committees, bookkeepers, and gender and development workers. Within three years the company had grown from 2000 to 8500 farmers; after four years the start-up loan was fully repaid; and after the second season, small bonuses from operating profits became feasible and added to the incentives for both pioneers and newcomers.

Kuapa Kokoo is now an organisation of some 35,000 farmers, around 30 per cent of whom are women, with village groups operating in more than 600 villages across most cocoa-growing areas of Ghana, and trading 7.2 per cent of Ghana's national production in 2000/01 (more than 30,000 tons). It has recorded a profit each year since 1994, which is distributed among its members, and more than US$850,000 has been paid out in bonuses derived from efficiency and from fair trade premiums to date. Kuapa Kokoo quickly outshone the competitors by focusing on 'small' but pivotal operational goals – for example, a reputation for not 'fixing' the scales (i.e. cheating), for cheques that do not bounce, and so on.

In parallel to its commercial activities, Kuapa Kokoo set up a separate Farmers' Trust, run by elected farmers, selected Ghanaian advisers (non-executive), and funded through grants, profits, and fair trade social premiums. To date the trust has sponsored medical programmes (with mobile clinics that have reached more than 100,000 individuals), scholarships, school and latrine construction, and fresh-water wells in members' villages. This means that while on average Kuapa Kokoo members make up around 7 to 10 per cent of farmers in a medium-sized village, the reach is beyond these farmers into the wider community. A recent DfID-funded evaluation notes that altruism is considered an indicator of wealth locally, and the ability to support such help to the sick was something 'new that could now be afforded'. Given the market context of low prices, and the relatively small amount of fair trade sales (5 per cent), the impacts of the institutional success of Kuapa Kokoo are apparently not fundamentally, or purely, material. This is in keeping with the original vision of rebuilding dignity for farmers and combating their sense of powerlessness and inability to influence their society.

Kuapa Kokoo is run for and by Ghanaians. Since 1996 no international staff or advisers have been part of the management teams or formal structures. Professional advisers operating on a voluntary or paid basis are drawn from both international and national networks, in fields such as cocoa agronomy or export marketing. Kuapa Kokoo has managed to attract and retain skilled Ghanaian professionals. There has also been significant advance in the representation and presence of women in all parts of the organisation – farmer-members, elected leaders, staff, and managers. But it is vital, if perhaps awkward to some, to acknowledge that colonial history and race did influence the farmers' perceptions and types of roles played by external (foreign) supporters at the outset. How?

- First, by example: the TWIN-SNV programme was at all stages a mixed-nationality team, from the UK and Ghana, with an innovative (adaptive, risk-taking) but cooperative approach and sensitive but firm leadership style. The early programme was run by two women – one Ghanaian, one British – and this clearly set a strong gender lead. The international partners and their support focused on the international dimension of the project – quality cocoa marketing.

- Second, by direct participation: farmers themselves have stated that, cheated so much by fellow Ghanaians up to 1993, the presence of impartial *obruni* or white people added to Kuapa Kokoo's credibility in their eyes. Some have reported to the author that they felt that made it more likely that the rules and policies – paying dues, delivering cocoa, membership terms, attendance at meetings, and so on – that they implemented would (have to) be adhered to by all. This was clearly not the norm, nor expected, despite its desirability. TWIN and SNV acknowledged this at the outset and did, periodically, 'take sides' to resolve conflicts. This was, arguably, atypical NGO behaviour, but the TWIN contribution was introduced in a 'commercial framework', not a developmental one: no grants, only loans.[2]

- Third, by simple 'appearances': the reappearance of foreigners in the cocoa villages added credence to the market reforms and made the planned trading activities of Kuapa Kokoo look more feasible.

Appreciation of the tradition of high-quality on-farm processing was directly expressed by visitors to farmers, who at last could take great pride in their skills and high cocoa quality. Kuapa Kokoo's slogan is: *pa pa pa!* ('the best of the best beans').

Sources of knowledge and learning behind the intervention

In the case of Ghana, there were a number of sources of learning and operational 'triggers' to the intervention. The comprehensiveness of the vision enabled the mobilisation, step by step, of sustained support for these cocoa farmers' efforts to organise and become dignified 'protagonists' in their own market. These included the empirical, the experiential, and the opportune:

a In 1989 we undertook research on SAPs and export-led growth for the Transnational Institute, funded by the Swiss government. It showed a paradigm with a dead-end for bulk commodities from sub-Saharan Africa. There was simply no market for all the extra supply or production being urged on these already skewed economies (see Barrett Brown and Tiffen 1990).

b Additionally, the research, which focused on the demand side, showed that in the view of the manufacturers interviewed, the cocoa market highly valued African, smallholder-produced cocoa ('the best basic cocoa worldwide'). But this market information came against a backdrop of its competitive destruction by heavy investment in Asian plantations!

c Twin Trading (the trading associate of TWIN) had had extensive previous experience helping coffee, sesame, and honey farmers in Latin America to become exporters, where liberalisation and the withdrawal of state subsidies preceded SAPs in Africa.

d Given the poor track record and performance of the marketing boards, it did not seem too difficult to help farmers set up a more rewarding alternative. This system, which became known at Kuapa Kokoo as 'pick up and pay', recognised a fundamental fact – that money costs more than cocoa when interest rates are above 45 per cent and loans are difficult to obtain. It was based on the modern manufacturing techniques of 'just-in-time' deliveries and the sometimes ignored fact that, while often illiterate, farmers are able to count.

e All the original operating systems were designed through a combined effort and aimed to reinforce village responsibility, not central or top-down control. The villagers held the key decision on who to employ as 'recorder' (or group bookkeeper), a position requiring the absolute trust of the many illiterate farmers in the community, and therefore not to be imposed from 'outside' as before. Where effective, these experiences created virtuous circles and were refreshingly different and inspiring for the farmers who first mobilised.

f Twin Trading founded a new coffee coalition in the UK (Cafédirect, launched in 1990) and by 1993, it had national distribution, a reasonable market share (3 per cent), and was approaching profitability. Cafédirect represented an outlet and opportunity for many smallholder cooperative suppliers to 'apprentice', or make their 'first-time' exports, without fear of penalty or losses.

g It seemed likely, as 'fair trade' markets were growing, that the same essential, sympathetic market space could be developed for cocoa farmers. Fair trade cocoa was just starting (1993/94) in The Netherlands and Switzerland.

h The coffee market-development work had taken place against a similar discouraging and adverse market background, including historically low prices (1992 saw the lowest coffee prices since the 1930s, until the drop to below 50 cents per pound in August 2001).

i International development agencies, including the UK's Overseas Development Agency (now DfID), were concerned about the impact of SAPs on farmers, and encouraged TWIN – which had no direct cocoa trading experience – with a small 'experimental' grant to build on its Latin American experiences and to explore the consequences of liberalisation and possible interventions in two sub-Saharan African countries.[3]

In Ghana, TWIN found a willing partner in SNV, with its focus on rural development, gender, and participatory techniques. SNV, an NGO modelled on VSO, also financed (locally and through TWIN) a number of personnel to take up posts *within* the emerging Kuapa Kokoo structures, until the organisation could afford to fill these posts itself. This facilitated the development of a highly professional, but accountable, management culture in the organisation, which still persists. Similarly, apprehension among local professionals about the wisdom of joining the new farmers' venture – suspicion was at least as high as among the banking community – was more easily mitigated with initial mediation between the farmers and these professionals by foreign third parties. The bad practices of the past by state cocoa 'clerks' – mainly stealing but also being disrespectful to farmers – were aggressively combated. Training opportunities were offered to farmers and staff. The staff of Kuapa Kokoo Ltd are also shareholders in the company and have rights to join the credit union (founded in 2000), just like the farmers themselves, and thus benefit directly from good financial performance.

Later partners have included Conservation International, a US NGO bringing support for integrated and organic farming pilots, and The Body Shop International, which has significantly contributed to Kuapa Kokoo's ability to finance development activities in its members' villages, through the sourcing of all its cocoa butter from the cooperative at fair trade prices.[4]

The chocolate market

Competition in the marketplace and the battle for shelf space

Mounting an effective export programme for small-volume shippers of cocoa beans is challenging for a number of reasons, which distinguish cocoa from other commodities. First, the number of buyers is limited. Second, there are diminishing numbers of processing facilities and relatively few end-users in the market. Two trends exemplify this: (a) increasing bulk, loose, and non-containerised shipping; and (b) the concentration of ownership (of factories and consumer brands). Just a few large companies – five in Europe overall, two in the USA, and three in the UK – account for 75 per cent of the chocolate market. They are: Cadbury-Schweppes, Nestlé, Mars, Hershey, and Philip Morris-Jacobs-Suchard. The UK market for chocolate is worth over US$5.6 billion a year. The market is dominated by brands. Difficult to evaluate and intangible, product 'branding' clearly does add value. The most valuable brands have had a long life: Mars Bars and Kit Kats, for example, have been around since the 1930s.

Entering this market looked more daunting than the coffee market had been (and the conventional wisdom at the time of the launch of Cafédirect was that 'it could not be done'). Marketing expenditure on these household names is considerable, part of a wider trend perhaps to imbue products with other meanings. (Some US$300 billion is spent on advertising globally to conserve these kinds of product differences – US$16 billion in the UK alone.) Brand values are the means by which market leaders seek to find a competitive edge among otherwise similar ranges of products. Some estimates indicate that more than 12 per cent of corporate wealth is now tied up in the intangibility of brands (Tiffen 2000). It is perhaps difficult to contemplate that the product empire nestling under a brand name such as 'Heinz' is worth more than US$13 billion, an amount equivalent to the total annual sales of chocolate in the USA.

Big chocolate brands do not feature cocoa origins as part of the message. And the big companies have resisted any direct association with or claims for the sustainability of their brands based on the fair trade model – namely, buying from cooperatives, through auditable or traceable chains, and ensuring terms that reward the farmers for their work. The market is mature – all sorts of people of all ages eat chocolate, know what it is, and can be subject to marketing. There are many failed chocolate launches and the old favourites often 'see off' newcomers through anti-competitive pricing, exclusive distribution deals, and so on.

When Kuapa Kokoo and its partners in the UK, Twin Trading, The Body Shop, and other fair trade supporters, joined together to make a link with chocolate lovers, setting up a new and unprecedented international joint venture called the Day Chocolate Company in 1998, the initiative received a resounding counter-attack from giant rivals. The product quality was impeccable and received no adverse comment, but Nestlé and Cadbury in particular took very firm public positions to counter the claims of fair trade companies like Day and insisted that their own activities were fair and in the long-term interests of producers. Nestlé went on record at the launch of Divine (Day's first chocolate bar) with spokeswoman Hilary Parsons stating:

> Yorkie and all our other chocolate products are produced fairly. Nestlé cocoa is fairly traded. It is in Nestlé's interest as well as the growers' to ensure a guaranteed supply of quality cocoa. To this end we work closely with cocoa farmers. In many countries we supply them with extensive agricultural and technical advice and training to help them improve their crops and hence their income ... ultimately the price paid to growers depended on the balance between supply and demand. But developing and sustaining world demand for cocoa products Nestlé supports the price paid to all growers and their opportunities for development.

(Hilary Parsons cited in *York Evening Press* 3 October 1998)

In the same article Terry's spokesperson Richard Johnson defended his company's record claiming: 'Significant resources had been invested to help cocoa producers improve the quality of their product and protect against disease.' However, when this article was shown to a representative of Kuapa Kokoo visiting the UK in March 1999, his response was unequivocal: 'When these companies say producers or growers they do not mean us, the farmers!'

And this contrasting understanding epitomises some of the fundamental institutional questions and prejudices that were encountered at the outset of the cocoa work and that still prevent interventions based upon seeing farmers as legitimate participants in international commercial trading projects in their own right. For example:

- Viewing farmers as worthy counterparts or partners is considered too costly and infeasible for large companies.

- Since liberalisation, no systematic attempt has been made to support organisational development in rural areas to enable farmers to take up the challenge of trading in place of parastatals.

- Direct work with farmers as trading counterparts by the mainstream chocolate industry would require significant changes in trading chains and practices, which large companies are simply not prepared to make.[5]

- The equation of free trade – the balance between supply and demand – with fair trade looks implausible, not least because there is an emerging and verified definition for the words 'fairly traded' in consumer marketing. Fair trade mark initiatives have high profiles and ranges of 'certified' products in most G-8 countries. Mainstream chocolate company practices do not come close to such standards and guidelines for trading partnerships that benefit smallholders.

- Cocoa and chocolate markets are increasingly so dominated by a few companies that they are clearly uncontested and uncontestable – new entrants have to be as large as the smallest transnational chocolate company to succeed.

The Day Chocolate Company was launched with part of the company's financing underpinned by a guarantee facility provided by DfID. DfID's intervention reflects the realisation that market-based poverty-reduction initiatives are of developmental interest and suited for experimental support. This guarantee was provided to overcome a market failure, i.e. the gap between the necessary rate of return from financing of high-risk ventures – launches into mature and 'hard-to-contest' markets – and efforts to improve producers' livelihoods.

Why did setting up a chocolate company become a part of the overall project? In fact the Day Chocolate Company is a response to a number of problems and the need for new international business models that connect smallholders and very poor farmers more appropriately into global markets. Many point to the fact that liberalisation has increased the share of the market price for cocoa that a farmer can get – from around 30 per cent in the early 1980s to more than 65 per cent in the late 1990s in the case of Ghana. But when this is a share of a shrinking pie, i.e. a highly depressed market price, and when it is placed in the context of the overall value generated by the cocoa component in processed chocolate products – less than one penny in an average 100g bar – it looks inequitable.

But this is more than 'unjust'. A dichotomy is emerging for a number of tropical commodities such as coffee, cotton, and cocoa, between the high retail prices charged on the one hand, and farm-gate prices on the other, which are now falling well below the cost of production for even the most efficient farmer. This is a severe market detachment or 'disconnect', one that enables coffee beans to retail at US$10 per pound versus the US$50 cents paid to the Guatemalan who grew and exported the beans (*San Francisco Chronicle* March 2001) or that allows for only nine pence of every pound sterling spent on food in the UK to return to farmers, compared with 50 to 60 pence 50 years ago (cited in the *Guardian* 3 March 2001). The Day Chocolate Company explicitly confronts this reality by making farmers the equity owners of the brands and upstream added-value chocolate and cocoa products that are on sale.

Farming as a business is about permanent investment and perpetual risk from price and climatic volatility. The low level of return on labour and investment by farmers is being extracted because of how the market is controlled, not just as a result of supply and demand. It cannot be justified given the enormous and widening gap between rich and poor. And this perception is increasingly widely held, not just in the chocolate chain, but in vocal parts of 'active' civil society, for example. In the protests at WTO meetings in and since Seattle, one of the most prominent slogans has been: 'Free trade is not fair trade!'

Supply and demand as a neutral mechanism of price setting has not been a part of the Ghana cocoa story in any farmer's living memory; value has not trickled down and bargaining power is dissipated, since most farmers are not organised. Social and economic formations like Kuapa Kokoo are the exception – conventional trading practices and marketing chains do not encourage the formation of 'good' farmers' organisations; rather, they prey on farmers' weaknesses, illiteracy, and distance from urban centres, and frequently prevent their development and evolution. The macro-level impacts of large mainstream market players – whether in the government or the private sector – cannot be assumed to have positive consequences for micro-groupings of farmers unless specifically designed to do so.

Struggle and new forms of social and economic relations

It would be unrealistic to expect no response from the 'choc giants' as initiatives like Day capture the public imagination. Chocolate is a deeply emotive product in any case! Day celebrated three years of trading in October 2001. It has certainly touched many pulses in civil society, offering a new, and arguably irresistible, alternative – tasty, gratifying, and involving practical individual action – to a prevailing and harmful mainstream business model.

Day has mobilised support at many levels, with outreach and practices relevant for both consumers and Kuapa Kokoo. Partnership and the harnessing of social capital is part of its essential strength, for example:

- Public messages and 'marketing' are part of Kuapa Kokoo's support for the company – farmers have visited cities all over the UK where local authorities and church, campaign, and fair trade groups come together and declare the place a 'Divine town'.

- Kuapa Kokoo has two representatives on the Board to oversee policy and strategy. They attend all meetings and at least one Board meeting a year is held in Ghana.

- Comic Relief organised a competition to design a new chocolate bar – a product for children by children. There were 16,000 entries and the winner visited Kuapa Kokoo (with her mother). Comic Relief is piloting teachers' packs (for pupils aged 4 to 14 years) and Internet links between teachers in the UK and schools in Kuapa Kokoo villages within the framework of the UK national curriculum.[6]

- Christian Aid and other trade campaigners have mobilised their effective debt campaign networks to lobby other chocolate companies and buy the product in supermarkets.

- Trade unions, MPs, student unions, the Women's Institute – all forms of civil society – have 'adopted' Day's chocolate and its partnership message as a symbol of their commitment to social or economic justice and fair trade.

- National distribution – in more than 10,000 outlets – was achieved within less than one year, including outlets not previously engaged in fair trade or 'sustainable' product promotion, e.g. garage forecourts and the large cash and carry (wholesalers) which reach the smallest 'corner shops'.

- A process of transition to the USA has begun, with fair trade coming onto the consumer agenda and a coalition of alternative and sustainable business supporters, human rights activists, and trade campaigners coming together around this unusual political and commercial proposition.

The company has also been validated in other ways, receiving a number of awards for its innovation and example. When Kuapa Kokoo won a prestigious Government Millennium award for innovation, the 'difference' was summarised as follows:

> There is nothing earth shattering about forward-thinking companies recognising the need to innovate. The real thorny issue surrounds the way companies put good intentions into practice. Theory proliferates yet success is far more difficult to achieve ... [The] Day Chocolate [Co.] was awarded the Millennium Product accolade not so much for their chocolate – which has the same taste qualities of many of Britain's most popular chocolates – but because of their innovative approach in giving cocoa farmers at the beginning of the production chain a significant stake in the operation.
> (Duncan 1999)

Lessons and challenges

The lessons of the cocoa-to-chocolate chain experience need to be articulated because the problems that were overcome are widespread and the scope for replication and the specific challenges they represent need to be addressed. They can be divided into three areas.

Producer organisations: purpose and context

Ghana faced a particular experience of atomisation: the state dominated and did not promote (or enforce) cooperative organisations at village level, in contrast with many other African experiences, which led to a quick recognition of the importance of each individual (cocoa farmer) as a player within voluntary groupings. The groupings that emerged after liberalisation were therefore quite mixed and spontaneously formed – big farmers worked alongside small and tenant farmers. As such, they are even now very diverse in nature and style, while still operating within a common framework. This made a focus on effective and profitable business the main entry point. Social-oriented activities, gender opportunity, and 'developmental' discourse in Ghana took place within the fabric of business development and farmer participation, not as ends in themselves. Efforts to 'use' the cocoa business structure for purely development projects – e.g. by well-meaning NGOs – have seldom worked and are frequently rejected by farmers.

In countries where cooperatives were supported and artificially sustained, often gaining a poor reputation in the process, the dilemmas may differ – for example, whether to reform or start again – but the internal dynamics and development processes and challenges are similar to those faced in Ghana. There are significant prejudices about cooperatives at all levels. Yet new NGO-sponsored producer organisations often do not last much beyond the usually finite duration of direct external technical assistance. There is little systematic or strategic work on the challenge of developing viable producer organisations for business activities. Credit in rural areas for cash-crop production, has more or less dried up, microfinance has not reached many rural areas, and the high and sometimes exploitative nature of informal finance systems erode farmers' earnings further. In addition, there are few state institutions or NGOs with the capacity to underpin rural development programmes with market analysis, finance, investment decision-making skills, and an understanding of commodity market fundamentals.

The lack of a farmer-to-market connection

An estimated 11 million smallholders grow cocoa in West Africa.[7] Large cocoa plantations, for example, have not flourished in much of West Africa, and private, smallholder production has remained the norm and accounted for most of the large increase in production and export from the Ivory Coast in the 1990s. Small in this context means less than 10 hectares. But few cocoa farmers in Ivory Coast, Ghana, and elsewhere are aware of the destination of their beans beyond the village. Few have any concept of chocolate, have not tasted or seen it, and have no awareness of consumers or their concerns. They do not use cocoa beans locally at all. Conversely, despite long commercial track records in the producing countries, trading houses have little or no connection or contact with farmers, working mainly through subsidiaries and middlemen or agents. Commercial intermediation is usually local, by indigenous companies or individuals, as indeed it was during the colonial era. So the margins and terms of trade between all the parties in a cocoa-to-chocolate chain are not subject, at first sight, to the chocolate manufacturers' direct control, and it is the local intermediaries who have the access and 'relationship' with farmers. State-sponsored or private, it is hardly ever a developmental or mutually beneficial relationship. It is not yet one prepared or equipped to mediate fairly between consumer interests and farmers' needs.

The role of consumers

Consumers also play a role in the 'disconnect'. While most consumers know that cocoa is 'tropical', until recently few could trace the cocoa content of their favourite chocolate product back to its origins: Côte d'Ivoire, Ghana, Nigeria, Sierra Leone, etc.[8] And the connotations are not positive. Chocolate contrasts starkly and unfortunately with wines, coffees, teas, and cotton, as well as with the added-value and cachet derived from their place of origin. Efforts to change this rely on long-term investment in consumer awareness and responsible and articulate marketing – far from existing chocolate style. But, with the support of loyal and aware consumers, there can be a move away from an emphasis on purely voluntary initiatives, towards an obligation on the part of all chocolate companies to demonstrate purchasing systems that deliver fairer and more sustainable trade for all smallholder cocoa farmers.

Conclusions

Globalisation has led to stronger transnational companies and global brands but not necessarily to more integration of commodity marketing chains. This makes it more difficult for newcomers into these markets to succeed. Current commodity chains and prevailing practices are entrenched. The existing trading model for cash crops is harmful to the interests of smallholders, and it does not respect their needs and right to economic return for their labour or investment. Farmers are disconnected from the consumers, and they fall outside the reach of the social protection that is offered under ethical or other supply-chain management schemes. Supply-chain management work does not address structural inequity or power relations *per se*. The weaker players are losing the means to negotiate a return on their investment.

Mainstream commodity and food-branding companies, the most significant purchasers of cocoa, coffee, and cotton from smallholders, are not openly addressing this problem. All have eschewed the fair trade, direct-to-farmer model, and they have even openly criticised it. Codes of conduct do not reach farmers or influence the terms of trade between parties in the supply chain. Therefore they do not address the unequal bargaining relationship between the farmers and these global giants.

The problem needs to be acknowledged because to focus only on the 'local' will make interventions less effective. SME and other organisational support must be adapted and positioned firmly within the context of the global marketing chains of which low-income smallholders are now part.

Globalisation, strong civil society groupings, and information technology also have other effects. They make networking and international partnerships less abstract and more feasible. The Ghanaian cocoa farmers and Day Chocolate Company cooperation show that linkages can be built within a development framework: trading is the focus and the means, the call to action but not the end. Successful trading means successful human development for farmers and their neighbours as well as for 'empowered' consumers. This also contests the market norm. There are significant barriers to changing the commodity markets but there is a need to do so because of the vast numbers of farmers involved – and there are many opportunities.

The Day Chocolate Company model is more than material – prices, tons, units sold. It is psychological and also remedial – helping to overcome the worst aspects of the past, and aiming to overcome the 'disconnect' in conventional business chains. Counter-arguments of 'scale' and 'unfeasibility' seem weak. Increasingly, consumers are aware that if large companies do not know for certain where their primary products or raw materials are sourced, they are not in a position to satisfy consumer concerns about a range of issues as diverse as genetic modification (of lecithin in chocolate), social welfare, child and forced labour, sustainable farming practices, and good quality raw materials.

Examples like Day and Kuapa Kokoo can therefore have an impact beyond their sales figures, numbers of households, or sacks of cocoa. Now development organisations are being approached by large companies to assist with reviewing and assessing their 'social impact'. Rural areas in particular need significant but appropriate attention. Clearly, SME skills and capacity-building projects are needed to support farmers in their efforts to organise and 'relate' to their clients' and the end-consumers' concerns (for quality, for pesticide-free production, and so on). Complex and costly structures for top-down auditing and scrutiny do not necessarily assist farmers to improve their status. Other writers on corporate social responsibility have commented on the unintentional adverse impacts of large companies adopting codes of conduct, for example, when this has resulted in their 'removing' the smaller companies and commercial entities from the supplier list because they could not afford to 'comply' quickly.

Traditional focus on SME and purely localised support will not empower farmers but rather consolidate existing trading chains and their characteristics if they lack components aimed to challenge the status quo and create alternatives such as:

- empowerment and awareness raising about the market;
- synchronised programmes (consumers and farmers are part of an integrated chain, even though operating at a distance, separated only by middlemen);
- interventions to create more bargaining power and access to fairly priced finance for the smaller, weaker player at the point of purchase or sale into the international market;
- financial and commercial realism, including attention to cost and scale;
- recognition of the competitive and concentrated nature of the global markets in which even the smallest farmers and growers of commodities now operate.

Development interventions need to address the whole value chain – relative power, worth, and weaknesses – from the perspective of allocation of value. This requires a clear strategic goal or vision, 'staying power', and multi-layered and international partnerships. The Kuapa–Day Chocolate experience, while still at its early stages, points to some ways in which leverage can be gained at different stages, from village to final customer, and how some of the broader goals of empowerment and 'voice', so often sought in development projects and so needed by millions of atomised cash-crop farmers, can be incorporated.

Notes

1 The expansion of cocoa production was similar in magnitude and impact to the recent Vietnamese coffee producers' leap to second place in world production of coffee. There was no comparable public attention to the social and economic consequences for cocoa farmers then as there is now for coffee growers.

2 All outstanding loans for the start-up were repaid to TWIN within four years of the launch. Interest was charged at a rate of 12 per cent.

3 The grant in 1993 was for three years, and totalled US$50,000. Other smaller donors included the Max Havelaar Foundation (US$15,000) and Comic Relief (US$60,000 in year 2). An 'outcome' was the formation of Kuapa Kokoo in Ghana and the establishment of export departments at a number of coffee farmer cooperative unions in Tanzania – all of which survive to this day. A more recent grant from DfID has assisted in the documentation of these experiences in a number of essays and case studies (see Tiffen and Murray 2000).

4 The fair trade minimum or floor price is currently US$1600 per ton with an additional US$150 per ton as a social premium, totalling US$1750. This compares with prevailing market prices averaging less than US$1000 in recent years. Fair trade in practice also means democratic and accountable organisations, pre-finance facilities, and direct and long-term relationships.

5 Recent allegations of abusive child labour on cocoa plantations in West Africa are stimulating debate on the roles and opportunities of private companies, governments, and NGOs to improve conditions, and a joint industry and NGO taskforce is being formed to look at the practices and possibilities of eradicating such exploitation from the chocolate chain. Direct farmer trading on an alternative or fair trade model is to date not viewed as a feasible option by the chocolate trade.

6 See www.divinechocolate.com or www.dubble.co.uk (the joint product with Comic Relief and education-teacher link-up site).

7 George Foulkes, MP, speech to the International Cocoa Organisation, London, 1999.

8 See numerous articles since late 2000 on forced labour and slavery in cocoa plantations, e.g. 'Malians work to free child laborers' (*Miami Herald* 25 June 2001); 'Help End Child Slave Labour' at www.oneworld.org/ni/issue304/contents.html; in addition to BBC documentaries and many campaign websites promoting action over revelations in the cocoa sector (e.g. www.act.actforchange.com/).

References and further reading

Barratt Brown, Michael and Pauline Tiffen (1990) *Short Changed: Africa and World Trade*, London: Pluto Press.

Clairmonte, Frederick and John Cavanagh (1988) *Merchants of Drink: Transnational Control of World Beverages*, Penang: Third World Network.

Duncan, Shona (1999) 'Thinking outside the box', in *Millennium Products*, London: Confederation of British Industry News-Design Council Report.

Eagles, Caroline (2001) 'Analysis: with coffee producers unable to solve coffee crisis has the time come for renewed producer-consumer market coordination?', available at www.reports@commodityexpert.com (accessed 13 August 2001).

Giovanucci, Daniele (May 2001) 'Sustainable Coffee Survey of the North American Speciality Coffee Industry', a survey conducted for the Summit Foundation, the Nature Conservancy, North American Commission for Environmental Cooperation, Specialty Coffee Association of America, and the World Bank, available in English and Spanish at www.scaa.org.

Gladwell, Malcolm (2001) 'Java man: how caffeine created the modern world', *The New Yorker* 30 July 2001.

Krugman, Paul (1997) 'In praise of cheap labor: bad jobs at bad wages are better than no jobs at all', *The Dismal Science* 20 March 1997.

Oxfam GB (2001) 'Developing a Socially Responsible Portfolio', unpublished paper, Oxford: Oxfam GB.

Peel, Quentin (2001) 'NGOs find success brings problems', *Financial Times* 12 July 2001.

Price, Caroline (2001) 'It's official: organic box schemes are more than twice as wealth-creating as supermarkets', *Radical Economics* July-August.

Rabo International Advisory Services (RIAS) (2000) 'Cooperatives and Cooperative Banks: Their Contribution to Economic and Rural Development', Utrecht: Rabobank International.

Rifkin, Jeremy (1995) *The End of Work: The Decline of the Global Labor Force and The Dawn of the Post-market era*, New York, NY: Putnam.

Rosselson, Ruth and Joe Ryan (2001) 'Superficial supermarket in going green? Supermarkets' ethical claims under the spotlight', *Ethical Consumer Magazine* 71 (June–July).

Stone, Adrian (2001) 'DfID's Support for Fair Trade', unpublished paper, London: DfID.

Tiffen, Pauline (2000) 'Small change, big difference', *New Internationalist* (April).

Tiffen, Pauline and Robin Murray (eds.) (2000) *Understanding and Expanding Fair Trade*, London: TWIN.

World Bank (2001) 'Delivering Commodity Price Insurance: Lessons Learned from Four Case Studies', Commodity Risk Management Group of Rural Development Department, unpublished report, Washington, DC: World Bank.

Zadek, Simon, Sanjiv Lingayah and Maya Forstater (1998) 'Communicating Ethical Trade: Understanding How Social Labels Work', unpublished report for the European Commission, London: New Economics Foundation.

This article was first published in Development in Practice *(12/3&4:383–397) in 2002.*

Learning leaders:
the key to learning organisations

John Hailey and Rick James

Introduction

Learning and knowledge management are crucial capacities for any NGO expecting to survive and thrive in the uncertain global development environment of the new millennium. Creating the learning organisation is increasingly seen as being synonymous with capacity building, organisational development, and managing change. This recent focus on learning immediately raises a number of questions for NGOs:

- Why is learning seen as so important for NGOs?

- Are NGOs natural learners?

- How do successful NGOs actually learn? What do they do differently from others?

- What drives this quest for learning? What role do key individuals play in this process?

This article attempts to answer these questions by analysing the role of learning and knowledge creation in NGOs, how they are promoted, and what role the leadership plays in this process. It draws heavily on the findings of a major study of nine 'successful' South Asian NGOs including BRAC and PROSHIKA in Bangladesh, BAIF and Sadguru in India, and AKRSP and IUCN in Pakistan (Smillie and Hailey 2001).[1] The research highlighted the importance of organisational learning in local development NGOs, and the role of leaders in promoting a learning culture in such organisations. One of the major conclusions was that the success of these NGOs was in part attributable to their willingness to embrace new learning and invest in developing their capacity as 'learning NGOs'.

The article highlights the many different ways in which these organisations consciously learn, and goes on to explore what is driving this quest for learning. The research suggests that effective learning is a hard-won goal, which depends as much on formal training, effective information systems, and human resource management strategies as on informal, participatory processes. These findings also question the myth that learning is a distinctive process that is inherent in the values and activities of NGOs. In reality, NGOs are no different from other types of organisation having to work hard at promoting learning.

We shall see that an organisation's ability to learn is dependent on its organisational culture[2] and in particular the development of an internal culture of learning. The case studies from South Asia reveal that the creation of this 'learning culture' derives primarily from the attitude of the leadership towards learning.[3] At the heart of a learning organisation is a 'learning leader'.

What is so important about learning for NGOs?

The importance of learning as a key organisational capacity has become increasingly apparent in the changing and volatile economic and political environment of the 1990s. Learning is considered to be vital if organisations are to be able continuously to adapt to an uncertain future. Reg Revans (1993) pointed out that an organisation's very survival is dependent on its capacity to learn. He argued that in a turbulent environment, an organisation's rate of learning has to be equal to, or greater than, the rate of change in its external environment if it is to remain relevant and effective. If NGOs fail to learn at such a pace, then they will be 'destined for insignificance' (Fowler 1997:64).

The difficult reality for most NGOs is that the economic, social, and political environment in which they operate is increasingly complex and volatile. NGOs have seen their roles and perceived importance shift radically in the last few years. New political thinking on the roles of civil society and the State, inclusive national planning processes, and democratisation has challenged NGOs to take on very different roles and relationships to traditional service provision. Conflict and terrorism can suddenly and very powerfully transform the context in which NGOs operate. On the social side, the devastating 'attrition rate' from HIV/AIDS in many parts of the world, particularly sub-Saharan Africa, places yet further demands on NGOs. In the face of such pervasive change, it is a priority for any NGO to invest in building its capacity to manage knowledge, promote learning, and become a 'learning organisation' (Edwards 1997; Lewis 2001).

The 1990s have been called the decade of the learning organisation and this present decade is likely to reinforce this trend. There is a close link between learning and organisational change. Peter Senge (1990), one of the early advocates of organisational learning, defined a learning organisation as one that is 'continuously expanding its capacity to create its future'; similarly, Pedler *et al.* (1991:2) defined it as 'an organisation which facilitates the learning of all its members and continuously transforms itself'. The learning organisation can therefore be seen as being synonymous with any ongoing process of individual learning, capacity building, and organisation development. Alan Fowler identifies the challenge for NGOs as how best they can 'bring together facts and personal learning as primary information sources, then collectively make sense of what they mean and then translate the results into a greater capacity to be agile' (Fowler 2000:138). In other words, how can they transform information into organisational change? In both the private and the non-profit sector, the term 'learning organisation' has arguably become a metaphor for managing change.

The effective use of learning and knowledge has been the hallmark of many successful organisations in the 1990s (Dixon 2000). Learning is about linking knowledge with effective and sustainable action. Knowledge is therefore a key resource that all leading organisations, in both the private and the non-profit sectors, must manage and exploit if they are to maintain their position (Handy 1994; Kluge *et al.* 2001; Senge 1990). Similarly, there is more appreciation of the role of knowledge management and learning in the development process (World Bank 1998). Development is essentially a knowledge-based process, and as a result learning and knowledge management are now recognised as key elements in development work. One of the challenges for development NGOs is how they share and disseminate knowledge and learning. As Ian Smillie commented, 'knowing what works and why is essential to the success of NGOs, yet knowing what does not work is equally important. Knowledge involves awareness, memory and familiarity that develops with experience and learning' (Smillie 1995:23). NGOs increasingly appreciate that knowledge, and the dissemination of knowledge and learning, are key to their effectiveness and, as David Korten concluded, their success depends on the suitability of their systems, their ability to embrace error, and their willingness to learn from the local communities with whom they work (Korten 1980).

Are NGOs naturally good learners?

Most NGOs are committed to the learning of their beneficiaries. It is often enshrined or implicit in their mission statements. There is a strong emphasis within most NGO programmes on training and capacity building of their 'clients', rather than just provision of infrastructure. And yet this emphasis on learning is often not emphasised internally. There is sometimes a dissonance between what NGOs promote with their beneficiaries and what they apply to themselves. There are many NGOs who claim to be 'learning organisations', but our understanding of how they promote shared learning and engage their staff is very unclear. Research indicates that many smaller NGOs fail to learn from experience or mistakes and commonly fail to adapt the way they work (Smillie 1995). Fowler even goes as far as to suggest that a universal weakness of development NGOs is actually a 'limited capacity to learn, adapt, and continuously improve the quality of what they do' (Fowler 1997:64). But why should this be so?

The capacity for NGOs to promote learning is limited by a number of external barriers such as the competition for funds and the consequent pressure to show low rates of administrative overheads. There are also structural barriers such as departmental rivalries and the short-termist project culture that militate against shared learning. There is deep-rooted resistance to investing scarce resources in such an intangible concept as learning, in addition to the difficulty of identifying attributable and tangible impact indicators. Other barriers include the unwillingness of individuals to engage in new ideas, new technologies, new ways of working, and the hassle of dealing with the quantity of documentation generated. There is also a reluctance to admit to, or analyse, mistakes because of the fear that this will attract criticism and provoke a backlash from donors and government. The task- or action-oriented culture of many NGOs also does little to encourage the self-assessment or critical reflection that is essential if learning is to take place (Britton 1998; Smillie and Hailey 2001).

These barriers mean that NGOs have to work hard at learning. It does not come naturally or easily. It does not simply arise from their developmental orientation. They have no particular monopoly on being learning organisations. Such learning is not some innate process that is inherent in the culture of development NGOs. Instead, it is commonly the result of conscious investment in a variety of formal and informal learning processes. Those NGOs that exhibit the characteristics of learning organisations have worked hard and spent considerable time and money in overcoming the inherent barriers to learning and developing new learning processes and systems. It is to some of these 'success stories' to which we should turn and from which we should ourselves try to learn.

How do 'successful' NGOs learn?

The recent research into what made the largest NGOs in Bangladesh, India, and Pakistan successful concluded that their success depends, in part, on their willingness to embrace new learning and invest in developing their capacity as 'learning NGOs'. This research was concerned with the management practices of NGOs in South Asia, and in particular how such organisations have managed change and handled growth. It was based on detailed case studies of nine NGOs – two in Bangladesh (BRAC and PROSHIKA), three in India (the AKRSPI, BAIF, and Sadguru), and four in Pakistan (AKRSPP, IUCN, SRSC, and Sungi). These organisations represent a cross-section of medium to large NGOs that have expanded their activities and undergone significant change in recent years. They all work with local community organisations, are funded by a range of international donors, and are involved in a variety of activities including primary healthcare, education, microcredit, agro-development, irrigation, and environmental programmes. The case studies were based on extensive research undertaken by local researchers between 1998 and 2000, which drew on both archival materials and interviews with a wide range of staff, beneficiaries, and other key stakeholders (Smillie and Hailey 2001).

In particular, the study analysed how these organisations managed their external relations, handled strategic planning processes, developed their organisational culture, and how they were shaped by the vision, commitment, and character of their 'founder leader'. These individuals could be characterised as 'development leaders', whose leadership style was value driven, knowledge based, and responsive. The study also analysed the process by which such development NGOs promoted learning among their staff, and concluded that they used a range of informal processes to generate new learning, reflect on past experience, and experiment with new approaches. They also invested heavily in more formal learning processes such as training and research. We shall now outline the different methods these successful NGOs employed in order to learn.

Learning from the poor

The importance of the role of personal engagement, listening, and dialogue that lie at the heart of the way many NGOs learn is exemplified by Sadguru (India). When Sadguru started working with tribal communities in Eastern Gujarat in 1974, its founders, Harnath and Sharmistha Jagawat, spent the first two years of the organisation's existence walking up to 30km a day in order to meet with local people. They listened to their concerns and discussed how best to meet their needs. In this way they learnt of the immediate needs of local people, and developed friendships, built trust, and gained the credibility on which their future work could be based.

Virtually all the NGOs in the Hailey and Smillie study relied on similar village-based processes of dialogue to spearhead internal learning about the authentic needs of the communities. These NGOs see the poor as the main source of organisational learning. With AKRSP in Pakistan, most early staff training took place through village dialogues between a team of AKRSP staff and local people. The informal 'training sessions' were held outdoors and were open to everyone, not just village elders and other notables. As these discussions were recorded and analysed, they became the basis of future interventions. Even today, 'staff look back on the village dialogues as the most effective training they received' (Smillie and Hailey 2001:75).

Learning from practice

The primary means of learning for most successful NGOs is the conscious reflection and analysis of their own implementation experiences (particularly where things have gone wrong) in order to learn and improve. Barry Underwood, then Chief Executive of AKRSP (India), identified the 'importance of embracing one's mistakes and learning from them, creating in the process a culture which accepts criticism'. A number of organisations have institutionalised meetings to reflect and learn from experience. PROSHIKA, for example, holds quarterly meetings where 200 staff and group representatives get together to review performance and discuss appropriate changes. Such systems need to be developed if learning from practice is to take place.

The founder and Chief Executive of BRAC, Dr Fazle Hasen Abed, similarly sees mistakes as an inherent part of an iterative learning process, and he recognises that BRAC had many failures from which it was able to learn. He relates:

... you go to a woman's house to find that the loan you have given her is taken away by her husband, or a child comes to school and suddenly has to drop out because the parents have moved away, and the child doesn't learn anymore. These are all failures ... little failures are, of course, inherent in any successful programme. You must accept that for they are part of the learning process.

(Smillie and Hailey 2001:76)

Similarly, in an effort to expand the impact and scope of its health programmes, BRAC staff were 'mobilised with motorbikes'. They became so focused on meeting quantitative project objectives that they had little time to sit and talk with local people. It soon became apparent that 'when we walked or went by bicycle, we did much better'. So BRAC reintroduced slower, more time-consuming ways of working with local communities. The challenge for many NGOs is whether such a decline in performance would actually 'become apparent' as it did with BRAC.

Learning through staff participation

The NGOs in the study responded to the challenge of sharing learning internally so that individual learning became organisational learning. For some, like PROSHIKA, institutional learning is a function of participation. As Faruque Ahmed, the President of PROSHIKA, points out, 'If I as the head of the organisation had to remember everything, then probably there would not be much remembered. But if you use participation in the decision-making process then there is much more chance of institutional memory' (Smillie and Hailey 2001:77).

Most of the NGOs in the study used a mix of regular meetings, retreats, workshops, and seminars to promote shared learning and to disseminate new ideas. Sadguru, for example, holds regular meetings on the last Saturday of the month, allowing staff to share experiences and to give feedback from other meetings or courses they have attended. These meetings are quite structured and characterised by a high degree of mutual respect. This in turn allows for more open dialogue and constructive discussion. BAIF has gone further in its efforts to ensure that staff learn from each other, and systematically moves staff around the organisation or assigns them to new projects as part of its strategy to encourage cross-functional learning. It transfers staff from research posts to field positions and from specialist to management positions in an attempt to disseminate and institutionalise learning.

Learning from external actors

Many of the NGOs in the study have consciously learned from each other's experiences as well as their own. They have been keen to visit specific programmes and have arranged a series of attachments for their staff. All the largest South Asian NGOs have visited BRAC and PROSHIKA and in turn BRAC and PROSHIKA invest in learning from others. According to Dr Abed, BRAC is an 'unashamed replicator' of other people's good work, and he attributes much of its remarkable success to its ability to learn from other agencies.

One of the strengths of many of the NGOs in this study is the way they have actively used external specialists and outside consultants. Despite their cost, there is a recognition that such external actors play a crucial role as a source of new learning because of their ability to challenge the status quo. For example, the major organisational and operational changes at IUCN (Pakistan) in the last five years have been the product of two major external management reviews conducted by consultants. Similarly, the Director of Sadguru, Harnath Jagawat, attributes part of its success as a development agency to 'continuous appraisals by external consultants and academics'.

Learning from formal training

The successful South Asian NGOs have invested in a number of formal processes to capture and disseminate learning. They have spent considerable sums on training, research, and new information-management systems even in the early years of their existence, and they continue to be heavily engaged in training and staff development. This investment in formal training complements informal processes for learning from the poor. As AKRSP, for example, grew and as training needs became more sophisticated and specialised, the organisation gradually became more reliant on formal courses and structured training processes.

Many NGOs have invested in purpose-built training centres and, in the case of BRAC and PROSHIKA, increased their training capacity enough to be able to train nearly a million people a year. BRAC has established 12 Training and Resource Centres that employ 150 trainers and offer management, human resource development, and skills-based training courses, primarily for BRAC employees. Considering its size (over 58,000 full- and part-time staff) BRAC invests a remarkable 7 per cent of its overall salary budget on staff development and has now established its own university in Dhaka.

Learning through research

There is a growing understanding of the benefits that can be gained from sponsoring relevant and applied research, and both BRAC and PROSHIKA in Bangladesh, and AKRSP and BAIF in India have established specialist research departments. According to BAIF, 'development without research is outdated, and research without development is irrelevant' (Smillie and Hailey 2001:82). Since its inception, BAIF has recognised the importance of research, and was one of the first Ghandian organisations to recruit scientists and other research professionals. Its founder, Dr Manibhai Desai, created a climate in which there was an understanding that the organisation needed to invest heavily in an ongoing programme of research. This is reflected not just in the quality of its research, but also in the way BAIF staff are actively encouraged to publish their research findings in academic journals and to present papers at national conferences. The 1996/97 Annual Report provides detailed abstracts of 20 publications produced during that year alone. Even BRAC, which is more recognised for its emphasis on learning by doing, invests heavily in research: by 1997, BRAC employed 52 full-time researchers, ten of whom had PhDs.

Learning from monitoring and evaluation

Closely linked with research work are the formal management processes and systems developed by NGOs to monitor and evaluate their work and learn from their performance. Many of the NGOs in the study have developed sophisticated internal management information and monitoring systems, which are increasingly computerised. For example, PROSHIKA uses an Impact Monitoring and Evaluation Cell (IMEC) to monitor its work. Others, like BAIF, have instituted an integrated review system across the organisation at both district and state levels, incorporating input from its own researchers and outside specialists.

The extent to which donor-led evaluation processes contributed to learning was mixed, with the incentive to cover up mistakes in order to maintain funding undermining the learning process. The older and more established NGOs appeared sufficiently confident to treat the process more positively, and so were better able to take advantage of the outside perspectives of donors and their consultants. But, in general, there appears to be a growing understanding that such evaluation reviews are as much an opportunity to capture and synthesise new learning as they are a mechanism to assess whether goals have been attained or funds have been well spent.

What drives this desire for learning?

We have seen that successful NGOs are intellectually fit enough to handle change, and agile enough to drive change forward. This is a direct result of their preoccupation with learning. Although they all learn in different ways, with some emphasising informal methods and others more formal approaches, what is common to all is their fundamental commitment to learning. Learning is one of their core values and pervades their organisational culture. As a result, their staff demonstrate a willingness to reflect, a curiosity, a capacity to innovate and experiment, as well as to embrace new thinking. Thus, learning is not just a resource or asset to be invested in, it is also a crucial part of the values and culture of the organisation. But where does this culture of learning come from?

Learning leaders

The culture of learning in these NGOs, apparent even in their early years, can be directly attributed to the personal views of their leader. Learning organisations have learning leaders. Senge (1990) points out that leadership is central to organisational learning and that learning organisations have leaders who are facilitators and educators. Organisations, particularly in their founder phase[4] (though not exclusively), tend to be very much moulded in the image of the leaders. Not only do founders tend to choose the organisation's mission and vision, but they also choose the staff. According to Schein (1992), founder leaders tend to have a high level of self-confidence and determination, and strong assumptions about the world, organisations, and human nature (and learning!). They are usually quite comfortable in imposing (albeit unconsciously) these views on the rest of the organisation. Their strong theories get tested early. If the leader's solutions fail, then the organisation dies quickly. If they succeed, the organisation grows and develops with yet greater belief in its original assumptions and solutions. There is, therefore, particularly in founder-led organisations, a very close connection between the leader's ideas and the way an organisation functions. Even as organisations mature and develop, the importance of leadership in determining how an organisation functions remains paramount. The leader still controls many of the key levers for influencing the organisational culture.

The case studies we have looked at bear this out. It was the drive and insight of key individuals in a leadership position who, with the support of their management team, actively promoted the strategic role of learning and championed new learning throughout the organisation. BRAC's commitment to learning can be directly traced to the personal commitment to learning of its founder, Dr Abed. It was his views and learning example that laid the foundation for the commitment of BRAC to become a learning NGO. Right from the outset, Dr Abed would go to the field for at least four to seven days, live there, and talk with BRAC staff. 'We would then discuss and analyse strategies and problems, and take vital decisions on the spot. This is how we learnt ... in fact BRAC started learning while doing things, and the excitement was that everybody was learning too. It was like a "little university"' (Smillie and Hailey 2001:75). His commitment to learning, acceptance of error, and active promotion of education, training, and shared learning across the organisation have been there from the outset. Even the research and evaluation department was established after only three years.

With Sadguru, it was the founder leaders' two years' 'walking and talking' with the people that not only proved of immense immediate operational benefit, but also was symbolic of their commitment to learning from local people themselves. This process is the foundation on which Sadguru's relationship with the local community is based, and it created a culture of shared learning which has marked the development of the organisation and the way it works with the local community. But it is not merely founders who influence the culture of learning in an NGO. Barry Underwood, an expatriate appointed as successor to the founder of AKRSP (India), 'personally emphasised learning and research, and because of the pressures for change, he placed great emphasis on training, organisation development and strategic planning' (Smillie and Hailey 2001:155).

The research did not bear out any specific gender dimensions to leadership and learning (possibly because there was only one woman out of the 16 past and present Chief Executives in the case studies considered, and the issue was not a primary focus of the research). There was, however, a sense that women who do get into leadership positions are better equipped to deal with the constantly changing challenges, as they have taken more bruises along the way. Efforts to promote women to senior positions are actively pursued, and a number of special initiatives have been introduced to overcome some of the deep-rooted resistance to women being recruited to senior positions. Many of these NGOs have made women the focal point of their activities, and have learnt over the years that empowerment is a gender issue that relates as much to men as to women. Consequently, gender programming has been the subject of considerable research and analysis. These organisations have learnt that any efforts to promote women to leadership positions have to be seen as a strategic priority, backed with a considerable investment of time and resources, and actively supported by senior managers. In short, such efforts have to be mainstreamed across the organisation and endorsed at the highest level.

Efforts to promote such new initiatives, encourage innovation, and support new learning are normally seen at an organisational level. However, it should be noted that 'learning leaders' are not just interested in promoting *organisational* learning *per se*, but are also keen to develop their own *personal* learning and initiate individual change. Organisational learning is not an impersonal process. Merely creating a learning culture or developing a knowledge strategy is insufficient. It requires human beings to learn and change. All the evidence suggests that organisational learning is dependent upon individuals being both open to new ideas and willing to engage in new learning (Swieringa and Wierdsma 1992; Cross and Israelit 2000). 'Learning leaders', who can draw on their power and prestige in the organisation to drive this learning process forward, often have a personal commitment to learning, a natural curiosity, and an understanding of the value of research and education generally. The commitment of such leaders to organisational learning is often a consequence of a personal commitment to developing their own learning. The leaders in the case studies we have reviewed had a fascination with knowledge and learning. It was the leaders who went out to learn from the people in the early days, and the same leaders have consciously and systematically created the means by which they can learn from their staff. Thus, it appears you cannot have a learning organisation without a learning leader who is open to personal change. As Hailey concluded, 'what has been striking ... has been the ability of their founder leaders to change and adapt' (Hailey 1999:3).

These findings are reinforced by the academic literature on leadership, learning, and management. It is persuasively argued that the ability to promote learning and instil a learning mindset in an organisation is 'the trademark competency of future leaders' (Conger and Benjamin 1999:242). Senge (1990) concluded that leaders in a learning organisation should have a facilitative role rather than an inspirational or technical one, and as such should be seen as designers, stewards, or teachers. Such managers have specific learning competencies such as a learning orientation, a proactive stance towards problems, the ability to reflect critically, and a tolerance of critical feedback (McCauley 2001).

Conclusion

There are many different methods by which NGOs can learn, as the cases we have looked at illustrate. These NGOs relied on informal processes to generate new learning, reflect on past experience, and experiment with new approaches. They also invested heavily in more formal learning processes such as training and research.

But what is common to all is that learning organisations are staffed by learning people and are led by learning leaders. Learning is a key characteristic of their organisational culture. Organisations are made up of the people within them. Organisational learning cannot happen without individual learning. Leaders are particularly influential members of organisations. A crucial characteristic of such learning organisations is that their leadership and senior management team are willing to invest in developing the organisation's learning, and recognise its role as a catalyst for change. But more than being committed to organisational learning, they have to be committed to their personal learning.

All the learning leaders reflect different facets of the learning process. Although they place a different emphasis on formal or informal learning processes, their willingness to invest time and money in new learning highlights the importance of their role as founders who inculcated a learning culture in their fledgling organisations. Manibhai Desai, of BAIF, emphasises the importance of learning from new technologies and applied research to help the rural poor. The Jagawatis from Sadguru created an organisational culture that is marked by learning through dialogue, and the need to build trust and relations before genuine learning can take place. Dr Abed of BRAC, while actively encouraging direct investment in formal learning and knowledge-generating activities, also recognises the role of team building and experimentation in promoting organisational learning.

Such leaders have married sound organisational design and effective management with strong personal values. These 'development leaders' have a distinct character and leadership style that can be characterised as being value driven, knowledge based, and responsive. They have ambitious development aspirations and an ability to understand and work within an uncertain and changing external environment. In practice, this has meant that they have a clear vision, a firm value-set, and a strong sense of commitment to helping the rural poor which they were able to share with, and which could inspire, others. Second, they have had a willingness to learn and experiment, to apply new technologies or organisational forms, and to draw on science or other sources of applied or professional knowledge. Third, they have a curiosity and ability to analyse the external environment, follow trends, and respond to changing circumstances. Fourth, these leaders also possess communication and interpersonal skills that have enabled them to motivate staff and engage with a cross-section of society. Fifth, they have displayed the ability to balance diverse demands and play different roles. They have demonstrated a chameleon-like ability to adapt to different roles, styles, or organisational needs. They have therefore been able to combine ideals and values with analysis, technical expertise, and professionalism, while still being able to communicate a vision and motivate a range of staff, stakeholders, and beneficiaries. Right at their core, they passionately believe in the importance of learning and knowledge in shaping the future of their organisation.

Notes

1   For a description of this book, see the Resources section of this Reader.
2   We define organisational culture as a pattern of learned assumptions about appropriate behaviour, or more colloquially 'how things get done round here'.
3   We use the word 'leader' to refer to the Director or Chief Executive of an organisation, and see leadership as a process through which the senior management and the Board influence group members to attain group or organisational goals and so shape the direction and culture of an organisation.
4   The early stage of an organisation's growth where the pioneer provides many of the ideas and much of the energy and direction to an organisation.

References

Britton, B. (1998) *The Learning NGO*, Occasional Paper 17, Oxford: INTRAC.

Conger, J. A. and B. Benjamin (1999) *Building Leaders: How Successful Companies Develop the Next Generation*, San Francisco, CA: Jossey-Bass.

Cross, R. and S. Israelit (2000) *Strategic Learning in a Knowledge Economy: Individual, Collective, and Organisational Learning Process*, Oxford: Butterworth-Heinemann.

Dixon, N. (2000) *Common Knowledge: How Companies Thrive by Sharing What They Know*, Cambridge, MA: Harvard Business School Press.

Edwards, M. (1997) 'Organizational learning in NGOs', *Public Administration and Development* 17:223–234.

Fowler, A. (1997) *Striking a Balance: A Guide to Enhancing the Effectiveness of NGOs in International Development*, London: Earthscan.

Fowler, A. (2000) *The Virtuous Spiral: A Guide to Sustainability for NGOs in International Development*, London: Earthscan.

Hailey, J. (1999) 'Charismatic autocrats or development leaders', paper presented to DSA Conference, Bath.

Handy, C. (1994) *The Empty Raincoat*, London: Hutchinson.

Kluge. J., W. Steen, and T. Licht (2001) *Knowledge Unplugged*, Basingstoke: Palgrave.

Korten, D. (1980) 'Community organization and rural development: a learning process approach', *Public Administration Review* 40:480-511.

Lewis, D. (2001) *Management of Non-governmental Development Organisations: An Introduction*, London: Routledge.

McCauley, C.D. (2001) 'Leader training and development', in S. J. Zaccaro and R. J. Klimoski (eds.) *The Nature of Organizational Leadership*, San Francisco, CA: Jossey-Bass.

Pedler. M., J. Burgoyne and T. Boydell (1991) *The Learning Company*, London: McGraw Hill.

Revans, R. (1993) *The ABC of Action Learning*, Manchester: International Federation of Action Learning.

Schein, E. (1992) *Organizational Culture and Leadership*, San Francisco, CA: Jossey-Bass.

Senge, P. (1990) *The Fifth Discipline: The Art and Practice of the Learning Organisation*, London: Century Business.

Smillie, I. (1995) *The Alms Bazaar*, London: IT Publications.

Smillie, I. and J. Hailey, (2001) *Managing for Change: Leadership, Strategy, and Management in South Asian NGOs*, London: Earthscan.

Swieringa, J. and A. Wierdsma (1992) *Becoming a Learning Organisation*, Wokingham: Addison Wesley.

World Bank (1998) *World Development Report: Knowledge for Development*, Oxford: OUP.

This article was first published in Development in Practice *(12/3&4:398–408) in 2002.*

Leading learning and change from the middle: reconceptualising strategy's purpose, content, and measures

Colin Beckwith, Kent Glenzer, and Alan Fowler

Introduction

The last decade has witnessed significant changes in the system of international development and aid – changes that have strategic implications for NGOs. This introduction briefly describes the pressures for major change in NGOs. Subsequent sections explain how one unit of CARE International is responding by rethinking strategic planning to support organisational transformation more effectively.

Far-reaching attempts at reform to improve performance now pervade the aid system. For example, in addition to a stricter focus on reducing poverty, accompanied by numerical targets with increased concentration on the poorest countries and groups (OECD 1996, 1998), bilateral and multilateral agencies now emphasise the importance of involving a wider array of non-state actors in development processes (see, for example, United Nations 2000). Furthermore, they are taking greater account of differences in country-specific conditions as well as ensuring the 'ownership' of development policies and processes by those for whom change is intended. In addition, they recognise that global forces are accelerating the pace of change that confronts developing countries. Consequently, institutional reforms in aid are taking place that learn from past lessons and deal with fast-emerging, new realities.[1]

One result of this change is a growth in official funding to NGOs with policies favouring the direct financing of domestic organisations in developing countries (INTRAC 1998). Another result is the priority given to improving NGO achievement and measurable impact within a framework of increasing coordination of, and coherence between, a greater diversity of actors (e.g. Wolfensohn 1999). This heightened pressure to demonstrate effectiveness and improve inter-agency collaboration raises urgent organisational questions and relational challenges for NGOs. For example, the degree to which NGOs can or should operate as 'partners' or (as constituents of civil society) more autonomously of the priorities and practices of governments and official aid is the subject of critical discussion, as is the issue of NGO roles, responsibilities, and accountability (Fowler 2000), particularly in relation to (international) governance, advocacy, and civic participation (Edwards 2000).

Such conditions demand heightened professionalism, better demonstration of results, and stronger inter-organisational relations. They call for more speedy and reliable processes for organisational learning, gaining multi-actor collaboration, sharing knowledge externally, and adapting global strategy. Yet 'standard' approaches to strategising are based on individual organisational goals and results, clear distinctions between 'strategic' and 'operational', reliance on top leadership to translate vision into concrete actions, and long-term commitments of resources to unchanging priorities. Such an approach may impede rather than assist necessary learning and reform. Instead, global non-profit organisations may need to take more seriously what may be called a new consensus on strategic planning, one that assumes that:

- strategy is about effective learning processes as much as results (De Geus 1997; Senge 1990);
- it is difficult to determine *a priori* what is strategic versus what is operational (Mintzberg 1994);
- top-level leaders have no innate competence or location to translate global vision into locally appropriate, concrete action (Collins and Porras 1991); and
- the 'top-down cascade' of multi-level, multi-year, nested organisational strategies can inhibit learning and innovation.

This paper describes how one sub-unit of CARE International – the Latin America Regional Management Unit (LARMU) – centralised these assumptions and developed a lighter, more flexible strategic learning tool: not another layer of planning, but a 'management framework' which (a) makes explicit cause-and-effect relationships between CARE efforts and wider poverty reduction; (b) translates global vision into region-specific, measurable, desired outcomes; and (c) serves as a critical node for *both* guiding strategy creation at the country office and local levels without imposing inappropriate priorities *and*, eventually, feeding learning into future strategy revision at the global level. Although still in a pilot stage, we argue that such a tool is one way to conceptualise and integrate multiple levels of strategic planning more flexibly, as well as to focus organisational learning.

The paper has five sections. The first describes CARE International and outlines its 18-month global visioning process. The second summarises challenges that typically confront mid-level managers in global NGOs once a new overarching vision and strategy are defined. It discusses how LARMU rethought and reframed middle-level strategy to better operationalise a collective global vision, created the conditions for improved organisational learning, and initiated a process of leading corporate change from the middle of the organisation. The third section describes the process LARMU followed to shape its management framework. This is followed by a presentation of the framework itself as well as its internal logic. The paper concludes by identifying strengths, weaknesses, and future challenges for using the framework to drive ongoing learning and organisational change.

Establishing a guiding framework for organisational reform

Founded in the USA in 1945 to provide relief to war-torn Europe, CARE has evolved from a single US entity to a multinational non-profit organisation, CARE International (CI), with headquarters in Brussels. Now, ten national organisations (NOs) located in OECD countries annually raise some US$450 million, and these funds are distributed for relief and development work through CARE country offices (COs) in 65 developing countries. CARE NOs are legally independent entities, united by a common brand and shared intentions. By designating an NO as the Lead Member for operational work, it is ensured that there is only one CARE office in each developing country. Although the single CO model prevents duplication, it does have drawbacks (Edwards 1997). While these are not crucial to this article, an important conclusion recognised by the CI board in 1997 is of relevance: that resolution of many intra-organisational issues would require CARE's constituent parts to reach a common understanding of their collective identity and role in a rapidly evolving context.

CARE is highly decentralised. Responsibility for determining and carrying out programmes resides with the Country Directors. Consequently, most organisational learning required for innovation and adaptation originates at country level. Country offices enjoy support from NOs for resource acquisition, technical support, and human resources. Structurally, CARE International divides its work into five geographic regions: Asia, Southern and West Africa, East Africa, Eastern Europe and the Middle East, and Latin America and the Caribbean.[2] All country offices depend on the CI Federation for the development of organisation-wide standards, policies, procedures, and systems. It was therefore vital to initiate a process of collective visioning, described below, which optimised the participation of all parts of the organisation.

Creating a new vision and mission: the process

In 1998, CARE International embarked on a process to outline a shared vision and mission. The International Secretariat was given responsibility for defining and guiding the initiative, aided by an external adviser. From the outset, it was agreed that the method should be as participatory as resources would allow. The process evolved as described below.

Establishing critical preconditions

While the International Board had initiated and mandated a 'vision' and 'mission' process, it was important that members agree on what these terms actually meant. Consequently, a period was allocated at a board meeting to consider the criteria that would be used to judge a 'good' collective vision and mission. These criteria formed one input to determining components of an appropriate visioning exercise.

Second, to ensure good two-way communication within the geographically widespread parts of the whole organisation, both NOs and COs were asked to nominate members of a steering committee. The task of the committee was four-fold: to communicate views and comments from the field, to share intermediate outputs, to provide decentralised reference points, and to act as a resource for responding to queries.

Finally, in explicit recognition that CI faced *both* conceptual *and* linguistic challenges, a key element of the process was to ask all COs and NOs to submit proposed visions, and the CI Secretariat produced practical guidelines and support information to assist them. To help frame this activity, the Secretariat commissioned a UK development think tank to produce a forward-looking study of development to 2015. This was circulated to all offices, and participants were asked to consider their outputs in relation and response to this analysis. Respondents were also asked to provide a detailed interpretive narrative for their submissions. In this way, the steering committee was able to gain a more concrete idea of how diverse parts of CARE saw the future in practical terms.

Combining and selecting the results

Vision and mission statements from NOs and COs were brought together by the Secretariat and then redistributed to the steering committee, whose members were asked to rank their preferences. The top five were used as the starting input for a five-day seminar. Some 40 people participated, including a member of the International Board of each NO. The task was to arrive at an agreed proposal of vision, mission, and concrete indications of 'what CARE should look like in 2010' for consideration by the International Board. Areas where no consensus could be reached were clearly signalled, together with reasons for contention.

Reaching corporate agreement

The board of each CARE NO discussed the draft statements and implications. The objective was for the members of the International Board to obtain a mandate for, or suggest revisions to, the draft arising from the conference. Not least due to the participatory nature of the process itself, the International Board speedily reached agreement on the corporate vision and mission as well as on many of the implications:

CARE International Vision Statement

We seek a world of hope, tolerance, and social justice, where poverty has been overcome and people live in dignity and security. CARE International will be a global force and a partner of choice within a worldwide movement dedicated to ending poverty. We will be known everywhere for our unshakable commitment to the dignity of people.

CARE International Mission Statement

CARE International's mission is to serve individuals and families in the poorest communities in the world. Drawing strength from our global diversity, resources, and experience, we promote innovative solutions and are advocates for global responsibility. We facilitate lasting change by:

- *strengthening capacity for self-help;*
- *providing economic opportunity;*
- *delivering relief in emergencies;*
- *influencing policy decisions at all levels; and*
- *addressing discrimination in all its forms.*

Guided by the aspirations of local communities, we pursue our mission with both excellence and compassion because the people whom we serve deserve nothing less.

How LARMU translated this vision and mission into a tangible, regional set of priorities and measures – and how these in turn influenced CARE as a whole – is the subject of the remainder of this paper.

Planning as learning: operationalising global guiding ideas

The literature on non-profit planning and strategy is thin regarding mid-level strategic planning. Yet most global NGOs have intermediate, regional management structures that straddle and bridge global and country levels. Typically, these geographically-based structures serve basic administrative and oversight functions, but their contribution is potentially much greater. We argue that regional management structures are crucial for operationalising a global vision by linking levels of planning and strategy. Furthermore, in a world in which the dynamics of poverty reduction differ significantly between continents and also between countries within continents, we suggest that the 'region' is a critical unit both for measuring progress towards a global vision and for feeding in revisions to global strategy. In other words, 'the region' is a pivotal pole of organisational learning, uniquely positioned both to ground lofty ideas and to elevate lessons learned to higher levels of the organisation.

While this potential exists, common systems of strategic planning that seek to integrate multiple levels of action within an organisation actually make this difficult.[3] Strategy is commonly implemented through a 'cascade method', where corporate vision, strategies, and goals are gradually passed down through the organisation, resulting in layer after layer of strategic plans. At its best, this basic process is open to iteration to adopt 'bottom-up' feedback that may include local partners and other stakeholders. But problems commonly remain. Those encountered in the past in CARE include *elapsed time* (months or years can pass while lower organisational levels await strategy decisions or revisions), *conflicting or too many priorities* (managers near the bottom of the cascade get inundated), and *under-specification* (global visions and strategies cannot – and should not try to – accommodate country, regional, and continental specifics). But perhaps most importantly, as Kaplan and Norton (1996a) have stated, no matter what planning model is adopted, cause-and-effect relationships between vision achievement, goals, strategies, resources, and organisational capabilities are rarely made explicit. In the absence of such shared, public, organisational consensus regarding cause-and-effect relationships (in short, in the absence of an explicit 'hypothesis'), strategic learning is extremely difficult.

To address these weaknesses, LARMU adopted three innovations to a 'cascade' process:

- re-imagining what constitutes ethical performance in a global NGO;
- inverting the normal sequencing of the 'cascade' model; and
- eschewing the notion of a regional *strategic plan* in favour of a *strategic learning framework* that makes explicit the region's hypothesis regarding poverty reduction.

Ethics and measures

Most strategic planning literature agrees on one fundamental tenet: organisations should specify results that *are fully within their control*. This leads non-profit organisations to spend much time and energy trying to discern *their own* contribution to change in clients or geographical areas. Not only is this difficult given the multitude of intervening variables but, more importantly, on critical measures of poverty reduction and human rights, *no* single organisation can achieve 'breakthrough' results.

LARMU turned such advice on its head. Instead of concentrating on CARE's particular and unique contribution, LARMU adopted the OECD's 50 per cent poverty-reduction target as the most fundamental measure of 'success'. LARMU felt that CARE and other organisations had spent decades trying to be very precise about *their own* outputs and results, and yet poverty was expanding, not decreasing. Instead, LARMU determined that the only *ethical* measure of CARE's perform-ance was industry-wide success. At root, LARMU hoped that such a measure would initiate a deeper learning process, prompting new organisational initiatives and approaches, particularly ones which would encourage staff to think beyond projects, beyond programmes, and to reflect deeply on their own (and CARE's) roles, mandates, and priorities. LARMU sought to inculcate a critical creative tension (Senge *et al.* 1994:195–196) in which even outstanding 'CARE' performance was simply not good enough if poverty in the region continued to grow.

The sequencing dilemma

LARMU rejected the 'cascade' method. Hoping to capitalise on the energy and excitement created by the CARE International vision, LARMU deliberately ran ahead of higher levels of strategy creation. It presented its process to higher management as a 'space' in which staff would try to translate the vision and mission into practical, concrete priorities *before* this was done at the global level. LARMU ensured that key senior CO and NO managers attended workshops both to express their own ideas in a relatively risk-free atmosphere and to signal emergent, non-negotiable 'bottom lines'. Throughout the process, e-mail exchanges and individual meetings were included to keep senior management informed about emerging ideas. In effect, leaders had an early opportunity to test and refine ideas that they would later propose as vital to the organisation's global strategy. Indeed, the global CI strategy – finalised after the LARMU process – incorporated most priorities that staff in the region had identified. It also adopted LARMU's poverty-reduction goal as CI's overarching goal. By reversing the 'cascade', LARMU senior managers, country office staff, and external experts were able to shape the organisation's global strategy in tangible ways.

From 'strategic planning' to 'strategic learning': the management framework

Rather than add a layer of priorities, objectives, and results that country offices would adhere to, LARMU sought to create a 'management framework' loosely based on the balanced scorecard and strategy-map concepts (Kaplan and Norton 1996a, 2000). That is, the framework's goal was to translate CARE International's global vision into an *explicit cause-and-effect hypothesis* of how CARE could contribute to poverty reduction in the Latin American context. It did not establish non-negotiable 'objectives' or 'priorities' or 'strategies' for specific Latin American COs. Rather, it offered a high-level, guiding, strategic logic chain linking CARE to wider poverty-reduction results in the region. The framework would focus field managers' attention on two critical tasks. First, it would ask them to consider the framework's logic and priorities while leaving open the question of locally appropriate goals, objectives, and strategies. Second, the framework would ask managers to have local conversations about whether the framework's cause-and-effect logic is accurate – what Argyris and Schön (1996) call 'double-loop learning', that is, conversations about performance that ask not so much 'are we accomplishing our goals and objectives?' but rather 'are our goals and objectives correct to begin with?'. The management framework, when finalised, would tell COs not so much *what* to do, nor *when* to do it, but rather *how* and *why* to attack poverty reduction.

Crafting a management framework for the region

In late 1998, LARMU initiated conversations to define both the process and product for the management framework. The core process was a series of three conferences. The first, held in February 2000, included LARMU, Country Directors (CDs), and representatives from NOs. A second, in September 2000, included some CDs, representatives from CI, LARMU, and 15 CO senior managers. The final conference in November 2000 included the full complement of regional CDs and Assistant CDs, representatives of CI, and LARMU.

Prior to the February 2000 meeting, LARMU developed and distributed a regional poverty analysis that looked back 20 years and forward 10 years. Focused more on structural than technical factors, this document set the stage for frank discussions about NGOs' abilities to address poverty reduction. Senior CI leaders emphasised that the new vision implied radical changes in CARE's role and programme approaches, outlined that regional field staff were best placed to identify these changes, and encouraged staff to consider a 10 to 15-year time horizon. The remainder of the workshop was devoted to identifying such changes. Participants delineated five areas of transformation (the Breakthrough Arenas, described below) that CARE would have to adopt across the entire region, what such changes might look like if successfully carried out, and some of the broad implications for CARE programming.

Following this meeting, LARMU developed a draft management framework, which included a ten-year poverty-reduction target as a working goal, the five Breakthrough Arenas, and a set of 'Measures of Success' and 'Indicative Actions' for each arena, and the draft was circulated for feedback. This was the first time participants had seen the framework, and many responses reflected concern regarding the role and use of the framework itself and wariness regarding the poverty-reduction goal. In short, the framework's intermediary role to bridge global *vision* and CO *strategy* needed more dialogue and discussion.

A second draft incorporating feedback was circulated to the same audience. LARMU management focused on explaining the role, function, and use of the framework. Most importantly, between the first workshop and second framework draft, LARMU decided to adopt the OECD's 50 per cent poverty-reduction target as its own. The revised draft was then discussed at the second conference in September 2000.

Participants in this conference included 15 CO senior managers. In addition, representatives from the Comisión Económica para América Latina y el Caribe (CEPAL), the Asociación Latinoamericana de Organizaciones de Promoción (ALOP), and the Instituto Centroamericano Empresarial (INCAE) were present. Prior to the conference, they had been asked to review the draft framework and to present their reactions. These outside opinions were invaluable for helping LARMU get beyond buzzwords and jargon. They were also crucial in validating the framework's logic and its role as a bridge between global vision and CO strategy. The conference then undertook a risk-and-barriers analysis of the proposed changes.

From the analysis, LARMU developed a set of critical actions or initiatives required in order to succeed in advancing each of the Breakthrough Arenas. Three important shifts in thinking occurred during this meeting. First, there was general acceptance of the poverty-reduction goal and a shared understanding that the goal was meant to spur learning and thinking rather than to measure CARE's specific work. Second, there was more energetic acceptance that the Breakthrough Arenas were vital to CARE's future. Third, the arenas were explicitly recognised as important *organisational capabilities* that CARE would need to develop or enhance in order to make a significant contribution to poverty reduction in the region. Understanding the Breakthrough Arenas as future organisational capabilities (rather than as a list of 'what CARE does') made the bridging role of the management framework clearer to CO staff.

Based on the second conference, LARMU developed and circulated a third draft, firmly positioning the framework within a 15-year time horizon. Responses indicated that the framework was clearer in spirit, intent, and content. In developing this third draft, LARMU introduced the notion of the management framework as comprising two 'hypotheses' that would serve as the foundation for organisational learning over the next three to five years. The first, LARMU's 'development hypothesis', is:

> *Poverty should drop in the Latin America Region if CARE demonstrates excellence in each of the five Breakthrough Arenas.*

The second 'organisational hypothesis' is:

> *In order to excel in the Breakthrough Arenas, LARMU needs the support of the wider organisation in terms of changes in policies, measures of individual performance, and resource allocation.*

Although simple and straightforward, these clear statements of causal logic, eminently measurable and therefore disprovable, constituted an important final step to permit CO staff and CI representatives to embrace and take ownership of the framework.

The focus, spirit, and intent of the management framework

LARMU's management framework for 2000–2015 has four major components: a Strategic Target, five Breakthrough Arenas, programme implications, and internal changes required.

The Strategic Target

LARMU has adopted as its own most fundamental performance measure the OECD Strategic Target of a 50 per cent reduction in poverty by the year 2015 in those countries where CARE operates.[4] The Strategic Target is explicitly intended to communicate that poverty reduction is 'larger than CARE' in that no matter how good CARE's results are, alone they are insufficient to make lasting and positive impacts on poverty. The target tells CARE that reduction can occur only through cooperation with a wide range of local, regional, and international actors; acting and thinking 'outside' projects; and opening up CARE's boundaries to social change coalitions. LARMU will use the Strategic Target to create vital space for critical reflection and organisational learning about the systemic and structural nature of poverty and about its effective reduction. In other words, overall poverty reduction is the fundamental yardstick by which CARE's regional performance is assessed and new priorities identified.

Breakthrough Arenas

Breakthrough Arena 1: Developing and promoting learning processes
LARMU's projects and programmes will no longer be designed solely to deliver social services to target populations. They will also serve to contribute and make accessible new knowledge, technologies, and approaches that can be used by a wide range of social service providers and that can be used to influence decision makers at all levels.

Initial qualitative measures

- All programming includes explicit learning objectives and poverty-reduction hypotheses.
- Hypotheses are systematically tested in the field and results shared with other social actors.

- Approaches that are successful in addressing the systemic and structural causes of poverty are replicated or adapted at larger scales.

Breakthrough Arena 2: Influencing public policy and attitudes

LARMU must explicitly focus on influencing public policy and attitudes concerning poverty reduction at local, national, regional, or international levels.

Initial qualitative measures

- CARE's on-the-ground programming experience will be made formally accessible to key stakeholders.
- Tangible evidence that innovations inform policy dialogue.
- Tangible evidence that innovations contribute to policy implementation and reform.
- Tangible evidence that policy and attitudinal influence lead to a larger constituency base committed and contributing to poverty-reduction initiatives.

Breakthrough Arena 3: Expanding and deepening inter-institutional relationships

During the life of a project or programme, LARMU will seek to engage with social actors and stakeholders from all segments and levels of civil society in relationships that go well beyond the transfer of resources with those directly involved in implementation.

Initial qualitative measures

- LARMU's involvement in networks, coalitions, strategic alliances, and partnerships emphasises quality-of-relationship criteria such as mutual interest, mutual benefit, and mutual control.
- Agreed upon institutional and programmatic objectives and expected results are attained.

Breakthrough Arena 4: Integrating within local society

LARMU will expand its definition of whom it is accountable to and in what ways. This will imply moving beyond the more traditional donors-partners-beneficiaries construct.

Initial qualitative measures

- A significantly wider range of local stakeholders have influence on our decisions, in setting expectations, and in monitoring our performance and effectiveness.
- Local stakeholders' perceptions and testimony qualify CARE as an integral part of the social fabric.

Breakthrough Arena 5: Mobilising new and diverse resources into local economies

LARMU will mobilise increased amounts of new and varied resources, both financial and non-financial, and leverage them to generate increased social benefit towards poverty reduction. These efforts are not intended solely to benefit CARE or our direct partners. The larger intent is to attract and/or inject increased amounts of more flexible and more diverse types of financial and non-financial resources.

Initial qualitative measures

• Additional and more diverse resources dedicated to poverty reduction are available for CARE and others.

• The local economy, socially oriented businesses, local organisations, and poor people have greater access to, and effectively utilise, a wider array of resources.

The five Breakthrough Arenas are linked through cause-and-effect relationships, with progress in one arena feeding success into others. The internal logic of the framework is schematised in Figure 1.

As can be seen in the figure, these cause-and-effect relationships are not linear. Rather, the logic is that of a dynamic system in which progress in all five Breakthrough Arenas is required, and failure to move forward in one of the arenas will affect success in several others.

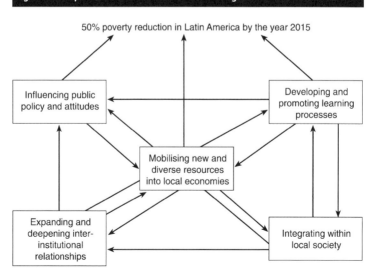

Figure 1: Component relations in the LARMU management framework

In very broad terms, progress in these five organisational capabilities would be demonstrated by:

- a working system that transfers learning between CARE, its collaborators, decision makers, and Northern constituencies;
- increasing instances of lessons from CARE's experience influencing public policy and attitudes towards poverty reduction;
- increasing instances of CARE being invited to join social movements, networks, and coalitions committed to improving governmental and donor policies on poverty reduction;
- new models of governance for country offices that increase CARE's accountability through strong local oversight and evaluation of programmes;
- a demonstrable broadening and increase in financial and non-financial resources for poverty reduction.

Internal changes required

Participants in the process were insistent on one point: all five Breakthrough Arenas demanded internal organisational changes *before* CARE could achieve better external impact. These internal changes and their intent in terms of expectations about organisational performance over the next two to three years include:

Reconceptualising the purpose of projects and programmes

Projects and programmes must shift from a predominant role of CARE as the 'doer' towards that of a 'facilitator' and 'enabler'. In such new roles, CARE identifies, designs, and evaluates its core business in terms of:

- actively engaging with and acting upon *systemic and structural issues* that underlie poverty;
- contributing *new knowledge and innovative approaches* that expand the capacity or effectiveness of poverty-reduction strategies;
- establishing alliances to *generate and share knowledge* and to influence and leverage macro-level change; and
- measuring success in terms of *linking social actors, their knowledge and resources* in more mutually supportive ways.

Redefining the essential tasks of CO managers

One of LARMU's main roles will be to advocate within CARE itself to redesign project staff's responsibilities and internal operating environment to permit them to fulfil the new approaches to development work listed above.

Becoming more interdependent

LARMU, as a regional management unit and organisational layer, must establish ways for CO managers to reflect on and discuss 'big picture' issues with the many other parts of CARE International as well as play a lead role in building the strength of connections between country offices. LARMU must also take the lead in connecting country offices with wider social movements across the region, with think tanks and research organisations, and with Northern constituencies.

Conclusions: strengths, weaknesses, and future challenges

The management framework is currently in its first year of implementation. As such, it is difficult to evaluate its success in any summative manner. So far, it has served its purpose as a bridge between two layers of formal strategy: global and local (country specific). The process of developing the framework made the lofty aspirations of CI's new global vision and mission more concrete and measurable without adding yet another set of objectives or goals that COs would have to adopt. By preceding CI's global strategy-creation efforts, the framework's development process offered CI senior managers a relatively safe location for testing and refining ideas that later were embedded in CI's strategy. In addition, a single region was able to radically alter how the global organisation thinks about its impact, as shown by CI's adoption of the OECD poverty-reduction target as its own measure of success. The framework speaks upwards to higher reaches of the organisation, summarising regional results within an explicit poverty-reduction logic, thus providing an empirical basis for altering global strategy.

LARMU's adoption of the OECD poverty-reduction goal has significantly altered the terms of strategic discussions and assumptions about what constitutes ethical performance standards in a global NGO. The identification of region-specific Breakthrough Arenas, their intent, and performance expectations, has served to ground CI's global vision in Latin American realities while providing an overarching logical framework within which country offices have ample latitude to develop locally relevant strategic plans. The wide, participatory process which resulted in the identification of internal organisational changes required to support such transformation has given LARMU management solid backing and a clear poverty-reduction rationale for overhauling internal systems, policies, and procedures. Within this progress, the following strengths, weaknesses, and future challenges will be likely to determine the framework's success as a guide to leading organisational change.

Strengths

The management framework highlights key areas for organisational change and learning, and makes explicit the cause-and-effect assumptions linking global vision and more concrete, regional action. More importantly, the framework was crafted in a highly participatory manner with field staff themselves identifying the vast majority of its eventual contents. It was crafted as a strategic management tool to bridge and influence both global and country levels. It also creates a middle ground (in philosophy, conception, and design), providing a poverty-reduction hypothesis that COs must respect and consider but which does not impose specific results or timetables.

The nature and intended use of the Strategic Target forces CARE managers to think beyond their project or programme boxes to how they might better link CARE with wider networks, alliances, and movements. It also forces thinking about deep structural and historical causes of poverty. The Breakthrough Arenas and initial measures of success provide COs with categories to consider in their own strategic planning processes but leaves them free to determine how they will be pursued.

Most importantly, the implementation of the framework is focused on 'double-loop learning' and not simply 'single-loop' problem solving – to separate the causal wood from the symptomatic trees. Key questions become not so much 'what's wrong with our implementation?' (an archetypal single-loop learning question), but rather 'is our strategic hypothesis correct? Have we identified the right targets or focus to begin with? Have we got the cause-and-effect links right?' (classic double-loop learning questions).

Weaknesses

The conception of the management framework described above was not present from the start of the process. LARMU took the adventurous decision, in effect, to learn in public about its own emerging ideas. This resulted in rocky patches as CO and NO staff tried to understand LARMU's evolving intent with the framework concept. In addition, CO staff often felt put off by jargon coming from the literature of learning organisations and the balanced scorecard and, worse, they did not see its relevance to the day-to-day challenges faced by frontline managers. A second weakness was that efforts to fully define region-wide measures of success and performance indicators were not brought to full closure. The framework, at the time of writing, is still work in progress (not necessarily a bad thing) and LARMU faces significant challenges in finalising these two critical components. Eventually, once they have been piloted for a year or two, LARMU will begin using them to make strategic resource-allocation decisions across the region's country offices.

Finally, despite LARMU's efforts, the framework's role, purpose, and function are still perceived differently across the whole organisation. There is general awareness and acceptance of the framework at CARE's global level. However, there has been insufficient dialogue regarding how LARMU experimentation and adaptation of CARE's management systems, policies, and processes will be supported by other parts of the organisation. In one instance already, senior CI staff publicly refuted parts of the framework's logic regarding internal organisational changes required to support poverty-reduction efforts in Latin America, stating that LARMU was basing its conclusions on 'mere' hypotheses without substantive data to support them. Furthermore, despite LARMU's constant assurance to CO staff that the framework provides a guiding logic and a menu of options, some staff still worry that the framework represents more 'mandates from above' albeit, perhaps, in a kinder form. Country Office staff are unclear (as well they should be) about how the framework will influence both individual and CO performance evaluation by LARMU management; how, explicitly, the framework should be incorporated into their own strategic planning processes; and, more pragmatically, how the framework will influence their collaboration and coordination with country-level clients, partners, and stakeholders.

Future challenges

A major challenge for LARMU will be to build internal coalitions to support necessary changes to CARE's management systems, processes, and structures. CARE International gave LARMU considerable latitude to translate the global vision into practical and measurable actions at the regional level. Subsequently, many of the issues incorporated into the management framework were adopted by the global organisation in its strategy process. However, there is significant disagreement on just how much CARE must change its internal policies, systems, and decision-making processes to deliver on the new vision. The same leaders who provided LARMU with freedom and support to develop the framework's Breakthrough Arenas are, understandably and correctly, more wary about transforming organisation-wide policies and procedures that extend well beyond a single region. This is not unusual, nor is it cause for undue alarm. However, it will demand that LARMU spend significant time building understanding and support inside CARE for such changes, and that it actively and openly listen to alternative ideas.

A second challenge lies in LARMU's ability to maintain the creative tension necessary to lead wider organisational learning 'from the middle'. There are no guarantees that the uptake of lessons learned from the region will be able to alter established global CI strategy. LARMU faces serious challenges in 'translating up' country-level innovation and learning to influence global priorities. While the framework can provide the data and conceptual foundations for improving upward learning, in general such cross-organisational learning requires subtle political, negotiation, and communication skills that LARMU staff must learn. Similarly, while the framework may guide innovation at the country level, the concrete practices, mechanisms, and conversations between LARMU and CO managers to profit from this opportunity have still to be developed.

While challenges of bridging and negotiation exist between LARMU and the wider organisation and between LARMU and CO managers, perhaps the most difficult challenge is linking the management framework to lower levels of the organisation, i.e. to projects, programmes, partners, and participants in specific countries. The reconceptualisation of the purpose of projects and programmes described above is the most concrete link between the framework and grassroots efforts. LARMU also believes that the framework, by asking CO staff to consider and explain their poverty-reduction causal logic, will result in new kinds of country-specific programmes. It will also inform local choices about partnering and collaborative relationships with other social actors.

Like similar NGOs, CARE is vulnerable to high turnover of management staff. Therefore, a final, and perhaps the most critical, challenge will be to maintain momentum and continuity through the next five to ten years. To be successful, a 'middle-ground' management model – one capable of guiding an ongoing and evolving process – must enjoy broad-based understanding and ownership that is vertically integrated within CARE. Only then can we make sure that the framework becomes embedded within the organisation, with LARMU managers continuing to be open and supportive of ongoing adaptations to ensure that necessary enabling conditions exist for maintaining and sustaining change over time. Building these preconditions for long-term strategic learning is, perhaps, the most critical short-term task that LARMU now faces.

Notes

1 For example, Poverty Reduction Strategy Papers (PRSPs), now required in order to qualify for funding from the World Bank and the International Monetary Fund, are premised on widespread local ownership of definition and implementation.

2 The Latin America and Caribbean Region comprises COs in Bolivia, Brazil, Ecuador, El Salvador, Guatemala, Haiti, Honduras, and Peru. In this paper, the acronym 'LARMU' refers to the management unit that supervises these CO programmes and consists of a Regional Director and two Deputies.

3 Bryson (1995:194–200) summarises these 'standard' models well. The 'layered or stacked units' model requires visioning, overarching goals, objectives, and strategies to be established at the highest corporate level, and sub-units are then asked to develop strategic plans within this framework. The 'strategic issues management' model eschews detailed coordination across organisational levels in favour of agreement on the key issues facing the entire organisation and relative freedom of business units to address these as they see fit. 'Portfolio' planning models largely borrow from for-profit marketing approaches, basing strategy creation on identifying and exploiting 'niches' for specific products and services. 'Goal or benchmark' models, often used in

multiple stakeholder environments, limit themselves to the identification of overarching goals or clusters of indicators, and individual organisations design action plans independently.

4 Acknowledging that poverty is multi-dimensional, LARMU will initially track six different measures of poverty in the region.

References

Argyris, Chris and Donald Schön (1996) 'Single- and double-loop learning', in *Organizational Learning II*, Reading, MA: Addison-Wesley.

Bryson, John M. (1995) *Strategic Planning for Public and Non-profit Organizations*, San Francisco, CA: Jossey-Bass.

Collins, James and Jerry I. Porras (1991) 'Organizational vision and visionary organizations', *California Management Review* (October):30–52.

De Geus, Arie (1997) *The Living Company*, Boston, MA: Harvard Business School Press.

Edwards, Michael (1997) 'Structure, Governance and Accountability in CARE-International: Options for the Future. A Report to the Lead Member Model Review Group', unpublished report, Brussels: CARE International.

Edwards, Michael (2000) *NGO Rights and Responsibilities: A New Deal for Global Governance*, London: Foreign Policy Centre.

Fowler, Alan (ed.) (2000) 'NGO futures: beyond aid', *Third World Quarterly* (special issue) 21(4).

INTRAC (1998) *Direct Funding from a Southern Perspective: Strengthening Civil Society?*, Oxford: INTRAC.

Kaplan, Robert S. and David P. Norton (1996a) *The Balanced Scorecard*, Boston, MA: Harvard Business School Press.

Kaplan, Robert S. and David P. Norton (2000) 'Having trouble with your strategy? Then map it', *Harvard Business Review* (September-October):167–176.

Mintzberg, Henry (1994) *The Rise and Fall of Strategic Planning*, New York, NY: Free Press.

OECD (1996) *Shaping the Twenty-first Century: The Contribution of Development Cooperation*, Paris: OECD.

OECD (1998) *Measuring Development Progress: A Working Set of Core Indicators*, Paris: OECD.

Senge, Peter (1990) *The Fifth Discipline: The Art and Practice of the Learning Organization*, New York, NY: Currency Doubleday.

Senge, Peter M., Charlotte Roberts, Richard B. Ross, Bryan J. Smith and Art Kleiner (1994) *The Fifth Discipline Fieldbook: Strategies and Tools for Building a Learning Organization*, New York, NY: Doubleday Dell.

United Nations (2000) *We the Peoples: Executive Summary*, New York, NY: United Nations.

Wolfensohn, James (1999) *A Proposal for a Comprehensive Development Framework*, Washington, DC: World Bank.

The struggle for organisational change: how the ActionAid Accountability, Learning and Planning System emerged

Patta Scott-Villiers

Introduction

How does a development agency make real its belief in the rights of the poor? ActionAid is one NGO that has made space and time to change its organisation and relationships in quite a different way, involving a leap of faith in what it means to run a development agency.[1] The opportunity for a new approach came about when, after a period of upheaval, the organisation's beliefs about the rights of the poor and marginalised, its anti-poverty objectives, and its aid delivery structures all began to align with one another. Introduced in 2000, ActionAid's Accountability, Learning and Planning System (ALPS) is part of this change. It details processes for appraisal, strategy formulation, programme review, and regular reflection across the organisation's programmes, departments, and partnerships. The system is different because it seeks to increase accountability to the poor and to ActionAid's partners, while maintaining traditional accountability to sponsors and donors. It is important because it explicitly recognises the contribution the procedure is hoping to make to the quality and style of the organisation's relationships and the impact of those relationships on ActionAid's goal of eradicating poverty.

It is too early to say whether this new system will succeed in contributing to global anti-poverty efforts or to increasing the access of poor people to their rights. A critique of ALPS, identifying its contradictions and strengths, will be the subject of later studies once the system has matured and inquiry into it has deepened. Nevertheless, we can say that it has already succeeded in generating spirit, enthusiasm, and debate among many ActionAid staff, and the partners and community organisations with whom they cooperate.

The article opens with an introduction to ALPS, its non-negotiable principles, and what it looks like in practice, at least in a few of its diverse manifestations around the world; and I ask why it seems to be worthy of our attention. The main part of the article will look at what was going on in the organisation in the decade before the new system arrived and what the key developments were during those years. Finally, I use this history to ask why innovation took so long and what this tells us about organisational change.

Background

This article is a result of collaboration between the Participation Group at the Institute of Development Studies (IDS) and ActionAid's Impact Assessment Unit, which started in October 2000. In order to learn about both ALPS and the wider organisational dynamic of which it is a part, we adopted an action-research methodology that involves taking part in the change process itself – supporting, criticising, and learning at the same time. Four members of the IDS Group, Garett Pratt, Andrea Cornwall, Robert Chambers, and the author have all spent time in different ActionAid programmes in India, Kenya, Ethiopia, and Brazil. We took part in initial workshops where staff and partners considered the new system. We also joined in early stages of work with partners, communities, and community organisations, where the reality of the new ideas of accountability to the poor began to become apparent. As the system matures, the team will collaborate in continued action-research to learn in greater depth about this particular organisational learning and change enterprise.

Introduction to ALPS

> I suggest inclusion of the now often espoused principle that poor communities are our 'principal stakeholders'. The implications of this would be that their views, aspirations, evaluations, would be the paramount driving force behind our work, and how we design and assess it. Not many organisations or individuals could honestly say that this is the case. So while dropping the hypocrisy of the phrase 'primary stakeholder', we need to introduce instruments of real community accountability.
> (Harsh Mander, ActionAid India)

ALPS is about procedures, but it is also about fundamental changes to relationships. It is based on a set of beliefs and principles regarding the rights of the poor to criticise and influence poverty eradication efforts. Instead of information flowing only upwards in the organisation, and requests and guidelines flowing downwards, the system tries to achieve

360 degree accountability, opening up formal channels for *direction* to originate from the poor as well as from management. In order to do this, the system requires that staff at all levels dedicate time to transparency, learning, and negotiation with partners, the poor and one another. ALPS involves consistent and deliberate reflection, which needs to be nourished by accurate and useful information and followed by negotiation on changing procedures, strategies, priorities, and relationships.

ALPS replaces ActionAid's old Annual Planning and Reporting System (APRS). It includes advice on behaviours and attitudes to emphasise that the way in which staff members relate to each other and to others is more important than the documents that are produced. 'ALPS aims to liberate staff and partners from the tyranny of endless forms and writing lengthy plans and reports which mostly adorn some shelf or archive' (ActionAid 2001:iii). An annual report from countries, programmes, or departments, traditionally the mainstay of the organisation's accountability and memory system, is no longer required. Instead, in the spirit of increasing accountability to the poor and to partners, the system asks each of these entities to carry out a set of participatory reviews and reflections with stakeholder groups on the quality of their mutual programmes.

Box 1: An ALPS reflection meeting with some 30 women and men of the Manja clan (an excluded minority) at Gendo village, Ethiopia

The ActionAid facilitator invites the group to choose their own agenda as part of a review of their work together. The debate is raw and truthful; it is about people's rights. ActionAid is challenged on its own behaviour:

> Manja man: *There is just one minority person working for ActionAid, a cleaner. But is there anyone of our clan working with you as a programme person? No. Do we live a life of baboons, eating fruit and roots? A permanent remedy will be when our representatives get positions in government. Other remedies appear and disappear …*

> Project officer (later): *We've never had a conversation like that before.*

Box 2: Khema, a community organisation, speaks after ActionAid has presented the budget for the last three years, Kwale, Kenya

The analysis of spending over the last three years is broken down to show money spent by ActionAid on itself in the local office against how much has been spent on programmes. It also shows how the community organisations decided to use the money for different activities:

> Khema secretary: *Can we take this [financial] information away and analyse it further? We should have had this information before. It has a benefit. I feel that we are like a child growing up, when the child gets real information from an elder, then he knows he is growing. This has opened our eyes and given us a picture. It satisfies us about the work we did and helps us see the gaps. These astronomical figures! When we go back to the village it will be very difficult to explain, so we have to look into how we do it. It could cause problems and conflict. There are some suspicions of the community organisations; at times we have not been transparent.*

As ALPS is based on principles rather than on a blueprint of required actions and procedures, there will be a wide diversity of interpretations in each context. Where ActionAid funds community organisations, ALPS may take the form of critical reflection meetings including poor people, staff, and government representatives. Where a programme supports anti-poverty advocacy efforts by social movements, there may be joint action-learning activities. Inside ActionAid itself, it could be new transparent and reflective approaches to managing meetings or staff-appraisal systems. Each of these will lead to different ways of ensuring change happens after reflection and that the organisation is held to account.

Principles of ALPS

- *360 degrees accountability, emphasising accountability to the poor and marginalised, women, men, boys and girls;*
- *Commitment to gender equity;*
- *Application to the whole organisation at all levels, not just to the frontline;*
- *Relevance of information to both the people who supply and those who receive it;*
- *Feedback to the information provider on reaction to information;*
- *Learning rather than writing long reports;*
- *Linking financial expenditures to quality of actions;*
- *Critical reflection: learning from success and failure.*
  (ActionAid 2000:3)

Through aligning *principles* of rights with *procedures* for accountability, ALPS offers an elegant procedural solution to making rights real. In ALPS there are no centrally dictated rules, just principles. They echo the principles set out in ActionAid's overall strategy and the strategies of individual country offices, which staff use and refer to often, at many levels and in many contexts. In each case, people have the opportunity to discover the implications of these principles and decide upon actions that fit with local realities. ALPS offers no specific guidelines about how this should happen, as the essence is that it should be invented and reinvented to suit each relationship and context.

ALPS is coherent with what ActionAid is saying about the rights of the poor to have influence and the role of that influence in reducing poverty. It aligns the organisation's use of resources and its reporting procedures with its rhetoric. On the merits of being consistent, a

Buddhist monk once said: 'If you're going to over-eat then over-eat. If you're going to meditate then meditate. Just don't wobble!' Alignment of what an organisation believes in, what it does, and what works well in a given social, political, economic, or physical environment is a successful strategy. The Community Development Resource Association (CDRA) (1998) argues that the most important element in organisational capacity is 'a conceptual framework which reflects the organisation's understanding of the world' and procedures and resources come at the other end of the scale. Organisational effectiveness, it says, results from coherence between these elements. Coherence smoothes the progress of work and the organisation becomes easier for outsiders to understand and work with.

Of course, alignment can make an organisation more effective, but it doesn't always make it good. An overly coherent organisation is a tyranny. In the words of Harrison (1995:101):

> I am somewhat suspicious of the aligned organisation because of its potential for exploiting or 'taking over' organisation members, and because of its prevalence in war and the military. The aligned organisation is not noted for its sensitivity to nuances of communication from its environment, nor for its harmony and adaptation to the ecosystems of which it is a part. Rather it tends to be aggressive and 'daimonic' in its proclivity for expanding beyond all limits which are imposed from the outside. In other words, it appears to need checks and balances and these are not provided from within.

So ALPS is new, unpredictable, and risky. People can feel lost without guidelines, especially if they are familiar with a more directive style of management. Having no rules, the new accountability system could be susceptible to unscrupulous manipulation and corruption, so each office needs to negotiate which rules of accountability they need for all parties: the poor, the sponsors, and donors. Because of the diversity of interpretation, the relationships between the activities of each level or location will also need to be negotiated. It is quite possible for the result to be a rapid descent into misalignment, as the organisation splits into factions or regions, where particular leaders take advantage of the freedom to devise new methods of reporting and acting that take no account of the needs of others. There are other areas, too, where things could go wrong, depending on how the principles are interpreted and accounted for. For example, the issue of gender equity requires active attention – has ActionAid ensured a means of accountability for something that perhaps the poor themselves may not stress?

All these potential problems could easily lead to more bureaucracy than before. Avoiding the two extremes of excessive bureaucracy and excessive freedom is a question of balance, requiring attention to detail, negotiation, and resources. But since ALPS generates a degree of interest and commitment among a range of stakeholders previously excluded from information and decision making, it may liberate skills, resources, and trust that can be used to maintain the balance.

A selective history[2]

In the 1980s, Northern development agencies generally believed that development would be achieved through the delivery of projects. At the time, ActionAid's bureaucratic approach was aligned with this belief. As understanding of development changed in the 1990s, procedures continued to be bureaucratic and the organisation became misaligned. Looking back over a period of 13 years, it is possible to see how ActionAid moved through stages of misalignment and deepening contradiction before it reached its current state of realignment. The progression is visible – there was decreasing confidence in the way things were being done, attempts to change, failures, learning, and more failures, all of which eventually led to a new idea and a newly energised and coherent organisation.

A bureaucratic approach

In 1988, ActionAid managers, concluding that they needed systematic information to inform the appropriateness of their decisions and the effectiveness of their fundraising, introduced an organisation-wide system called the Annual Planning and Reporting System (APRS). At that time, the UK Board of Trustees was required to supervise all activities quite closely, through a group of international managers who directed the efforts of country directors and their staff in 26 countries. The Board used information provided to them through APRS to authorise programme decisions. This included deciding on even relatively local matters, such as the plan for moving into a new geographical area within an existing country programme. To show its progress towards its goals, the organisation used just three global indicators: levels of child mortality, nutritional status of children, and community literacy. Goals were enunciated in terms of significant benefits to children sponsored by ActionAid's supporters, and APRS aimed to provide information on these benefits.

Parallel to APRS were two other systems, the financial reporting system and sponsorship system. Finances were tracked according to budgets and expenditures and were not explicitly linked to impacts. Individuals in Europe would give money to sponsor individual children and their communities in the South, and would receive regular letters from that child. This would be accompanied by annual reports from the sponsorship department as to the overall impact and direction of the work, based on missions undertaken by the department's own staff from the UK.

APRS was part of the bureaucratic approach. It was an upward accountability system that requested regular and systematic information from the field up through the hierarchy to the Trustees. As a procedure, it was congruent with the organisation's sense of itself and its other systems. It reflected the organisation's belief that efficient delivery of basic services, such as health, education, and water, would bring about manifest reduction in the poverty of children and communities receiving these benefits. Donors could be informed by APRS of these improvements and would continue to finance the efforts. Managers could use the system to understand results and guide fieldworkers and middle managers to make appropriate adjustments, through introducing policies, rewarding beneficial practices, and chastising error.

ActionAid's programme-delivery system and its reporting system both helped to reinforce the style of relations between staff and partners and between staff and poor communities. This was a relationship of benefactor and beneficiary, in which the beneficiary's room for manoeuvre was limited to acceptance of the conditions imposed in exchange for the valuable services offered, peppered with some acts of resistance. In the late 1980s this was in alignment with the philosophy of service delivery, which was supported by a mechanistic approach to management. However, things changed.

A period of misalignment

A few years after the introduction of APRS, ActionAid began to change dramatically as thinking about development changed in the early 1990s. It was proposed that the role of a development NGO was to support the rights of the poor not only to services but also to decision making in development and governance. This idea suggests that being 'developed' means being influential and responsible (as well as having resources) and suggests that poor people have the right to be heard and responded to. In effect, poverty will be reduced if poor and marginalised people find ways to have significant influence over the forces that affect their lives.

An understanding of rights had begun to take a strong hold in the organisation in the early 1990s, when many field operations began using forms of participatory rural appraisal (PRA) in their work with communities. From this emerged a frustration: how was it that poor people were supposed to use PRA to take control of, or at least influence, decisions, while ActionAid made its plans and allocations thousands of miles away, based on its own ideas of poverty, accountability, sectors, and timeframes? Since the sponsors and other donors, on whose money everyone relied, were the ones to be kept happy first, the poor would never have real influence. While participatory approaches were contributing to narrowing the communication gap between frontline staff and the poor, they did not reverse the pecking order. The right of poor people and their organisations to influence decisions was hardly being met and a misalignment between the idea and the action began to emerge.

Between 1990 and 1998 ActionAid's budget more than doubled, from £20.2 million (US$28 million) to £49.6 million (US$70 million) as the organisation expanded to new countries, new activities, and took on more staff. It became increasingly unworkable for Trustees to absorb all the information and make decisions on small and essentially local matters. In 1995, moves were made towards decentralisation: a number of decisions were devolved to new regional directors in Latin America, Africa, and Asia and the bulk of power was devolved to country directors. In some cases, decentralisation allowed country directors to put their own ambitions before the organisation, and in others they moved so far ahead conceptually that they left their staff behind. Mostly, however, the effect was to liberate innovation and diversity.

Meanwhile the reporting and other procedures remained essentially the same, so staff found themselves spending time 'satisfying bureaucratic demands for reports with irrelevant information, while carrying out programme work based on the needs and situations on the ground' (ActionAid staff member, Mombasa ALPS Review Workshop, May 2001). In general there was a tendency for much to be written by fieldworkers that was not used, many decisions to be made by management that were avoided in the field, and much energy expended which could have been better spent. People said they felt they were being pulled in two directions. Participation was increasing stress and mendacity rather than creating influence among the poor and marginalised. Bureaucracy was winning.

One staff member describes the APRS annual reporting period as 'a time of no sleep' (Dharitri Pasternaik, ActionAid India). As much as three months in each year would be spent on reporting and budgeting. Because the processes took so long, reviews had no bearing on the plan for the following year. Planning would start in July; projects and programmes would be submitted for approval in September; in December they were approved; and in January work started. Meanwhile the annual reporting time was December. Annual reports and plans were very thick documents, yet a project officer would find herself also answering 'endless requests for information from headquarters, where managers expected their questions to be answered' (ActionAid staff member, Brazil).

Efforts to change

We have a culture in the institution for the demands of the higher level ... 25 emails a day are requests for information. We have a problem. It is not an ideological problem, not about the relationship of power between us and communities, it is a problem of the higher level ... it is an organisational problem, of time, hierarchy, demands for the quantity of information.
(ActionAid staff member, Brazil)

By 1998, ten years after APRS was introduced, demands for a new accountability system were reaching boiling point. A number of attempts to modify the system had already been tried, but to no avail. In 1997, for example, a rewrite of APRS tried to incorporate indicators on gender for the first time, but that just increased the burden on staff to include a section on gender as well as all the other requirements. It did not help to focus action on gender or clarify gender issues. The Trustees were still weighed down with paper, little of which helped them to a clear view of realities of the poor or progress towards eradicating poverty. An international meeting in Addis Ababa in early 1998 recommended urgent action. An internal team, suggesting that the entire mindset surrounding an accountability system needed to change, produced a new system. The ActionAid Accountability System (AAS) contained some of the principles that we see later in ALPS, but fundamentally broke no new ground because it was still a bureaucratic system for reporting up the hierarchy and controlling frontline workers, partners, and the poor. ActionAid had not yet found the point of leverage that it later found with downward accountability. AAS was never ratified.

Immediately a new effort was launched and a system called the Core Accountability System (ACAS) was drafted. It took almost a year to produce, with different working groups mapping the organisation, undertaking benchmarking with other agencies, holding workshops, and producing the plan. But meanwhile there were other changes underway that were to kill ACAS before it was even born.

A new strategy and vision

It was only after the organisation had thoroughly reviewed and transformed its strategic direction and faced up to the truth of how muddled and unprincipled some of its actions actually were, that it became clear that procedures had to change not incrementally, but radically and extensively.

In 1999, after a massive undertaking involving months of wide-ranging consultation right across the organisation, a global team created a new document, *Fighting Poverty Together*, outlining a compelling new vision and strategy (ActionAid 1999). It seems to have been a rallying point for the organisation, providing members with a sense of direction and a set of principles for their work. The new strategic direction was understood and agreed by the majority of staff, particularly those at the top. Those who didn't agree were forced out or left. Between 1998 and 2001 the leadership changed and many new managers were appointed. They brought with them new perspectives and innovation.

Box 3: Fighting Poverty Together

ActionAid's mission is to work with poor and marginalized people to eradicate poverty by overcoming the injustice and inequity that cause it.

Fighting Poverty Together is about change–about recognising and understanding change in the wider world, and committing ourselves to change in the way we go about eradicating poverty. Key among these changes is:

- *Recognising that poor people have a right to life's essentials, including food, water, healthcare, and education.*

- *Working increasingly in partnership with others in order to achieve greater impact.*

- *Promoting change internationally in favour or poor people–particularly in relation to private companies, government in the North, and international institutions.*

- *Improving gender equity to counteract discrimination against women and girls. (ActionAid 1999)*

The mission and goals had been transformed, decision making had shifted away from the centre, new people had joined, and after a number of attempts to adjust what had become entrenched procedures, the organisation's systems began to align.

'Taking Stock'

It is possible that there would have been no significant change at all without one further catalytic factor – an excoriating, devastating external review. *Taking Stock*, a global assessment of ActionAid commissioned by the director, was published in June 1999 some months after the new strategy was produced. Insiders have described it as brutal, but true. The external consultants called it a medical examination – looking at the organisation's state of health before it embarked on the difficult journey towards making real its new and powerful strategy, *Fighting Poverty Together*. They said that ActionAid's health was not up to the journey. They pointed out that its actions were contradictory to its rhetoric. Sophisticated analysis of the multi-faceted nature of poverty had led the organisation to think that it must attack on all fronts at once. There was a tendency to 'add on' rather than to make strategic choices. On the questions of control and accountability, the report described APRS as one that involved so much paper that it obscured and limited accountability and that the new revisions did not solve the problem. ActionAid, it said, was neither transparent, as claimed in its strategy, nor did it account to the poor and its partners. *Taking Stock* pointed out ActionAid's complacency. In the words of Antonella Mancini, an ActionAid staff member in London, 'We realised we had been patting ourselves on the back.' The organisation used the review to drive the organisation forward, rather than rejecting its shattering description of their cosy world.

Leadership

Over the years, executive directors had contributed by putting in place, one by one, the building blocks of change – Martin Griffiths in 1992 wrote the manifesto for the move from service delivery to rights-based work (ActionAid 1992); John Batten in 1995 began the process of decentralisation and reducing the demand for information at the top; and in 1998, Salil Shetty made it possible for staff to create *Fighting Poverty Together*. Then, despite demands to design a new reporting system immediately, Shetty postponed the decision for over a year, waiting for the right conditions. The new strategy needed to be understood by all, or any new procedures would simply be modified to serve the old direction. Perhaps, too, he was waiting for those who would contest the new approach to move on. It was a period of recriminations and angry departures.

In 2000, Rosalind David, leading the Impact Assessment Unit, an organisation-wide network, met Robert Chambers, an ActionAid trustee, and they brainstormed a system whose primary objective would be learning for all, based on transparent and reflective processes and involving only short reports. The idea of learning about rather than controlling change aligned with the ideas set forth in *Fighting Poverty Together*: poor people should decide themselves what successful development is and in so doing make success more likely. In March 2000, Colin Williams (Africa Director), Ephraim Dhlembeu (Africa Programme Coordinator), Lubna Ehsan (Gender Policy Analyst, Pakistan), Nigel Saxby Soffe (Director of Finance), Robert Chambers, and Rosalind David met in Harare and designed the Accountability, Learning and Planning System (ALPS). It called for improving strategy and programme quality by opening up to scrutiny and criticism by the poor, reducing reporting, and integrating finance with programmes.

Diffusing ALPS

What staff in London refer to as the 'roll-out' of ALPS started in mid-2000, but most country programmes only began to give it thought in early 2001. Programme staff as far apart as Orissa and Rio de Janeiro said ALPS was asking them to do what they were already doing: 'At last', one said, 'our organisation is catching up with us!' Another said, 'It is the operationalisation of transparency, of democracy.' During the first half of 2001, most ActionAid country offices began to adapt its principles to their local operation and culture. Those who had come up with the idea felt a sense of urgency. In response there was some resentment: it seemed like yet another change invented by the centre that was coming hard on the heels of last year's great idea. Many were critical of its top-down origins:

> *I particularly dislike the term 'rolling out', which implies pushing a way of doing things. It evokes, for me, the image of rolling out a carpet: a red carpet, for Important ActionAid who has the knowledge and power, rolling out over what's already there on the ground, and providing a direct route of passage to communities that rolls over the heads of partners.*
> (Andrea Cornwall, IDS, Learning and Support Team member)

> *We never get time to review and evaluate any change we make, before a new one takes its place. Anyway it takes time to implement new procedures, it requires so many people to understand them and adjust. We have to hold workshops and pilots, all at the same time as fulfilling so many other plans.*
> (ActionAid staff member, Ethiopia)

The reaction to ALPS from country directors and programme managers was mixed. The response was in general positive, particularly among those who had seen the effect that transparency had on their relations with partners and communities. Some said it was what they had been waiting for, a chance to get aligned and reduce the tension between the needs of the field and the sponsors, and for ActionAid to become an honest learning organisation. Others said that it was 'an anticlimax – it didn't go far enough'. Others looked at it and saw useful, if imperfect, accountability systems being swept away and replaced by noble ideas, which would be dangerously vulnerable to manipulation and abuse.

Inbuilt assumptions, based on years of experience of the working culture, meant that many people thought that the system was only for field programmes. Human resources managers, finance directors, sponsorship staff, and policy advocates, did not initially get involved even though the idea was to integrate organisational procedures with accountability and change. First steps across the inter-departmental divide were made by the Finance Department. Their accounts were needed for partners and communities to examine. For example in Kenya, the chief financial officer joined teams which sat with community organisations to review and reflect together. As he did this, he and his colleagues realised some of the problems their systems were causing to the realisation of rights and participation. Debate is now going on about to how and what to change in financial procedures to ensure continued careful accountability for funds, while allowing influence over budgets by the poor and their organisations. The sponsorship people were not sure that ALPS was going to serve their needs and did not join the teams. But, in Kenya, it wasn't long before they were called to come and account for a system of which local people were deeply suspicious.

Analysis

ALPS is creating a degree of energy and enthusiasm inside the organisation, which is unusual for a reporting system. Many who have begun to put it into practice are feeling relieved – it seems better than the old system, it is hardly bureaucratic, more creative, and in greater harmony with their beliefs. But this raises two questions: why did it take ActionAid so long to achieve a new system? And, can we relax now?

Why did it take so long?

In the development sector, there is considerable confusion as to what to believe in, what the purpose of development is, and therefore what to do. Over the decades development has aimed at spiritual salvation, technical improvement, economic growth, poverty alleviation, citizen empowerment, rights, good governance and more. It is hard to keep creating procedures for a mission that is so nebulous and changeable. Deciding the organisation's development stance takes frequent applications of time, resources, and skilful enquiry by a range of stakeholders. People may not be able to see things differently if wrapped up in their current vision of reality, so outsiders and new people are needed. Bringing in new people and 'letting go' of others, as ActionAid did, is a painful process that takes time and introduces a difficult dynamic. If people are not included, change exercises may produce just a repackaging of previous frameworks and systems. As ActionAid found with *Fighting Poverty Together*, taking time to understand and agree the organisation's purpose is the first step towards creating coherence and clarifying how associated systems need to change. But it took a great deal of time and energy to develop.

A workable change initiative needs to generate commitment among those who need to appropriate it. Only a few people will agitate for change when all is going well. As the ALPS case shows, decision makers may not even see the contradictions and misalignments that are growing beneath the surface. Yet, because change takes so long in a global organisation, it needs to be considered early if it is to come on-stream at the right moment. When work is running successfully, there are energy, confidence, and resources that could be used to consider how to maintain comparative advantage. Most organisations spend that energy in expansion, taking on new locations and new sectors, replicating successful models, and consolidating systems. Aid organisations are particularly prone to doing too much. The diversity of locations and sectors introduces complexity and the bureaucracy finds it hard to adapt. All too often, new mechanisms are imposed to try and keep control, so new procedures are applied and old ones are also retained, to cover all the eventualities. People spend more time satisfying the bureaucracy than thinking. Energy, confidence, and resources can then drain away, making it much more difficult to contemplate radical change. As we saw in the numerous attempts to revise APRS, changes may then be defensive and additive rather than transformative.

For many individuals, change is very risky, particularly for those at the bottom of a hierarchy. They may have spent years understanding the system and working out strategies for making the best of it. There are many frontline workers in ActionAid who worry a great deal about keeping their jobs, who are not in a position to change radically. Confident people, comfortable with power, will often be those to embrace change with most enthusiasm and they can become exasperated with the resistance they encounter. All through the system interests will inevitably conflict and powers will be used on all sides. Change in these circumstances can be unsystematic, slow, and difficult.

Now we've got a vision and a matching reporting system can we relax?

Development is about change and development organisations cannot operate without the ability to adapt to change. ActionAid was built as a bureaucracy. Gareth Morgan (1998) points out that while bureaucratic approaches to organisation work well when the environment is stable and predictable, the problem is that, like machines, bureaucracies are designed to achieve predetermined goals, and they have difficulty adapting to change. Over the last decade, ideas of development have changed radically and continue to do so. In response to this, ActionAid has introduced a system of accountability that commits it to responding to issues raised by the poor and their advocates, meaning that it is *committing* to being a changeable and diverse organisation.

ActionAid is more or less coherent at present, but it is a balancing act between diversity and unity, participation and leadership, principles and rules. As the internal and external environments continue to change, this balancing and alignment process will continue. But it may not be without its periods of inertia and frustration. While misalignment may generate confusion, alignment generates complacency and dominance. These negative states create dynamism between the two. Towards the extremes of either state, people can get anxious and exploitative or anxious and creative. When an organisation's systems get out of step with its environment, or if upon examining and updating its beliefs it fails to update its procedures across the board, the result will be tension. Anxiety generates an impulse for more supervision, more information, and more hesitation. This leads to conflict. This in turn creates frustration and, often, an energetic search for new understanding and new approaches. Frustration leads to a drive towards realignment. Ironically, a new alignment will produce success, which will lead in due course to complacency, conflict, and misalignment once again. Vaill (1996) uses an image of keeping a canoe upright in white water to describe how people and organisations have to keep alert and to learn in order to maintain balance and alignment in a fast-changing internal and external world.

Conclusion

Confusion and exasperation seem to play an essential energising part in the learning process. It took more than a decade of trying to change before ActionAid managed to put a congruent set of changes in motion. Procedures in particular often endure long after the conditions and aspirations for which they were created have moved on. Many people in many development organisations are aware that their procedures for dealing with partners, funders, and the poor are sending out messages that are contradictory to their own current thinking.

Organisational change is born of tension and succeeds best when it aims for alignment of purpose and action and attunement of the internal and external environment. It is impossible to avoid conflict, inertia, and confusion in this process; the only option is to make use of these forces by being aware of their potential. If a development organisation makes it possible for its staff and partners to thrive on change, then it will be, in essence, a learning organisation. Although the jury is still out on ALPS, as an organisation-wide system that tries to promote good relationships and critical awareness, it seems to have potential. In being transparent and listening properly to poor people and partners, the organisation is attempting to be honest, which helps it to learn and change. In being accountable to these same constituencies, ActionAid is trying to align its principles with its practice, which is an effective strategy. In combination, learning and effectiveness have a fair chance of coping with the forces of inertia and conflict that counter them. As such, ALPS may make it easier for staff and partners to work through and resolve more quickly the next stages of misalignment that they will inevitably encounter.

Notes

1   Founded in 1972, ActionAid is one of the UK's largest development agencies, with decentralised operations in over 30 countries across Asia, Africa, Latin America, and the Caribbean.

2   This, like all histories, is a selective one; it is based on a timeline made by a group of 22 people who met at Mombasa in May 2001. The meeting brought together programme and finance staff from ActionAid offices in Ethiopia, Gambia, India, Kenya, Latin America, and the UK. It was convened by the ALPS Learning and Support Team, a collaboration between the Participation Group at IDS and ActionAid's Impact Assessment Unit.

References

ActionAid (1992) *Moving Forward into the Nineties*, London: ActionAid.

ActionAid (1999) *Fighting Poverty Together: ActionAid's Strategy 1999–2003*, London: ActionAid.

ActionAid (2000) *Accountability Learning and Planning System,* London: ActionAid.

ActionAid (2001) *Notes to Accompany ALPS,* London: ActionAid.

Community Development Resource Association (CDRA) (1998) 'Crossroads: A Development Reading. The CDRA Annual Report 1997–1998', available at www.cdra.org.za (accessed July 2001).

Harrison, Roger (1995) *The Collected Papers of Roger Harrison,* San Francisco, CA: Jossey-Bass.

Morgan, Gareth (1998) *Images of Organization,* Thousand Oaks, CA: Sage.

Vaill, Peter B. (1996) *Learning as a Way of Being: Strategies for Survival in a World of Permanent White Water,* San Francisco, CA: Jossey-Bass.

This article was first published in Development in Practice *(12/3&4:424–435) in 2002.*

Heifer International:
growing a learning organisation

Thomas S. Dierolf, Rienzzie Kern,
Tim Ogborn, Mark Protti, and
Marvin Schwartz

Introduction

Heifer International (HI) has been applying participatory approaches to rural development for nearly 60 years. Although HI did not intentionally set out to be a learning organisation, this characteristic is inherent to its grassroots approach. HI uses livestock distribution as a means of building self-reliance and enabling smallholder farm families to make better decisions about their land and lives. Organisationally, HI focuses on building the capacity of its country programme offices and local NGO partners to work independently towards a unifying mission. An open structure allows HI to validate and incorporate the rich and diverse experience of its project holders and country offices into organisational planning and daily operations. By using a participatory approach, HI has evolved into an organisation with the capacity to facilitate and respond to change; one that co-evolves in its relationship with a dynamic and complex environment. This paper presents a review of HI's evolution as a mission-driven learning organisation, and the learning processes responsible for that evolution.

Flexibility is essential to HI's global operations across diverse and changing contexts. Flexibility without systemisation, however, tends to result in case-by-case decision making that restricts or even prohibits cross-fertilisation and organisational learning (Suzuki 1998:133–134). In the last ten years, HI has grown from an organisation operating in 24 countries with a budget of US$8.3 million to one with programme offices in 37 countries and an annual budget of nearly US$40 million. In this decade of exponential growth, the informal networking and shared decision making that had served HI well in the past were overwhelmed. Organisational learning that relied primarily upon the hierarchy of line management or project-donor relationships and informal (and quite limited) staff networks, was no longer adequate.

Recently, HI has been more intentionally creating an enabling, flexible environment for organisational learning. This stems mostly from an ongoing decentralisation process that was initiated partly as a response to a funding crisis in the late 1980s, with the rapid growth mentioned above providing an additional impulse. HI is complementing the decentralisation process by increasingly applying its own mission of empowerment and self-reliance to itself and its country programmes. The goal is to build the capacity of country programmes to operate more independently, while creating a more horizontal and interdependent relationship between them and the central office.

Even as HI develops or adopts mechanisms to institutionalise best practices, shared values, norms, and lessons learned, there is the danger that the systems themselves will limit learning in a kind of self-denying paradox (Argyris and Schön 1978). Without deliberately considering the learning process, organisations may limit field-level input only to contributions to outcomes set by the organisation.

This paper uses three case studies to highlight HI's effort to build systems that maintain flexibility and maximise organisational learning. An essential feature of the case studies is the attempt to cut across hierarchical lines by selecting and applying different learning mechanisms, including learning communities, councils, participatory planning, and best practice workshops. These systems create space for practitioners to share new insights and build mechanisms to integrate new learning. They ensure an appropriate means to share experience and understanding through genuine participation that directly informs implementation across the organisation.

Background to case studies

Context

HI used a series of USAID Matching Grants through the 1980s and early 1990s to strengthen capacity in several areas including training, gender, participatory development, and evaluation. As part of this process, HI developed the Cornerstones Model (CM) for community planning (Aaker and Shumaker 1996), which derives its name from HI's core values (referred to as Cornerstones). The model is a participatory community planning and management framework that incorporates several years of practitioner assessment of best practices in rural project planning. The CM is an iterative framework consisting of four components: situation definition; envisioning the future;

planning; and implementation, monitoring, and evaluation. Unique features of the CM are that it is values-based and vision-based, rather than the more conventional problem-based model. The model incorporates participants' collectively identified core values throughout the planning process.

In 1997, HI sought and obtained a three-and-a-half-year Matching Grant (MG) from USAID to help integrate the participatory process outlined in the CM throughout the organisation. The MG primarily addressed HI's challenge to enable its partner organisations to be more self-reliant and to promote sustainable community development. The grant funded three country offices (in Indonesia, Zimbabwe, and Bolivia) to implement the CM in depth and share their experience with the entire organisation.

HI initially developed the CM to build the capacity of rural, community-based organisations (CBOs) to plan and manage small-holder livestock projects. The first case study, provided by the Indonesia country programme staff, demonstrates how the CM was adapted and revised to fit their local context, and how this facilitated learning by local CBOs and NGOs and eventually throughout HI. Throughout the grant period, and driven by experiences in the pilot countries, the CM took on increasing importance as a strategic planning framework. HI eventually adopted the CM for strategic planning in all departments and country programmes, and this process is presented in the second case study. Heifer International's Agroecology Initiative, presented as the third case study, also used the CM.

Learning framework

The learning processes presented in the case studies highlight the participatory nature of the efforts, and the design and selection of appropriate mechanisms to feed back rapidly into the processes themselves. While each case study demonstrates a different approach to institutional learning, they all aim to create opportunities for practitioners to reflect on their practice in relation to others in the organisation. Examples include the creation of a learning community; the deliberate, iterative process of practice and reflection (*praxis*) used in the strategic planning process; and the organisation-wide, case-study approach employed by the Agroecology Initiative. By employing diverse learning mechanisms, HI is refining its capacity to determine those that work best in different circumstances. In this setting practitioners are both active learners and are committed to sharing and learning in ways that allow consensual understanding or new meaning to be reached. Furthermore, in this system the learning individual is reconceptualised as part of the learning organisation.

Each case study describes a deliberate, facilitated, two-way learning process rather than an incidental or unexpected one. The primary intention is to learn from participants who are then responsible for passing on the learning to others. In the first case study, the central office initiated CM planning, and then control of the process gradually shifted to country programme staff and project partners. This critical shift in ownership allowed the CM to take on a life of its own and, as will be demonstrated, to contribute directly to organisational learning. HI intends to promote sustainability and organisational learning through a similar transfer of ownership in both the strategic planning and the Agroecology Initiative. In the Indonesian and strategic planning case studies, the central office instituted learning mechanisms through programme design: each of the programmes began with training workshops, followed by field practice, and then by structured events to stimulate reflection. In the case of the Agroecology Initiative, the learning process began by gathering and interpreting lessons from the field.

The case studies show how learning from the field can directly inform organisation-wide practice. For example, the Indonesia experience led to the use of the CM as the foundations of the strategic planning process in HI, and the Agroecology Initiative brought values and perspectives from the field, which led to a renewed organisational commitment to environmental education and protection. This is especially evident in the planning and design of HI's proposed new Global Village project, an interactive public-education facility.

Finally, the case studies illustrate how the HI central office gradually changed from simply instigating and managing institutional initiatives to deliberately facilitating and systematising organisational learning.

Case 1: Heifer Project Indonesia country programme

This case study highlights Heifer Project Indonesia's (HPIndonesia's) proactive learning approach. The focus is on learning from applying the CM in NGOs and CBOs, because this eventually influenced HI-wide activities (discussed in the second case study). HPIndonesia is one of eight country offices in the Asia and South Pacific Area. Each office has between 10 and 15 staff who develop their programme based on the local situation. HPIndonesia came into being as a full-time country office in October 1997, coinciding with the start of the MG, and currently has eight staff.

The MG significantly influenced the new HPIndonesia country programme, providing a conducive environment for HPIndonesia to experiment with an atypical approach. A typical HI approach is to solicit, screen, and approve project proposals, with capacity building often carried out around these binding relationships. HPIndonesia, however, believes that capacity building for many small NGOs, especially in community planning, should precede a project's approval. Managing a project is considered to be only one organisational capacity. HPIndonesia made use of this freedom to be a proactive learner, building upon the basic training and guidance provided by HI through the MG. Finally, because it was a new country office, there was no resistance to change.

Indonesia context

Factors shaping the direction and evolution of the HPIndonesia programme include the newness of the country office, the MG, and the local political context and its effect on the situation of local NGOs.

Indonesia was under the dictatorship of Suharto for 32 years. The Asian economic crisis which began in mid-1997 helped lead to his demise in May 1998. Three decades of Suharto's rule, however, had drastically suppressed the development of civil society leaving the corrupt, centralised government as the main role model for development. Its approach was predominantly top down, paternalistic, and required little accountability. The repressive political situation also led NGOs to follow survival strategies. Especially on Sumatra, this involved staying small and silent to avoid attracting attention. Often, NGOs remained one-person shows, which would collapse if that individual left, and frequently they simply replicated much or part of the government's approach to development. CBOs were often temporary organisations formed to access resources provided by government programmes. With the change of government in 1998, more funds were made available, resulting in a flourishing of organisations created simply to access these funds. The government, however, mainly considered NGOs as contractors to carry out its own programmes.

HI chose Indonesia as one of the three MG country programmes primarily to see its impact on a new programme. The MG was designed with some input from the HPIndonesia country representative before the office developed a strategic plan. The grant authorised activities that focused on developing capacity in HPIndonesia and partner organisations involving the CM, learner-centred education, and gender.

Given this background, HPIndonesia decided to work through local NGOs to reach families in need and to have a sustainable impact. After visiting and surveying local NGOs in Sumatra, however, it saw a great need for organisational capacity building and that going straight into funding farm-level projects with local NGOs risked a high failure rate. As a new programme, HPIndonesia was aware that it too needed capacity building in many areas. The challenge was to determine the most appropriate approach to address these needs, and the solution was to form a Learning Community of local NGOs (discussed below).

Indonesia learning framework

Two concepts guide HPIndonesia's approach to learning. First, the programme focuses on the organisation, not the individual or the project, as the unit of development (Holloway 1997). HPIndonesia's experience is that many development and capacity-building efforts are not sustainable because they focus on either the individual or on projects. For example, individuals are trained in a particular issue, but do not share this within the organisation. Most activities are project-oriented, with little thought given to building organisational capacity to continue beyond the project. Thus, instead of immediately funding projects, programme staff sought means to help local NGOs build their capacity to facilitate community development. This mode of thinking is not typical of most development efforts with Sumatran NGOs. In fact, because of frustrations in trying to develop local NGO capacity, a large local support NGO (Bina Desa) switched, a few years ago, from working with local NGOs to training a cadre of individuals to work directly with CBOs.

HPIndonesia uses the onion model of an organisation, among others, to discuss organisational issues. An organisation, like an onion, grows from the inside outwards. At the heart of the organisation lie its values, identity, and worldview. Many local NGOs focus more on the outer layers, such as physical and financial resources, often neglecting the important core issues.

Second, HPIndonesia encourages organisations (including itself) and trainees to embark on an ongoing cycle of application and reflection (*praxis*) of new skills and knowledge in their own work, before they train others (e.g. in using the CM, or gender awareness and sensitivity). Often, NGO staff attend a training event and immediately want to train CBO members in the topic, without applying what they have learned to themselves first. This can result in rapidly decreasing depth and effectiveness of subsequent training activities.

Country programme development

In November 1997, a month after the full-time country office was established, HI held the first CM training in Indonesia for HI country programmes in the Asia and the South Pacific Area. This was the first CM training organised by the HI central office which was then promoting the CM to use with CBOs for livestock project development. HPIndonesia, being a new programme, did not have a ready testing ground of NGOs and CBOs to implement the model, but the country programme did need to develop a strategic plan, and programme staff quickly realised that the CM was an appropriate tool.

The CM framework itself is a learning process when it is participatory and iterative (i.e. not just done once in order to plan a project and apply for funding). HPIndonesia developed and reviewed its strategic plan every six months, eight times in total from March 1998 to November 2001. As a new country programme they considered this essential because the iterative nature of the CM allows for internal learning about the organisation itself. New and old staff gain and maintain ownership because it is a participatory process. Using the CM for strategic planning also allowed programme staff to learn more about the model before trying to train others in its use. For example, they developed methods on how to better integrate values into all aspects of the CM, and how to undertake issue identification and analysis that was tied directly to the vision.

Learning community

Instead of using projects to develop relationships with NGOs, programme staff formed a Learning Community (LC) of 20 local NGOs (including HI). NGOs could belong if they worked in community development in rural areas and if they formed and strengthened CBOs. In the LC, NGO staff practised using the CM in a membership organisation. This also allowed HPIndonesia to learn with other NGOs, which is essential for a new programme. At first, MG-supported activities (i.e. the CM, learner-centred education, and gender) mostly determined the agenda. Initially, HPIndonesia did not fund any of the LC members, except for one NGO that the HI central office had directly related to previously.

The LC uses training, follow-up workshops, mentoring, external consultants, study visits, a newsletter, and informal meetings to share experiences among members. The full LC also shares experiences in an Annual Learning Community Consultation (ALCC), and every two years an administrative group focuses on rules, membership, and strategic planning. Thus far, programme staff have applied and shared experiences about the CM, gender, learner-centred education, and organisational self-assessment.

The first item that HPIndonesia introduced at the first ALCC in late 1998 was the CM. HPIndonesia knew from experience that NGO staff would need to apply the basic CM training themselves, before working with CBOs. Thus, the LC used the CM to develop its strategic plan during the initial ALCC. The main benefits from this approach were that NGOs learned more about the CM by applying it in this way, and it quickly became a well-known term, although not fully understood initially.

NGOs only began to understand the CM better after a few of them tried using it with CBOs during 1999. NGOs are usually tempted to use the CM first with CBOs, without applying it in their own NGO (many see this as a way to get HPIndonesia project funding). HPIndonesia helped the NGOs facilitate these workshops, because there was not yet any experience within the LC of using the CM with CBOs. This learning was captured in a training module for CBO-level workshops, developed directly from these early workshops. A lot of interest was generated when NGOs shared their experiences during the third ALCC in 2000.

HPIndonesia also developed a series of *learning grants* to assist selected NGOs to use the CM with CBOs. These comprised *planning grants* (of US$80) to help NGOs try out the model with two CBOs initially; *mentoring grants* (US$25) which paid for travel and accommodation for an experienced NGO staff member to co-facilitate the CM with one CBO partner of another NGO; and *pilot grants* (of US$425), one per NGO, to support a small livestock-based activity arising from a planning grant. Eleven NGOs eventually conducted workshops with over 20 CBOs, and some of this learning was incorporated into the training module (now called the 'CM Toolkit for CBOs'). The NGOs shared this field experience during the fourth ALCC in October 2001.

Many of the NGOs have developed a deeper understanding of the CM through using it with CBOs. This has directly resulted in four NGOs requesting HPIndonesia staff to help them use it for their own strategic planning. The experience of using the CM for strategic planning in these NGOs and in HPIndonesia has been compiled into the 'Cornerstones Model Toolkit for NGO Strategic Planning', reflecting our own improved understanding of how NGOs can use the CM for this purpose.

Short-term effects

The LC will conduct an evaluation in two years' time to measure the effects on their own organisations and, more importantly, what effect it has had on CBOs. Currently, HPIndonesia has only some short-term observations to share.

There are noticeable attitudinal changes among the LC members. A combination of learning approaches, mentioned above, have influenced most members to direct their focus away from the outer to the inner layers of the onion (strategic planning, gender, governance, fundraising strategies, etc.). By continually stressing that the LC is for learning at an organisational level, NGOs have also moved from seeing HPIndonesia simply as a potential project funder, to being also a learning partner. They have shifted from thinking that they had to train CBOs in every topic they learned about, to focusing on applying these topics to themselves as well, if not first. As one female NGO director said in closing the fourth ALCC: ' ... before, we thought gender was only for others, now we realise that it is also for ourselves'.

At the fourth ALCC, in addition to five NGOs already using the CM, 13 NGOs planned to use it to develop a strategic plan in 2002. Fourteen NGOs have already used the CM with over 70 CBOs. Recognising that the CM is an iterative process, these NGOs plan to continue using it in the future.

To ensure the LC was based on members' needs, rather than on what the MG supported, the LC began an Organisational Capacity Assessment (OCA) in March 2001, which led to the formulation of an OCA tool. This process was facilitated by PACT-Indonesia, which visited each of the 16 participating NGOs to help them carry out a confidential self-assessment using the OCA tool. Each organisation then developed an action plan that it could execute by itself. At the fourth ALCC, each NGO shared their unmet needs to attain a vision of a high-capacity NGO. In addition to following up on the CM and gender, new LC learning topics (the agenda is no longer driven by HPIndonesia) include fundraising strategies, governance, and documentation and reporting systems. Each learning topic focuses on the innermost parts of the onion model, indicating that LC members realise the importance of the inner layers in developing sustainable, effective organisations.

Intra-HI learning

HPIndonesia's use and adoption of the CM provided the foundation for an HI-wide movement in CM-based strategic planning.

HPIndonesia realised that the initial strategic planning outline provided was not congruent with using the CM. Indeed, HI had developed the strategic plan outline before the CM and did not immediately integrate the two methods. HPIndonesia suggested that HI modify the strategic planning outline to fit the CM results. It also encouraged the central office to use the CM internally, instead of simply teaching others how to use it. Programme staff shared their experiences in using the CM and some of the techniques they developed in internal working papers and at a CM reflection workshop held in Bolivia in 2000. A booklet highlighting the learning from the Bolivia workshop, including an outline of how HPIndonesia uses the CM for strategic planning, was distributed throughout HI. An HPIndonesia staff member shared their experience with the CM by co-facilitating the HI international training workshop on strategic planning, discussed in the next case study.

Case 2: HI strategic planning

Strategic planning context

HI initiated strategic planning processes in the early 1990s by adapting a model developed in the banking industry. The central office disseminated the model to country programmes with little or no training in its use, and incorporated only minimal feedback into its design. Consequently, most strategic plans submitted to the central office looked alike, were of short duration, and were more operational than strategic. They fell short of portraying the unique characteristics and needs of each country programme due to the strict adherence to a predefined structure.

Several factors led HI to adopt the CM for strategic planning throughout the organisation. These include the parallel development of the CM for community planning and its implementation throughout the organisation for use with partner organisations, the experience of the Indonesia programme in applying the CM for its own strategic planning, dissatisfaction with the existing planning model, and HI's move towards applying to itself the practices and philosophy that it applies in its projects and with its partners. The CM-based strategic planning process was field tested during 2000 in South Africa and Nepal and with the Asia and South Pacific Area team. Learning from these initial trials led to its further refinement and the initiation of the process described below.

Participatory methods for strategic planning demand greater capacity. HI soon realised that flying staff out from the central office to conduct strategic planning workshops around the world was not feasible. This resulted in the recruitment of field-based Planning, Evaluation, and Training Coordinators (PETs) and the development of a resource manual with guidelines and a design for a strategic planning workshop.

Strategic planning learning framework

Figure 1 depicts the model that HI used to learn from the strategic planning initiative. The learning took place in four phases: training on the use of the resource manual; testing; feedback; and revision. Beyond these are three virtual phases that take place in the context of organisation-wide learning and reflection: the use of the resource manual, identification and documentation of best practices, and revisions to the resource manual to incorporate best practice.

The first phase was an international training workshop for the PETs in December 2000 to introduce the resource manual and workshop design for strategic planning. The workshop used the methodology

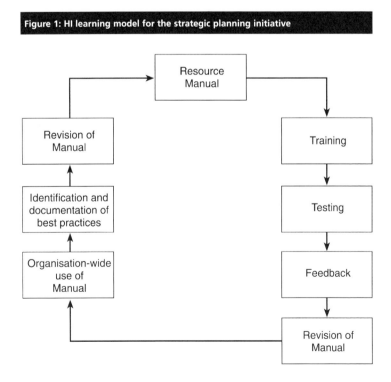

Figure 1: HI learning model for the strategic planning initiative

developed for the strategic planning workshops to train the participants in its use. At the end of each workshop session, participants commented on what had gone well and suggested improvements. The PETs received a revised version of the manual shortly after the workshop.

In the second phase, the PETs and central office staff jointly tested the resource manual and the workshop design in six countries over six months. The PETs were in a good position to capture and articulate the learning from their field-based workshops. After they facilitated workshops, they e-mailed comments and feedback to all participants. This gave everyone the opportunity to benefit immediately from the experiences of fellow facilitators.

The third phase occurred in July 2001, when staff who had tested the resource manual met for a second workshop, capturing the experience of the test phase to further refine the manual. The greatest benefit of this meeting was the opportunity to discover the diversity of understanding and application of strategic planning and terminology in different contexts.

The final phase is the incorporation into the resource manual of feedback obtained during the second workshop and lessons learned from the test phase.

Key lessons from the field-based learning process

The PETs provided and enhanced the opportunity for learning. With their multi-country responsibilities, they capture learning from across the organisation. The use of *praxis*, as in Indonesia, was a critical part of the learning process. The HI Planning and Evaluation Team created and used learning space. The ongoing dialogue and documentation of lessons ensured that the learning became part of the institutional memory.

International workshops involving skilled staff from all areas of the organisation provided the learning space necessary for intra-institutional learning to take place. The documentation and rapid dissemination of the workshop outcomes through the flexible strategic planning resource manual institutionalises this learning and makes it available throughout the organisation very quickly. Working across several country programmes, PET Coordinators learn from diversity and bring that learning back to the learning space facilitated by central office staff.

Having benefited from this learning model, HI will need to extend it to other initiatives. The next step will be to use the same model for training facilitators to conduct Project Self Reviews and Programme

Reviews during 2002. Here again, the PET Coordinators have a critical role in the learning process. Eventually, they will build capacity in country programmes to enhance intra-country programme learning. This will help test area- and country-specific methodologies, and learning from the area and country levels will be incorporated into the overall learning of HI.

Another important space for learning will be annual PET meetings. These will be forums for a more active exchange of learning, for identifying areas that have potential for organisational learning, and for presenting unique situations from the field that can lead to organisation-wide learning.

Case 3: HI's Agroecology Initiative

Agroecology context

As part of its continuing efforts to improve its programmes, HI identified 2000 as its 'Year of the Environment'. In previous years, the choice of priorities had focused on, for example, gender and other areas of HI's programme. HI established an Agroecology Initiative to coordinate a range of new and existing programme activities and a new strategic emphasis. A member of the Organisational Development Department (ODD) coordinated the process, although the driving force came from the International Programmes Department. The specific focus on improving the environment is not new for HI – the concepts behind it reflect the organisation's core mission and values. Although these values have long been incorporated into its programmes, this has been achieved without a strong overarching strategy. Driving the Agroecology Initiative were the primary impact of agroecology project activity on HI country programmes, and a desire to learn from some of the best experiences from both within and outside HI to improve its programmes. The development of a field-driven initiative was highly appropriate for the new CM planning model that HI had been adopting.

The Agroecology Initiative built on HI's work with smallholder and subsistence farmers to improve agroecological practices that protect and enhance natural resources. The Initiative also included a significant educational element to raise public awareness of the values and opportunities for multiple aspects of sustainable agriculture. The new resources and focused alignment with ecological objectives helped the Initiative to integrate into all HI programmes.

HI formally launched the Agroecology Initiative in 2000 with financial support from the Sandy River Charitable Foundation, a funder that had previously established another new initiative in the area of disaster relief. The Sandy River funds specifically enabled the HI learning process, providing for a diverse range of research and documentation throughout the year. A consultant led the self-assessment, which included:

- 14 case studies and papers prepared on global Best Practices Models project activity;
- regional meetings in Tanzania, China, and Romania on sustainable agriculture and ecology;
- presentations to HI Board and staff on the findings of the case studies and the consultancy;
- a database summarising agroecological and environmental aspects of nearly 550 HI projects in more than 50 countries;
- an agroecology intranet site and listserve for international communication;
- a CD-ROM entitled 'Sustaining Life on Earth' used to disseminate the information collected;
- an agroecology video;
- pages dedicated to agroecology in the HI magazine *World Ark*.

A Global Roundtable held in Ecuador culminated a year of coordinated, organisation-wide learning. The meeting focused on sharing information and on developing the HI Agroecology Strategy. The 40 participants included HI staff and representatives of organisations collaborating in ecological and conservation activities covering diverse projects such as aquaculture and water quality monitoring in the Philippines, habitat preservation in the Amazonian rainforest, and sustainable agricultural practices (hillside terracing) as a defence against hurricane damage in Honduras. The Roundtable featured case studies from numerous HI country programmes, field trips to community practitioner sites, a cultural programme, and also addressed the spiritual dimensions of conservation work through a keynote speaker, Calvin DeWitt of the Au Sable Institute.

The Roundtable was a milestone experience for participants, most of whom are career professionals already dedicated to the issues. The success of the Roundtable, therefore, was its effectiveness in refocusing an existing and comprehensive global strategy to the agroecology framework. A new sense of mission, the idea that their work was indeed *saving the earth*, inspired the participants. The challenge then remained to disseminate this new vision to a global audience and gain the participation of all sections of HI for its full integration. An adaptation of the CM was the basis for the design of the Roundtable and contributed greatly to its success.

Agroecology learning framework

The learning framework followed by the Agroecology Initiative was composed of three main phases. The first captured existing experience and learning across the organisation. The second consisted in sharing that information during the Roundtable, and the development of an institutional strategy for agroecology. The third phase is the coordination and implementation of that strategy through the setting up of an Agroecology Council.

An essential aspect of the new learning framework for the Agroecology Initiative was its alignment with traditional HI programmes. All HI projects already include significant agroecology activities and they all address sustainable practices and natural resource management – HI has been doing this work for nearly 60 years. However, the new framework did more than just validate an existing strategy. It identified essential cross-organisational areas of planning, communication, and task assignment. It created a space for intra-organisational learning, and contributed to a significant area of institutional memory, which had previously not received much attention. The framework also revealed that an organisation-wide initiative required a new process of working together.

Participants at the Roundtable specifically identified the need for a learning strategy that allowed maximum interpretation from the field and minimal imposition of new organisational policy or structure from HI central office. The challenge was to establish a mechanism to achieve full representation and to facilitate cross-institutional learning, but which avoided creating new layers of administrative review and accountability. As an appropriate implementation technique the Agroecology Initiative selected the same process of decentralisation that HI was implementing to maintain its recent growth and expansion.

An Agroecology Council was established and has responsibility for the development of the Initiative's core strategy. Members of the nine-person Council included representatives from all HI divisions, including country programme directors, fundraisers, educators, and a Board member. The only new position assigned to the Initiative was a Programme Assistant. The Council's mission was to provide leadership for the Initiative and to recommend a strategy that used as many existing systems as possible in new and innovative ways. The matrix management structure of the Council was itself a learning process. The representation process demanded that all Council members be fully informed of their own division's strategic plans and that each member serve as an effective liaison to present Council and field decisions to central office staff.

Through the Council, the Agroecology Initiative has offered HI a unique opportunity to transform and adapt itself. In late 2001, the Council developed a strategic plan that assigned all components of the Initiative to appropriate divisions within HI, thereby ensuring its full integration.

The learning strategy here is one of a central goal with multiple objectives and activities. The Agroecology Initiative has established organisational goals and provided guidance on how to achieve them. However, their achievement is dependent on the integration of agroecology objectives at departmental levels so that agroecology does not become a separate activity, but is integrated into the regular planning mechanisms of HI. Examples of activities that are a consequence of this process are capacity building of country programme staff, new indicators for monitoring and evaluation systems, fundraising, building strategic alliances, and public policy. Current public policy issues include genetically modified food and the influence of transnational agricultural corporations.

Just as agroecology promotes diversity of species and habitat, so the HI strategy encourages a diversity of responses. As agroecology promotes sustainability and holistic systems, the HI strategy aims for an ongoing and comprehensive structure. Furthermore, it reflects the increasing decentralisation of HI, because field experiences and feedback define and drive the strategy. The impact is seen both in the field and in administration. The lessons are learned on multiple levels and will certainly influence the development of future thematic initiatives within HI.

Conclusions

The establishment of diverse learning mechanisms within HI has enabled initiatives emerging from both the central office and the field to have a major positive impact on HI's operations. The different learning mechanisms described here show how it has been possible for a growing organisation to learn from its experience and consequently reorient its processes. Critical to this success is the lack of central control over the content of these processes, even when the central office provided the resources to facilitate them.

Even when activities were initiated by the central office (such as in the Indonesia and Agroecology cases), the freedom provided to field staff to orient those initiatives to their own needs was critical to their success. In the Indonesia case, the HI central office provided a new country programme with the basic tools of the CM. HPIndonesia applied this and other basic tools provided by HI to develop and strengthen its own programme. This internal experience was then used to begin a capacity-building process with local NGOs and CBOs through the LC, which in turn further strengthened HPIndonesia's own capacity. Finally, they were able to pass back their experience in using the CM for strategic planning to the HI central office.

In the strategic planning case, the central office refined and promulgated an idea primarily promoted by the HPIndonesia country office. HI shared this idea with country programmes throughout the world, rather than having it remain in one field office. The learning process used with the strategic planning methodology led to rapid and effective institutional learning. It was possible to update and adapt the methodology within a period of six months from experience gained in five continents. The use of the PETs and the learning that they harnessed resulted in establishing centres of excellence. Without the PETs, the learning would have been a much slower and less rich process, as central office staff would not have been able to benefit from such a broad and diverse set of experiences.

In addition, although facilitators from the central or country programme offices initiated and facilitated the processes, responsibility and control gradually shifted, or is in the process of shifting, to the programme participants. This is especially evident in the Agroecology Initiative where a participatory Agroecology Council emerged to move the process forward and facilitate communication between the field and administration. In Indonesia, the LC is now determining the learning agenda, which was initially led by HPIndonesia. Country programmes, assisted by the newly-created PET Coordinators, are assuming greater responsibility for, and control over, the strategic planning process.

The HI experience demonstrates a potential role for the central office as initiators and facilitators of learning processes. The challenge is knowing how and when to step back so that the processes gain a life of their own. HI continues to strive to institutionalise learning systems without having the systems themselves limit the process.

Future directions at HI

The need to develop new ways of learning organisationally will continue to be a focus at HI. The ongoing challenge will be to adopt learning approaches that allow the organisation to respond to the diversity and complexity of rural development without restricting flexibility. The vision of HI in the future, consisting of a network of interdependent members, requires the development and integration of learning processes that will match the fluid nature and diverse needs of its constituency.

The ODD, developed as a consequence of the MGs mentioned above, is devoted to organisation-wide capacity building. The ODD develops and facilitates training and learning programmes in areas deemed critical to the organisation and now has specialist teams in the areas of planning and evaluation, training, gender, governance, and fundraising training. The ODD has the specific role of stimulating the creation of learning spaces across the whole organisation without controlling them. As a unit, the ODD is learning from the processes already in place, and will use its experience to help HI to move towards its vision of itself in the future. An essential component of this organisational role is for the ODD, together with its constituency, to reflect continually on its practice and to be aware of the inherent tendency for organisational systems to restrict learning. The commitment of significant resources in this area is a clear demonstration of HI's dedication to institutional learning.

Organisational learning systems must institutionalise ways of creating enabling space. They must allow practitioners to explore their own actions and ways of knowing in relation to those of others in the organisation. Thus, practitioners must not only be active learners, they must also be committed to sharing and learning in ways that allow consensual understanding or new meaning to be reached. The critical component of an effective learning organisation is to validate and prioritise these fresh insights and integrate them into, or allow them to transform, organisational practice. In this sense, the learning organisation and the learning individual are the same.

References

Aaker, J. and J. Shumaker (1996) *Cornerstones Model*, Little Rock, AK: Heifer Project International.

Argyris, C. and D. Schön (1978) *Organizational Learning*, San Francisco, CA: Jossey-Bass.

Holloway, R. (1997) *The Organization, Not the Project, as the Unit of Development*, Baltimore, MD: Johns Hopkins University.

Suzuki, N. (1998) *Inside NGOs: Managing Conflicts between Headquarters and the Field Offices in Non-governmental Organisations*, London: IT Publications.

This article was first published in Development in Practice *(12/3&4:436–448) in 2002.*

'New learning in old organisations':
children's participation in a school-based nutrition project in western Kenya

Charles Ogoye-Ndegwa, Domnic Abudho, and Jens Aagaard-Hansen

Introduction

Chambers (1983, 1997) has given numerous examples of the ways in which underprivileged segments of populations worldwide can be empowered to take an active part in the development of their own communities. Among children, the Child-to-Child Approach (CtC) has been implemented in several countries around the world, representing an innovative and action-oriented way of encouraging the active participation of children in the dissemination of information on health-related issues. In this approach, children are at centre stage, either through caring for their younger brothers and sisters or through working among children in their own age groups to improve health practices in the school, the home, and the community. In a worldwide network of over 60 countries, CtC focuses on health education and primary healthcare (Bailey *et al.* 1992). However, although many CtC interventions have been implemented throughout the world, few researchers have made any critical studies. Pridmore (1997) studied a CtC programme in Botswana and Onyango-Ouma (2001) conducted extensive research within our study area in western Kenya on the potential of children as health-change agents based on a CtC intervention. Meinert (2001) explored the interaction between schooling and children's roles as resource people in their homesteads in eastern Uganda.

Recently, scholars have focused on children's 'action competence' as a critical element in health education in particular and life skills in general (Jensen and Schnack 1994a). The concept of 'action competence' builds on the premise that children can influence their surroundings, thereby partly changing their own lives, and partly influencing their community in a positive direction. This potential can be realised by empowering children to take charge of their own health and that of the entire community (Wals 1994). (For a more theoretical approach to the agency of children, see James *et al.* (1998)).

In 2000 it was estimated that sub-clinical vitamin A deficiency (serum retinol <0.70 μmol/l) affected up to 250 million pre-school children, and iron deficiency and its anaemia affected more than 3.5 billion (all age groups) in the world (Sub-Committee on Nutrition 2000:v). This is in accordance with research findings in western Kenya, where 62 per cent of pre-school children and 24 per cent of school children were found to have sub-clinical vitamin A deficiency (Friis *et al.* 1997).[1]

Measures such as diet diversification, supplementation, and fortification are needed to alleviate these severe problems, although 'strategies to increase the income of the poor are the most sustainable means of improving the household food security' (Sub-Committee on Nutrition 1997:84–87). As a measure towards increasing the amount of micronutrient-rich foods, Leemon and Samman (1998:24) recommend the application of the food-based systems approach, which involves 'the development of a community garden and small household plots, containing many indigenous plant species, as a practical and a sustainable solution'. They go on to argue that 'a food system is dynamic and has the potential to influence a community's consumption of micronutrient-rich foods. This intervention is more economically and culturally feasible, and is a more sustainable way of improving micronutrient status' (*ibid.*:8). The Committee on Micronutrient Deficiencies (1998) states that: 'experience to date has shown that "how" an intervention is implemented may be as important, or in some cases more important, than "what" is implemented'.[2]

The action-research project[3] reported here has a two-fold purpose: to explore ways of empowering Kenyan primary school pupils in order to make them change agents for community development and thereby transform traditional primary schools into active resource centres for community change; and to (re-)introduce locally available, traditional vegetables[4] in teaching about agriculture at the primary school level with a view to improving the food and nutrition security in a rural community in Kenya. The article will focus on the processes of the first part of the project since the nutritional aspects are described elsewhere (Ogoye-Ndegwa and Aagaard-Hansen forthcoming).

Materials and methods

Study area

The study was conducted in Bondo District, Nyanza Province in western Kenya, in a Luo community along the shores of Lake Victoria. The main rainfall season is between February and June, when the land is cultivated, and there is usually a shorter period of rain in October and November. The Lake Victoria basin receives an average annual rainfall of 750–1000mm. The area experiences temperatures varying between 14 and 30°C and the altitude is between 1140 and 1300m. The landscape is characterised by dispersed homesteads intersected by bush and the soil is mostly black cotton soil with rocky areas in between.

Study population

The Luo are among the largest ethnic groups in Kenya – estimated to number about three million. The main occupation of the Luo is subsistence farming, with maize, sorghum, millet, and cassava as the staple crops. The Luo, who were originally predominantly pastoralists, still keep a substantial number of goats, cows, and poultry, and sheep and donkeys are also common. In addition, petty trade, fishing, and remittances from migrant workers supplement the household economy. The population is far from prosperous and is consequently vulnerable to drought periods and decline in agricultural produce and cash income. The majority belongs either to the Anglican Church of Kenya, the Roman Catholic Church, or the Seventh Day Adventists, although there are several smaller sects as well.

Educational system

All children in Kenya are supposed to go to primary school for eight years (plus an optional nursery class). Teachers' salaries are paid by the government, but all other expenses (buildings, desks, uniforms, chalk, books, etc.) are paid for by the parents. Although the fees are moderate from a Northern perspective (approximately US$10 per annum), the cost still means that some children don't attend school.

Teaching methods are traditional: 'Classroom activities are ritualistic and cyclical following a laid out timetable ... Teaching methods are mostly didactic with pupils on the receiving end and the knowledge hierarchy is quite clear' (Onyango-Ouma 2001:132). Discipline is strict: ' ... the first thing that strikes a visitor in rural primary schools is the rate at which teachers use corporal punishment as a mode of punishment for various mistakes. Pupils in my study schools got corporal punishment for such offences as not running when summoned by a teacher, coming to school late, failure to answer a question during a lesson' (Onyango-Ouma 2001:28).

Methods of data collection

The researchers conducted semi-structured interviews and 'field walks' with 27 key informants, elderly people who knew about traditional vegetables. Together with input from the research pupils, these data formed the basis for the compilation of an inventory of traditional vegetables.

During the time when the school gardens were tended, pupils wrote so-called 'plot diaries'. They were provided with books and pens, and trained field assistants (secondary school leavers) later translated what they had recorded in the local language (*Dholuo*) into English. The research pupils recorded data for each traditional vegetable on areas such as the length of time each vegetable takes to germinate, resistance to infections, drought resilience, maturation duration, and difficulties in general care (e.g. pruning and weeding).

Over a two-week period, field assistants recorded dietary intake among 24 pupils based on structured question guides. The exercise was conducted during a rainy month (May 1999) as well as during the dry season (March 2000). The children were purposively selected from Classes 4 to 7 in the school ensuring equal distribution in terms of gender, age, and geography. Data were collected daily based on 24-hour recall.

Based on his own observation, the teacher made research notes on the pupils' competencies and learning abilities with regard to classroom learning of agriculture and practical work in the school garden as well as in participatory research.

In addition, market surveillance was conducted, involving repeated visits to markets within and around the community where traditional vegetables are for sale. The markets were monitored during a full year, covering both the wet and the dry seasons. Interviews were also conducted with hawkers who went from house to house selling traditional vegetables. During two sessions of community interaction ('vegetable fairs'), data were collected regarding palatability of the vegetables and various methods of preparation.

Sequence of events

The study involved the researchers, the local primary school, and the community as part of a stepwise action research-cum-development project. We believe that each of these steps was essential for the success of the project.

Initial planning

The idea was originally conceived by the researchers, who at that time had already been conducting research in the community for three years. Thus, a close link between the researchers and the community had already been established and a relatively reliable picture of community needs as well as its development potential had been identified. The researchers approached the school administration of the local Mbeka Primary School (MPS) explaining the objectives and scope of the study. The project was endorsed and the headmaster appointed a teacher (based on his keen interest in agriculture) who has subsequently participated in the project planning and implementation.[5] Then, informed consent was sought from the Parents and Teachers Association (PTA) committee, which also endorsed the project. Furthermore, the local educational authorities at division and district level were kept informed and strongly supported the project throughout. The role of the headmaster as a bridge to the community in societies where the adherence to formal rules is valued should not be underestimated. In this case, the headmaster showed a lot of personal interest and allowed the Class 6 pupils to be exempted from normal school duties in order to give them time to concentrate on their school gardens.

Teacher training

On two different occasions the project teacher was trained on horticulture farming at 'Care for the Earth' (CftE), a local agricultural self-help project carrying out training and consultancy on organic farming systems involving the management and conservation of natural resources. The overall objective of CftE is to increase food-production capabilities, especially among low-income, small-scale farmers in a bid to reduce nutrition-related diseases among children. The training covered mainly courses on horticulture, traditional vegetables, inter-cropping, manure production, and poultry, but specific topics such as soil management, seed harvesting, and storage, as well as how to apply manure using locally available materials, were also taught.[6] An important topic was pest behaviour and pest management using naturally available, easily obtained, and affordable plant leaves and bark. Plants usually used as pest sprays are pounded and mixed in water. Given the high costs of commercial pesticides, these techniques reduce costs greatly.

The teacher was not given any formal training on participatory teaching methods. Nevertheless, the school-based horticulture activities developed in a mode of dialogue between the teacher and the pupils. Primarily we found that the practical mode of teaching gave the teacher a chance to realise the pupils' potential. Whether there was an element of the teacher's personality, the influence of the researchers, or a combination of the two, it is difficult to say. However, with hindsight we realise that this is a crucial element both in selecting and training the teachers. Apart from the project's support for the training (including payment of a per diem during the course), no financial incentives were given. However, the training (for which a certificate was provided) served as a strong incentive in its own right, partly because of the new knowledge gained and partly because it was a rare chance for in-service training, which can facilitate career development.

Recruitment of children

According to the Kenyan Primary School syllabus, agriculture is taught as a subject in grades 4 to 8.[7] Class 6 was chosen as the research class because this is the stage where children have already been exposed to most horticulture-related topics. The selection of pupils, who are referred to as 'the research pupils', was based on their previous year's examination performance, particularly in agriculture, and on their outspokenness, inquisitiveness, and willingness and ability to record research data neatly. Based on information about the project, the children were then asked whether they would like to participate.[8]

The 'research pupils' were responsible for part of the data collection such as the daily recordings in each respective plot and also market surveillance. This selection has been repeated at the start of each school year when the new Class 6 takes over the project. The number of research pupils varied from 14 (in 1998) to 18 (in 1999), with an equal balance of boys and girls. However, there was no sharp distinction between participants and non-participants. This was partly because all the Class 6 pupils were teaching other classes within MPS and beyond, and partly because, as the project developed over the years, new pupils reached Class 6 while those going on to Classes 7 and 8 still had the skills and some even expressed nostalgia about the fact that new pupils had taken centre stage.[9]

Data collection

Initially, a list of all the 72 locally available, traditional vegetables was constructed. Market surveillance was initiated and continued for more than a year (1999–2000). Data on dietary intake recall based on structured interviews were collected during two sessions. In addition the various school-based activities and the community-dissemination process have been documented throughout.

Agriculture teaching and school gardening

According to the way agriculture teaching in Kenyan primary schools is conceived, there should be a practical as well as a theoretical element. In real life, however, the teaching is mostly theory- and classroom-based. Based on the existing inventory of traditional vegetables derived from interviews with key informants, a selection of traditional vegetables was made by the pupils in collaboration with the teachers and the researchers. The school garden was prepared and fenced and compost manure was prepared using locally available materials. The garden was divided into several small plots in which different vegetables were cultivated. Some pupils were assigned to each plot, and a research pupil made daily records of all the activities in that particular plot on behalf of the other pupils. After the training in methods for organic horticulture farming at 'Care for the Earth', the agriculture teacher was a facilitator for the Class 6 pupils. Among the most important points was the introduction of the new methods for production of manure based on locally available materials. During the four years, the horticultural activities have been carried out intermittently, depending on periods of school holidays and lack of rainfall. The project provided the stationery and at a later stage a few farm implements, and once a year it facilitated the Class 6 pupils' visit to CftE.

Community involvement

Two 'vegetable fairs' (1998 and 1999) were organised in which the Class 6 pupils acted as hosts to the other pupils from MPS, the teachers, parents, PTA committee members, as well as teachers' and pupils' representatives from neighbouring schools, members of the community, area educational officers, and other local opinion leaders. These were days in which the vegetables were cooked and eaten in the school. The fairs served a double purpose: to give feedback to the community and to collect more data. In terms of community feedback, visitors were encouraged to change their own attitudes towards increased consumption, while the fairs provided opportunities to collect additional information on palatability ranking and how best to cook specific traditional vegetables. In addition to the fairs, two community meetings were held in 1999 and 2000, to which about 70 key people were invited in order to tell them about the study findings and give feedback.

During the school year 2000,[10] Class 6 was divided into two streams, which meant that an additional teacher was introduced to the project. The emphasis is now on seed production and dissemination of knowledge to the community. In this process, the research project has chosen the establishment of home-based gardens with traditional vegetables as an indicator of community dissemination, irrespective of whether they are made by the pupils or other community members. The fact that there are now two Classes 6 at MPS has introduced an element of competition regarding the success of dissemination.

Several meetings between the pupils, the teacher(s), and the researchers were held over the years to monitor the whole process jointly and identify future strategies.

Further expansion

In 2001 there was an encouraging development pointing to the sustainability of the project. In parallel to the ongoing horticultural activities at MPS, three other schools in the vicinity showed interest in becoming part of the project. Consequently, a new group of teachers was sent for training at CftE and the activities are now in various stages of being implemented in the three new schools. An informal network has been established ensuring communication between the now eight horticulture teachers, and supervision by CftE resource staff was planned for 2002.[11]

Results

Horticultural aspects

A total of 72 different traditional vegetables were identified, the majority of which (57) are believed to be uncultivable. Extensive data have been collected on procurement, preparation, and medicinal uses, and related perceptions and practices will be described elsewhere (Ogoye-Ndegwa and Aagaard-Hansen forthcoming). These data served as the starting point for the school- and community-based activities that are described in this article.

In total, 19 different species of traditional vegetables have been cultivated in the school gardens. Of these, seven were perceived as cultivable, whereas 12 had never been cultivated before. All 72 traditional vegetables thrive during the wet season (February to June) even though they are not all consumed during this time of abundance. In contrast, the dry season (September to January) presents a limited variety of 38 different species. Data from the food-recall activities indicate high consumption of traditional vegetables during the rainy period and hardly any during the dry season. It should be borne in mind that the rainy season is usually 'the hungry period' when the granaries are empty and the new harvest is not yet ready, so the availability of the many traditional vegetables is timely.

There were 13 traditional vegetables that were commercially available. Seasonality was a strong determining factor in the availability of traditional vegetables in the local markets. Since the vegetables are available only in small quantities during the dry season, none of them are sold in the local markets, and community members procure them only for direct household consumption.

The data showed that the use of vegetables was declining rapidly and it was mainly the community's elders who had the knowledge about the procurement and utilisation of herbs.[12] However, the data from the dietary intake recall showed a clear trend that the consumption of traditional herbs was higher in the households of the Class 6 pupils who had been exposed to the project.

There are indications that several of these traditional vegetables contain large quantities of micronutrients such as iron and vitamin A (FAO 1968). Botanical and biochemical studies are currently looking further into these issues. However, the specific nutritional aspects are not the main focus of the present article.

Participatory aspects

Pupil involvement

Usually the relationship between pupils and teachers is characterised by large differences in status and power. Teachers are looked up to with a combination of reverence (because of their knowledge) and fear (because of their authority which is often expressed in corporal punishment). After the inception of the project, the pupils were becoming more open and inquisitive, as they could challenge the teachers in various discussions – something that never happened before.

The action-oriented modes of learning took the pupils away from the monotonous, rote-learning of the classroom and gave them motivation and satisfaction since they were actively involved in community development. The agriculture teacher made the following observation:

> The research pupils' performance has been commendable and this is attributable to their active participation in the school gardens; and partly because they have always acted as 'knowledgeable persons' regarding all aspects of the project at school. Agriculture teaching has been made more realistic and easier for the agriculture teachers than ever before. The open dialogue and empowering of the pupils as really 'knowledgeable' made them speak more freely and engage in lively discussions.

The teacher noted that pupils were livelier to teach, that they were more active and outspoken after the introduction of the project, and that their participation in class was much enhanced. From the practical work they were engaged in, most of them became more familiar with concepts in agriculture than before:

> The idea of having a school garden made the classroom more lively as most things became so vivid and practical to the pupils. The classroom teaching has greatly been more meaningful through demonstrations in the garden. This means that even the less bright pupils are also given a chance to prove their worth in the practical lessons that went alongside theoretical learning. This greatly boosts their motivation.

From the academic point of view both girls and boys did well. However, girls tended to do better and showed more commitment than the boys, for example working during odd hours and watering during drought. There is a cultural dimension to this. Traditionally and even today vegetable cultivation, gathering, and cooking are seen as exclusively a female domain and males who venture into it are pejoratively regarded as 'women'. So the significant issue here is that the boys participated at all.

The community's involvement

During the vegetable fairs, traditional vegetables were tasted and compared and the guests engaged in lively discussions regarding the various dishes that had been prepared by the pupils. This formed the basis of the data collection on palatability ranking as well as presentation as a means to raise awareness. In line with the cultural perception that cultivating vegetables falls within the female domain, most informants were women. Community members expressed amazement that 72 varieties of local vegetables were locally available – an unknown and under-used resource, which was often thrown away when weeding the 'real' crops.

Community members expressed their satisfaction that for the first time in their lives they realised that education should not be divorced from community participation, and that children have a significant role to play. As one parent stated:

> I have never known what my child learns at school until he came to teach us and demonstrate to our neighbours how to cultivate these traditional vegetables we have lived with for a long time and assumed uncultivable.

The mere fact that meetings were convened where vegetables were the main focus and no meat or staple food was served to go with them, was seen as extraordinary. According to local attitudes, vegetables compare very unfavourably with other food items such as meat or fish. Among the Luo, it is usually considered undignified to serve only vegetables to a visitor. The Area Educational Officer (AEO) who attended one of the vegetable fairs remarked:

> I had a lot of commitment and meetings to attend, but I could not fail to attend this day. It is the first time in my lifetime to be invited to eat vegetables. I wouldn't have come if it were a feast on beef, chicken, etc.

Class 6 pupils were looked upon as knowledge holders and became instructors to pupils from other (and even higher) classes and guests from other schools, who occasionally visited the MPS. In one of the neighbouring schools, which had been exposed to the teaching of the study pupils, school gardens were introduced in which traditional vegetables were grown and sold to the local community. Funds collected were used on school building and other projects.

The new role of the research pupils was clearly shown when the District Educational Officer of Bondo District visited the study school in 1999 specifically to see the horticulture project. It should be borne in mind that, seen from the 'grassroots perspective' of an ordinary primary school, the DEO is a very powerful person who, on rare visits, mostly inspects and looks out for faults that are commented on mercilessly. So the scene of the DEO walking around with the Class 6 pupils and learning from them was rather extraordinary. The headmaster expressed it thus:

I thank Class 6 for their role in the school, always acting as a bridge between the school and the community. More so, we are very proud that on several occasions we receive visitors from our Educational Offices who come to see what they are doing in the project, and even hosting other schools on behalf of the whole school.

We see these statements as indications that the horticulture activities did not take place in isolation, but influenced educational opinion leaders and thereby the school in a more general sense.

As a means of reaching a wider community, the pupils continue to cultivate traditional vegetables in their individual kitchen gardens and in the school to provide the seeds and offer demonstrations to community members on gardening, how to use manure, and other practical aspects of cultivating the herbs. The Class 6 pupils have played a key role in this respect. A girl who was one of the research pupils had this to say:

When I started preparing my plot, my mother used to quarrel me that I was wasting time, but now ugali *can be cooked in our house even before vegetables are looked for.*

What is implicit here is that, unlike in the past, it is now easy to obtain vegetables within the homestead so that they do not need to be looked for before *ugali* (the staple food of the Luo prepared from maize and sometimes sorghum flour) can be cooked.

The agriculture teachers continue to act as external advisers and to supervise the process. They visit pupils in their homes and offer them advice wherever necessary. This kind of follow-up motivates and guides the pupils and increases acceptance within the community. Pupils continue to record the entire process of community dissemination – for example, the kind of information they give to community members, problems as seen from community members' perspective, acceptability to the community, problems they encounter in the process of dissemination, etc. The data have shown that kitchen gardens have been introduced in many homesteads thanks to the efforts of the horticulture classes.

Needless to say, the project has faced major problems as well, mainly of a practical nature. Rainfall is a crucial factor, and the unpredictability of the amount as well as the time at which it may come make farming an uncertain way of subsistence. There are no irrigation schemes in the area. Water has to be fetched from the lakeshore a few kilometres away and carried either by the pupils themselves or by donkey. Thus, the watering of a school garden of about 1000m² during an extended dry spell can pose a major challenge to the participating pupils, not least during the holidays when the school is deserted and other children are playing. This has had a negative influence by discouraging the pupils and forcing them to start afresh.

Another practical problem was the interference of animals and outsiders destroying the plots. Fencing of the school plots was needed in order to keep out goats and cows. However, the fence constantly had to be maintained as some people in the neighbourhood snatched dry wood from the fence to use it for fuel.

Conclusion

During a period of about four years we have gathered experiences from the action-research project described here, which has involved a primary school, community members, and researchers. We believe that a number of practical lessons can be learnt from the study:

- The importance of having good knowledge of the community prior to introducing the project cannot be overemphasised. This enables practitioners to address the actual needs of the community and to operate in a way that is compatible with local structures of power and status. While this may sound a banal truism, it should always be borne in mind.

- Careful selection of potential change agents (in this case the Class 6 research pupils and the teacher) based on thoroughly considered criteria is significant.

- Involvement of all relevant key players from the start (e.g. the PTA committee, the education authorities, opinion leaders of the community, and parents) broadens the ownership of the project and increases the likelihood of successful dissemination of the results.

- The delegation to the pupils of responsibility for key project activities (e.g. cultivation, data collection, and teaching) empowered them to play a more active role, which increased their personal learning and enabled them to act as development change agents.

- Only very limited financial input is needed from the outside provided that it is appropriate and comes at the right time (in this case project funding for teacher training, pupils visits to CftE, stationery, and a few farm implements).

- The combination of research (to provide relevant new knowledge and to document ongoing activities in a systematic way) and community development (to apply the research findings and introduce sustainable change) has many advantages.

Provided that these steps are taken, human resources (i.e. pupils and teachers) can be mobilised, and institutions (in this case primary schools) which previously were mainly reproducing traditional values and academic knowledge can be used as resource centres for participatory and sustainable community change. The keywords are: locally adapted, evidence-based planning, collaboration on equal terms, and a long-term perspective – tenets which may be troublesome to developers at the macro level, but are the only way to achieve sustainable change.

Acknowledgements

This study was conducted within the framework of the Kenyan–Danish Health Research Project (KEDAHR) and with funding from the Danish Bilharziasis Laboratory. We acknowledge the support from Mbeka Primary School, and particularly the headmaster, Jeremiah Nyamezi, and the 1998, 1999, 2000, and 2001 Class 6 pupils, the local community, the area and district educational authorities, the National Museum of Kenya, and the local NGO 'Care for the Earth' for their support of this study. Also thanks to Bjarne Bruun Jensen at the Research Centre for Environmental and Health Education, Danish University of Education, for substantial help during planning and analysis. Finally, we are grateful to anonymous reviewers at *Development in Practice* for constructive comments.

Notes

1 The project forms part of the Kenyan–Danish Health Research Project (KEDAHR), which is an interdisciplinary research project operating at the interface between health and education and with focus on research capacity building and applied research.

2 The implicit assumption is, of course, that intake of nutritious herbs can counter micronutrient deficiencies. However, there is an important added advantage. The herbs can serve as an important source of income generation not least for vulnerable groups such as orphans or elderly people without support.

3 By action-research we understand an endeavour which used research as a tool to improve the living conditions of a given population in a concrete way and with their active involvement in at least some stages of the process. Although this term is often used in a more comprehensive way, addressing fundamental issues in society, we still find that our project falls within the same category.

4 To clarify the terminology, by 'traditional' we mean something that has been an integrated part of a culture

for about a generation or more. The term 'wild' alludes to something that can be procured in nature (although some of the herbs in this study were both wild and cultivated). A 'food item' is anything edible (in this study we are concentrating on plants, but some insects also belong to this category). According to Southgate (2000:349), vegetables can be divided into the categories of tubers, roots, leafy vegetables, legumes (or pulses), and fruits commonly considered as vegetables. Vegetables belong to the more general category of 'plants' or 'herbs', but do not include fungi (two of which we discuss in the present study). Consequently, the correct term for the topic of the present study would be 'edible, mostly leafy, and mostly wild growing, green plants plus a few fungi, that have been part of the Luo culture for a long timespan'. So, although slightly imprecise, we have chosen to use the term 'traditional vegetables'!

5 The teacher, Domnic Abudho, who was at MPS for the first three years, is a co-author of this article and is presently working in a neighbouring school where he is in the process of introducing a similar project.

6 Innovatively, one notable, newly acquired piece of knowledge was on the preparation of compost manure. Briefly, three separate holes were dug into which plant leaves and animal wastes were sequentially put and turned. A long stick of about 1.5m, referred to as the 'thermometer', was stuck into the second hole in which almost ready manure was placed. This stick was felt and a rise in soil temperature could be detected. A rise in temperature meant that soil organisms were active and decomposition was taking place, which by implication meant that no water

needed to be added to the hole. When it was very hot, water was added. A fall in temperature meant that soil organisms were not active, and the soil needed turning. This new technology has served as a major contributing factor to the success of the project and has been adopted in neighbouring farms.

7 One year ago a national reform of the educational system made agriculture non-examinable – much to the regret of the teachers as it is feared the pupils will be less motivated in an educational environment where competition and good marks are usually seen as a strong incentive.

8 Some readers may question the selection criteria and advocate for a more random choice. However, we maintain the importance of selecting the most suitable for the project to get the best possible start.

9 There were even cases where some of the pupils who had to repeat Class 6 expressed satisfaction that they could now be actively involved in the horticulture activities for one more year.

10 The school year in Kenya runs from January to November and is divided into three terms.

11 Based on the accumulated experience, CftE and the researchers have provisional plans for a further expansion into another ten schools.

12 The reasons for this can only be guessed. Partly, the natural habitats of the traditional vegetables are reduced in many parts of Luoland because of increased population pressure and subsequent increase of cultivated land. Partly, modernisation has introduced new vegetables (e.g. *sukuma wiki*), which (although less nutritious) have marginalised the traditional herbs.

References

Bailey, D., H. Hawes and G. Bonati (1992) *Child-to-Child: A Resource Book, Part 1*, London: Child-to-Child Trust.

Chambers, R. (1983) *Rural Development: Putting the Last First*, Harlow: Longman.

Chambers, R. (1997) *Whose Reality Counts? Putting the First Last*, London: IT Publications.

Committee of Micronutrient Deficiencies (1998) *Prevention of Micronutrient Deficiencies: Tools for Policymakers and Public Health Workers*, Committee of Micronutrient Deficiencies, Board on International Health, Institute of Medicine, Washington, DC: National Academy Press.

Food and Agricultural Organisation (FAO) (1968) *Food Consumption Table for Use in Africa*, Geneva: Division of Nutrition, FAO.

Friis, H., D. Mwaniki, B. Omondi, E. Muniu, P. Magnussen, W. Geissler, F. Thiong'o, K. Michaelsen and F. Michaelsen (1997) 'Serum retinol concentrations and Schistosoma mansoni, intestinal helminths, and malaria parasitemia: a cross-sectional study in Kenyan preschool and primary school children', *American Journal of Clinical Nutrition* 66:665–671.

James, A., C. Jenks and A. Prout (1998) *Theorising Childhood*, Cambridge: Polity Press.

Jensen, B. B. and K. Schnack (eds.) (1994a) *Action and Action Competence as Key Concepts in Critical Pedagogy*, Studies in Educational Theory and Curriculum, Volume 12, Copenhagen: Royal Danish School of Educational Studies.

Leemon, M. and S. Samman (1998) 'A food-based systems approach to improve the nutritional status of Australian aborigines: a focus on zinc', *Ecology of Food and Nutrition* 10:1–33.

Meinert, L. (2001) 'The quest for a good life: health and education among children in eastern Uganda', unpublished PhD thesis, University of Copenhagen and Danish Bilharziasis Laboratory.

Ogoye-Ndegwa, C. and J. Aagaard-Hansen (forthcoming) 'Luo traditional vegetables: an anthropological nutrition project in western Kenya', *Ecology of Food and Nutrition*.

Onyango-Ouma, W. (2001) 'Children and health communication: learning about health in everyday relationships among the Luo of western Kenya', unpublished PhD thesis, University of Copenhagen and Danish Bilharziasis Laboratory.

Pridmore, P. J. (1997) 'Children as health educators: the child-to-child approach', unpublished PhD thesis, London: University of London.

Southgate, D. A. T. (2000) 'Vegetables, fruits, fungi and their products', in J. S. Garrow, W. P. T. James and A. Ralph (eds.) *Human Nutrition and Dietetics*, London: Churchill Livingstone.

Sub-Committee on Nutrition (ACC/SCN) (1997) *Third Report on The World Nutrition Situation*, Geneva: WHO.

Sub-Committee on Nutrition (ACC/SCN) (2000) *Nutrition Throughout the Life Cycle: Fourth Report on The World Nutrition Situation*, Geneva: WHO.

Wals, E. J. A. (1994) 'Action taking and environmental problem solving in environmental education', in B. B. Jensen and K. Schnack (eds.) *Action and Action Competence as Key Concepts in Critical Pedagogy*, Studies in Educational Theory and Curriculum, Volume 12, Copenhagen: Royal Danish School of Educational Studies.

This article was first published in Development in Practice *(12/3&4:449–460) in 2002.*

Organisational learning in NGOs:
an example of an intervention based on the work of Chris Argyris

Didier Bloch and Nora Borges

Introduction

Ten years after the publication of Peter Senge's bestseller *The Fifth Discipline*, organisational learning (OL) appears to be awakening considerable interest in the non-governmental world. 'The learning organisation' and 'learning to learn' are phrases that are increasingly heard in discussions about the third sector. But do the principles of OL as applied in various large corporations over the last 30 years apply to non-profit organisations?[1] Our experience in Brazil might give us some pointers and allow us to draw some initial lessons, though it is not a basis upon which to claim to deal with this complex subject in an exhaustive manner.

The first section of this paper will be limited to a brief description, without any academic pretensions, of the pertinence for NGOs of OL principles, as outlined by the US researcher Chris Argyris.[2] Following this, we will describe a concrete intervention that uses this conceptual framework, based upon work funded by the International Women's Health Coalition (IWHC) that began in February 2001 with Grupo Curumim, an NGO based in north-east Brazil.

Organisational learning: what relevance for NGOs?

A brief overview of the theory

For many years, and to a great extent still today, an organisation was understood as the 'rational coordination of activities of a set of people who have a common explicit goal, through the division of work and function, and a hierarchy of control and authority' (Schein 1965, quoted in Weick 1973:2). Organisational theorists such as Karl Weick took a radically different approach, teaching us to see organisations as dynamic systems, analysed in terms of behaviour, processes, and the interactions between actors (Weick 1973).

An interesting point in Weick's perspective is that he lays the major responsibility for an organisation's acts and problems at the feet of its people. We find something similar in the search for professional effectiveness put forward by Argyris and Donald Schön (1974) or in the systems thinking approach presented by Senge (1990): each member of the system should seek to understand his/her responsibility for mistakes; in other words, s/he should see her/himself as a causative agent rather than trying to put the blame on people outside the system. In this way, learning does not just mean the accumulation of information and knowledge, or the solution of problems. Above all, the members of an organisation should 'reflect critically on their behaviour, and identify the ways in which, inadvertently and frequently, they contribute to the organisation's problems, and on that basis change the way they act' (Argyris 2000:186).

Put more simply, we can say that an OL intervention seeks to increase professional effectiveness within the organisation, providing tools to enable people to reflect periodically on their behaviour. In this way organisation members analyse what Argyris terms their 'theories in action' – their assumptions and intentions, strategies and results, and, above all, the deepest held values and beliefs that govern their behaviour.

Argyris suggests three theoretical models of action, which we can call authoritarian (Model 1), paternalist (the opposite of Model 1) and participatory (Model 2). While Model 1 is characterised by unilateral control, intransigence, and open competition, in its opposite, competition and control are camouflaged by the appearance of empathy and open discourse (Valença 1997). Model 2, which the author clearly prefers, has three underlying values: the production of valid information, freedom of choice, and internal commitment to action.

According to Argyris, every person who intervenes should follow these values exactly, trying to ensure that the group is increasingly able to analyse and solve its problems, take decisions, and act on them. For him it is impossible to solve problems without the relevant information. In turn, taking a decision requires not only information but also an environment of trust and free choice. For successful implementation, people need to feel completely committed to these decisions. Helping the group to generate valid and useful information and developing an environment of free choice and internal commitment are what Argyris calls the 'primary tasks' which guide each and every OL intervention (Argyris 1970: Chapter 2). Apart from this, interveners should ensure they enable people to become fully independent. Thus it is not just a question of applying tools and following principles, but also of ensuring that the organisation can use them effectively, without the presence of external consultants.

Argyris, who led hundreds of interventions in companies and developed theories based on his practice in more that 30 books, affirms that organisations are effective and can learn when they can detect and correct their mistakes. It is worth noting the complete lack of any moral undertone in his notion of mistake. For Argyris, a mistake is simply the difference between the original intention and the actual outcome of the action, the discrepancy between the idealised project and the results. There are thus two kinds of errors. This was well summed up by Antônio Carlos Valença, one of the leading Brazilian academics focusing on the work of Argyris. On the one hand there are those mistakes that are 'linked to operational procedures' and on the other 'those that involve questions that are threatening and embarrassing, ambiguous, paradoxical, contradictory or politically unmentionable' (Valença 1999:16). For Valença, the latter are 'the most serious errors which have the greatest impact, errors which merit the most skilled intervention'.

Lack of information on learning in NGOs

Our impression is that there are still few, or certainly few accessible, publications on the actual experiences of applying OL in the third sector. On the one hand, the great majority of case studies that are used to illustrate the work of Argyris, Senge, and other theorists refers to large private corporations from the northern hemisphere and, to a lesser degree, to public sector bodies. On the other hand, as noted by Michael Edwards (1997), there is a small but growing volume of NGO literature addressing the process of learning and its results.

One reason for this lack of material is the fact that, despite existing for many years, it has only been since the 1990s that the third sector has been regarded as 'a strategic area for the harmonious development of modern society' (Merege 2000). Management schools have started including specialised courses for third-sector organisations, but this interest is very recent. In Brazil the Getúlio Vargas Foundation was a pioneer in establishing the first such course in 1996, with the justification that:

> [T]raditional management techniques applied to both public and private
> sectors demonstrate real limitations when they are simply transferred across
> to the third sector. The absence of shareholders and profit as the main

objectives [of the organisation] mean that other values dominate, such as the
form of participative management, commitment with the mission and the
prioritisation of principles that guide the service to the target group, and
where valuing the human person and commitment to others stand out most.
(Merege 2000)

The need for an approach that focuses on values

This focus on values, which is used to justify the founding of specialised training courses, seems to us to strengthen the pertinence of an OL approach in NGOs. In other words, we believe that OL, which has been so well tested in the business world, can also be a relevant approach for NGOs.

We will start by referring to the comments made by Edwards of the World Bank on the subject of learning in international NGOs whose head offices are in the industrialised world (Edwards 1997). Edwards, who has also worked for Save the Children Fund-UK and Oxfam GB, argues that, because of the nature of development and its 'inherently unstable and uncertain contexts, their complexity and diversity ... means that to develop capacity for learning and to make the connections is even more important than accumulating information'. It is a question of learning from experience, rooted in 'solid feedback mechanisms that link information, knowledge, and action', and on skills in 'reflection-through-action'.

Edwards also notes that NGOs 'have a values system that, in theory, encourages learning and communication', which gives them a certain advantage in relation to other organisations. Nevertheless, like their counterparts in the private and public sector, NGOs 'do not like to admit failure or ignorance', and he concludes that ' ... if NGOs still wish to have a distinct identity as value-based organisations, then they should be particularly well equipped to develop in this aspect'. We interpret these comments as arguments for the relevance of a values-based organisational approach for NGOs.

The difference between stated values and actual behaviour

An important contribution made by Argyris is the distinction between the theory of stated action (through its discourse and publicly stated values) and the theory of action in practice (the values actually practised, those that shape behaviour). There is always a difference between the stated values and actual behaviour, which he calls 'incongruence'.

For example, when Chris Roche, head of Programme Policy at Oxfam GB, writes that 'NGOs espouse partnership and the need for synergy' but that 'just like other organisations, they tend to blame others and/or the context when things go wrong' (Roche 2000:50), he is pointing to an inconsistency: I espouse partnership but my concrete action is based on values that do not favour partnership. Roche offers another example when he summarises various critiques of NGOs in the image of a vicious circle made up of five elements, including 'the nascent learning and institutional responsibility'. He agrees that 'these elements come together to produce a large vacuum between the rhetoric of the agencies and what they actually accomplish' (Roche 2000:15), and also notes critiques that highlight the 'inadequacy of the majority of current attempts to promote institutional learning', viewing the exposure of 'the mistakes and uncertainties that are inherent in development work' as a possible way out (Roche 2000:15–16).

Search for approaches that reduce inconsistencies

NGOs openly defend values such as participation, democracy, citizenship, and respect for diversity. This is their discourse, their 'stated theory'. The question is: how are these values put into practice in the day-to-day life of these organisations? Among NGOs? With their partners? Between members of the same organisation?

We agree with Roche that there is a significant difference between the stated values and actual behaviour of NGOs. It is true that no individual, group, or organisation is wholly consistent. Nevertheless, this is a much more sensitive topic for NGOs than for organisations from the first and second sector, for a variety of reasons.

The first reason is that it is precisely these values and their defence in practice that in large part justifies the very existence of NGOs. Take, for example, a piece from the charter of principles of the Brazilian Association of NGOs: 'ABONG and its members commit themselves to apply the following principles in their daily practice: ethics, impartiality, morality, publicity, and solidarity; to identify and defend alternatives for sustainable human development that take into account equity, social justice, and environmental balance for present and future generations' (ABONG 2000). These values and principles are commitments made by the most respected Brazilian NGOs, without any doubt made with the best intentions. But we also need to recognise the difficulties inherent in putting these values into practice. Unfortunately, in the absence of certain interpersonal and group skills that are not particularly prevalent (listening, dialogue, shared decision making, etc.), the best of intentions may not prevent the appearance of undesired and dysfunctional results. Without deep reflection on the 'error' (i.e. the difference between the intention and actual performance), these undesired consequences are all too likely to occur. For example, apart from proclaiming solidarity between organisations, it would be useful to encourage critical reflection on the specific process of engagement between NGOs. This, in turn, could lead to the gradual development of competencies that seldom emerge spontaneously.

The second reason is exactly the fact that, in most organisations in the third sector, the necessary attention is not given to actual behaviour, individual and collective. Hence, the inevitable contradictions between stated values and practice are rarely raised and even more rarely addressed. Given that the values that NGOs defend are their very *raison d'être*, should we not think of mechanisms that could minimise the gap between discourse and behaviour?

Going back to Argyris, learning means to identify and correct mistakes. This can happen in two ways: either by just changing operational procedures, the 'action strategies' (single-loop learning), or, going deeper, by questioning and gradually changing the values and beliefs that in practice govern these strategies (double-loop learning) – though we shouldn't forget that overcoming personal and organisational barriers and acquiring new behavioural skills are very lengthy processes.

Thus NGOs that evaluate the impact of development actions and reflect on their fieldwork with a view to improving operational procedures are engaged in important single-loop learning (external). However, it is equally or perhaps more important to check behavioural realities (internal) and start a processs of double-loop learning. Concretely it is worth asking how an organisation that supports participation or the rights of all to have a say deals with cases of arbitrary, controlling, or authoritarian behaviour that may occur in its everyday life. Ignoring such practices would expose the organisation to all kinds of criticism, and we know that NGOs are increasingly subject to attack, whether malicious or well-meaning. Working on actual behaviour and underlying values is thus vital. It just remains to explore how best to do it.

So we come to the third reason why discrepancy between stated goals and actual practice is so sensitive for NGOs. We believe that the tools currently used by NGOs (evaluation, planning, monitoring, etc.)

are often inappropriate for dealing with these contradictions or tackling behavioural issues. They certainly help to improve external operational procedures (single-loop learning). Ideally, they enable the organisation to identify certain symptoms (unproductive meetings, failures in internal communication, lack of trust, etc.), but people are rarely equipped to deal with them effectively. Often they do not even realise that there are certain things that can help them to do so. The result: the same problems keep occurring and the group has increasing difficulty in confronting them. The tendency is to develop dysfunctional patterns of behaviour which become increasingly difficult to challenge and deal with, a phenomenon that Argyris calls 'skilled incompetence'.

Rethinking professional practice in relation to organisational development

Some NGOs would like to become alternative reference points for organisational issues as well. In ABONG's charter of principles we find phrases like 'internal democratic participation', 'partnership between members', 'harmony and respect', 'point of reference for society'. Internal democracy and participation are, however, the result of processes; they always have to be (re)-constructed. To this extent we believe that a critical examination of external actions and internal contradictions that underlie OL interventions can be of great help.

All of this demonstrates, in our view, the need to find appropriate approaches, to stop and think, to put aside a time and space to reflect on the *action strategies that are actually used* and on *the values that in fact govern these strategies.* We believe that OL is a relevant approach, with its educational perspective, its emphasis on continuous improvement of the (inevitable) mistakes, and its focus on practice and on the values that shape this practice, which can help in generating a more participatory democracy and in promoting a less competitive and more open interaction. Essentially, it can bring discourse and practice closer together in interpersonal relations within NGOs, between NGOs, and between them and the various groups and organisations with whom they engage (beneficiaries, governments, other NGOs, etc.).

And this is precisely what we are trying to do in our work with Grupo Curumim.

The intervention process in Grupo Curumim

To bring all the above ideas to life, we now describe the first six months of the two-year intervention process with Curumim.

Curumim, a feminist NGO

Curumim is a Brazilian feminist NGO with its headquarters in Recife in the state of Pernambuco. The group has been working for 12 years in the area of humanising childbirth and women's health, in a country where maternal mortality remains high, and where the rate of Caesarean delivery is one of the highest in the world. Most of Curumim's work is done alongside traditional midwives in north-east and north Brazil.

The team draws on a range of skills (a medical doctor, a sociologist, midwives, health education workers) and works at both a technical level (training of midwives, antenatal care) and at policy level (participation in national and international feminist networks, interventions in public policy) in what is often a hostile context. We should underline that in Brazil, and particularly in the region in which Curumim works, there are many traditional midwives who, despite their unparalleled role serving the poorer population particularly in remote areas, are not officially recognised within the health system. A part of Curumim's work is undertaken in pilot municipalities and consists of organising the midwives in order to ensure their integration into the health system, with the aim of controlling maternal, neonatal, and perinatal mortality in the whole municipality. Furthermore, the study of practices in various municipalities should facilitate the development of a new model of service. Despite the difficult context, it is worth noting that Curumim works within the scope of reproductive rights and women's health, an area in which the Brazilian feminist movement has achieved significant advances over the last two decades.

Having said this, we will see that the plan for the first months of OL intervention was designed above all in relation to the behavioural and organisational issues raised in the initial diagnosis. This diagnosis involved the midwives, who for technical and geographic reasons and lack of finances are not participating directly in the OL process. However, they are benefiting indirectly from this intervention given that Curumim is adapting some of the tools of OL for use in its meetings with the midwives.

The initial diagnosis: organise the variables

The OL work formally began in February 2001. In reality, however, the work with Curumim started in the first half of 2000, with the examination and diagnosis of the Traditional Midwives Programme, which, as with the whole of the intervention, took place at the request of Curumim and was financed by the US-based feminist organisation IWHC.

This diagnosis took about two months, during which time information was collected through individual interviews with the members and partners of Curumim and through the reading of reports and publications. There were also several workshops with the whole team, which comprised eight people. A part of the information collected related to the external environment, to Curumim's partnerships, to the influence of the institution on public policy, and its overall effectiveness. Besides this, specific organisational aspects linked to working methods were looked at (planning, monitoring, meetings, etc.) including internal environment (e.g. relations within the team, decision making), human resources (size of the team, skills, training needs, etc.), financial aspects (funding, salaries), and infrastructure (physical space, equipment).

At the final workshop, when the results of the diagnosis were fed back for checking and approval, the long list of variables that reflected the organisation was examined. An exercise of systemic visioning helped to reveal the relation of cause and effect between these variables. Four variables stood out from the mass of information collected, and we called them overall determining factors – those with the most impact on the 'Curumim system'. These four generic variables – internal communication, management model, socio-political training, and resources – and their specific importance for Curumim formed a first set of important information to guide the intervention. In addition, the diagnosis highlighted problems with planning (carried out competently but easily hijacked by immediate demands) and monitoring (which was not systematic). Overall the diagnosis pointed to difficulties in following long-range objectives and agreed procedures.

Between Argyris' three models of action theory, Curumim certainly showed a desire to move towards Model 2 (participatory); however, the diagnosis showed that its practice put it nearer the opposite to Model 1 (paternalistic). Far from being dispirited, the Curumim team saw this situation as an opportunity for growth. After various conversations with the consultants, it was unanimously decided to undergo an OL intervention. Initial funding was requested from IWHC to cover one year's intervention, with the option to renew for one further year. For us, the consultants, the next step was to design this intervention.

From diagnosis to design

One of the key ideas in learning is to enable the organisation to reflect on its performance in concrete situations. In the case of Curumim, this does not mean to encourage an abstract reflection on the concept of monitoring but rather to propose a gradual change of behaviour in practice. Thus when working on operational procedures (fundraising, for example), we can encourage the group to monitor the planned actions (developing and monitoring relevant indicators) and at the same time create an environment that favours reflection on their behaviour in the monitoring process. Can the group define appropriate indicators? Does it encounter difficulties? What is the documentation of the indicators like? Is it worth doing? What is the group learning through doing this?

Basically, the intervention tries to make the group reflect on certain operational questions (fundraising, public policy for midwives, etc.), while the principal focus is on behavioural and relational questions (the effect of personal issues on group dynamics; the ability to listen, discuss, and argue; the fulfilment of planned tasks; the expression of ideas and feelings; decision making; etc.). These questions are not just dealt with in an abstract way – reading a text on leadership, for example – but are worked on by the group through periodic analysis of their own practice and filmed on video.

On the basis of the diagnosis and applying the theoretical principles espoused by Argyris and others, we decided to suggest two consecutive modules of ten months each. For the initial module we suggested a 'backcloth' with various themes: mental models, theory of action, personal and group competencies, effective teams, mistakes and defensiveness, systems thinking – not necessarily in that order, depending on the response of the group and on the progress of the intervention.

We also decided to hold monthly two-day sessions with the group, including the following activities. After a short period of relaxation and concentration the participants talk about the 'current moment' – and for about an hour, each person can find out about the internal and external comings and goings of their colleagues, about the ideas and feelings of that moment, and about the development of projects and aspirations, be they individual or collective. Thus there is what one of the members of the group described as an 'unfreezing of the images that we have of other people'. Usually, the consultants then give a *theoretical presentation* of OL. This more reflective part is complemented by the *observation and analysis of behaviour*, be it of characters in fiction films or of the team itself in experiential exercises linked to the theory being presented. Additionally, the monthly programme includes a *collective clinic* (a filmed session of structured dialogue) to deal with problems raised through the diagnosis, or coming up in the group's daily business. To close the seminar, participants carry out a written *self-evaluation* and *group evaluation*, using a standard form, and take part in a final evaluation, where each one speaks in turn. Finally, between sessions *theoretical tasks* (study and presentation by Curumim of texts on learning) and *practicals* (continuation of the work on operational procedures) are introduced, and the times for feedback during the following monthly sessions are scheduled.

In order to accompany and measure how the group's performance evolved, we foresaw three types of more formal evaluation. The first takes place monthly through a self-evaluation and group evaluation form, in which each participant marks (on a scale of 0 to 4) variables such as listening, focus on the task, free expression of ideas, and so on. The second type of evaluation is also behavioural; however, this time it is carried out by the consultants. In this case the interaction between the members of the group is carefully observed in video-filmed laboratory exercises. Finally, the third type of evaluation takes place each time an operational theme that came up in the diagnosis is dealt with (communication, fundraising, etc.). The group thus develops operational indicators and is charged with monitoring them.

This, at least, is the plan. In practice, in the 'live system', the agenda remains an important point of reference; however, sometimes there are diversions, upsets, or surprises that turn into raw material for the intervention. Below we present some reflections on the experience that is still 'work in progress'.

Slow handcrafted work, enriched by feedback from the group

During the first seminar, group norms (confidentiality of the sessions, respect for the timetable, etc.) and the calendar of monthly meetings were discussed. The group was also filmed talking about internal communication, dwelling in particular on the irregularity of team meetings.

Between the first and second seminar the team had to produce a plan for internal communication, together with specific indicators. They failed to do so, and this non-action was excellent raw material to develop a preliminary simplified map of the theory of group action. This map showed the assumptions, strategies used (in this case the non-fulfilment of the agreed task), as well as the consequences for the group. This mapping had almost immediate effects: the following day Curumim met to produce an action plan for internal communication. One of our principal hypotheses was that assumptions such as 'I don't have time' or 'this isn't my responsibility' pointed to more general and deeper behavioural patterns that inhibited the group's effective action. In fact, in another situation three months later, very similar behaviour was repeated and was again mapped and discussed.

This is an obvious but nevertheless essential point: it is not enough to point out behavioural patterns only once if you are trying to promote profound change in the group's behaviour. There are no miracles: changes take time. They do not depend solely on individual or group decisions but require the acquisition of new skills – hence the length of the OL intervention, which in this case will take place over 20 months. Overcoming 'defensive routines' and changing the 'master programme' represent a long journey during which new forms of communication need to be worked on – defending one's viewpoint by reference to observable facts, inviting the others to challenge our reasoning, contributing incrementally – which form part of what Argyris calls Model 2 of theory in practice.

We designed the intervention from one seminar to the next in a very handcrafted way, tailoring it to the group, taking into consideration the context, the theoretical norms (in particular Model 2 participatory and democratic), and the response of the group.

The logic that developed in relation to the four overarching variables we had identified was as follows. First, it was necessary to deal with internal communication at least to ensure that the monthly team meeting would take place. Without such meetings there would be no way the group could deal with any topic. Later on, the second theme proposed was financial resources, given its critical nature – specifically the forthcoming end of core funding. Without some sense of the group's continuation, there was no way one could think of OL or any other type of organisational work.

This is the point we have reached after six months, dealing gradually with these two variables, trying to encourage the group to develop indicators and monitor them. However, often other themes arise during these sessions, altering the order envisaged. This was how a structured discussion developed about the feeling of belonging to the group, for example. On another occasion, we felt it opportune to include in the programme the study of a chapter of Peter Senge's recent work referring to overcoming the challenge of 'lack of time' in the processes of OL (Senge 2000: Chapter 3).

In the near future, we will address socio-political training and the model of the institutional management, though this plan remains provisional. In truth the dynamic of the intervention means that one variable can hide others and new themes emerge during the process. Thus it is useless to try to predict everything in detail in advance.

Monitoring as a learning tool

Between the first introductory seminar and the sixth, which was designed as a special moment of feedback from the consultants to the group and vice versa, only four monthly seminars took place. Four months is a very short time in which to see significant behavioural change. But that doesn't mean one can't reflect on some preliminary results, difficulties encountered, and challenges.

At the sixth seminar, a whole day was dedicated to the results of the first six months. The collective interpretation of how the behavioural variables had evolved show that Curumim feels at ease with the experimental environment, but cannot yet change certain behaviour patterns: without the presence of the facilitators. There is still a tendency not to listen and to lose focus, as the group educator admits: 'I am really clear that something very good has happened, principally in relation to self-confidence and respect for differences. The word "building" is key; I am not yet ready to solve certain problems without the help of the consultants.'

Despite the difficulties, the group attributes some qualitative advances to the intervention of OL; for example, members cite greater confidence in negotiations with funders, or the unprecedented integration of the whole team in the strategic planning process. The overall feeling is of empowerment, thanks to the greater alignment of the group around its institutional project, which its members have experienced more intensely as group building: 'At the end of the second day of the seminar, there is certainly a shared sense of building an ever clearer vision of what we need to do to reach new levels of relationship, and to be more effective in our work and in internal and external communication.' The first tangible advance was when the group, for the first time in years, managed to meet for a whole day each month for three months in succession. It doesn't seem much, but the physical presence of everyone in the same space at the same time is a first condition for the existence of a group, especially a small group like Curumim.

Other advances related to the way Curumim works with the beneficiary groups were also noted. Curumim, which campaigns to make childbirth more humane, seeks to change practices which are deeply engrained among doctors and midwives. After six months the OL intervention triggered reflections about the importance of *experiencing* changes and not just preaching about them. From that point, one idea that came to the group members was to promote deeper work on the values underlying the practice of health professionals. Thus, without this being explicitly planned, the concepts, principles, and instruments proposed during the OL intervention were adapted and used not only within, but also beyond, Curumim. The coordinator of Curumim thinks, for example, that the session on the current moment 'was a huge discovery: we have always used it in activities within and outside Curumim. This has really improved interaction and we can see a greater effectiveness when dealing with operational issues.'

One of the greatest difficulties of the group is still the design and use of operational indicators. After four sessions dealing with the theme of internal communication, nothing emerged that would enable the monitoring of the development of team meetings. There is a veiled reluctance in this domain: nobody openly opposes the value of such monitoring; however, nobody takes any initiatives in this direction. For this reason we find the reaction of the group to the feedback of the self-evaluation at the sixth seminar interesting. For this session we made a simple table of the facts registered by the team members themselves, who at the end of each seminar had filled out a form marking themselves and the wider group against various criteria. Graphs showing the development of each of these dimensions (ability to set objectives and reach them, focus on tasks, contributions made, etc.) and in various situations (seminars, everyday work, preparatory tasks) were discussed.

This feedback session aroused a lot of interest and seemed almost to shock the team. 'I thought it was boring filling in the form, doing it because I had to, but from now on I will pay a lot more attention to it' is the comment which best captures the overall feeling. With the table the group was shown all the potential that creating and accompanying indicators can have, so long as this task is considered a moment of reflection on the team's practice. In other words, the team realised that if monitoring is understood and practised as a learning exercise, it could become a powerful tool to analyse their achievements. However, in order to reach this conclusion the group has to *experience* a positive 'laboratory' experience. From then on, we believe that they can value monitoring in other spheres, internal and external, or even challenge the relevance of monitoring, but this time with solid arguments based on actually doing it. The most important step is to move away from a pattern of defensiveness and omission to a point where they can actually feel the relevance (or lack thereof) of monitoring in practice.

We can conclude, then, that the group has undergone some behavioural advances, but that these do not yet clearly appear in the formal evaluations. As a team member put it: 'we are still learning what not to do, then we can discover what to do differently'. After six months of work, encouraging indicators emerged, such as, for example, 'less dispersion in day-to-day activities and a greater sensitivity in relation to shared decision making'. It remains to be seen what the impact of this learning will be in terms of relationships with partners and beneficiaries, i.e. how behavioural advances translate in terms of how effectively the institution's mission is achieved. Some advances can already be seen by the coordinator:

> Looking at the negative points raised by the diagnosis, we feel that we have improved a lot in our communication with other NGOs and with our interlocutors in the municipalities, and we are dividing our time better between the women's movement and the work in the municipalities. On the other hand we still need to improve in terms of recording and systematising, as well as in monitoring our activities.

We would add that before being able to note significant changes, Curumim faces one of the greatest challenges of OL ahead: to express intentions through better strategies will call for the development of new skills.

Developing new skills

An initial impression by any outside observer would suggest that interpersonal relationships in Curumim could be classified as 'good'. But this assessment would be different if we took effectiveness as a criterion, defined as 'more productivity with less psychological cost' (Valença 1997:45) or if we used Argyris's Model 2 as our guide, in which participation means listening and dialogue, taking on one's responsibility and skilled analysis of others' actions. From this perspective, new personal and interpersonal skills should be developed, for example, to deal better with information (ideas and feelings) minimising inferences, ambiguities, and contradictions.

The development of skills, which already forms part of the ten seminars, will be a special focus of the second module. Identifying the technical and relational skills and gaps already existing in the team, and developing new skills (of relating, analytical reasoning, etc), and seeking skills outside the group to carry out certain tasks in partnership – these are some of the challenges for the next phase of work with Curumim.

The second module will also focus on two huge topics: explicit monitoring of external activities that the group considers are critical, and the progressive building of a new management model.

Encouraging the pendulum swing between research and action

We are optimistic regarding the future of OL in NGOs. On the one hand we believe that there is in Curumim, as in various other third-sector organisations, a real commitment to its stated values and a certain willingness to question its own practices. On the other hand, while private-sector companies are caught up in fierce competition and the public sector is tied up in legislative strictures, the third sector faces fewer such constraints. NGOs' flexibility and their defence of public interests together form a powerful duo, in harmony with the criteria which according to Argyris should guide the interventions of OL: effectiveness and justice – and, of course, *learning*.

Developing mechanisms through which to analyse one's own actions, learning through mistakes, equipping oneself to reduce the distance between stated values and concrete actions, promoting a system of norms and rewards that favour learning, are all favourite themes in OL, which we believe offer principles and tools that match the lofty ambitions of the third sector.

Model 2 of participatory, democratic behaviour remains utopian. As with all utopias, it is a kind of distant star that one never reaches, but which shows the direction forward. For Argyris, conflicts, mistakes, and problems – the raw material of an OL intervention – will never stop happening: once one error is corrected it is inevitable that another will appear. Learning means just not repeating the same mistake all the time. It means, above all, learning to learn, learning to deal in a group, and, with a constantly changing environment, establishing mechanisms for collective feedback and action.

We believe that Curumim is learning little by little, and learning to learn about itself. Our experience is that in the medium term this learning will spread to the activities carried out with the midwives and other groups with whom Curumim works. We hope that this article provokes reflection and critical reaction that can help us correct our mistakes, improve our practice, and refine our thinking. As Argyris himself suggests, the theory will continue in this way to be tested in the real world, in a continuous movement of the pendulum between research and action, thus generating new knowledge.

Acknowledgement

This paper was translated from Portuguese by Frances Rubin. A copy of the original is available on request from: editor@developmentinpractice.org.

Notes

1 We use the terms 'non-governmental organisation', 'third-sector organisation', and 'non-profit organisation' interchangeably.
2 'To intervene is to enter a system of relationships already in process, come clear to people, groups or objects with the aim of helping them' (Argyris 1970: Chapter 1).

References

ABONG (2000) *Carta de princípios da Associação Brasileira de ONGs*, São Paulo: ABONG, available at www.abong.org.br/abong/documentos/cartaprincipios.htm (accessed June 2001).

Argyris, Chris (1970) *Intervention, Theory and Method*, Reading, MA: Addison Wesley.

Argyris, Chris (2000) 'Ensinando pessoas inteligentes a aprender', in Robert Howard *et al. Aprendizado Organizacional*, Rio de Janeiro: Campus.

Argyris, Chris and Donald Schön (1974) *Theory in Practice: Increasing Professional Effectiveness*, San Francisco, CA: Jossey-Bass.

Edwards, Michael (1997) 'Organisational learning in non-governmental organisations: what have we learned?', available at www.worldbank.org/essd/essd.nsf (accessed June 2001).

Merege, Luiz Carlos (2000) 'Administração do terceiro setor: um novo e próspero campo de trabalho', *Valor Econômico*, São Paulo, 31 August 2000.

Roche, Chris (2000) *Avaliação de Impacto dos Trabalhos de ONGs: Aprendendo a Valorizar as Mudanças*, São Paulo: Cortez (Portuguese translation of *Impact Assessment for Development Agencies Learning to Value Change*, Oxford: Oxfam, 1999).

Schein, E. H. (1965) *Organizational Psychology*, Englewood Cliffs, NJ: Prentice Hall.

Senge, Peter (1990) *The Fifth Discipline*, New York, NY: Doubleday.

Senge, Peter (trans.) (2000) *A Dança das Mudanças*, Rio de Janeiro: Campus.

Valença, Antônio Carlos (1997) *Eficácia Profissional*, Rio de Janeiro: Qualitymark.

Valença, Antônio Carlos (1999) 'Prefácio', in *Pensamento Sistêmico*, Recife: Valença e Associados.

Weick, Karl (1973) *A Psicologia Social da Organização*, São Paulo: University of São Paulo.

This article was first published in Development in Practice *(12/3&4: 461–472) in 2002.*

Mainstreaming disaster mitigation: challenges to organisational learning in NGOs

John Twigg and Diane Steiner

Introduction, research aims, and method

Our paper looks at the implications for organisational learning of a recent study of the nature and extent of NGO activity to protect people in the South against so-called 'natural' disasters.[1] In particular, we discuss whether the mechanisms by which NGOs normally learn support the promotion of disaster mitigation and preparedness (DMP) within them. We believe our findings will be useful to those seeking to push other new or marginal issues and approaches into the mainstream of development work.

There are two main reasons why NGOs should be extensively involved in DMP. First, disasters triggered by natural hazards (such as cyclones, droughts, earthquakes, and floods) are a major threat to sustainable development. Between 1971 and 1995 they caused each year, on average, over 128,000 deaths and affected 136 million people, and 99 per cent of those affected lived in the South. Between 1991 and 1995 the economic cost of such disasters worldwide was US$439 billion (IFRC 1997). Second, poor and socially disadvantaged people, whom NGOs support through their development programmes, are usually the most vulnerable to such disasters (Blaikie *et al.* 1994).

Our research aimed to understand the scope and nature of relevant activities, identify good practices for replication elsewhere, and examine institutional and other factors influencing the work of NGOs.[2] An international research team collected evidence from a sample of organisations: 22 international relief and development NGOs with headquarters in the UK and 40 NGOs in Bangladesh, Nicaragua, the Philippines, and Zimbabwe. More than 200 semi-structured interviews were carried out with operational staff and managers, and hundreds of internal documents were collected. The results were written up as five detailed reports (Twigg *et al.* 2000;

Matin and Taher 2000; Rocha and Christoplos 2000; Luna 2000; Shumba 2000).

The following discussion is based on evidence gathered from the study of the 22 international NGOs with headquarters in the UK (Twigg *et al.* 2000): four were relief agencies, nine were development agencies, and nine were involved in both relief and development. We focus on this study because it examined issues of organisational learning in more depth than the other four country studies, which put greater emphasis on DMP activities in the field. However, the discussion also presents important complementary or contradictory findings from those studies.

Findings on organisational learning

Overall, the research shows that DMP has not established itself in the mainstream of NGO work. Thinking about disasters and vulnerability is beginning to penetrate NGO consciousness at policy level but this is not being translated to the operational level, where disaster risk-reduction activity tends to be sporadic, poorly integrated with development planning, and largely unsupported by institutional structures and systems.

Analysis of the reasons for this sheds light on the mechanisms that NGOs use to acquire and apply knowledge. While there are external barriers to mainstreaming disaster mitigation in NGOs, in particular the limited interest among donors, much of the problem is internal and relates to different dimensions of organisational learning. We set out the main features of this in the following paragraphs.

Influences on learning at policy level

Natural disaster preparedness and mitigation are not addressed at policy level in most of the NGOs studied. Only three have a formal preparedness or mitigation policy. However, there are signs in several NGOs that disasters, vulnerability, and disaster mitigation are rising or are likely to rise in the strategy agenda.

It was difficult to assess the influence of intellectual debates and new concepts on policy change. We found indications of shifts in attitude, with the old view of disasters as one-off events being replaced by awareness that development processes can influence the impact of disasters. This suggests that extensive academic debates on this subject in the 1980s and early 1990s (Blaikie *et al.* 1994) have found their way into NGO thinking in very general terms.

However, the main influence on NGO thinking is recent disasters themselves, because of their impact on NGOs' own work and target groups. Hurricane Mitch in October 1998 was particularly significant: its massive impact on Central America's development – 9200 lives lost and economic losses totalling U$5 billion (Munich Re 1998) – has forced NGOs working in the region to reconsider their approach to disaster risk. We were struck by how many NGO staff spoke of disasters as opportunities for change in thinking and the adoption of new approaches. Yet this potential can be overstated: even in Nicaragua it is not clear that Mitch has led to much fresh analysis by NGOs of the complex issues involved in vulnerability reduction, and discussion of DMP is largely overshadowed by the national debate over different development models.

We were unable to reach firm conclusions about the influence of international NGO partnerships and networks on the policies of British NGOs towards DMP, as these vary considerably between individual organisations, but recent discussion of the subject in European NGO networks may be opening up what we term 'policy space' for discussing the issues and providing a mandate to take the work further. The Bangladesh study found that affiliations with international organisations involved in disasters have influenced the policy positions of some NGOs (although operational guidelines are far less up to date). One would expect local NGOs to be more sensitive to hazard risk and the need for mitigation and preparedness, but we found no evidence of Southern NGOs influencing their British partners' disaster mitigation policy.

Influences on operational learning: structures and systems

At country and especially project level, we found a lack of hazard risk assessment in planning, showing that NGOs' systems have failed to incorporate this issue. Awareness of risk is, predictably, much higher in sub-Saharan African countries where droughts are frequent and affect wide areas. Sudden-onset disasters in other regions are more likely to be seen as one-off events.

NGOs' operational and funding guidelines have little to say about DMP. Where the subject does feature, it is just as likely to do so in development guidelines as in those for emergencies. In any case, the documents vary in range and depth, and in general such documents tend to contain limited practical guidance on planning and implementing projects. This gives desk and programme officers considerable leeway in applying guidelines, thereby making them influential players within NGOs, especially development NGOs. They may also have great influence over the development of country plans, project approval, and in some cases choice of local partners. They could play a major role in promoting DMP but they have very heavy workloads and are generally too busy with their ongoing concerns to reflect on or absorb new ideas. One of the most significant, and emphatic, findings of our research is that overwork and pressures of work are not minor factors in NGO operations and performance but *systemic weaknesses*. In our view, this is a major obstacle to the uptake of new approaches.

Emergency units and advisory teams have grown rapidly in recent years, which is potentially significant for disaster mitigation because discussion of DMP has traditionally taken place in the emergencies arena. However, in NGOs working in both relief and development, institutional and cultural tension between emergency and development departments is evident, fuelled by lack of clarity about the mandates of emergency teams. One development worker spoke of the 'fear of relief culture' in their NGO. Where emergencies specialists lead debates about disaster mitigation, this may act as a brake on the willingness of other staff to become involved. The research team in Bangladesh, where several NGOs have set up separate disaster units, also questioned whether this separation is a strength (in promoting DMP ideas) or a weakness (in marginalising them).

At programme and project level we did not see signs that Southern partners are pressing for greater activity in mitigation – if anything, the limited evidence available suggests that partners needed pushing by the British NGOs and are sometimes resistant. The reasons for this remain unclear, although it is likely that time and work pressures play a part. Even in a country as hazard-prone as Bangladesh, NGOs' approach to disasters tends to be responsive.

Institutional memory, learning and information mechanisms

Several factors hinder NGO learning about good practice. Project documentation is poor overall, often difficult to find, and of varying quality. This is significant, since we found that internal project documentation makes up a significant part of interviewees' reading.

Monitoring and evaluation of DMP is weak, focusing on performance of activities, not on projects' impact in reducing disaster risk. Most of the few projects that attempted to assess their impact did so at a relatively early stage. NGOs are comfortable with indicators of output, especially where these are quantitative, but shy away from indicators of impact and seem unsure of how to apply them.

Evaluation of disaster mitigation is problematic because of what one NGO worker referred to as its 'preventive logic': the measure of success is that something – the disaster – does *not* take place. More work is needed to develop appropriate indicators. However, the consequence of poor evaluation is a lack of evidence that mitigation can be effective, making it much more difficult to persuade other NGOs and donors of the value of investing in mitigation measures. Added to this is the problem that evaluations are rarely shared outside the organisations that commission them.

We discovered a handful of strategic initiatives to train NGO staff, local partners, and other NGOs in mitigation and preparedness theory and practice on a regional basis. Such training is expensive. There is some evidence that it has influenced individuals who took part in it, but there are clearly challenges to 'internalising' training at the organisational level, and more attention to long-term follow-up is required. We sensed that demand for training courses and materials is high, although we noted one NGO's perception that its partners were putting too much effort into new courses and materials to the detriment of local capacity building.

The issue of information supply and use is a thread running through the study. Work pressures clearly leave NGO staff very little time for reading and thinking. However, it does not necessarily follow that they are not well informed: in fact, they draw on a variety of information sources, selecting those that best meet the practical needs of their job.

Unsurprisingly, books and academic journals do not have a wide readership among NGO staff, who prefer short case studies and similar material on lessons learned from experience. The Bangladesh study highlighted an additional problem in that most material on disasters is in English and therefore particularly inaccessible at the grassroots level.

Conferences, seminars and the like are not considered significant sources of information: interviewees are aware of such events, but rarely attend them (possibly because of the pressures of work). However, internal workshops or lunchtime debates are recognised as a valuable means of communication and awareness-raising.

Personal contacts, in the same NGO or partner organisations, are a very important source of information. Learning from other individuals is often immediate, to the point, and happens in the course of operational work. Some interviewees pointed to key individuals in NGOs whose personality, enthusiasm, role, or history within an organisation make them important information conduits. E-mail plays an important role in maintaining such personal contacts, especially with partner organisations overseas.

On the other hand, knowledge of what non-partner NGOs are doing is limited: NGO workers want to know, but are too busy to spend much time finding out. This seems to be in contrast to NGO staff in Bangladesh and the Philippines, who find personal and operational contacts with other organisations to be important sources of information (and like their Zimbabwean counterparts seem generally more keen to attend workshops and seminars).

Language and its limitations

Like many other professional and academic disciplines, disaster studies and management have developed a number of theories and an extensive vocabulary of technical terms. We investigated how NGO staff understood some of these concepts and terms. In particular, interviewees were asked how they defined two key terms: 'preparedness' and 'mitigation'.[3] The replies brought home to us how important terminology is in the take-up of ideas.

Few of those we spoke to are comfortable with the terms, especially 'mitigation'. Several see such terms as jargon or over-academic, and find them off-putting. Unsurprisingly, people working in emergency relief are most likely to use the words, while those working in development are least at ease with them. Policy workers tend to be relatively conversant with the terminology, although this does not necessarily make them any happier to use it. People working on food security issues have an alternative set of terms, including 'shock' (for 'disaster') and 'risk/vulnerability reduction' (for 'mitigation').

'Mitigation' and 'preparedness' are understood or were explained in a variety of ways, with a substantial overlap between the two. Many interviewees preferred to give examples of what they considered to be mitigation and preparedness (e.g. 'cyclone shelters', 'crop diversification', 'contingency plans') instead of definitions. This preference for the concrete over the abstract, which we found again when we asked the interviewees what sources and types of information they used in their work, has significant implications for the promotion of new approaches.

Zimbabwean NGOs are also uncomfortable with the terms 'preparedness' and 'mitigation', and, since drought is the main natural hazard they are addressing, are more likely to adopt terms used in food security and natural resource management. The difficulty in clarifying terms and concepts may be partly due to the fact that many have no equivalent in local languages. In the Philippines, understanding of the two key terms is better, perhaps because of the higher proportion of disaster specialists interviewed, but the term 'disaster management' causes some confusion. Elsewhere there is a tendency to re-label other types of work (relief/rehabilitation in Bangladesh, development in Nicaragua) as 'mitigation' or 'preparedness', showing that there has been little or no thinking about what these concepts mean.

The formal language of DMP may be valuable in academic circles and among some full-time disaster professionals, but we believe that the use of such technical terminology in writing and discourse acts is a barrier to many more who are unfamiliar with it, preventing their engagement with the issues – especially since NGO workers are often extremely busy. This does not mean that they do not understand the main issues if these can be explained in a more appropriate manner. It may be time to discard the old terminology and adopt the more accessible language of 'risk' and 'risk reduction', which is already in common use and more readily understood.

The human factor

Greater emphasis on the human factor may be one key to progress. Organisations are not just structures but communities of people, and our study showed that determined and well-placed individuals can push significant innovations through, even at policy level and in large and highly structured NGOs. It also demonstrated that investment in good personal contacts can help defuse institutional tensions between emergencies and development structures. In addition, a growing army of technical advisers of every kind is building up within larger NGOs. They operate across intra-institutional boundaries and they have a mandate – and, crucially, time – to think. They are potentially important figures in bridging the gap between policy and operational practice.

We found that the influence of such individuals depends as much on cultural factors – the time they have been in the organisation, their personality, and their personal networks – as on their formal position within the structure, but can be considerable. High rates of staff turnover in British NGOs, shown in our study and other research (Wallace *et al.* 1997:5-6), probably amplify the influence of a core of long-serving staff, particularly as guardians of institutional memory.

A similar picture appears among NGOs in the South, although here formal seniority in the organisation plays a more important role. In Bangladeshi NGOs, experienced senior managers are influential in setting disaster policy, while NGOs in the Philippines benefit from a substantial cadre of long-serving staff experienced in DMP (as well as relatively low staff turnover). Nicaraguan NGOs have recruited experienced disaster planners and managers who lost their jobs in government as a result of recent retrenchment. However, among Zimbabwean NGOs it is felt that senior management in headquarters is too dominant in decision making, and does not always understand the situation on the ground.

This suggests that targeting key individuals in organisations has potential as a means of disseminating ideas and good practice, although it may be difficult for outsiders to identify them.

Conclusion: ways forward

Our research shows that NGOs, as learning organisations, face considerable challenges in bringing marginalised issues such as DMP into the development mainstream, but the studies also indicate how learning about such issues can be stimulated. We have three main recommendations to make here.

First, NGOs must recognise that organisational learning is much more than a matter of making information available. NGO staff must be given time and opportunity to learn.

Second, advocates of alternative theories and approaches need to think of NGOs as communities, not merely as formal structures. They should identify and target key individuals within NGOs who can share information, promote ideas, and influence policy and practice.

Third, there should be greater emphasis on practical aspects of learning. It is relatively easy to argue a new idea successfully, especially if it is presented in everyday language, but much more difficult to explain how to put it into effect operationally. It is here, crossing the boundary from policy to practice, that NGOs want to learn more.

Notes

1   The term 'natural disaster' is widely used to refer to the impact of natural hazards (e.g. cyclones, earthquakes, floods) on society. This is misleading because the impact of such hazards is profoundly influenced by the extent of society's vulnerability to them, which is influenced by socio-economic conditions and trends (i.e. development processes).

2   The research was funded by the Department for International Development (DfID) and managed by the British Red Cross, but undertaken by a team of independent researchers who are solely responsible for the outputs and the views contained in them.

3   The technical literature gives a range of definitions. We have interpreted them broadly as follows. 'Mitigation': any action before, during, or after a disaster to minimise its impact or potential impact (ranging from physical measures such as flood defences or building reinforcement to non-structural measures such as training, land use regulation, legislation, and public awareness raising). 'Preparedness': specific measures before disasters strike, usually to forecast and warn against them, take precautions when they threaten, and arrange for the appropriate response (e.g. organising evacuations, stockpiling food supplies, and training rescue services).

References

Blaikie, Piers, Terry Cannon, Ian Davis, and Ben Wisner (1994) *At Risk: Natural Hazards, People's Vulnerability and Disasters*, London: Routledge.

International Federation of Red Cross and Red Crescent Societies (IFRC) (1997) *World Disasters Report 1997*, Geneva and Oxford: IFRC and OUP.

Luna, Emmanuel (2000) 'NGO Natural Disaster Mitigation and Preparedness: The Philippine Case Study', available at www.redcross.org.uk/dmp (accessed 3 August 2001).

Matin, Nilufar and Muhammad Taher (2000) 'Disaster Mitigation in Bangladesh: Country Case Study of NGO Activities', available at www.redcross.org.uk/dmp (accessed 3 August 2001).

Munich Re (1998) *Annual Review of Natural Catastrophes 1998*, Munich: Munich Reinsurance.

Rocha, José, Luis and Ian Christoplos (2000) 'Disaster Mitigation and Preparedness in Nicaragua after Hurricane Mitch', available at www.redcross.org.uk/dmp (accessed 3 August 2001).

Shumba, Owen (2000) 'An Assessment of NGO Disaster Mitigation and Preparedness Activities in Zimbabwe: Country Survey Report', available at www.redcross.org.uk/dmp (accessed 3 August 2001).

Twigg, John, Diane Steiner, Mary Myers, and Charlotte Benson (2000) 'NGO Natural Disaster Mitigation and Preparedness Projects: A Study of International Development and Relief NGOs based in the UK', available at www.redcross.org.uk/dmp (accessed 3 August 2001).

Wallace, Tina, Sarah Crowther and Andrew Shepherd (1997) *Standardising Development: Influences on UK NGOs' Policies and Procedures*, Oxford: WorldView.

This article was first published in Development in Practice *(12/3&4:473–479)* in 2002.

The learning process of the Local Capacities for Peace Project

Marshall Wallace

Where does the Local Capacities for Peace Project come from?

The changes in the world in the wake of the Cold War have altered the circumstances in which humanitarian and development agencies work. Violent conflicts surfaced in many countries – conflicts that the international powers did not or would not support or mediate. The roles of humanitarian agencies began to shift. Aid agencies either identified new roles for themselves or were asked by their donors to take on functions they had not previously filled.

The new circumstances propelled aid workers into situations of increasing danger that affected them, their projects, and the beneficiaries of aid. It became increasingly apparent that aid given in a context of conflict is itself a part of that context. This is simply unavoidable. Further, it was clear that the way in which aid is given can, under some circumstances, have exacerbating effects on the conflict.

The negative effects of aid are inadvertent and unintentional, but that does not diminish the need to avoid them. Rather, it sends a call to all our colleagues to be aware of these effects and to do our work in such a way as to minimise them – to 'do no harm'. It is also possible in some cases to give aid in a way that can help mitigate violence and provide the people involved in the conflict with the space – the breathing room – to build their peace.

If aid is found to support a war effort, should aid agencies and practitioners continue to give it? The resounding answer given by aid workers all over the world is that the needs of suffering people are too important to ignore and, further, that there can be no justification for not assisting suffering people. Inevitably, the next question is: how can one provide aid in the context of conflict without exacerbating the conflict?

The Local Capacities for Peace Project (LCPP) was formed in 1994 to address this concern. If aid becomes a part of the context, how does this happen? The LCPP was created to learn how aid and conflict interact in order to help aid workers find a way to address human needs in conflict situations without feeding conflict.[1]

What does this paper do?

This paper will not repeat the lessons learned through the LCPP in any depth. Those have been amply detailed elsewhere.[2] Rather, it will discuss the processes and approaches of the LCPP. It will show how the methodology of the LCPP was designed to address an issue of serious concern to aid practitioners and to generate lessons based on experience that could be translated into a practical and useable tool to improve the impacts of aid programming. The paper will also discuss how the learning process of the LCPP was designed and what results were gained at each step. Finally, it will show how the results were fed back to the participating organisations.

Inductive process of the LCPP

The LCPP was designed to gather its results inductively, working from the experience of people in the field towards a general application of the lessons. Why use an inductive process? What are its advantages and what can be learned by using this approach?

The inductive process is engaging. It starts where the people are, with their daily experiences, their dilemmas, and their observations. The inductive process is cumulative. It proceeds from the particular to the general by taking many individual experiences and comparing them in the search for patterns. The inductive process is wide ranging and realist. It accepts the validity of everyone's experiences and follows where these lead. The inductive process is pragmatic. As patterns are found, lessons can be drawn about options for action available in similar situations.

Furthermore, for humanitarian professionals there is an additional reason to use an inductive learning process. Humanitarian work has a direct impact on the quality of people's lives. It is, therefore, essential to base a learning process that is intended to improve humanitarian work on people's actual lives and actual experiences.

How did the LCPP use an inductive process? The LCPP involved four phases. The first gathered information about the relationships between aid programmes and conflict and the experiences were written up as case

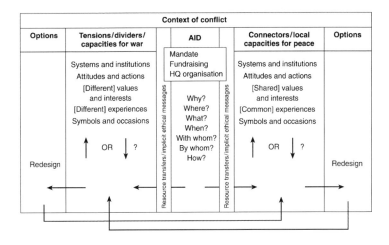

studies. The second phase added to the learning through 'feedback workshops' where these earlier experiences were shared with aid practitioners in a variety of venues. In these workshops, participants added their experiences and insights through their confirmations of, and challenges to, the lessons drawn from the case studies. In the course of the second phase a practical tool in the form of a framework for understanding and predicting the relations between aid and conflict was developed. The third phase focused on implementing the lessons learned and the application of the framework at the field level in ongoing projects in situations of conflict. Field staff used the framework tool to analyse the impact of their project in situations of conflict (see Figure 1). Twice-yearly consultations with representatives from all of the project sites supported the generalisation of lessons learned by specific projects. The fourth and current phase is that of mainstreaming the lessons and approaches of the LCPP in a number of participating organisations. Each of the four stages has contributed to understanding the issues and to learning how to improve humanitarian work. The following sections describe each phase in more detail.

Experience-based learning Phase I: case studies (1994–1996)

In order to learn about the interaction of aid in conflict, it was necessary to gather an initial set of information and to see if there were common experiences among aid practitioners. The LCPP began by looking at the activities and projects of 15 agencies in 14 conflict zones and by writing up these stories as case studies. The studies covered a wide range of agencies and types of intervention, as well as a number of different regions of the world and types of conflict in the expectation that breadth of coverage is necessary for generalisable learning.[3]

The case study writers were people in the aid community who had expressed concerns about aid in the context of conflict and wanted to learn more about how the two interact. Some wrote about their own experiences or those of their organisation; others were 'outsiders' to the project they examined. Writers were charged with a straightforward task. They were asked, first, to describe the context of the conflict; second, to describe the aid intervention; and, third, to describe the interactions between the conflict and the aid. Finally, they were asked to discuss the reasons for what had happened from their perspective, as well as from the points of view of people in the field (aid workers, beneficiaries, and others).

The case study writers made site visits and had extensive conversations with practitioners on the ground, both expatriate and local staff. They talked with people who were beneficiaries of the project and with people who did not benefit directly. The writers did not work with pre-set interview protocols or questionnaires but engaged people to tell their own stories in their own way.

The organisations about whom the case studies were written were involved in the LCPP in a number of different ways. Some had been asked by their donors to participate. In other cases, the headquarters either suggested a field site or their field staff lobbied to be included. All were motivated by the shared concern about the interactions of aid with conflict. They were willing to risk 'exposure' in the expectation that the learning gathered would be of practical use. Encouraging as many organisations as possible to join the project ensured that the ownership was broadly spread and that the learning was representative.

Case studies take a snapshot of experience. Putting a series of snapshots side by side allows common themes and patterns to appear. It also makes it possible to identify contextual differences. Distilling the commonalities and the particularities is the challenge to learning from case studies. The LCPP convened groups to read and analyse the cases. These groups consisted of the case writers, people from the war zones where the studies had been written, and other aid practitioners. They began the process of sorting the information for its practical application.

The process identified enough patterns about the impact of aid on situations of conflict to agree to the production of a booklet for broader consideration. This booklet, *Do No Harm: Supporting Local Capacities for Peace through Aid*, was conceived as a work-in-progress and invited readers to contact the LCPP 'with your own ideas and insights so these can be incorporated into the lessons learned to be widely shared among the assistance community at work in conflict settings' (Anderson 1996:i).[4] It was recognised that the case studies were not sufficient in and of themselves to provide much more than a starting point, identifying some common themes. While the cases had amply confirmed the fact that aid and conflict interact with each other, they had barely begun to chart the mechanisms involved in how these interactions take place.

Experience-based learning Phase II: feedback workshops (1996–1998)

Accepting its own challenge as presented in the booklet, the LCPP set out to involve many more people in testing and adding to what had been learned through the case studies. 'Feedback workshops' were used to introduce more people and all of their experiences into the mix. These workshops were arranged in collaboration with aid agency personnel in the field and at headquarters. Over an 18-month period, over 25 feedback workshops were run in 20 settings. Most of these were in regions of conflict, including some in the locations where case studies had been written. Others were held in agency headquarters in European and North American cities.

The LCPP recruited and trained a cadre of workshop facilitators. Some of these were aid agency staff whose time was donated to this effort. All the facilitators had had experience in humanitarian or development assistance and, along with LCPP staff, put together a manual for trainers. This manual was designed for use by aid agencies in their own training programmes so that the process could continue beyond the availability of the cadre of LCPP trainers.

Feedback workshops usually lasted three days and included a series of sessions designed to elicit participants' own experiences of working with aid in conflict situations. Participants were asked to challenge, support, add to, and amend the learning from the case studies. The facilitators led the sessions and gathered the results of discussions, feeding them back into the LCPP learning process.

This phase of the LCPP's inductive process directly involved over 750 additional practitioners from about 100 agencies in generating ideas and insights. One or two organisations hosted each workshop, but all agencies in the area were invited to participate and to send someone to share their own and the agency's experiences. People in the workshops often told the LCPP that these events gave them a rare opportunity to step away from their daily work and, with colleagues from other agencies, to consider the impacts that their aid programmes were having. They often found that the sharing of these ideas led to creative responses to some of the difficulties they were encountering.

Engaging this wide range of people with their broad variety of experience ensured that the learning was both grounded in the complexity of real life and relevant across many circumstances. Introducing additional people into the LCPP through the feedback workshops was equivalent in some ways to adding a further 750 case studies (or more, because many participants had experience of providing aid in more than one conflict area). This testing of and adding to the patterns and commonalities identified by the case studies focused and improved the quality of the learning.

Involving more people and agencies in the learning process also ensured that the ownership of ideas would be more widely disseminated. It was never anticipated that the findings of the LCPP would 'belong' solely to the project. It was intended from the beginning that aid agencies and practitioners would take up whatever information was generated by the project. The feedback workshops were a part of the process of spreading and increasing ownership through the dissemination of ideas and also the challenging of those ideas. At the end of every workshop, the learning of the project was greater than before.

At the end of the feedback-workshop phase, the LCPP was able to produce a workable and generalisable tool for analysing the impacts of aid on conflict. The 'Do No Harm Framework' came from the people participating in the workshops, as together they applied their wide range of experiences to the issue. In order to further the spread of the knowledge gained by the project, the LCPP produced a book detailing this tool.[5]

The feedback workshops transformed the patterns emerging from the information in the case studies into a general and common framework of knowledge for understanding the impacts that aid projects can have on conflict. Useful and necessary as this was, the challenge remained to take these general lessons and apply them to particular situations. If the patterns identified and confirmed during the first two phases of the LCPP were, in fact, relevant for aid practitioners, they needed to be translatable into a form that was practical for use in the daily activities of aid workers.

Experience-based learning Phase III: implementation (1998–2000)

The LCPP is about aid agencies doing their work better. The third phase of the project set out to apply the knowledge gained through the first two phases and the LCPP proposed implementing the 'Do No Harm Framework' in actual field sites. The purpose of this effort was to demonstrate the usefulness of the framework to inform and improve the day-to-day decisions made by project staff in difficult situations around the world.

Fourteen agencies collaborated directly with the LCPP in testing the usefulness and practicality of the framework. They used it in their project design, implementation, monitoring, evaluation, and redesign. In order to ensure that everybody involved in a project was working from a common understanding, training sessions in the material and the use of the framework were held. Many agencies included local staff and the staff of local partner organisations in this training.

The projects were selected in a variety of ways. In some organisations, the headquarters picked a project to implement the framework and requested that the team in the field make themselves available to participate in the LCPP. Some of the projects were picked by people who were themselves running projects and had heard about or been exposed to the LCPP and found it interesting and worthwhile to attempt to apply it to their own work.

The LCPP's role was to provide a 'liaison' person for each project. The role of this person was, first, to run training sessions on the lessons learned for the people at the project site. Second, s/he served as an adviser on how to use the framework and to help focus the discussions. Third, the liaison person was responsible for returning to the project site every three months to perform additional facilitating or training as needed, and to keep the approach in the forefront of the project team's minds. And, fourth, s/he was responsible for documenting the learning and feeding the experience gathered back into the project.

In addition to supporting the liaison work at the project sites, the LCPP convened biannual consultations. These consultations gathered the liaison people together with people participating in the projects from the field, as well as with people from the headquarters of the agencies involved, and even some donors. Participants shared their experiences of using the framework. The most interesting discussions involved using the whole group to generate ideas and options to deal with the difficulties faced by a particular project.

The implementation phase covered a full three years. It was felt that this was the minimum time needed to be able to assess the impacts of the use of the tool. Three years were sufficient to establish some indications about aid's impacts on conflict and to identify the *significant* impacts on conflict of six major types of decisions made by aid projects.[6] A manual was produced discussing the impact of these decisions and offering several options for aid projects.

Implementation served to test the framework produced from the two preceding phases and also generated a new set of experiences that added to and tested the learning. Furthermore, it provided a way to check on the knowledge gained and the lessons learned in the previous two phases of the project.

The implementation incorporated the general and common lessons and provided the opportunity to use those lessons in a particular place to achieve a particular result. The learning process, in some sense, came full circle, though it did not cease. Several hundred more aid practitioners were involved in the implementation phase of the LCPP. They too challenged, tested, and added to the learning. The continuing addition of people exposed to the LCPP and involved in refining the framework, as well as adding to its basis, further spread the ownership of these ideas among the aid community.

The power of the learning process of the LCPP as embodied in the Framework

The Do No Harm Framework is an evolving tool. While its overall structure has remained the same since it was first developed out of the feedback workshops, using it in practice has further refined the details which the framework can emphasise. Also, several agencies have adapted it to better integrate it into their own procedures. This constant testing under practical conditions goes on and so continues to push the development and usefulness of the tool.

The experience of using this framework has allowed agencies to map the interactions of their aid within contexts of conflict. It has also offered three interrelated benefits. First, it has helped aid workers develop specific criteria for making decisions and be able to articulate clearly the reasons for those decisions in a manner that can be shared easily. Field staff are responsible for making good decisions and they often need to be able to explain these decisions to their headquarters and donors, as well as to the local communities. In situations of uncertainty, where levels of fear and distrust are high, being able to communicate clearly and transparently can greatly improve the ability to do the work well.

Second, the framework has encouraged a rigorous emphasis on facts. This leads agencies to make their implicit decisions explicit and helps prevent misguided assumptions. It also encourages agencies to rely on the knowledge of their local staff. Several agencies have commented that involving local staff in the LCPP sessions has led to greater understanding of the context for all involved as well as steering the programming in clearer directions.

Third, the framework has supported a continuous critical inquiry into the way in which agencies do their work. Agencies have reported that in using the Do No Harm Framework they can see their actual impacts more clearly and therefore can make informed decisions, rather than decisions based on an assumed impact. Organisations want to do their work well and the framework has encouraged an honest appraisal of good work. Many agencies have reported uncovering 'honest mistakes' on their part, which has led them to change their programming procedures to avoid such pitfalls in the future.

Experience-based learning Phase IV: mainstreaming (2001)

Three related issues raised in the consultations encouraged the continuation of the LCPP into a fourth phase. All three concerned the interactions of work in the field with responses of headquarters and donors.

The first issue was a difficulty raised by the field staff using the framework. They found that donor policies and agency headquarters policies could themselves have an exacerbating influence on conflict. This led to a paper produced by the LCPP about the responsibilities of donors and headquarters staff when dealing with projects in conflict situations (Anderson 1999b).

The second issue was also a concern raised by field staff. They found that donors and headquarters staff often had attitudes and policies that hampered the uptake of the Do No Harm Framework by field staff – even if the field staff were interested in doing so. This concern was also expressed in a broader fashion, encompassing a general concern by field staff about the influence of donors and headquarters on the uptake of any new idea or method.

The third issue sprang from the acknowledgement by agency headquarters of their influence on the uptake of ideas. Headquarters staff were interested in spreading the concepts of the LCPP throughout their organisations. The implementation efforts had succeeded in imparting the existing lessons learned by the LCPP to the staff directly involved in a particular field site. However, the organisations themselves had not been sufficiently exposed to the broad learning in a way that would ensure the framework could be adopted in other areas. This was also expressed in a broader fashion, concerning the ways in which humanitarian agencies as a whole learn and implement new ideas and methods.

A fourth phase of the LCPP was proposed to address these three concerns. It was decided to focus on the third of these issues, the issue of organisational learning, and to address the other two as adjunct to this process. This fourth phase of the LCPP was named the 'mainstreaming' phase to reflect its concern with bringing the LCPP to the mainstream of humanitarian practice.

The purpose of this phase was conceived of in two ways. By exposing more people to the Do No Harm Framework, the knowledge base of the LCPP could again be extended and expanded through involving more people from the aid community. In addition, the LCPP would use the framework as a test case to learn about organisational learning in humanitarian agencies.

The agencies involved looked upon this as an opportunity to increase the integration of the framework tool into their operational procedures. While the third phase of the LCPP had in large part limited the use of the framework to one field project, the mainstreaming phase would engage a wider range of staff, both in the field and at the headquarters. It was remarked that this process would put the field and the headquarters 'on the same page'.

How an organisation establishes these linkages within itself to promote the uptake of an idea or a tool – and the incorporation of the tool into their operations – was also seen as a desired outcome by the agencies. A varied approach was taken to answer this question. The LCPP began a wide-ranging discussion with agencies about how to proceed. Agencies were encouraged to think about their own strategies for mainstreaming other ideas (e.g. gender, the environment, the use of computers). This prior experience informed the strategies that agencies could use in the course of the fourth phase of the LCPP.

Each participating agency identified its own way to proceed. These varied quite a bit, depending on a number of factors including agency size, partnering strategies, and types of field activity. The LCPP offered support to the agencies through conversations about prior and current strategies. The LCPP also offered continuing training, but in this phase with an emphasis on integrating it into an organisation-wide strategy.

All of the strategies identified and used by agencies built upon existing linkages between people in the field and the headquarters staff. These relationships vary from agency to agency on a range of issues such as differing perspectives on autonomy and direction, policy and implementation, and impact of donor decisions.

The mainstreaming phase was scheduled to last only one year. It was understood by the LCPP and the agencies that such a short time is not sufficient to mainstream an idea. However, it was felt to be long enough to begin the mainstreaming process and to learn important lessons about how humanitarian organisations learn and implement their learning.

Again, two biannual consultations were scheduled to gather the experience of the agencies involved. The second of these was held at the end of November 2001, and will be followed by an LCPP publication outlining what was learned in this phase of the project, and ways in which people think about how their organisation can take up and implement any idea.[7]

An additional note on the consultations

The consultations have been found to be among the most important parts of the process. They have provided a supportive setting in which to discuss issues that were being raised on the ground. The wide range of experiences of participants encouraged the flow of ideas and facilitated problem solving.

Agencies brought their problems of working in contexts of conflict to the consultations and the group was always able to generate some options. Agencies also brought their solutions, which would soon be tested at other project sites. The consultations always had an emphasis on the refinement of the learning and allowed for the constant practice of using the methodology. The consultations also provided a forum for developing and deepening professional relationships. Information and techniques continue to be disseminated among the people who participated in the consultations.

Summary

The learning process of the LCPP demonstrates four things. First, it demonstrates how a large amount of experience can be gathered in a fairly short period of time. Second, it shows how that experience and data can be transformed into a useful and practical tool. Third, it shows how such a process can be designed to increase and refine learning over time, while also leading to actions that improve project impacts. And, fourth, it shows how a process can be organised to engage many people to increase ownership of the learning process, and, therefore, the use of the lessons once learned.

Case studies are limited – only so many can be written, and this limited set of information seldom leads to an acceptable platform for generating practical responses to the issues raised. They can serve to establish the existence of common, general themes across a range of specific experience. However, in order to develop practical responses to the lessons outlined in case studies, it is necessary to take further steps.

Once a series of experiences has been collected, in this instance through case studies, it is equally important to involve as many people as possible into the process of gathering the lessons from those experiences. There is a continuing responsibility to involve as much experience as possible in the project. Engaging people with an issue they have identified as important ensures that the project will benefit from this experience. It also ensures that the outcomes will be relevant to the experience of the people involved.

Implementing the findings tests their operational practicality. The process of putting something into practice reveals the limitations and the strengths of the prior learning. The practical application of the lessons highlights concerns and demonstrates where the project can have an immediate impact. It also highlights those places where more work needs to be done in the project. Furthermore, implementation involves another set of people in the process and the project continues to learn from their experience.

The aid field has a vast number of highly intelligent and thoughtful people who are involved in discussions about how to work better. Engaging these people can only improve the quality of all our work. The challenges that people bring to bear on an issue from their own experience open up great possibilities for learning and for acting.

Notes

1   The funding of the LCPP was a two-part process. Funds came from both existing donors and from participating agencies. By design, the LCPP was funded by a large number of the donor governments and agencies. This encouraged the agencies from those countries to be involved, which also spread knowledge

around the world. Further, the information and lessons coming out of the LCPP could not be seen as belonging to one country or reflective of one country's experience. Spreading the funding over a wide number of donors encouraged a wide sense of ownership. It was also understood that donors give more than money. Their encouragement of a project can increase the involvement of NGOs. The LCPP encouraged donors to take an active part in the project through participation in the consultations and some work in the field. Some of the donors have done so in the course of the LCPP. These additional elements increase donor ownership of the project and its results, and provide valuable insights throughout the process.

The agencies involved in the LCPP were encouraged to offer some of the time of their staff as in-kind payments. The project estimates that 30 per cent of the LCPP budget has come from donations from agencies, both cash and in kind. For a list of donors please refer to the Collaborative for Development Action, Inc. (CDA) website at: www.cdainc.com.

2 Mary B. Anderson has written numerous pieces on the lessons learned by the LCPP. See the References for some examples, as well as CDA's website.

3 The case studies were written about 15 projects in 14 conflict zones, including Bosnia, Burundi, Guatemala, Lebanon, Somalia, and Tajikistan. For a complete list and the text of some of the cases, please refer to the CDA website.

4 This booklet, the first titled *Do No Harm*, has been superseded by the 1999 book. CDA does not 'stand behind' this booklet, as it was never intended to produce a final document. If you possess a copy, CDA requests that you recycle it. Do not use it as a reference. Quotations from this work-in-progress have led to many misunderstandings about the nature of the LCPP.

5 See Anderson (1999a: Chapter 6) for an introduction to the 'Do No Harm Framework for Analysing the Impact of Aid on Conflict'.

6 The six major types of decisions faced by aid agencies are detailed in Anderson (2000: Sections 2–7). Briefly, they are decisions about who should receive aid; about staffing of field programmes; about local partners; about what to provide; about how to provide aid; and about working with local authorities.

7 Heinrich and Wallace (2000) have collected the experience of agencies in mainstreaming the 'Do No Harm Framework' into their organisational experience.

References

Anderson, Mary B. (1996) *Do No Harm: Supporting Local Capacities for Peace Through Aid*, Cambridge, MA: Collaborative for Development Action, Inc.

Anderson, Mary B. (1999a) *Do No Harm: How Aid Can Support Peace – Or War*, Boulder, CO: Lynne Rienner.

Anderson, Mary B. (1999b) 'The Implications of Do No Harm for Donors and Aid Agency Headquarters', available at www.cdainc.com/lcpp-policy.htm.

Anderson, Mary B. (ed.) (2000) *Options for Aid in Conflict: Lessons from Field Experience*, Cambridge, MA: Collaborative for Development Action, Inc.

Heinrich, Wolfgang and Marshall Wallace (2000) 'Helpful Hints for Mainstreaming: NGO Mainstreaming in Practice', available at www.cdainc.com/lcpp-mainstreaming.htm.

This article was first published in Development in Practice *(12/3&4: 480–489) in 2002.*

Humanitarian principles and organisational culture: everyday practice in Médecins Sans Frontières-Holland

Dorothea Hilhorst and Nadja Schmiemann

Introduction

Until recently, it would have been nonsensical, or at least counter-intuitive, to write a paper on humanitarian principles for a publication devoted to learning organisations. Principles of humanity, neutrality, and impartiality were considered universal, not evolving or contextual. These principles were thought to be enshrined in international humanitarian law and embodied in the practices of the Red Cross movement. But in the last decade, this has changed dramatically. Changes in the nature of conflict, the complex contexts in which humanitarian work is undertaken, and the proliferation of humanitarian organisations have contributed to a situation in which humanitarian principles are being debated and negotiated. One of the signalling events that set these changes in motion was the formation of Médecins Sans Frontières (MSF) in 1971. This offshoot of the International Committee of the Red Cross (ICRC) came about in response to experiences during the war in Biafra. It was a deliberate challenge to the perceived rigidity of some of the principles and hierarchical workstyle of the ICRC. The founders of MSF considered *témoignage* (the witnessing and shaming of humanitarian law abuses) an important complement to providing relief, but nonetheless compatible with the principles of impartiality and neutrality. MSF also stands for a different workstyle. By employing volunteers for humanitarian work, the organisation provides people who are motivated by the humanitarian spirit with the opportunity to contribute to worthwhile action, and it thus maintains a strong embeddedness in society.

While in the last few years there have been a number of conferences and publications on humanitarian principles in response to changing political contexts, this paper focuses on the meaning of principles for humanitarian workers in their everyday practice. Principles are declared and are formally negotiated in codes of conduct and in working arrangements between the parties involved in situations of complex crisis. However, what difference these make in practice depends on how they are translated by the people who put them to use. How they are implemented in the running of a field hospital or in responding to numerous small events encountered in providing assistance depends on staff members' interpretation of the situation and the principles. To understand how principles work in practice, it is therefore important to take into account that these operate through patterns of organisational culture.

Principles do not only work in regulating actions and relations with external stakeholders of humanitarian organisations, they also have a bearing upon organisational life and motivation. It was this latter aspect in particular that triggered the research informing this paper, which examines the way organisational principles are experienced by MSF volunteers in the field, and how this influences their decision to stay with or leave the organisation.[1] This question was identified by the MSF management who wanted to find out the extent to which MSF's specific principles make a difference for the people working for the organisation. The core of the research consisted of in-depth interviews with 14 volunteers who had just returned after one to three missions lasting anywhere between six months and two years. Half of the interviewees were medical personnel and the others were logistics experts.

The first part of this paper introduces humanitarian principles and the recent discussions that have evolved around them, followed by some theoretical notes on the meaning of principles in organisational practice and culture. Everyday field experience will be illustrated by a fictional account of a day in the life of a volunteer, which was constructed on the basis of interview material. We then elaborate how volunteers redefine and renegotiate principles in practice. As we shall argue, the implementation of principles in humanitarian action is patterned by organisational culture where all actors use their own agency to learn, redefine, and negotiate what happens.

Humanitarian principles

Humanitarian action finds its essential motivation in the principle of humanity, defined by the International Federation of Red Cross and Red Crescent Societies (IFRC) as 'the desire to prevent and alleviate human suffering wherever it may be found ... to protect life and health and to ensure respect for the human being' (IFRC 2001). Humanitarian action addresses human suffering, whether resulting from disasters caused by natural hazards or by situations of conflict. Humanitarian principles that guide assistance, such as the principles of impartiality and neutrality, find their rationale in international humanitarian law and stem specifically from experiences in war situations. Henry Dunant initiated the formal regulation of warfare after the Battle of Solferino in 1859. Wars in those days were typically between competing nation-state armies, and the idea of reducing suffering was appealing as a means of legitimising warfare in increasingly democratising societies. Humanitarianism started with the Geneva Convention of 1864 and the recognition of the ICRC, which was given space to operate on the condition of neutrality and impartiality (Leader 2000:12) After the massive abuse of humanitarian ideals in the Second World War, four more Geneva Conventions elaborated the rules of war. It is important to note that the term 'humanitarian principles' refers to moral principles to mitigate the destructive impact of war, but it is also used to refer to principles of humanitarian action. This paper is concerned with the latter. Principles of humanitarian action are *derived* from international humanitarian law but are not *integral* to the conventions that regulate warfare among belligerents (Leader 1998).

In the last two decades, humanitarian principles have generated extensive debate and undergone much change. This development is related to several factors. First, the nature of conflict has increasingly moved away from the wars between nations that inspired international humanitarian law. Today's conflicts are mostly intra-state in nature. They occur in societies where the legitimacy and representational capacity of the State is low or even non-existent, at least in the eyes of certain sectors of society. Civilians are often the direct targets of violence and account for 90 per cent of all victims. Warfare is spread over a large area and fragmented in nature. In the 'battlefield', use is made of light weaponry and small arms, while common techniques include methods such as rape, 'ethnic cleansing', and starvation, which are specifically directed against the civilian population. International conventions and rules for warfare in these cases hardly apply, and humanitarian organisations have had likewise to reconsider their working principles. In particular, the principle of neutrality has come to be renegotiated in humanitarian politics, varying across both situations and organisations. Leader (2000) identifies three different positions in this respect: 'neutrality elevated', 'neutrality abandoned', and 'third-way humanitarianism' seeking a middle way.

Second, there has been a proliferation of organisations which are active in humanitarian operations. Even when they nominally embrace the same principles, the way these principles are translated into practice may differ substantially. Among others, organisations have different positions in the status they accord to principles, varying between the view that they are universal and imperative (people have the universal right to humanitarian assistance) to the view that they are relative (Macrae 1996:34). These different meanings come to the surface and clash when organisations want to define a coordinated response to a particular crisis, as for instance in South Sudan and Liberia (Atkinson and Leader 2000; Bradbury *et al.* 2000). Third, humanitarian principles have been further elaborated, thus creating more potential for diversity. On the basis of a survey among humanitarian organisations, Minear and Weiss (1993) found that eight principles were included by most agencies in the package of humanitarian principles. Apart from the so-called classic principles, humanitarian organisations, partly affected by notions from development but mainly learning from their own experiences, had come to adopt a new generation of principles including accountability and the need for appropriateness and contextualisation. Fourth, humanitarian organisations to different degrees have taken on additional, but not always equally compatible, sets of principles, such as human rights, justice (directed at fair and equal relationships), development and peace building, and staff protection. Finally, humanitarian principles have come to be debated as a result of increasing doubts about the effectiveness and impact of humanitarian aid. Some consider humanitarian action liable to be part of the problem rather than the solution by actually feeding into the economies of war, acting as diversion for political solutions, or undermining people's coping and livelihood capacities (see, for instance, Anderson 1996; Prendergast 1996; de Waal 1997).

Changing political and military contexts of conflict and the proliferation of organisations and principles have all contributed to revealing the negotiated nature of principles. Humanitarian principles have lost their universality and their aura as radiant beacons in the storms of humanitarian crises. This has led to what some have labelled an ethical crisis in humanitarianism. We do not wish to add to this debate on ethics, but would rather approach the problem in a more empirical way. Having realised that principles are relative rather than absolute, one then has to ask: What do principles *do* for organisations? What constitutes the relation between principles and practice? Are humanitarians simply drifting around? How can humanitarian workers distinguish right from wrong in the minutiae of their everyday work? These questions direct attention to the importance of organisational culture for understanding humanitarian work in practice.

Organisational principles and culture

Principles, in classic organisational thinking, precede policy, which in turn precedes implementation. Principles, in this view, are defined or declared by the founders or trustees of an organisation; management translates them into policies; and staff deal with their implementation. Recent thinking about organisations, on the other hand, views principles and policy as processes rather than entities. Colebatch (1998:111), for instance, sees policy and principles as 'continuing patterns of events and understanding'. Indeed, as the above discussion illustrates, principles find expression in historically specific ways and evolve in response to organisational experience. The relation between principle and practice ceases to be sequential and becomes mutually informing: principles shape practice but at the same time only become alive through everyday practice where they are interpreted and reshaped. The translation of principles into practice is not the prerogative of management but happens through the combined actions of *all* staff members and other involved actors. It is, therefore, not enough to follow formal declarations of principles and policy. Rather to understand the working of principles we must look at the actions of fieldworkers (Long 1989).

The processes by which principles are assessed in order to identify which are the more appropriate ones for a given situation and then applying them are not rational. How actors understand principles and the situations in which they apply is mediated by their institutional experiences, expectations, and 'lifeworld'. (The concept of lifeworld denotes the world as immediately or directly experienced in the subjectivity of everyday life.) The interpretation of principles is, furthermore, a social process: it is through interaction that individuals make sense of principles and practice. Much of this happens implicitly and routinely: in the course of time, patterns evolve from which fieldworkers derive their decisions. These can be called patterns of organisational culture.

Such cultural patterns evolve in the first place in the field teams of humanitarian organisations. MSF volunteers on mission experience conditions that are very different from 'normal' work situations. The volunteers have to make sense of a new environment, in tense security situations, where they face unprecedented experiences that often take place in the context of, or have, emotional impact. Family and friends are left behind and life on mission is so extraordinary that volunteers often think that people at home cannot relate to them. In the field there is hardly any space or time separating work from non-work. The team frequently forms the volunteers' only social network: they do not go home and cannot reflect on their work with outsiders. This situation has a strong resemblance to what Erving Goffman (1961) called 'closed communities'. Much importance is attached to a local team that largely coincides with the lifeworld of volunteers at that moment. Social interaction with immediate colleagues becomes a major reference point for making sense of the situation and of experiences at work.

Similar patterns may be identified in a broader context, whether MSF-wide or across the humanitarian sector. This sector is characterised by a rapid staff turnover. Knowledge and experience thus travel around within it and result to some extent in shared patterns of practice. However, culture too is a process. Organisational culture is not a piece of luggage that humanitarian workers carry around with them. Evolving patterns are never final: they change in response to situations. Besides, there are always competing patterns and alternative actions. Implicitly or explicitly, fieldworkers use their agency to select and apply certain courses of action over others. Yet, while such cultural patterns are not totally voluntary, they do serve to order organisational life wherein ideas become institutionalised and practices take on habitual or ritual properties (Hilhorst forthcoming).

Once we acknowledge that every staff member contributes to the shaping of organisational principles through everyday practice, it becomes clear that the set of principles that an organisation adopts may change considerably in the experience of its staff. As we shall argue below, MSF volunteers not only reinterpret principles, but also adhere to other ordering principles they deem typical for MSF and more determinant of their life in the field. Likewise, staff members find their own channels for negotiating principles outside formal communications, for instance through informal interaction and 'gossip'.

Although organisational principles are renegotiated in practice, they remain important for the organisation. They may not dictate practice, but do help to order humanitarian action in many, perhaps unexpected, ways. They serve as anchor points expressing what an organisation wants to achieve and on what values its actions are based. Besides having the potential to prescribe action, they provide fieldworkers with clues about how to accord meaning to their interactions, the environment, and the events around them. In addition, principles are identity markers that help organisations to distinguish themselves from others working in the same field (Rokebach 1973:159). Furthermore, principles can serve to boost motivation. People want to give meaning to their actions and make sense of their interactions with others. Principles can thus add some higher meaning to otherwise tedious or tense work (Sims *et al.* 1993:269). Finally, principles can work as 'glue' when they bind members of an organisation together (Barnard and Walker 1994:57). Principles thus remain important in different ways. How they work in practice depends on how actors understand and employ them in the field. Therefore we stress the need for an ethnographic approach to the study of principles.

MSF-Holland

MSF was founded in 1971 and MSF-Holland (MSF-H) followed in 1984. MSF has five operational centres in Europe and 13 support offices. Canada, the UK, and Germany function as partner sections of MSF-H. MSF-H supervises about 34 missions (in 30 countries), is responsible for sending out almost 800 people each year, and has about 2800 local staff members. In the countries in which MSF-H has projects, country managers and their teams are responsible for setting up and establishing the aims and functioning of the projects. Each project has a coordinator who is responsible for the team and reports to the country coordinator, who in turn reports to the operational manager at headquarters. With 700,000 contributors and an annual turnover of around DFL150 million (US$67 million), MSF-H has become one of the best-known humanitarian aid organisations in the world.

The set of principles defined by MSF, as in other organisations, is a mix of old- and new-generation humanitarian principles (MSF 1996, 1999a). MSF embraces *impartiality, independence,* and *neutrality.* Through direct contact with the victims of crisis, MSF expresses its compassion and guarantees *proximity. Transparency* and *accountability* stand for the belief that all information should be available to everyone inside and outside the organisation.

What makes MSF distinct from other organisations are the principles of *advocacy, voluntarism,* and *association.* Being neutral does not forbid MSF-H to speak out about abuses of international humanitarian law witnessed in the field. Advocacy for MSF-H implies drawing attention whenever possible to abuses of humanitarian law, either through silent diplomacy or with the help of the media (MSF 1998). MSF-H director Austen Davis explained this (when addressing an introductory course for volunteers in 1999) as a 'moral duty to speak out' and is the point distinguishing MSF from other organisations. MSF is committed to the principles of voluntarism and association to fulfil a social mission (MSF 1999a). The organisation is an association based on volunteer members, who make up part of the mission teams.

Principles, for MSF, are clearly not universal. A 1999 policy document states that there is a challenge in principled action:

> These principles are there to help us debate and structure relevant and meaningful action – but should never serve as barriers, hindering our direct action. These values and principles are still relevant and alive and they must be nurtured and sustained and lived through – with all the compromises inherent in human social life.
> (MSF 1999b)

This also means that MSF emphasises the need to learn and to change its principles when appropriate. MSF-H states in its *Medium-term Policy Document* (1999a,b) that the organisation 'must constantly seek to bring in new members to bring in new ideas and question old wisdom, principles and policies'.

Although principles are not seen as universal, they are nonetheless regarded as important, and are emphasised during the Preparation Primary Departure (PPD) course for volunteers. This course lasts between one and two weeks and introduces volunteers to the MSF philosophy as much as to the everyday life of a mission.

Anna's day

To illustrate the daily work of one MSF volunteer, let us describe a day from Anna's life in the field. Anna (a pseudonym) is a 30-year-old Dutch nurse who has been on a six-month mission in Africa. Anna's day is a compilation from excerpts of the interview we had with her.

> Anna knows when she wakes up that another hectic day lies ahead of her. Although the real emergency is over, and the vaccination campaign has become routine, it is still a lot of work. The other members of the team are out there already. When she goes to the toilet somebody knocks on the door and asks her where she had put a particular medicine the day before. The day starts. Still sleepy, she gets a cup of coffee. But there is no way to drink it in peace. Local staff are running around, getting to work, looking for papers

and medicine while she tries to have breakfast. The first patients are already waiting outside. After having been here for three months, her wish for some privacy should have disappeared and she should know better. Instead, she gets bad tempered and wants to go back to bed. The fact that she has had maybe three hours to herself in the last three months does not help. And the doctor, who came some three weeks ago for a short mission, is already working, waiting eagerly for her to start as well. She leaves her coffee and starts the daily work.

First, she works alongside the newly arrived doctor. She has noticed that this doctor does not want to listen to anything about how his predecessors did the job; he wants to do it his own way and to find things out by himself. For Anna this is an inefficient 'learning-by-doing' approach that fails to take into consideration the experiences of others. With the high staff turnover in this emergency project, knowledge just slips away. After a while, Anna leaves the doctor as she has to get in touch with colleagues in the capital. She asks another nurse to take over, ignoring her resentment, as this woman does not get along with the doctor. While Anna observes this, she finds it again remarkable that personal matters are so important in the team and that they cannot put these to one side and just get on with the work. Despite having problems with each other, she knows that the doctor and nurse will start now to talk about her. Gossip is the most common thing in this project.

Anna goes to the office and contacts the capital. While waiting for the telephone to work, she looks out of the window and sees some of her expatriate colleagues talking with the local staff. From this distance she can see the discomfort of the local staff caused by the nonchalant behaviour of the expats, who have obviously not been around long enough to become sensitive to the local culture. Thinking about the last few months, Anna realises that morale in the project has gone down. It seems that the problems never bothered them in the beginning. Then they were all on an adrenaline 'high', and everybody had the same goal and knew what to do. But now it is a matter of maintaining the project, which involves more routine work. This seems much harder for the volunteers to deal with than an emergency.

The Country Manager calls again and tells Anna that she will come after work to meet with the team to discuss the importance of MSF principles. Anna sits back and thinks that it is good to talk about principles once in a while. Their team is losing perspective regarding MSF. Although the local staff always remind her of this identity by calling her 'Sister Anna from MSF', she feels increasingly distant from the values and policies of the organisation. When she had just completed her PPD course she felt strongly connected to the principles MSF stands for. She knows these matter, but here in the field the staff are just busy with work and team problems.

When she leaves the office to announce that evening's meeting, she sees another volunteer arrive unexpectedly. This volunteer works in another project but was with Anna in the emergency phase of the same project. She helped Anna a lot in her first weeks, when there were no other experienced people around. They are happy to see each other and Anna wants to chat immediately with her about her experiences and the dilemmas she faces. But of course, there is no time. Finally, after work and before the Country Manager arrives, Anna and her friend can have a beer together. Anna always knew that MSF people work hard and in a close team, but she had not anticipated the almost total lack of privacy. For lack of any alternative, Anna and her friend lock themselves in the toilet to have their beer and chat. Here Anna tells her friend how difficult it was a few days ago, when a female genital circumcision had taken place in a nearby village. Local people had carried it out under terribly unhygienic circumstances. MSF has a strict 'hands off' policy on this matter. It is opposed to the practice and does not want to contribute in any way to the procedure. Anna tells her how bad she had felt and that she had given the woman clean tools to make the operation less dangerous. Now, some days later, she still feels bothered, as she basically agrees with the MSF policy. But after all she has her medical ethics too. Talking about it helps to make Anna feel better. There is much more to discuss, but after a while they have to vacate the toilet.

Unfortunately, the discussion with the Country Manager about organisational principles turns out to be perfunctory. After a 12-hour working day, the team members are not interested and want to go to bed. Besides, the topic is remote to their experiences, as there is no space to discuss team issues. Sometimes, Anna no longer knows why she is so committed to MSF and her work. Often she feels she gives a lot and gets little in return from the organisation, although she feels very rewarded by the responses of the local people. Nonetheless, she wants to give it another try. Her loyalty to MSF is high and even though she does not always see them put into practice, she agrees with MSF's values and principles.

Principles in everyday practice

Anna's account strikingly underlines the closed character of mission teams that come to occupy to a large extent the lifeworld of those belonging to them. A lack of privacy, extensive gossiping, and small irritations seem to dominate especially, as Anna explains, when an acute emergency is over and the operation starts to be more dictated by routine. Other interviewees also pointed to the relatively mundane nature of their experiences in comparison to the principled mission they had hoped to join. As one said, 'We never talked about principles or ideology, the conversations were always about things like getting stuck in the mud and the latest local plane crash.' A first comment about principles, then, is that in terms of their importance in discussions about humanitarian assistance, they may fade away in the routines of everyday experience of humanitarian work.

When asked how principles ordered their action, it was remarkable that volunteers more often referred to what may be termed organisational ordering principles than to the humanitarian values normally associated with the notion of principles. On the basis of the interviews, four such ordering principles were identified: an unbureaucratic attitude, a focus on emergency relief, democracy, and ownership. Democracy applies to the notion that each person has a voice in the organisation, and ownership implies that 'we are all a big family'. Here, we shall elaborate the two most frequently cited, namely the unbureaucratic attitude and the focus on emergency relief. They are both thought to distinguish MSF from other organisations in a positive way, while also having their more negative sides.

The 'unbureaucratic' attitude is considered to typify MSF's culture. Characteristics such as responsibility, freedom, and flexibility have a major and positive impact on volunteers: 'I liked the horizontal organisation, that fitted me'; 'unbureaucratic and independent, that is what attracted me'; 'with MSF I could do what I felt was right, with another organisation that would have been impossible'; 'we are special: there is a kind of dynamic atmosphere that I don't see in other organisations. While the others spend time writing reports we are out there, thinking what else we can do.' On the other hand, the positive image of an unbureaucratic organisation can be overtaken by negative experiences. The borderline between a highly appreciated lack of bureaucracy and a criticised lack of professionalism appears to be thin. Some volunteers complained about managers or colleagues abusing their discretion or being unable to live up to their obligations. Some were also frustrated by a lack of clarity about tasks and responsibilities.

The focus on emergency work very much shapes the image of MSF and the everyday practices of fieldworkers. Would-be volunteers are most attracted by the idea of relieving distress when they join the organisation. In practice, this may lead to several problems. First, as

Anna made clear, volunteers may be disappointed to find that they will not be working in an immediate emergency. One interviewee also noted that the expatriate staff were bored by daily routines: 'They wanted action and [to] move fast.' In fact, however, only about a third of all MSF projects relate to immediate emergencies. Second, interviewees note the work style and pressure associated with this principle. They feel that MSF staff display an emergency work style even in non-emergency situations, and there is strong peer pressure to work long hours and to ignore local holidays. As one individual put it: 'It is so hard to stop working when others in the team continue. They keep asking questions and you just don't feel good when you don't work.'

These aspects of MSF are important. They are considered more 'typically MSF' than, for instance, the emphasis on advocacy. They also make a difference to the well-being of volunteers. When these aspects work well they add to the motivation, but they can also be a liability when they result in unrealistic expectations or when shortcomings inherent in these principles become apparent. Finally, they make a difference for the character and effectiveness of the humanitarian operation. The way in which staff perceive and organise their work affects their relations with other stakeholders, the quality of services delivered, their accountability, and the level of beneficiary participation they achieve. In short, they have a direct bearing on the quality and impact of humanitarian assistance.

What about the classic humanitarian principles such as neutrality and impartiality? From the interviews, it appears that when volunteers encounter dilemmas or are faced with making decisions, they have different ways of dealing with principles. They usually treat them, in line with MSF's view, as helpful guidelines that can be adapted according to the situation in question. There are two ways in which volunteers circumvent policies and principles when they consider these inappropriate. First, they refer to the pragmatic requirements of the situation: 'We knew we had no mandate to negotiate with the military, but we did it every day, how else could we have done our job?' ' ... I was not allowed to give rides, but I always gave the customs officer a lift to the airport because I needed this man to get the cargo through customs'.

In making these kinds of everyday decisions, volunteers often put the need to get their job done ahead of the policies. The other way in which volunteers negotiate principles is by justifying their actions by referring to higher or parallel principles. When Anna breaches the hands-off policy on circumcision, she defends this by invoking her medical ethics.

In one case, an interviewee explained how the team found ways to extend assistance to the local population even though this was against the organisation's policy, which stipulated that only the refugees should be given aid. Since the volunteers considered this policy against the (higher) principle of neutrality, they circumvented it in practice.

MSF policy, as we explained above, incorporates a processual and iterative notion of organisational principles. It encourages the idea that principles be debated in their context. The organisation is also aware of the importance of dynamics in field teams, and several measures are built into the operations to deal with such dynamics. Normally, more experienced fieldworkers guide new volunteers and there is room to evaluate and discuss issues related to the team. The loneliness and sense of isolation that Anna experienced may thus be more the exception than the rule in the organisation.

The purpose of this paper is not to determine whether or not MSF lives up to its principles, but to use the case of MSF to illustrate the importance of taking into account everyday practice and patterns of organisational culture when discussing humanitarian principles. According to feedback from MSF management on our research, our findings resonate well with the experience in the organisation that continuously endeavours to be a reflective and learning organisation. Our concern is whether the knowledge of the importance of everyday practice for the working of humanitarian principles, as corroborated by experienced humanitarian workers, is sufficiently taken into account in discussions and initiatives regarding these principles.

Conclusion

Humanitarian assistance is not very conducive to standardised practice owing to its emergency character and the volatile political context in which it is given. Short-term projects and rapid staff turnover further limit processes of organisational learning. As developments over recent decades have made clear, these problems cannot be remedied by declaring ever-expanding sets of principles to dictate practice. MSF and other agencies, well aware of the dilemmas faced in offering humanitarian assistance, have taken this into account and invested in expanding their organisational learning capacities. There has been a marked increase in human resource development programmes and attention to monitoring and evaluation.

Interestingly, the very same speed of operations and staff turnover that hinder organisational learning also facilitate institutional learning, if this is understood to mean learning *across* the humanitarian sector (Brabant 1997). A number of experienced individuals have worked in and obtained an overview of a large range of crises and humanitarian organisations. They have developed social networks of humanitarian workers across agencies in which they exchange experience and ideas. Thanks to these humanitarian troubadours, one might say that an imagined humanitarian community (see Anderson 1993) is evolving in which humanitarians learn from each other and start to develop common agendas for change, despite differences that continue to exist between agencies.

In the last five years, this has resulted in a number of initiatives taken by changing alliances of humanitarian organisations that all, one way or another, aim to enhance the quality and the learning capacity of humanitarian organisations (Hilhorst 2001). Worthy of mention here are the development of the Code of Conduct for the International Red Cross and Red Crescent Movement and NGOs in Disaster Relief; the Active Learning Network of Accountability and Performance in Humanitarian Assistance Programmes (ALNAP), which focuses on the improvement of evaluation and learning; the Ombudsman Project and, more recently, the Humanitarian Accountability Project, which deal with accountability to beneficiaries; the Sphere project, which has developed standards for humanitarian aid; the People in Aid programme to enhance human resource policies in organisations; and the Humanitarian Quality Platform, which brings together a number of French and international humanitarian NGOs.

Taken together, these projects represent an enormous capacity to learn and improve humanitarian assistance programmes, provided they become part of humanitarian organisations in practice. What this paper argues is the importance of grounding these initiatives in analyses of the everyday practice of humanitarian programmes and especially of involving the stories of the fieldworkers who are responsible for their implementation. New policies and standards should reflect the experiences of these frontline workers and be relevant to their practice. Without knowing how ordinary staff members translate and negotiate principles in their everyday practice, discussions regarding principles tend to become abstract. Without taking into account informal learning mechanisms (both positive and negative) that evolve among staff members who actively try to make sense of their actions and the programmes in which they work, it will be difficult to close the gaps between thinking and implementation.

Note

1   This research was undertaken by Nadja Schmiemann and supervised by Thea Hilhorst and Georg Frerks of the Department of Disaster Studies at Wageningen University, and Austen Davis and Paul van het Wout of MSF-H. It resulted in an MSc thesis (Schmiemann 2000). We thank Davis and Frerks for their comments on the paper and Laura Roper for her encouragement.

References

Anderson, B. (1991, rev. 1993) *Imagined Communities*, London: Verso.

Anderson, M. B. (1996) *Do No Harm: Supporting Local Capacities for Peace*, Cambridge, MA: Collaborative for Development Action, Inc.

Atkinson, P. and N. Leader (2000) *The 'Joint Policy Operation' and the 'Principles and Protocols of Humanitarian Operation' in Liberia*, HPG Report 3, London: Overseas Development Institute.

Barnard, H. and P. Walker (1994) *Strategies for Success: A Self-help Guide to Strategic Planning for Voluntary Organisations*, London: NCVO.

Brabant, K. van (1997) 'Organisational and institutional learning in the humanitarian sector: opening the dialogue', unpublished paper, London: ALNAP.

Bradbury, M., N. Leader, and K. Mackintosh (2000) *The 'Agreement on Ground Rules' in South Sudan*, HPG Report 4, London: Overseas Development Institute.

Colebatch, H. K. (1998) *Policy: Concepts in Social Thought*, Minneapolis, MN: University of Minnesota Press.

de Waal, A. (1997) *Famine Crimes: Politics and the Disaster Relief Industry in Africa*, Oxford: James Currey.

Goffman, E. (1961) *Asylums: Essays on the Social Situation of Mental Patients and Other Inmates*, Harmondsworth: Penguin.

Hilhorst, D. (2001) 'Being good at doing good? Review of debates and initiatives concerning the quality of humanitarian assistance', paper presented at Netherlands Ministry of Foreign Affairs conference 'Enhancing the Quality of Humanitarian Assistance', The Hague, 12 October.

Hilhorst, D. (forthcoming) *Discourse, Diversity and Development: The Real World of NGOs*, London: Zed Books.

International Federation of Red Cross and Red Crescent Societies (IFRC) (2001) *Principles*, available at www.ifrc.org/what/values/principles/index.asp (consulted 8 January 2002).

Leader, N. (1998) 'Proliferating principles or how to sup with the devil without getting eaten', paper presented at ECHO/ODI conference 'Principled Aid in an Unprincipled World: Relief, War, and Humanitarian Principles', London, 7 April.

Leader, N. (2000) *The Politics of Principle: The Principle of Humanitarian Action in Practice*, HPG Report 2, London: Overseas Development Institute.

Long, N. (1989) *Encounters at the Interface: A Perspective on Social Discontinuities in Rural Development*, Wageningen Studies in Sociology 27, Wageningen: Wageningen Agricultural University.

Macrae, J. (1996) 'The Origins of Unease: Setting the Context of Current Ethical Debates', Dublin: Non-governmental Organisations Forum: Ethics in Humanitarian Aid, December.

Minear, L. and T. G. Weiss (1993) *Humanitarian Action in Times of War: A Handbook for Practitioners*, Boulder, CO: Lynne Rienner.

MSF (1996) *Medium-term Policy Document*, Amsterdam: MSF-H.

MSF (1998) 'Mission Manual', HRM department internal document, Amsterdam: MSF-H.

MSF (1999a) *Medium-term Policy Document, First Draft*, Amsterdam: MSF-H.

MSF (1999b) *Medium-term Policy Document, Third Draft*, Amsterdam: MSF-H.

Prendergast, J. (1996) *Frontline Diplomacy: Humanitarian Aid and Conflict in Africa*, Boulder, CO: Lynne Rienner.

Rokebach, M. (1973) *The Nature of Human Values*, New York, NY: Free Press.

Schmiemann, N. (2000) 'MSF principles in practice: a volunteers' perspective. The effects of MSF-principles on the first/third mission volunteers' decision to stay or leave the organisation', unpublished MSc thesis, University of Wageningen.

Sims, H., S. Fineman, and Y. Gabriel (1993) *Organizing and Organizations: An Introduction*, London: Sage.

This article was first published in Development in Practice *(12/3&4:490–500) in 2002.*

Perceptions and practices of monitoring and evaluation:

international NGO experiences in Ethiopia

Esther Mebrahtu

Introduction

In an era in which accountability and cost effectiveness are at a premium, international NGOs (INGOs) are under pressure not only to improve their performance but also to be able to demonstrate this improvement. Indeed, criticisms of 'weak accountability mechanisms' and 'poor institutional learning' within INGOs are widespread. Such pressures can be traced back to several factors, including changes in management trends and the growing scarcity of donor funding in the face of the proliferation of Southern NGOs (Estrella and Gaventa 1998:3).

The division between INGO rhetoric and practice has also caused widespread concern within development circles, placing INGOs under further pressure to bridge this gap.[1] This pressure has focused INGO attention on the need to develop monitoring and evaluation (M&E) systems that are capable of ensuring and demonstrating improved performance. It is against this background that the study reported in this paper analysed how eight large UK-based INGOs with programmes in Ethiopia have progressed along this M&E path.[2]

The findings support Oakley's (1996) general observation that a large gap exists between INGO assertions that M&E is a necessary and valuable activity and evidence of good quality practice in these areas, and suggest several reasons for this discrepancy. This paper explores the nature and interplay of such factors by reviewing current M&E policies among INGOs, perceptions of M&E held at different organisational levels within INGOs, and the translation of policies and perceptions into practice.

INGO monitoring and evaluation policies

The INGOs included in this study have a number of important differences in terms of size, professionalism, resources, number of staff, and, consequently, M&E policies and practices. Nevertheless, despite these and other organisational idiosyncrasies, a review of relevant documentation reveals several common trends and concerns. First, the heightened preoccupation with effectiveness on the part of international donors has had a real impact on INGOs. Indeed, terms such as 'impact', 'performance', 'results', and 'accountability' have assumed a new prominence in M&E documentation, and questions of 'how INGO effectiveness can be gauged' have become far more common in the last five years.

A second observation is that although ten years ago few INGOs had moved beyond a simplistic understanding of M&E issues (specifically concerning the assessment of social development objectives), recent policy documents indicate a palpable desire by INGOs to explore and extrapolate pertinent lessons from M&E activities. Some INGOs have even started to develop qualitative indicators for the 'measurement' of intangible processes, such as 'decision making' and 'women's access to resources'. While there is little doubt that orthodox approaches to M&E still predominate,[3] project documentation suggests that INGOs are currently experimenting with ways to develop more people-friendly and qualitatively oriented M&E systems.

The third observation highlights a fairly new trend within INGOs towards developing M&E systems at field level. In terms of rhetoric, at least, there appears to have been a slight shift away from the use of highly structured methods in favour of more flexible and participatory approaches. As Oakley *et al.* (1998:65) also concluded, the basis of evolving M&E systems appears to be 'perception, experience and proximity'. Policy papers confirm the gradual realisation by INGOs that M&E systems are more likely to be effective if they are made sensitive to, and developed within the immediate context of, projects themselves.

A more in-depth review reveals further interesting findings. For instance, although it is frequently assumed that 'monitoring' and 'evaluation' refer to the same activities across all INGOs, in fact INGOs do not have common definitions of, or approaches to, either of the two. Indeed, few INGOs have any definitions at all and a broad range of activities is assumed to constitute both types of activity. The policy documents of two INGOs studied, for instance, often used the term 'evaluation' interchangeably with 'review' and 'monitoring'. Further, although recognising that at the operational level M&E are separate tools, each with its own area of application and target groups, policy documents from at least three INGOs failed to make a clear distinction between the two.

Despite this lack of conceptual clarity, however, there is an underlying consensus on the importance of M&E functions. Hence, although few INGOs had specific policies in relation to M&E activities *per se*, all had attempted to outline official M&E-related requirements within their planning and reporting guidelines (e.g. ActionAid Ethiopia's 1995 *Report on the M&E Workshop* or ACORD's 1997 *Planning, Monitoring and Evaluation Guidance Manual*).

Surprisingly, only two INGOs studied had separate Policy and Evaluation Units in their head offices. In general, M&E functions were increasingly incorporated into the mandates of regional and country desk offices.[4] Despite such spatial differences, however, the procedures for M&E activities at the project level were actually structured along remarkably similar lines. Most INGOs had built-in hierarchical M&E frameworks that operated at four key organisational levels (i.e. Field, Country, Management, and Trustees) on the basis of indicators linked to the M&E objectives. Indeed, for the majority of INGOs, the process of 'monitoring' was part of a decentralised system of periodic data collection and reporting that frequently required the collation of quantitative data. Evaluations, on the other hand, were generally agreed to constitute data-collection processes that are performed mid-term through the project and/or at the end by staff from other programmes and external consultants.

At the time of this study, two INGOs[5] (Plan International and CARE International) were completely restructuring their M&E activities and making significant conceptual and practical modifications. In both cases, the decision to make these changes had emerged from a general dissatisfaction with how evaluations, in particular, were being undertaken. This point is illustrated by the comment of one senior official who claimed that:

> *Evaluations as they now stand tend to have an* ad hoc *character and their primary purpose is to justify the existence of ongoing projects or provide a basis for future funding ... nothing more.*

Indeed, this respondent referred to the previous M&E structure and procedures in his organisation as 'loose, open-ended, and detached' from the continuous programming processes and from the development of policy. Thus, in these two INGOs, although planning was still viewed as a critical prerequisite for evaluation, the new structures sought to shift emphasis towards evaluations and a results-oriented management system. Both were also introducing 'performance measurement systems' as a means of generating more information on impact. Indeed, there was a great deal of emphasis on impact assessment. In the case of CARE International, for example, the M&E system instituted in 1994 was comprised of 'organisational and sectoral objectives, with corresponding generic indicators, against which country and regional offices could report annually' (CARE International 1997, internal document).[6] By its very nature, therefore, this system did not include other context-specific indicators that might have been more appropriate to the information needs of the project community, i.e. managers, partners, and the local community. Indeed, fewer than half the INGOs in the study permitted field programmes to design locally appropriate M&E systems that were consistent with internal guidelines and procedures.

INGO policies on how to use information and feedback mechanisms

All INGO policy documents placed great importance on being able to obtain continuous feedback on information generated by their M&E systems. ActionAid provides a good case in point:

> Feedback is critically important if monitoring and evaluation is to have any meaning, and to be of any use to the organisation. Without feedback, we have just a reporting system and data gathering and forwarding is just an activity like other activities.
> (ActionAid 1995, internal document)

Most organisations further advocated that, whenever possible, the findings generated through M&E activities should be made available to all stakeholders, and that an efficient feedback system was a means through which INGOs could review M&E systems, thereby ' ... improving the quality of information generated as well as revising programme design, development and implementation' (ACORD 1997, internal document). Much greater clarity was needed, however, on key issues such as: Who needs what information? How often? In what form? While at least three policy documents identified 'feedback of M&E findings to the community' as a particularly weak link in the M&E chain, there was minimal discussion about how it could be improved, or what actions may result.

INGO policies on the participation of local actors in M&E

With one exception, all INGO policy documents explicitly expressed the need for some form of local participation within M&E procedures. A frequently unresolved issue, however, was the *nature* of the role that local people could or should play. While most INGOs required them 'to be involved in all M&E activities', only a third specified the precise form this should take, and the significance that would be attributed to their views. In fact, only one INGO considered that M&E activities should exclusively be the domain of local participants (including drawing up Terms of Reference). Far more common were obscure statements, which held that the various stakeholder agendas should be addressed in different ways using a variety of methods, as illustrated below:

> A participatory approach can be used to some extent in most types of evaluation. Indeed, all methods and approaches should be designed to make sure the perspectives of different groups including women and children are taken into account.
> (SCF 1996, internal document)

In summary, therefore, we observe that few of the INGOs sampled had separate policy documents on M&E and that fewer still had clear policies outlining how to prepare, implement, and follow up M&E procedures. The lack of sound M&E policies to which staff can refer could, therefore, mean that policy implementation effectively depends to some extent on processes of negotiation between managers and field staff. However, neither group is likely to comply with policy expectations if they neither know nor understand them. We shall therefore turn to an analysis of how various aspects of M&E are perceived and practised by different INGO actors.

INGO perceptions of M&E

When assessing perceptions of M&E at different organisational levels, the most obvious point is that 'monitoring' and 'evaluation' were frequently employed by respondents in a way that reflected the discussion of such terms within the policy documents of their respective organisations. For instance, in INGOs whose documentation failed to make a conceptual distinction between the terms, respondents were far more likely to pick up on the ambiguity and to use the terms interchangeably. What is more, it became apparent that previous experiences with M&E activities significantly framed people's perceptions concerning these processes. As these experiences were in turn determined by the hierarchical positioning of respondents within their organisation, perceptions of M&E tended to vary accordingly. This hierarchical variation is discussed in a little more depth below.

Perceptions of M&E at head office

Generally, staff at head office were greatly in favour of M&E goals and objectives. They perceived such activities to be one of the most important stages of the project cycle (if not the most important) and generally associated it with the notion of strengthening and sustaining institutional development. A typical comment here was that 'M&E is an internal tool for improving standards and strengthening practices, and as such, it is an increasingly essential component of the project cycle.'

Moreover, these respondents generally favoured the increased prominence of M&E and acknowledged the enormous potential benefits for strengthening institutional learning. However, a significant number also voiced concerns regarding the validity or reliability of M&E findings at the project level, as illustrated by the comment that 'M&E offers considerable scope for institutional learning but it is weakened by the fact that the information generated can be readily abused by those who may feel threatened by it.' Field-level M&E may be an important means of improving our learning but only if we can ensure that the data generated accurately reflect the situation on the ground.

On further questioning, respondents went on to discuss the influence which donors traditionally have over the M&E process and the potential constraints on the flow of reliable data imposed by their financing structures:

> Donors are in the strongest position to encourage the flow of reliable information from the INGOs they finance, but 'negative information' is still unlikely to appear in INGO reports unless staff are confident that such information cannot jeopardise future funding.

Perceptions of M&E in offices in Addis Ababa

Although Addis officials were rarely as enthusiastic about M&E and their respective functions as their counterparts at head office, they were generally in agreement with the need to assess their activities at some level. However, for many such respondents, an implicit acceptance of the necessity for M&E failed to mask their concerns that such processes were primarily being used as instruments of 'control' and 'judgement' against them. Although internal evaluations were generally tolerated, external evaluations were perceived to constitute significant threats to job security, as the following quotes illustrate:

They [external evaluation teams] come here for a week or so, speak to us as if they are our friends and are genuinely concerned about our daily struggles, then they go back and write terrible things about us ... making us seem incompetent ... it's not a fair system!

We have two types of external evaluations – intermediate independent evaluations which are carried out twice yearly by partners [local government] and end of term evaluations carried out by donors. Both give us headaches!

These statements allow a glimpse of the level of powerlessness felt by Addis staff at being unable to influence the outcome of M&E activities, and the weight of perceived pressure to produce 'the required results'. Indeed, in certain INGOs the notion of job security was strongly, albeit indirectly, linked to the outcome of M&E processes and thus was obviously a real issue for such staff. In addition to raising critical questions about the ownership and control of information generated by M&E systems, the prevalence of such perceptions also highlights an obvious weakness in the structure and design of current M&E frameworks.

Perceptions of M&E in field offices

The impact of the position of staff within the institutional hierarchy on their perceptions of M&E was particularly evident in discussions with INGO field staff – both senior (project and sector managers) and junior (development agents, village motivators, etc.). While the discourse of senior staff revealed a frequent association of 'monitoring' with 'financial assessment' and 'accountability', junior staff tended to associate such procedures with notions of 'external measurement' and 'judgement'. It was quite revealing that junior staff were responsible for undertaking daily reporting and monitoring activities (i.e. filling in 'daily report formats' and 'field diaries') yet not one respondent thought to include these activities in their descriptions of what the 'monitoring' process entails. Rather, such reporting systems were primarily viewed as instruments through which senior managers could assess the progress of junior staff, as the following comment illustrates:

... once in two days – sometimes every day – I fill in this report and give it to the [sector] manager at the end of the week, then every month or so we meet and review what I have written and he assesses it and helps me understand what I have done wrong in my job ...

Clearly, staff at this level perceived M&E procedures as a highly sophisticated and technical set of activities from which they were excluded by virtue of their inferior position. One respondent effectively summarised this perspective when he stated:

> We still tend to think of M&E as a set of complex and specialised procedures that are beyond our understanding and to tell the truth, beyond our duties within this organisation.

The idea that frontline staff could get involved in the design and planning of M&E systems (as suggested by the researcher) was generally met with some degree of consternation. It thus came as no surprise to learn that such activities held little interest for junior field staff and so were undertaken without much enthusiasm. It later emerged that such widespread feelings of 'detachment' at this level had been further exacerbated by the staff not knowing the purpose of the information collated and its potential relevance for them as frontline actors. The following quotation is a good example:

> We collect most of the data necessary but we don't see where or how it is used ... we write reports, collect them, and pass them on to the sector manager who writes more reports and sends them off – we don't learn anything from this process, then the whole thing starts again!

Indeed, failure to feed back relevant information to frontline staff appears to have led to a general confusion regarding the end use of collated data. Feelings of disengagement from the M&E process were by no means exclusive to junior staff. Some senior field staff also perceived the M&E process to be 'too technical' and 'too formal', in addition to being undertaken largely for the benefit of partners and donors, as expressed below:

> For those of us who work directly with communities, information from M&E could be used to correct our mistakes and improve practice, but in reality it is carried out for the benefit of our donors and partners, not ourselves.

Such feelings of exclusion were observed first-hand in three scheduled interviews with senior field staff during which the researcher arrived only to discover an 'M&E designate' present in addition to (or in place of) the expected interviewee. Senior staff generally felt ill-equipped to discuss M&E-related issues and therefore occasionally desired the presence of a well-informed respondent to deal with potentially 'problematic questions':

When you asked to meet me, I went around the office and they told me you asked a lot of questions about M&E. This is really not my field. I didn't want to waste your time so I asked X [M&E officer] to join us and help me out.

Such incidents reveal that the 'M&E arena' was not one in which field staff felt empowered. Indeed, our findings confirm that openness and trust are prerequisites for the meaningful practice of M&E. Regardless of their place in the hierarchy, staff need a 'safe' space in which to articulate their views and concerns. This in turn calls for greater trust between donors, managers, and operational staff. But, as Gaventa and Blauert (2000:239) point out, 'trust requires more than "permission" to give voice to opinions'. Indeed, it requires honest self-evaluation and transparency about failures and successes at every level.

Variations in perceived functions of M&E within INGOs

Despite the limited familiarity of some actors with M&E processes, the study found that approval was heavily biased in favour of monitoring as opposed to evaluation by staff at all organisational levels. The general feeling was that the lessons offered by evaluations were produced, in the words of one senior field official, 'too late to be of use to staff and to make a difference to the quality of work being implemented'. Further questioning on the perceived functions of M&E revealed a distinct pattern of responses as illustrated for INGO A in Table 1.

While most head office respondents emphasised the role that M&E plays in relation to enhancing institutional learning and accountability to donors, country- and field-level staff generally stressed its role as a means of improving internal practice and upwards accountability. At field-office levels, the stress was primarily on the role M&E plays in satisfying the bureaucratic demands of higher-level offices and in facilitating the identification of anomalies within projects. Such findings are not altogether surprising considering that UK offices operate relatively autonomously of the administrative boundaries of

Table 1: Different views on M&E among staff in INGO A		
INGO A–UK Office	**INGO A–Country Office (Addis Ababa)**	**INGO A–Field Office**
M&E contributes to the learning process within the INGO and if done correctly can also empower those who participate in it.	M&E is [a] useful tool for improving internal standards and [is] the means through which we continue to receive funding.	[M&E] keeps those above us happy and allows the project to get feedback on its overall performance.

field projects, while those in the field are 'closest to the firing-line' and thus are responsible for presenting the project as a successful and viable package to the rest of the organisation.

It was also observed, however, that perceptions of M&E functions are also occasionally framed by more socio-psychological motives, as illustrated below:

> When outside officials visit the various project sites, M&E work helps us to be able to tell them about improvements in repayment rates of microcredit programmes, improvements in numbers attending adult education classes, etc. It makes us look better informed so they will give us more respect.
> (INGO country staff)

> If we know or understand what the local people feel about the project and how they want to be involved in it, we become stronger and we can represent their views better to the INGO.
> (INGO field staff)

The first respondent highlights the importance of 'good' self-image and being able to present the 'right' image to outsiders. The second emphasises the importance of accurately portraying grassroots information as a means of better representing local views. Both statements, however, implicitly acknowledge the potentially empowering nature of the M&E process, i.e. how it can locate staff in positions of authority and provide a broader base of legitimacy for their viewpoints. Frontline staff, in particular, tended to view the M&E process not only as a means of increasing their legitimacy within the INGO, but also as a means of securing a greater degree of acceptance from the local communities with which they worked. As the next quote illustrates, frontline respondents explained how the monitoring-type activities they performed frequently acted as a barrier against potential hostility from local people:

> It is very difficult for me as a woman coming into this new environment. My mother is from this region and although I'm familiar with the customs I have never lived here. People tend to be rude to newcomers, especially female ones ... It is up to you to win their acceptance. It isn't always easy but I find that when I have a clipboard in my hands and I'm asking questions as a member of staff they respect me more and answer me in a polite voice.

Such statements remind us that frontline staff can encounter considerable resistance, and frequently struggle to define their role within host communities. The fact that many such staff live in the same villages in which they work and emulate the lifestyles of local inhabitants can serve to lower their perceived status as INGO staff. These workers thus come under pressure to re-establish their social status and employ various strategies to do this, including undertaking simple monitoring procedures. Hence, the motives for undertaking M&E-related activities may comprise more than the need simply to follow INGO directives in a straightforward implementation of policy.

INGO practice of M&E

In the previous section we explored the nature of M&E policies and how staff perceived these processes and their related functions (i.e. why M&E is undertaken). We now examine how such policies and perceptions translate into practice (i.e. what methods are used on the ground and who owns the results of M&E activities). Issues relating to practice are divided into three distinct categories which address (a) types of methodological approaches used by INGOs, (b) the formulation of indicators and selection procedures, and (c) information needs and feedback mechanisms.

Methodological tools and approaches to M&E

INGOs currently use three different kinds of M&E approach. These can be categorised broadly as participatory M&E, which is mainly carried out by those directly involved in project implementation; non-participatory M&E, in which the evaluation is conducted by external evaluators; and joint evaluation where it is conducted by a team including people from outside and inside the programme.[7] The latter two predominate among the INGOs studied, and it was apparent that many attempts were being made to develop and employ alternative and more participatory approaches to M&E. Numerous interviews (especially, but not exclusively, at UK offices) revealed a fundamental dissatisfaction with the 'dominant M&E paradigm' in which M&E is mostly perceived as a narrow, donor-initiated external activity focusing primarily on 'upwards' accountability and quantifiable achievement. As the quotes below illustrate, at the time of the study several INGOs were attempting to broaden definitions of M&E by increasing the number of stakeholders involved in the process:

> As much as possible we are trying hard to encourage the use of more participatory techniques into all forms of M&E undertaken in this organisation.
> (Senior UK official)

Table 2: Methods, tools, and techniques used in six INGO M&E procedures					
INGO A	**INGO B**	**INGO C**	**INGO D**	**INGO E**	**INGO F**
Formal surveys, cost–benefit analysis, PAR and PRA, and case-study reports.	Mainly PRA tools and semi-structured interviews.	Participatory M&E methods, informal techniques.	Logical Framework, questionnaire, structured interviews, and focus-group discussions.	Logical Framework, questionnaire, and surveys.	Focus groups, PRA, and semi-structured interviews.

As an organisation we have found that formal tools such as surveys have pre-determined questions that don't allow for flexibility, are very extractive giving little in return, produce very poor quality data, and are non-participatory. Therefore, we now advocate the use of more participatory tools like PRA, PAR, and other variations on the theme.
(UK M&E officer)

Although a small but determined cluster of two INGOs remained suspicious of so-called 'alternative methods' and continued to justify the use of more orthodox approaches, in the main, INGOs appeared to have embraced the use of more participatory approaches in M&E, as evidenced in Table 2.

It was also observed that the type of M&E being undertaken had an influence on the methods employed. End-of-term and mid-term evaluations, for instance, tended to be undertaken by outside consultants whose operational parameters were frequently defined by Logical Framework Analysis (LogFrame). Reports were subsequently written from the perspective of donors and their information needs. On the other hand, internal monitoring processes were undertaken more frequently and thus considered to be better suited to the use of PRA tools. The findings would then be documented with the intention of feeding back to those directly involved in the project and as such were viewed more favourably by field staff: 'Many of our staff believe that ongoing monitoring with local partners and beneficiaries could be more useful and important for the development of the project than external evaluations.'

However, it was readily apparent that certain contradictions exist in the selection of methods for use in M&E. First, there were contradictions between the desire of field offices to achieve their own specific objectives and the obligatory use of rational management tools imposed upon them from above: 'Our donors strongly favour the LFA mode of management but our staff find it really onerous so we are in a real dilemma ... we are under pressure to conform to all their paradigms and expectations', said one UK official.

Similarly, the obligatory use of LFA tools posed real problems for field offices trying accurately to relay local views to donors. The following statement highlights the inherent dissension that plague staff during M&E reporting:

> *DfID funding reports place a heavy emphasis on the use of LFA, but we find it very difficult translating the information given to us by beneficiaries on the ground into 'DfID language' ... DfIDs' list of objectives/goals/indicators and the objectives/goals/indicators that are appropriate for our partners and the community do not match.*
> (Addis official)

Finally, contradictions were also apparent between the desire of INGO offices to be both more accountable to donors and to strengthen organisational learning processes:

> *We've found that there are potential conflicts in attempting to be more accountable to donors and using M&E for improving our learning as we would wish ... We haven't yet found the right balance between the two in our activities.*

Plainly, the mechanical use of M&E systems was limiting organisational learning to immediate project outputs (e.g. progress, results, efficiency, etc. as defined by the indicators) rather than extending it to issues of power and power relationships within the project community. As such, there was a need for a radical rethinking about who initiates and undertakes the process, and who learns and benefits from its findings.

Selection of indicators and information needs

The process of selecting appropriate indicators for use in M&E systems is one that highlights, perhaps more accurately than any other, the need to acknowledge the existence of differing stakeholder information needs and multiple perspectives of reality within project interventions. Ricafort (1996) points out that this process is one that requires careful examination.

A review of INGO documentation revealed that the selection of indicators occurs in various ways within different INGOs. In the more devolved or decentralised INGOs, for example, appropriate process indicators were decided upon mostly at project or sectoral levels. However, this could be problematic:

Each project has to select or design indicators which they believe to be specific to their problems and environment ... This could mean that two separate projects either side of the same mountain have completely different sets of objectives and indicators. This makes it very difficult to establish a central reporting system but what's the alternative?

Impact indicators were generally decided upon at national or HQ levels. In the more centralised INGOs, however, field staff were required to use externally pre-designed and pre-selected indicators, which meant that there was frequently little or no consideration of the experiences, views, and opinions of field staff within this process:

Indicators are selected en masse *by a group of NGOs who also have projects that are funded by the same body. Projects are then issued with a checklist of indicators categorised by sector, and managers are expected to use only those indicators that are relevant to them.*

Quantitative indicators were greatly favoured by INGOs regardless of the organisational level at which they were formulated. Although the choice of either quantitative or qualitative indicators was dependent on the objectives of the M&E process and the information required by the various stakeholders, interviews revealed the prevalence of, and preference for, the use of pre-defined quantitative indicators. One HQ official rationalised his organisation's decision to maintain this traditional approach as follows:

Staff are a lot more comfortable with using quantitative indicators to measure activities because they're much easier to conceptualise and therefore, more useful as a whole. Qualitative methods and indicators tend to require a lot of work and are more time-consuming than we can afford.

Even when monitoring long-term social development objectives, most INGO staff indicated a preference for quantitative indicators as being 'less difficult to define'. Indeed, 75 per cent of all respondents felt that such indicators – if carefully identified and selected – could be effectively employed to assess even *qualitative* changes. Moreover, despite rhetorical evidence to the contrary,[8] respondents readily acknowledged that the widespread use of qualitative and/or grassroots indicators is a long way from being realised:

Indicators have so far been designed using our perceptions of what participation is and how much of it we require. We have to learn to develop 'negotiated indicators' that allow for the perceptions of beneficiaries to be taken into consideration. We are still some way off ...

In reality, then, the process of selecting indicators was undertaken with a considerable degree of rigidity, conformity, and fear of innovation.

Lower down in the organisational hierarchy, moreover, the researcher was somewhat surprised to discover that junior field staff would occasionally 'collude' with local people in the task of identifying 'appropriate' monitoring indicators in order to present an image of 'project success', 'approval of project activities' and/or 'effective local participation' to Addis officials and external evaluators. The following extract from the researcher's own diary, drawing on highlights from an informal discussion with a group of village health workers (VHWs) and traditional birth assistants (TBAs) in western Ethiopia, illustrates this point:

27 January 1998

> *Over the year, there had been ad hoc attempts to assess the level of beneficiary involvement in the health sector. Although never undertaken in any systematic way, local actors such as TBAs and VHWs were encouraged to get involved and to develop what they considered to be appropriate indicators for measuring local participation. The results of this effort, however, were, in the words of one sector manager, 'highly unsatisfactory'. Senior field staff complained that the (mostly) qualitative indicators that had been selected by local actors were 'too subjective', 'very open to abuse', and could ultimately present the 'new health facilities in a poor light'. A meeting was called and senior officials explained to local actors that if such indicators were used, they would 'show the health facilities to be offering a poor service and funding would eventually be withdrawn'. VHWs even claimed that these officials had reprimanded them for using 'the wrong definitions of participation'. Terrified of losing their newly acquired health facilities and hard-earned social status with the community as a result, VHWs and TBAs agreed to use another list of impact indicators that had previously been approved by senior field staff.*

This diary entry illustrates how fear of reprisals, possible loss of status in the community, and the pressure to appear successful encouraged field staff and local people to 'collude' in misrepresenting information about the quality of health facilities offered by the programme. If we assume that the M&E process (including the selection of indicators) exists to fulfil the information demands of a range of actors in the project community, then the above extract highlights the need to revise our assumptions and carefully examine what these information needs actually are.

The information needs and expectations of different INGO actors

In-depth discussion with INGO actors revealed that M&E processes were expected to fulfil four broad categories of 'information needs', which directly corresponded to the position of staff within the hierarchy. HQ staff, for example, expressed a particular preference for information that would demonstrate the comprehension and/or acceptance of project aims by local people and thus gain donor approval (i.e. the sustainability of project activities). As such, the information generated was expected to provide answers primarily to subjective questions such as, 'Do local people accept what we are doing? ... Are they doing it because we are pushing them or because they feel it is genuinely important for them?'

On the other hand, both country- and senior-level field staff appeared to be more concerned with collating data on the progress being made in relation to their goals, and the extent to which this progress may or may not meet donor expectations: 'We need to know what major mistakes we've made for which we can be criticised by donors such as why local people are not getting involved in certain activities as anticipated'.

Indeed, there was evidence to suggest that country staff occasionally 'colluded' with those in HQ to present a particular image or relay a specific message to donors:

> Often the pressures from donors were so great – at least in terms of timing –
> that field staff were sometimes unable to finish off their quarterly or half-
> yearly reports. These reports would end up on my desk and often I would
> have to somehow beef them up and complete them. (M&E officer)

Field staff – in particular frontline staff – however, appeared to be less concerned with meeting the expectations of donors, and were anxious for the information generated by M&E systems to indicate to them how local people had responded to their own personal interventions within the project context. One such incident was recounted to me by a senior water manager based in eastern Ethiopia:

> The success of the water sector in Jijiga depends very much on the
> community's capacity to manage and maintain their scarce water
> resources. Traditionally in Somali culture, water points are privately
> owned, but we wanted to implement community shared water points, so we
> weren't exactly sure how well this would be accepted. Anyway, we started
> the project but we were worried about its sustainability and the possible
> waste of our resources. Then without notifying us the junior water manager

*designed his own monitoring procedure and carried out regular
assessments. He assessed the various community management
mechanisms, i.e. who and what member of the community was responsible
for fencing, for electing water point guards, and for financing the water
points. This continued over a period of a few months and was very useful to
us in explaining how the community perceived water projects and whether
or not they could be sustainable.*

Although later discussions with the junior staff member in question
revealed marked differences between the 'perceived' and 'real'
intentions underlying his regular assessment of the water sector, this
case was an excellent illustration of how field staff can, and frequently
do, exercise unsanctioned discretion to promote their own interests
within the confines of the INGO policy framework. Thus, the
underlying message behind this (and many similar findings not
addressed here) is that the capacity for innovative thinking which
exists within INGOs, especially at the lower levels, needs to be further
explored. Indeed, INGOs would do well to adopt an interactive
approach to M&E that enables them to listen to, and learn from, even
the most junior of actors.

However, the identification of varying information needs without
sufficient feedback into development processes simply ensures that the
M&E process becomes an end in itself, rather than a means through
which improvements can be made (Abbot and Guijt 1997:44). Thus, we
now turn our attention to M&E feedback mechanisms within INGOs.

Use of feedback mechanisms in M&E

Discussions with INGO staff revealed an overall awareness of the
importance of efficient feedback mechanisms and significant
consensus on the general inadequacy of existing systems. However,
complaints were especially common at field levels, as junior staff often
lamented the lack of adequate supervision and feedback on their
activities by their seniors. For example, in two INGOs, junior staff (e.g.
community workers and village promoters) were given 'field diaries' in
which they had to report their daily activities as part of an internal day-
to-day monitoring system. These diaries revealed a 'blow-by-blow'
account of project activities as they unfolded and provided potentially
valuable opportunities to study changes throughout the course of an
intervention (Jackson 1997). However, respondents said that such
diaries were almost never read or reviewed by sector managers (or

above). Neither was there any significant discussion with, or feedback to, the staff member about the contents of their diary. Consequently, junior staff were beginning to lose the motivation to keep such diaries:

> *I was told to report my activities to this diary every day and I have tried to do so but no one has asked to see it yet ... I'm still waiting to be asked about it ... I'm not sure if what I have written is relevant any longer ... or if I should continue ...*

When questioned about this, the senior managers interviewed generally attributed the neglect of such duties to the sheer volume of data generated by such monitoring systems and the subsequent shortage of time:

> *Often the frequent nature of the reporting system we use results in a colossal amount of data being gathered. Our time is very restricted ... We haven't got time to read these diaries. Anyway, much of the information in them is quite personal and not very useful ... staff don't always focus on recording the type of hard data that I need to compile my own reports.*

In turn, senior field staff complained bitterly about the inadequate feedback they received on their reports from support offices in Addis, local government offices, and donors. Focus-group discussions held with senior field staff in four INGOs identified five common limitations in organisational M&E feedback systems:

- irregularity and inconsistency of feedback;
- lack of clarity on roles and authority;
- lack of motivation from sector managers;
- lack of intra- and inter-sectoral information sharing;
- lack of field-visit reports from HQ and programme managers.

Thus far, we have discussed the issue of feedback to INGO staff. However, if INGOs are serious about handing over the control of development interventions to local people, then they must be the central focus of all programmes and systems. The M&E system is no exception and must be centred around the needs, perceptions, and values of the affected community so that locally generated information filters up through the ranks of the organisation and leads to improved learning. With the exception of two INGOs, relaying information back to the local community was generally 'not viewed as an essential activity'.

In these two INGOs, however, feedback from M&E activities was relayed to local people through a combination of both formal and informal channels. The formal route included oral presentations by staff in regular community meetings, committee-group discussions, meetings with peasant-association members, and so on. Traditional or informal communication channels such as *ider*, *debo*,[9] and religious gatherings were then also employed to convey interesting or pertinent findings to the wider localities. The following statement by a farmer in the Meket province of northern Ethiopia demonstrates the potential value of such informal channels:

> In the previous Government extension package, a quota system was in place that meant farmers were only entitled to receive food aid from the Government [during food shortage periods] if we agreed to produce a certain amount of crops of a certain variety each season. Those who were unable to comply with this quota were forced to sell their animals during the lean periods, which was disastrous. The seeds promoted in the extension package had not been properly investigated but we were forced to use them without even having been included in the selection or planning process. Now that SOS-Sahel has introduced this new extension package, PADET, we are determined not to be left out a second time! Now we meet regularly and discuss the progress of the new seeds and decide for ourselves if they are appropriate. Any new farming techniques that we are taught by the DAs who work with us are passed on to neighbouring farmers. We also discuss about the coping strategies we may use if our crops fail because finally, we can only rely on ourselves.

So, while feeding information 'upwards' from the local level poses one set of challenges for INGOs, the above extract reaffirms the need for effective 'downwards' communication. Significant numbers of both field staff and local people indicated that they had very little idea why they were being consulted, or even about the purpose of M&E exercises. Moreover, they were rarely informed of the outcome of higher-level decisions that were subsequently taken. Without this knowledge, it was difficult for them to offer a considered view or to become fully engaged in the process. This may in turn explain the feelings of alienation from the whole M&E process experienced by such actors: failure to promote both 'upwards' and 'downwards' accountability is thus a serious flaw that hinders the potential for learning within INGOs.

Analysis of findings

In his study of government bureaucracies, Wilson (1989:39) claims that a well-defined and widely understood sense of purpose can lead to better internalisation of an organisation's goals by its employees. If we concede this point, it follows that lack of conceptual clarity and the general blurring of functional distinctions evidenced in some M&E policy documents, coupled with the complex and hierarchical nature of many M&E frameworks, will hinder the internalisation of M&E objectives by INGOs. In fact, while staff generally recognised the potential value of M&E, it was clear from our study that country and field staff in particular were unable to define their roles within such frameworks. This confusion indicates the need for an office-wide clarification of these concepts if M&E policy is to be implemented effectively.

We also observed the significant impact of the hierarchical positioning of INGO staff on their perceptions of M&E. Those furthest removed from practice tended to embrace a more analytical approach focusing on the potential for M&E to feed into organisational learning, while those closest to the ground emphasised 'upwards accountability' and therefore associated such activities with 'judgement', 'control', and 'external supervision'. Significant numbers of field staff were observed to feel rather disengaged from M&E activities, viewing them as complex, specialised, and hence exclusive procedures. How did these perceptions affect the actual practice of M&E?

If our discussion of M&E practice is analysed with an emphasis on organisational-structural factors, then we note that the current structures of many M&E systems constitute a major constraint on the effective implementation of policy directives. Such constraints include the predetermined nature of M&E methods and indicators; the obvious preference of donors and head offices for quantitative indicators and data; the lack of adequate supervision and training; the absence of effective feedback mechanisms; and the failure of M&E systems to provide relevant and timely information to the various actors.

Although an understanding of these structural factors constitutes an essential dimension to explaining M&E practice, the conditioning influence of this structure can only occur through interaction with the knowledge and capability of staff, i.e. staff 'agency'. Thus, while it may be critical, such a narrow organisational-structural perspective does not adequately explain practice. Indeed, conflicting perceptions of M&E activities (even within the same INGO) indicate that its practice is not simply the execution of an already specified plan of action but is rather 'an ongoing, socially constructed and negotiated process' (Long 1990:6). Focusing on the perspectives of different actors in the M&E system effectively draws attention to the fact that whatever the initial plans, when M&E systems are built into a project, they are likely to be framed and transformed by the strategies (based on their perceptions and interests) of these different actors.

We have already indicated the extent to which both country and field staff associated the M&E process with 'judgement', 'control', and 'job insecurity'. However, we also detected evidence of 'collusion' between both sets of actors (and local people) in the process of reporting their efforts 'upwards'. Such events illustrate that staff are not passive recipients of INGO interventions and are capable of employing unsanctioned discretion in seeking to promote their own interests within the confines of the policy framework. Similarly, junior staff proved capable of some clever manoeuvring in their attempts to generate information or data that were outside the formal demands of the M&E process and thereby improve their performance.

Conclusion

Three key lessons emerge from this study. First, M&E and its various functions are perceived in very different ways, emphasising particular aspects of the process in accordance with the functional interests and past experiences of those involved. As such, there is evidently a disturbing gap between how head office and other INGO staff perceive the key functions of M&E. This highlights the importance of intra-organisational communication about the objectives of the M&E process.

Second, we learned that efforts to modify M&E systems appear to be taking place within INGOs without sufficient thought as to how information thus generated can be used to fulfil the demands of key project actors (e.g. field staff and local people) and thereby strengthen institutional learning. It is probable that this 'information gap' could have contributed significantly to the lack of interest in M&E activities exhibited by INGO staff at the 'lower end' of the organisational hierarchy.

Lastly, we learnt that M&E practice at the various organisational levels is generally undertaken in an atmosphere of uncertainty and tension, such that M&E reporting can sometimes involve staff 'framing a story' that adheres more closely to donor guidelines than to reality (Craig and Porter 1997). Thus, there is a clear argument for increased rigour at the project level and the creation of an empowering organisational culture on a broader scale. As an ActionAid Strategy Paper acknowledged, however, this is not something at which INGOs have traditionally excelled:

While most INGOs have written about empowerment in their literature, most staff within them have suffered from centralist attitudes and disempowering restructuring processes and language from HQ.
(ActionAid 1999-2003:21, internal document)

Unfortunately, failure to empower staff has resulted in narrowing opportunities for them to participate in critical decisions. As such, INGOs have thus far failed the challenge of the 1990s which, according to Cornwall (2000:41), was 'to lever open spaces for participation'.

Such a finding does not bode well for INGOs currently attempting to scale up the impact of their interventions and carve out a space for themselves in an increasingly competitive environment. There is a clear need for organisational change with regards to M&E practice. But, as the case of ActionAid illustrates, INGOs striving to institute such changes may face many severe challenges.

ActionAid has now joined the ranks of INGOs in attempting to modify its M&E system by instituting the principles of participation and 'downwards' accountability. This entails rewriting the planning and reporting system – recently renamed 'Accountability Learning and Planning System' or ALPS (David and Owusa 2000; Scott-Villiers in this volume). As these changes take place, however, there should be awareness that they bring with them a degree of instability. Staff are likely to find it difficult to accomplish their new job specifications as familiar lines of communication disappear. Indeed, they are likely to feel unsure of what is expected of them and what they must do to fulfil the new mandates. Although the new policies may be clearly stated, the actual conditions may appear quite different from the ideals expressed. Consequently, it is possible that staff will begin to long for continuity, and eventually this may become a dominant tension. Fritz (1994:27) warns that it is frequently at this point in the 'change cycle' that an organisation is likely to return to 'business as usual' and the change effort will be recognised as a failure. It is therefore essential that managers anticipate this resistance and create the space necessary for staff to find their own entry points into the new system.

Notes

1 Evidence of this concern can be gathered from the 'INGO, states and donors' overview in Hulme and Edwards (1997:7–10).

2 These include ActionAid, ACORD, CARE International, Oxfam GB, Plan International, SCF, SOS-Sahel, and Tear Fund.

3   The term 'orthodox' refers to M&E
approaches that are oriented solely
to the needs of funding agencies and
policy makers. Many argue that such
approaches produce information that
is 'objective', 'value-free', and
'quantifiable', and hence outsiders
are normally contracted to undertake
them (Estrella *et al*. 2000:3).

4   While field offices tended to handle
project evaluations locally, head offices
were involved in broader programme
and country evaluations.

5   ActionAid has since joined these ranks
with the establishment of ALPS in 1998.

6   Generic indicators act as common
currency across programmes worldwide and are later passed up the system
and aggregated. Methods for identifying such indicators differ between
agencies. In CARE, key indicators were
established based on best practice
within sectors and through consultations with professional and technical
staff in regional offices and HQ.

7   Internal evaluations or self-
assessments are also carried out by
local organisations, but these are not
always categorised as evaluations since
they may not always result in written
products. The final production of an
'evaluation report' complies with
traditional expectations of M&E.

8   For example, CARE experimented
with the use of qualitative indicators
in the reproductive health sector.

9   Traditional self-help institutions (e.g.
ider, iquib, debo) have existed in Ethiopia
for as long as can be recalled, and they
continue to play an important role in
the life of ordinary Ethiopians. Some
have been registered as 'neighbourhood associations' since the 1960s
and, although little written documentation exists about such systems, these
are considered to be the forerunners of
what are currently labelled local
organisations or CBOs.

References

Abbot, S. and I. Guijt (1997) 'Changing
Views on Change: Participatory
Approaches to Monitoring the
Environment', SARL Discussion
Paper 2, London: IIED.

Cornwall, A. (2000) 'Beneficiary,
Consumer, Citizen: Perspectives on
Participation for Poverty Reduction',
SIDA Studies No. 2, Stockholm: SIDA.

Craig, D. and D. Porter (1997) 'Framing
participation: development projects,
professionals, and organisations',
Development in Practice 7(3):229–235.

David, R. and C. Owusa (2000) 'When the
mighty sunset, the stars can shine –
Monitoring empowerment with
ActionAid – A partial view', Mimeo,
London: ActionAid.

Estrella, M. and J. Gaventa (1998) 'Who
Counts Reality? Participatory
Monitoring and Evaluation: A
Literature Review', IDS Working
Paper 70, Brighton: IDS.

Estrella, M. *et al* (eds.) (2000) *Learning
from Change: Issues and Experiences
in Participatory Monitoring and
Evaluation*, London: IT Publications.

Fritz, R. (1994) *Corporate Tides:
Redesigning the Organisation*, Oxford:
Butterworth-Heinemann.

Gaventa, J. and J. Blauert (2000)
'Learning to Change by Learning
from Change: Going to Scale with
Participatory Monitoring and
Evaluation', in M. Estrella *et al*. (eds),
*Learning From Change: Participatory
Monitoring and Evaluation*, London:
IT Publications.

Hulme, D. and M. Edwards (eds.) (1997)
*Too Close for Comfort? NGOs, States
and Donors*, London: Macmillan.

Jackson, C. (1997) 'Sustainable
development at the sharp end:
fieldworker agency in a participatory
project', *Development in Practice*
7(3):237–247.

Long, N. (1990) 'From Paradigm Lost to
Paradigm Regained? The Case for an
Actor-oriented Sociology of
Development', *European Review of
Latin American and Caribbean Studies*,
49 (December): 3–24.

Oakley, P., D. Marsden, and B. Pratt
(1996) *Measuring the Process:
Guidelines for Evaluating Social
Development*, Oxford: INTRAC.

Oakley, P., B. Pratt, and A. Clayton (1998)
*Outcomes and Impact: Evaluating
Change in Social Development*, NGO
Management and Policy Series 6,
Oxford: INTRAC.

Ricafort, R. (1996) 'People, Realities and
Negotiations: Some Thoughts on
Participatory Monitoring and
Evaluation, Development Cooperation
and Funding Organisations',
unpublished report, Brighton: IDS.

Wilson, J. (1989) *Bureaucracy: What
Government Agencies Do and Why They
Do It*, New York, NY: Basic Books.

This article was first published in
Development in Practice *(12/3&4:501–517)
in 2002.*

Learning from complexity:
the International Development Research Centre's experience with Outcome Mapping

Sarah Earl and Fred Carden

Introduction

In its conceptual and practical work over the past few years, the Evaluation Unit of the International Development Research Centre (IDRC)[1] has encountered four fundamental challenges in assessing and reporting on development impact that inhibit learning by development-research organisations. First, while development-research organisations are under pressure to demonstrate that their programmes result in significant and lasting change in the well-being of large numbers of intended beneficiaries, such 'impact' is often the product of a confluence of events for which no single organisation can realistically claim full credit. Therefore, when an organisation sets out to demonstrate that its programmes are the 'cause' of development improvements, it runs into serious difficulties in terms of how to measure the impact of its work. Second, in order for change to truly take root, ownership and control must have shifted from the external organisation to exogenous actors and organisations. In other words, ideas and approaches must have become integrated with a range of events, activities, customs, laws, and policies within the local context so that they fall outside the purview of the external organisation. As noted by Terry Smutylo:

> [A] paradox exists for external agencies under pressure to take credit for results at the 'outcome' and 'impact' stages; for it is at these stages where their influence, if they have been successful, is low and decreasing relative to that of other actors. Attribution for results which naturally goes to the dominant influences associated with those results may empirically overlook antecedent project components.
> (Smutylo 2001:5)

Third, assessing long-term development impacts does not usually provide the kind of information and feedback required to improve a programme's performance. It provides 'clueless feedback', which neither tells the organisation about its specific contributions to change, nor provides data on how to improve its efforts (Smutylo 2001:6). Fourth, the heavy emphasis on demonstrating the impact of programmes has meant that the development of learning capacities within organisations themselves has been ignored. Consequently, assessing impacts on development, especially from the perspective of an external agency, is problematic both methodologically and in terms of the value of the findings for learning organisations. Nonetheless, many organisations continue to struggle to measure results far beyond the reach of their programmes.[2]

To address this problem, IDRC has been working with a number of organisations in Asia, Africa, and Latin America to develop and field test a methodology called Outcome Mapping which takes account of the complexity of development processes and focuses explicitly on learning.[3] It establishes a vision of the human, social, and environmental improvement to which a programme hopes to contribute and then focuses monitoring and evaluation on factors and actors within its sphere of influence. The richness of a programme's performance story is told using systematically collected qualitative data. Although outlining a complete case study of a programme's use of Outcome Mapping goes beyond the scope of this short article, this paper will show how the fundamental principles of Outcome Mapping relate to organisational learning theory and discuss some of the challenges associated with applying theory to practice. Our experience with a number of applied development-research programmes has demonstrated that, despite best intentions, learning does not happen naturally, but it can be built into work practices through data collection and reflection processes. Outcome Mapping has proved a robust methodology to help programme teams think holistically and strategically about the results they want to help bring about and also to learn from their experiences.

This article presents Outcome Mapping as it pertains to development programmes,[4] but it can also be adapted for use at the project or organisational levels. Regardless of the level, the fundamental 'learning agenda' of Outcome Mapping remains the same – to encourage evaluative thinking, participatory decision making, open sharing of successes and failures, and a willingness to engage in regular processes of thoughtful reflection and learning.

Outcome Mapping is based on three principles, which we view as essential to encourage learning:

- planning for and assessing both external results and internal performance;
- the cyclical nature of planning, monitoring, and evaluation; and,
- systematised self-assessment as a consciousness-raising, consensus-building, and empowerment tool for those working directly in a programme.

Each of these principles encourages a programme to think holistically about its work in order to improve, and offers more generalisable lessons about encouraging learning and reflection that may be of value to others, whether or not they are using Outcome Mapping.

What is Outcome Mapping?

Maps are cognitive guides. They locate us, helping us figure out where we are now in relation to where we have been and where we are going.
(Michael Quinn Patton in Earl *et al.* 2001)

Outcome Mapping is an integrated planning, monitoring, and evaluation methodology. It takes a learning-based and use-driven view of evaluation guided by principles of participation and iterative learning. As a process, it is embedded in organisational learning principles and offers strategies for increasing a programme's ability to improve its performance. It fosters programme learning by incorporating self-assessment and reflection processes throughout the planning, monitoring, and evaluation stages. It begins with a facilitated workshop to design a programme and monitoring system, followed by a series of self-assessment workshops to monitor change and refine strategies, with periodic evaluation studies as required.

In terms of measuring results, the originality of the methodology lies in its shift away from assessing the development impact of a programme (e.g. poverty alleviation, reduced conflict, etc.), to a focus on behavioural change. Outcome Mapping is built on the premise that behavioural change is fundamental to sustainable development. Outcomes are defined as changes in the behaviour, relationships, activities and/or actions of the people, groups, and organisations with whom a programme works directly. By using Outcome Mapping, a programme will not be claiming the achievement of development impacts but rather to have contributed to the achievement of outcomes. These outcomes, in turn, enhance the possibility of development impacts, but the relationship is not necessarily one of direct cause and effect. This shift significantly alters the way a programme understands its goals and assesses its performance and results: its contributions to development are planned and assessed based on its influence on the partners with whom it is working to effect change. Focusing monitoring and evaluation on changes in partners illustrates that, although a programme can influence the achievement of outcomes, it cannot control them because ultimate responsibility for change rests with its partners. In essence, development is accomplished through changes in people's behaviour – and this is the central concept of Outcome Mapping.

Planning for and assessing external results and internal performance

Outcome Mapping recognises that development is a complex process comprising three parallel dynamics: first, the changes in the behaviours, actions, activities, and/or relationships of the people, groups, and organisations with whom a programme works directly; second, the strategies that a programme employs to encourage change in its partners; and, third, the functioning of a programme as an organisational unit. It builds an understanding not only of changes in the development setting in which a programme is working, but also monitors and assesses its strategies and activities and the extent to which the programme is learning and adapting to new conditions. As such, Outcome Mapping assesses a programme holistically and is based on the premise that a programme needs to know not only about development results, but also about the processes by which they were attained, and about its internal effectiveness. It is through the combination of information and knowledge in these three areas that a programme can build a better understanding of what it is achieving and how it can improve its levels of success.

Through assessing these three elements of a programme, Outcome Mapping unites process and outcome evaluation. Therefore, Outcome Mapping is well suited to the complex functioning and long-term aspects of international development programmes, where outcomes are intermeshed and cannot be easily or usefully segregated from each other. By considering the myriad actors and factors that contribute to development processes, it focuses on how a programme facilitates rather than causes change and looks to assess contribution rather than attribution. Outcome Mapping encourages a programme to link itself explicitly to processes of transformation and provides it with the information it requires in order to change along with its partners. Looking at how the three elements interrelate and the context in which change occurs is essential to programme learning. A programme does not operate in isolation from other factors and actors, and therefore cannot plan and assess as though it did. Systems thinking is not simple and straightforward, however, and requires a commitment to ongoing reflection and analysis. As Peter Senge points out:

> Seeing interrelationships, not things, and processes, not snapshots. Most of us have been conditioned throughout our lives to focus on things and to see the world in static images. This leads us to linear explanations of systemic phenomena.
>
> (Senge 1990:15)

International development programmes are particularly prone to excluding themselves from the system in which development change occurs. By separating themselves from development processes (i.e. something 'we' help 'them' accomplish) and explaining change by using linear reasoning, programmes lose the opportunity to explore their full potential as change agents. Outcome Mapping encourages a programme to think of itself as part of the change process and to embrace complex reasoning and multiple logic systems. Raj Verma, of the Nagaland Empowerment of People Through Economic Development Programme (NEPED), described the change in the programme team's understanding of their role after using Outcome Mapping for a self-assessment of their first phase and the planning of their second phase as follows: 'The often repeated and echoing question in Outcome Mapping "what or who needs the change?" raised us from being providers of development, achieving outputs, to actually believing we were agents of change.'

The cyclical nature of planning, monitoring, and evaluation

> [T]he key differentiating factor in the success of an organization is not just the products and services, not just its technology or market share, but the organization's ability to elicit, harness, and focus the vast intellectual capital and goodwill resident in their members, employees and stakeholders. When that intellectual capital and goodwill get energized and focused, the organization becomes a powerful force for positive change in today's business and societal environments.
>
> (Kaner 1996:viii)

Outcome Mapping is a process in which programme staff engage, not a product that is provided to them. In it, planning, monitoring, and evaluation are not discrete events but are designed to be cyclical with each feeding the other. Monitoring and evaluation considerations are introduced at the planning stage and all programme staff are encouraged to think evaluatively throughout the programme cycle. That is, they are encouraged to think critically and ask questions about what they want to achieve and how they will know whether they have been successful. The cyclical nature of planning, monitoring, and evaluation is important because development programmes are part of an open system. The context in which a programme operates is continuously changing, so staff need to be engaged in ongoing reflection and learning so that the programme remains relevant and appropriate. It is impossible to plan for all eventualities; therefore, a successful programme is one that assesses and adapts to changing situations in an intelligent way based on thoughtful reflection. This idea resonates well with those engaged in international development programmes because they have often experienced a well-thought-out plan being thwarted by an unexpected 'external factor' – war, natural disaster, or a change in government – and therefore are adept at thinking about how to work in complex environments.

A key challenge is that despite the enthusiasm for iterative learning and active engagement in the planning processes, many programmes have difficulty putting in place an effective and consistent monitoring system. The problem does not appear to be a lack of commitment, sense of usefulness, or ownership of the process. Rather, it is lack of time as other work demands take over and there is no time for group reflection. This poses a fundamental challenge for those supporting the incorporation of reflective practices in programmes, because it is unavoidable that learning takes time. Furthermore, it cannot be outsourced! Outcome Mapping attempts to address this problem by encouraging programme teams to be realistic about what they can manage in terms of monitoring and evaluation and to prioritise their information needs based on intended use. Prioritising information needs is a difficult exercise because programme staff genuinely want to know about many aspects of their work and tend to be over-ambitious about what is feasible with the available resources. For example, a programme supporting research into tobacco control used Outcome Mapping to plan its second three-year phase, and chose to focus data collection on only one of its partners – researchers in developing countries. They felt that understanding changes in the researchers' behaviours (e.g. engaging marginalised groups in the research process, publishing articles in peer-reviewed journals, influencing tobacco-control policies and programmes in their countries), and the factors and actors that contributed to that, would best reflect the development outcomes the programme was helping to bring about in this nascent field. Furthermore, the programme team could use the data collected both to fulfil reporting requirements and to provide themselves with credible information and knowledge with which to improve the programme's activities and interventions.

Systematised self-assessment and group learning

Outcome Mapping is based on principles of participation and purposefully includes the programme implementers in both designing and undertaking the data collection so as to encourage ownership and use of findings. It is premised on the belief that those engaged in the programme can benefit from working as a group to systematically collect, analyse, and interpret data. It is intended as a consciousness-raising, consensus-building, and empowerment tool for those working directly in a development programme. By actively engaging the team in the monitoring and evaluation process, Outcome Mapping empowers them to articulate, with accurate and reliable data, what they do to support outcomes, and to harness group wisdom to improve their performance. In essence, it tries to implant the passion and enthusiasm of programming into the assessment process. Recognising this emotional element of learning is crucial to encouraging programmes to engage in learning and reflection processes. As noted by Senge, 'People's natural impulse to learn is unleashed when they are engaged in an endeavor they consider worthy of their fullest commitment' (Senge 1990:13). Outcome Mapping moves away from the notion that monitoring and evaluation are done *to* a programme and instead actively engages the programme team in the design of a monitoring framework and evaluation plan and promotes self-assessment. For example, a women's health and empowerment programme in India is using Outcome Mapping to document and assess its own capacity development in the areas of gender, monitoring and evaluation, and applied research. The women have identified behavioural markers that indicate progressive change and are using these to negotiate expectations among themselves, assess progress, and determine future strategies. Their self-assessment findings are not intended to be shared with others but will serve their own purposes as programme implementers.

Outcome Mapping is usually initiated through a participatory workshop led by an internal or external facilitator, and then regular monitoring workshops are held in which the programme team collects and analyses data in order to plan new, or refine existing, activities. Group learning is an essential component of the methodology because of its power to harness organisational knowledge. Michael Doyle states that the key to engendering learning in an organisation is:

> by creating psychologically safe and involving group environments where people can identify and solve problems, plan together, make collaborative decisions, resolve their own conflicts, trouble-shoot and self-manage as responsible adults. Facilitation enables the organization's teams, groups, and meeting to be much more productive. And the side benefits of facilitated or self-facilitated groups are terrific: empowerment, a deepening of personal commitment to decision and plans, increased organizational loyalty, and the building of esprit de corps.
> (Kaner 1996:viii)

Outcome Mapping workshops are intended to be participatory and, wherever feasible, can involve the full range of stakeholders, including the partners in whom behavioural change is sought. Nonetheless, genuine participation is not simple (especially in the context of an externally funded development programme) and hierarchy and politics can affect learning. A programme using Outcome Mapping needs to carefully consider who should participate and ensure that participants feel comfortable sharing their experiences (positive and negative), engaging in self-assessment, and brainstorming on how to move forward. In their desire to use participatory approaches, donor agencies sometimes ignore the power imbalances that necessarily exist between the institution funding a programme and its beneficiaries. In order to create the optimum space for critical assessment and learning by a programme team, participation needs to be considered in each instance and should be requested in a spirit of equitable collaboration, acknowledging the complexity of existing relationships.

Outcome Mapping has been developed in organisations where monitoring and evaluation are intended primarily to help programme learning and improvement. Making reflection an organisational priority has proved to be a prerequisite for the successful integration of the learning processes associated with Outcome Mapping. When incentives and rewards have instead been directed towards reporting for the purposes of accountability, Outcome Mapping has proved an inappropriate approach to monitoring and evaluation. Outcome Mapping can only be as empowering, participatory, and learning-oriented as the organisational context in which it is implemented.

Conclusion

Outcome Mapping helps a programme to be specific about the actors it targets, the changes it expects to see, the strategies it employs, and its effectiveness as an organisational unit. It is particularly valuable for monitoring and evaluating development programmes, whose results and achievements cannot be understood through quantitative indicators alone but also require the deeper insights of a qualitative, contextualised story of the development process. Outcome Mapping will not help a programme create generic lists of 'lessons learned' or 'best practices'. Instead, it will help it weave the plots of the three elements related to its work: first, the changes in the behaviours, actions, activities, and/or relationships of the people, groups, and organisations with whom a programme works directly; second, the strategies that a programme employs to encourage change in its partners; and third, the internal effectiveness of that programme. Outcome Mapping provides a programme with processes through which to collect data and to reflect on the change processes in order to guide its actions knowledgeably.

Notes

1   IDRC is a public corporation created in 1970 by the Parliament of Canada. Its mandate is to initiate, encourage, support, and conduct research into the problems of the developing regions of the world and into the means for applying and adapting scientific, technical, and other knowledge to the economic and social advancement of those regions.

2   For a full discussion of problems associated with measuring attribution and impact see Terry Smutylo (2001).

3   Dr Barry Kibel, Pacific Institute for Research and Evaluation, was instrumental in introducing his Outcome Engineering approach and working closely with us to adapt some of these ideas to the development research context. Methodological collaboration with the West Africa Rural Foundation (FRAO) and testing with the Nagaland Empowerment of People Through Economic Development Programme (NEPED) and the International Model Forest Network Secretariat (IMFNS) have greatly informed this adaptation process. Ongoing testing with a number of other initiatives continues to enrich the process.

4 For the purposes of this article, a programme is defined as a group of related projects and activities with a specified set of resources (human, capital, and financial) directed towards the achievement of a set of common goals within a specified period of time.

References

Earl, Sarah, Fred Carden and Terry Smutylo (2001) *Outcome Mapping: A Guide to Building Learning and Reflection into Development Programmes* (with a Foreword by Michael Quinn Patton), Ottawa: IDRC.

Kaner, Sam (1996) *Facilitator's Guide to Participatory Decision Making* (with a Foreword by Michael Doyle), British Columbia: New Society Publishers.

Senge, Peter M. (1990) 'The leader's new work: building learning organizations', *Sloan Management Review* 32(1):7–23.

Smutylo, Terry (2001) 'A crouching impact, hidden attribution: overcoming threats to learning in development organisations', paper presented at Block Island Workshop on Cross Portfolio Learning, 22–24 May, available at www.idrc.ca/evaluation/crouching_impact.pdf/

This article was first published in Development in Practice *(12/3&4:518–524) in 2002.*

Modelling learning programmes

Molly den Heyer

Introduction

An overwhelming majority of international development agencies requests that staff and/or recipients use programme logic models to plan and evaluate their programmes and projects. The most common such model is Logical Framework Analysis (LFA). While the models may vary in language, structure, and use, they consistently illustrate programmes as a fixed set of activities implemented in a given timespan. This 'blueprint approach' is challenged by the concept of organisational learning, which redefines structures (such as programmes and projects) as an evolutionary process of action, reflection, and adaptation.

This trend affects development in practice by creating a tension between programmes that are driven by organisational learning concepts and the traditional use of various tools and methods in programme implementation. It is argued that if a programme is grounded in the learning perspective then that perspective should inform every aspect of the programme. With regard to planning and evaluation, this requires more than just loosening LFA's constraints, it means restructuring the model to illustrate change over time.

The following note describes one attempt to update the programme logic models to incorporate organisational learning. It begins with a brief review of learning concepts, describes the traditional LFA, and concludes with a sketch of an alternative programme model, the Temporal Logic Model (TLM).

Theoretical background

Learning organisations are 'skilled at creating, acquiring, and transforming knowledge, and at modifying [their] behavior to reflect new knowledge and insights' (Garvin 1993). The learning is both incremental, in order to 'focus on refinements of current strategies', and transformative, so as to 'focus on creating strategy because people understand the organisation or its work in new, fundamentally different ways' (Watkins and Marsick 1993). These processes consist of continuous cycles of action, reflection, and adaptation, which are commonly referred to as 'learning loops'. Depending on the challenges faced by the group, these learning loops occur (often spontaneously) on a variety of different subjects, stages, and timings. In programme management, single-loop learning correlates with an iterative process of reflection on an issue within the programme, while double-loop learning correlates with a transformative reflection on programme design. Further, Gregory Bateson (1972) introduced 'deutero-learning' to integrate the capacity to sustain the process of single- and double-loop learning (Morgan 1999). In essence, deutero-learning describes a learning programme's ability to continually improve itself throughout the implementation phase.

The above concepts transform how programmes and projects are perceived. They are no longer a set of activities that should be implemented according to a predetermined plan, but an evolutionary process that changes and adapts over time. This process incorporates emerging lessons, responds to the environment, examines intended and unintended results, and actively refines the implementation theories embedded in the programme.

Logical Framework Analysis

Leon Rosenburg, with a team of consultants from Practical Concepts Incorporated (PCI), invented LFA in the early 1970s for USAID (McLaughlin and Jordan 1999). Although there are several variations in structure and language, the model is part of standard procedures for most major funding agencies, including USAID, the Canadian International Development Agency, the UK's Department for International Development, the German Agency for Technical Corporation, the Japan International Corporation Agency, the Belgian Administration for Development Cooperation, the Norwegian Agency for Development, the European Commission, and the Swedish International Development Agency (Gasper 2000) (see Figure 1).

The evaluation logic model is used primarily at the programme level to foster a common understanding, help in its design, test its logical linkages and objectives, possibly explain the placement of activities in the larger programme hierarchy, and assist in the structuring of the evaluation (McLaughlin and Jordan 1999).

Figure 1: Logical Framework Model

	Narrative summary	Objectively verifiable indicators	Means of verification	Assumptions
Goals				
Purpose				
Output				
Input				

Criticisms of such models have included claims that the framework reinforces hierarchies and can be used as a tool to control programmes; reduce programme vision to achievable results, with negative effects on motivation; impose the blueprint approach which focuses on intended results, thereby overlooking the learning process; and assume consensus on problems and solutions. A final criticism is that LFA does not capture the *unintended* results (Gasper 2000).

While most of LFA's weaknesses can be attributed to misuse and institutionalisation, there are several structural issues that inhibit its effectiveness in learning programmes. Specifically, the graphic design illustrates a fixed plan 'blueprint' or a closed system that ignores how the programme adapts over time. The following model was designed to address this issue.

The Temporal Logic Model

Modelling learning programmes requires the mimicking of an iterative process, recording how the programme responds to internal and external fluctuations, and continuous refinement of the theory that underpins implementation – while still remaining user-friendly. The TLM was intended to do this primarily by expanding the model vertically to represent change over time, as well as enhancing the content.

As seen in Figure 2, the TLM illustrates the programme as an iterative process through a series of stages. The first stage, entitled the 'programme planning stage', maps out the programme's context and its internal mechanisms. The subsequent stages, referred to as

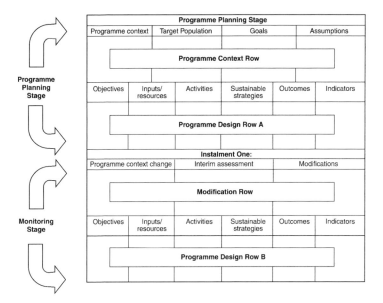

'monitoring stages or instalments', map out any internal or external changes to the programme, interim assessments, and necessary modifications. These modifications are incorporated into an adapted programme design row. The introduction of 'rolodex-type' instalments invites the stakeholders to track the learning loops by monitoring and reflecting on the programme and its environment (den Heyer 2001).

The programme context row acts as an anchor by being the only fixed statement in the model. It provides a general statement of the programme context, goals, target population, and underlying assumptions. It is intended to capture the common reasoning that underpins the programme. Once the broader issues are established, the stakeholders are then asked to fill in the programme design row. This links the internal programme mechanisms: objectives, resources, activities, sustainable strategies, outcomes, and indicators. The programme design row provides a more detailed account of how the programme's components are logically linked in order to produce a causal effect, often referred to as the implementation theory.

While most logic models stop at this still snapshot of the intended programme, the TLM invites the stakeholders periodically to monitor and reflect on the programme structure. The monitoring stages comprise a monitoring row and a subsequent programme design row. The modification row asks two reflective questions about changes in the programme context, interim assessments, and an analytical question about whether and how the stakeholders should modify the programme design on the basis of the previously noted reflections. These modifications are then recorded in the subsequent design row. The timeframe for the instalments should be determined on a case-by-case basis and may vary depending on the length, type, and structure of the programme. Programmes may wish to add extra instalments as the need arises.

The programme planning stage and subsequent monitoring instalments should correlate with the learning cycle of action, reflection, and adaptation at the level of double-loop learning (reflecting on the programme design), thereby creating an ongoing record of programme learning that can be shared with the wider organisation. Mapping the programme's change over time also reveals the evolutionary nature of its implementation. There is no defined end, simply instalments that monitor and support learning and adaptation throughout the process.

The LFA addresses the concept of being responsive to and interactive with the environment through assumptions that record potentially disruptive influences to the programme. However, the TLM further develops this concept by including a programme context row (which sets the stage for the programme implementation), and programme context changes in successive instalments corresponding to the monitoring stages. The addition of monitoring stages provides stakeholders with a flexible model to record changes in the context, interim assessments, and changes in the programme design, thereby creating an organic plan to capture the programme's interaction between contextual aspects and design.

The TLM also expands the concept of causation from LFA's presentation of linear and 'attributable' causality. As we saw above, LFA is criticised for assuming linear causality which undervalues the complexity of societal systems and the contribution of multiple causal factors (internal and external); assuming direct attribution for results; and promoting 'programme tunnel vision' by ignoring both positive and negative unintended results of the programme (Gasper 2000). The TLM approaches these issues both in terms of structure and content.

While it is impossible for a standardised model to map out each external contributory causal factor, it can illustrate the traditional intended causation between a set of activities and intended effects. The TLM adds to this normative illustration by expanding the model to allow the stakeholders to adapt the causation and incorporate unintended effects. This provides a mechanism to refine the implementation theory as the programme develops.

In terms of content, the TLM uses sustainable strategies and a behavioural definition of outcomes. Instead of asking for attribution of long-term impact in society years after the project has been completed, sustainable strategies ask the stakeholders to outline current strategies for ensuring that the programme's effects continue to exist in the target population after completion. This is complemented by outcome mapping's refined definition of outcomes as 'behavioural changes that contribute' to change (Earl *et al.* 2001; Earl and Carden this volume).

These modifications transform LFA into a tool designed for reflective practitioners to record programme modifications based on increased learning, evolving consensus, and contextual changes. In addition, it balances accountability with flexibility by allowing for change and providing space to justify changes in the programme design. It could be said that this results in a more 'accurate accounting' of what is actually happening on the ground.

Conclusion

The TLM was designed to address the gap between organisational learning theory and the practical application of logic models in programme planning and evaluation. It moves away from the traditional 'blueprint approach' by breaking open the standard '4 × 4 box' to include change over time. While there is a need for further field-testing, it is hoped that the TLM represents one more step in a wider effort to update and redesign traditional development tools for learning organisations.

References

Bateson, Gregory (1972) *Steps to an Ecology of Mind*, New York, NY: Ballantine.

den Heyer, Molly (2001) 'The development of the Temporal Logic Model', unpublished MSc thesis, University of Guelph, Canada.

Earl, Sarah and Fred Carden (2002) 'Learning from complexity: the International Development Research Centre's experience with Outcome Mapping', *Development in Practice* 12(3&4):518–524.

Earl, Sarah, Fred Carden and Terry Smutylo (2001) *Outcome Mapping: Building Learning and Reflection into Development Programmes*, Canada: IDRC.

Garvin, D. (1993) 'Building a learning organization', *Harvard Business Review* (July/August):18–91.

Gasper, Des (2000) 'Evaluating the "Logical Framework Approach": towards learning-oriented development evaluation', *Public Administration and Development* 20(1):17–28.

McLaughlin, John A. and Gretchen B. Jordan (1999) 'Logic models: a tool for telling your programme performance story', *Evaluation and Programme Planning* 22:65–72.

Morgan, Gareth (1999) *Creative Organization Theory: A Resource Book*, Thousand Oaks, CA: Sage.

Watkins, Karen and Victoria Marsick (1993) *Sculpting the Learning Organization: Lessons in the Art and Science of Systemic Change*, San Francisco, CA: Jossey-Bass.

This article was first published in Development in Practice *(12/3&4:525–529) in 2002.*

Learning for change: the art of assessing the impact of advocacy work

Barry Coates and Rosalind David

Introduction

Advocacy work has become the latest enthusiasm for most agencies involved in international aid and development. Over the past decade NGOs have dedicated more resources and given a higher priority to influencing and advocacy work at all levels (local, national, and international levels). These trends have been driven by a number of factors.

Perhaps the most fundamental of these has been a deeper understanding of the causes of poverty and marginalisation. NGOs and many donors have come to recognise that several decades of aid projects, even those using improved methodologies for intervention, are neither addressing the determinants of poverty nor alleviating its symptoms on a sufficient scale. Indeed, the underlying causes of poverty and social exclusion remain very much intact.

The context for development work has changed dramatically, as Southern NGOs have increased in size and capacity. In many cases, they have (legitimately) displaced Northern NGOs as implementers, or even as channels for aid from government or multilateral agencies. As democracy and political pluralism have spread, Southern NGOs and social movements have become more assertive in challenging power structures within their own countries and increasingly at the international level.

With a diminished role as aid implementers, many Northern NGOs have sought a new role in advocacy. The recent success of campaigns (such as those on landmines, some World Bank projects, debt, and the Multilateral Agreement on Investment or MAI) has stimulated interest among Northern NGOs. The media profile and potential for public involvement in such campaigns have added attraction as a source of profile and funding. More substantively, some Southern

NGOs have called on their Northern counterparts to change the policies of their own home governments, recognising that international policy is still largely driven by the OECD countries. In some countries, such as the UK, increased advocacy work has also been made possible by a relaxation in the interpretation of the legal framework governing charities.

On the heels of the enthusiasm for advocacy is an emerging enthusiasm for understanding whether the substantial devotion of resources to these activities is having an impact. NGOs are asking whether advocacy and influencing initiatives are cost effective and whether they are contributing to the fulfilment of their mission (i.e. improving the lives of their intended beneficiaries). These are important questions to ask, not only for accountability purposes (such as how NGOs are using donors' or the public's funds), but also to learn from experience and improve the way advocacy work is undertaken. Monitoring and evaluation (M&E) and impact assessment (IA) can also help NGOs understand how far their work is supporting the efforts of others, particularly in strengthening civil society, and the degree to which advocacy and influencing work results in lasting improvements in the lives of poor and marginalised people.

There are two major problems in M&E when applied to advocacy. First, there is currently little experience or capacity. The 'market' (of internal staff, research institutes, and/or consultants) is just starting to respond, recognising that M&E is set to become a growth industry. The multinational consultancy agencies are pursuing the potentially lucrative sector of monitoring the impact of companies on workers, local communities, and the environment, and attempting to establish themselves as credible verifiers. Smaller consultancy firms that have experience in M&E for project work are now eyeing the potential for evaluating advocacy activities. Meanwhile, NGOs are adding internal staff and starting internal training and capacity building in M&E for advocacy.

Yet a second problem remains: how do you do it? This paper suggests some deep pitfalls and some broad approaches to M&E/IA for advocacy.

What is advocacy and how is it changing?

The deepest pitfall of advocacy is failing to understand the nature of the work it involves. This is scarcely surprising, given the paucity of systematic research and analysis into its diverse forms, methods, institutional structures, and the dynamics of decision-making processes it seeks to influence. Further, the whole field of advocacy work is changing rapidly. The dominant role of major corporations, pressures to reduce the role of the State, new challenges for civil society, globalisation of media and entertainment, and new communications technologies are among the many factors introducing new challenges and new opportunities.

The complexity of the advocacy field can be illustrated across four dimensions:

- the increasing globalisation of advocacy work;
- the rise of a diverse civil society;
- the increasing diversity of advocacy structures;
- the increasing diversity in strategies.

The increasing globalisation of advocacy work

The last 20 years have seen the rapid internationalisation of economic activity and the commensurate growth in power of global economic institutions. In the past, civil society had a strong record of influencing human rights and social and environmental policies at the international level, particularly through UN processes. However, these 'soft' (aspirational) policies have largely been subordinated to the 'hard' (enforceable) rules made by international institutions and forums in the economic sphere. Economic decisions taken at the international level now affect the lives of much of the world's population. It is increasingly the case that ' ... major decisions affecting the lives of the disenfranchised, especially poor people, are being made in ever more distant places' (Watson 2001:123).

Patterns of development are being influenced by trade and financial flows and by the international rules that facilitate them. For example, the WTO provides a mechanism for governments to determine not only external trade rules, such as tariffs and quotas, but also national and local policies on subsidies, licensing laws, and a huge range of regulations across society. As the rules have become more pervasive and intrusive, civil society has increasingly challenged the underlying policies, the lack of transparency in decision making, and the very legitimacy of the institutions. Over the past two decades, such civil society advocacy has forced its way from the periphery to frame much of the discourse, and is now starting to change the policies and power structures.

The challenge of tackling these rules has necessitated a new approach to international advocacy work. New communications technologies, particularly the Internet, have allowed the formation of campaign networks that would have been unimaginable a decade ago. The interplay of local, national, and international campaigns means that there are many different campaign pathways and targets. Systems for coordination and accountability have been developed to encourage broad participation and a central role for the voices and demands of those primarily affected. It is important that M&E/IA systems recognise and support the huge diversity in forms of advocacy.

The rise of a diverse civil society

The strengthened capacity of civil society in the South has created new opportunities for effective advocacy across a wide range of local, national, regional, and international policies. The last ten years have seen the emergence of Southern NGOs as leading actors in international campaigns, including multinational advocacy groups from the South, such as the Third World Network. The traditional model of Northern NGO-led campaigns is changing rapidly to recognise that meaningful, sustainable policy change can only be achieved through strong Southern participation in all aspects of advocacy. Yet in many of the poorest countries, particularly in sub-Saharan Africa, there are few opportunities for civil society to exert influence and little capacity to do so. Some NGOs are therefore emphasising the need for advocacy work to include capacity building, support for coalitions and broad-based movements, and the expansion of democratic space for civil society. The challenge is to integrate the processes of strengthening the movement with the actions to achieve policy change. This requires a more insightful assessment of advocacy work, respecting its multiple aims.

The increasing diversity of advocacy structures

The organisational structures of advocacy work are also changing rapidly. New technologies and new forms of coalition are greatly enlarging the range of potential strategies and tactics that can be used by international coalitions. For example, *The Economist* in December 1999 likened the campaign against a new round of WTO negotiations in Seattle to a 'swarm', involving a diverse range of autonomous civil society organisations. Formal hierarchies and rigid structures have largely been displaced by multiple and overlapping networks and coalitions, with new ways to formulate joint strategies, share research, and act quickly on the basis of new information. This is a departure from the more traditional campaigns, where there has usually been a lead organisation and more clearly defined attribution of impact resulting from the work of any particular actor in the campaign.

The key ingredient that allows coalitions to function effectively across geographic, cultural, economic, and political divides is trust. Research on the success of civil society coalitions on the World Bank explains that these 'vertical coalitions' are facilitated by organisational chains of relatively short links that collectively span great distances (Brown and Fox 1999:8–11).

There is no doubt that information and communications technology has promoted a greater degree of specialisation among NGOs internationally, just as it has in the value chains of businesses in the international economy. It is no longer required that any particular group or organisation become an expert in all issues or cover all aspects in a particular campaign. For example, an important part of the strength of the anti-MAI campaign derived from the diversity of allies undertaking specialised advocacy roles in the coalition, such as 'insider' dialogue, research, public education, movement building, public campaigning, and networking. These roles also spanned issues that have often been perceived as distinct, such as international development, environment, human rights, the rights of workers, consumers, and women, faith-based social justice, local government, corporate social responsibility, etc. Within such coalitions, attribution of outcomes becomes impossible. Successes and failures are inherently shared by coalition members.

The increasing diversity in strategies

Alongside the increasing complexity of advocacy work is a greater appreciation of the diversity in strategies that can be used to achieve change. One of the most important insights in understanding the nature of advocacy work is that its success relies on the ability to transform the structures of power. The strategy adopted will therefore depend on the means by which the power has been created and maintained. A useful insight into different systems of power is provided by Gaventa (1995). Based on his work, we suggest three categories:

- A pluralist system, within which there is a relatively open competition for power.
- An élitist system, dominated by a privileged group that excludes and discriminates against others.

- An ideological system, relying on the dominance of political, economic, or religious beliefs to shape the consciousness of society.

These broad categories of the power structure require very different advocacy strategies. For example, professional lobbying may be effective within a pluralist system – a relatively open exchange of research and analysis lends itself to the development of specialist NGOs and research institutions, reasoned argument, and lobbying. However, such approaches are likely to be ineffective in a system dominated by élites, where the most effective advocacy strategies are likely to include subversion of the power structure through, for example, challenging its legitimacy or exposing it to ridicule. Similarly, advocacy in a system dominated by a particular ideology demands different strategies, such as mobilisation of those whose interests are excluded.

Likewise, different advocacy strategies are required in response to differing social, institutional, economic, and cultural circumstances. The diversity of advocacy approaches multiplies as campaigns cross national boundaries, involve new coalitions of civil society, and address new global challenges. A 'tick box' approach, listing the various components of a campaign that may have worked in a particular case, is clearly inappropriate. There is, or should be, an almost infinite range of different strategies and tactics that are used to achieve change.

The deep pitfalls of standard M&E/IA applied to advocacy work

The increasing power of civil society to influence policy has led to calls for NGOs to be more accountable. While the most vociferous calls often come from business leaders whose own accountability is limited to their largest shareholders, this does not detract from the need for NGOs to be more accountable, most importantly to their members and/or intended beneficiaries. In addition, the greater investment of resources in advocacy work has increased pressures for clear evaluation of its effectiveness. Therefore, NGOs are called upon to use the processes of M&E/IA to justify their advocacy work. This is a major challenge for most organisations. The traditional practices of M&E/IA are often inadequate and run the risk of providing misleading information. Some of the deepest pitfalls arise from potential misunderstandings of the nature of the advocacy process.

Advocacy is messy

The most common pitfall is to assume that political and institutional change occurs in a linear fashion, as in a recipe that is prepared through the addition of particular ingredients (research, lobbying, public concern, political pressure, etc.) and cooked (campaigned) for a certain period. This is rarely the case. Change often occurs in sudden leaps, in unexpected ways, and in response to the most unlikely circumstances. And campaigns typically evolve through a bewildering range of obstacles, opportunities, and responses. This is well illustrated in two case studies on the promotion of breastfeeding in Ghana and issues of child labour in the carpet industry in India (Chapman and Fisher 2000:152–157). These case studies make the point that campaigns cannot be understood as systematic, mechanistic, or pursuing a logical sequence. Typically, however, M&E/IA falls into this trap, assuming that impacts will be achieved within a given timeframe, based on an established plan (perhaps even a logical framework) with inputs producing outputs that result in impacts. The application of such a model may be misleading and even undermine the effectiveness of advocacy work. For example, undue emphasis on achieving targets against a plan may contribute to missing opportunities for achieving change in unexpected ways.

Advocacy relies on cooperation

A second pitfall is created by the obsession of many NGOs with assessing the impact of their own organisation in isolation from others. In some cases, for example, the impact of advocacy may be reduced to measuring the various forms of media coverage on a particular issue, with particular attention given to mentions of the NGO in question. While this may be important for institutional profile, such measures can encourage competitive rather than collaborative behaviour, providing incentives for campaigners to elevate their own profile over others or the coalition as a whole. More broadly, assessment of the impact of a single NGO as part of a coalition is difficult and all too often creates tensions. When international campaigns involve thousands of diverse civil society organisations from many different countries, it is difficult to attribute the impact of a campaign to any one type of campaigning method or national arena, let alone to a single NGO.

One size does not fit all

A third pitfall is the application of standardised M&E/IA tools, while different forms of advocacy may require different methods and timescales. Those engaged in longer-term research and intermittent policy influence may prefer formal systems that rely on annual reports, quantifiable indicators, and measurement against plans. By contrast, those using public mobilisation or direct action to influence a rapidly evolving issue may develop informal systems that assess progress each week, using subjective judgements and flexible plans that enable them to react quickly and take advantage of new opportunities. The use of standard approaches to M&E/IA will rarely provide the most effective information for decision making.

Advocacy is often adversarial

The type of decision-making system being influenced also needs to inform the types of M&E/IA used. For example, where there is a high degree of cooperation and trust between an NGO and a government department, as in the case of British NGOs lobbying for a larger aid budget, it can be useful to ask decision makers about advocacy impact and effectiveness (Development Initiatives 1996). However, if this is attempted when the relationship is adversarial, the information could be maliciously misleading.

Rome wasn't built in a day

A fifth pitfall is overemphasis on short-term aims over less visible long-term process goals. On the one hand, the achievement of tangible outcomes is an important part of most advocacy work. Not only does it demonstrate some degree of success and thereby gain more support and resources, it also plays an important role in building a wider base of participants in the advocacy work. But on the other hand, short-term successes may be won at the expense of longer-term goals. Most often these include the less visible aims of building capacity among partners and contribution to more fundamental change in future. An interim review of ActionAid's Food Rights campaign illustrates this point. In this case, shorter-term desires to influence the Seattle WTO process are shown to have initially compromised longer-term institutional aims of deepening the campaign, developing people-centred advocacy, and creating strong micro-macro links (Harding 2000).

The conclusion is that reductionist and standardised forms of M&E/IA are likely to be inappropriate for advocacy work, and may even create perverse incentives that undermine effective joint action. Just as Logical Frameworks have undermined participatory, process-oriented approaches to project work, pressure from donors to apply restrictive M&E/IA approaches will impede effective advocacy work. The challenge is to develop approaches that are useful to those engaged in advocacy and promote accountability to all stakeholders.

Broad approaches to effective M&E/IA for advocacy

So what can we say about the monitoring and evaluation of influencing and advocacy work? Four principles should guide the development of M&E/IA systems:

- Ensure that what the NGO values gets measured.
- Use methodological approaches that are appropriate to the type of advocacy work being carried out.
- Look at the whole – not just the parts.
- Make impact assessment an organisational priority.

Measuring what is valued

Clarity about the aims, strategies, and tactics of advocacy are essential for effective monitoring and evaluation. All too often an enthusiasm for advocacy means that NGOs 'work on' a particular issue without any clear idea of how their actions will achieve change. It is rare that NGOs are explicit about how advocacy will realistically achieve policy change, let alone clear about how that policy change will be translated into positive practice that helps poor people in the long term.

Even if advocacy is undertaken in a fluid and rapidly changing environment, it is important that each agency clearly articulates what it is trying to achieve and ensures what it values is measured (qualitative or indicative measures may be preferable to contrived ways to quantify the impact). One way of clarifying important process objectives is to identify and prioritise essential dimensions of the work at the outset. Policy or legislative change is one of the most obvious. However, depending on the type of advocacy (and the values of the NGO), a second dimension may be strengthening civil society by working in ways that create collaboration, trust, and unity among civil society groups. A third dimension could be helping to enlarge the 'democratic space' in which civil society groups can operate. And a fourth dimension could be the direct involvement of excluded people in advocacy to achieve their rights, rather than being 'consulted' by professional activists who are advocating on their behalf. Whatever the dimensions, each NGO should, at the outset, be clear about what it is trying to do and how this will be monitored.

Choose appropriate methodologies

What are the methodologies for assessing impact? As has been argued above, this needs to start from an understanding of the diversity in advocacy approaches. It is important to select appropriate methods for assessing change in different circumstances.

A wide range of stakeholders could be involved in an evaluation of advocacy work. These include NGO advocacy staff themselves, coalition members and partners, decision makers or influence targets, 'experts' (such as consultants or academics), the general public, representatives of those most affected, or those people themselves. Currently, standard methodological approaches involve semi-structured interviews, group-based discussions, surveys, and questionnaires, together with media records, internal reports of meetings, events and activities, mailing lists, and external reports.

Whom to involve in M&E/IA should reflect the type of advocacy work and the power structure being influenced. The intended beneficiaries of advocacy work should be involved wherever possible, though this may be impractical in campaigns involving large numbers of beneficiaries (e.g. the Jubilee 2000 debt campaign). A more practical approach would be to involve civil society representatives at the national and, where possible, local levels. This also is difficult in campaigns where a change is being prevented. For example, it is impossible to involve beneficiaries in a campaign to stop a new round of WTO negotiations – but the involvement of a range of NGOs, social movements, trade unions, and other civil society groups in a joint campaign evaluation would be possible.

In other cases, however, the direct involvement of the people most affected is vital. This is most likely to be meaningful when they have been closely involved in the campaign, when the policy change is local (rather than international), and where there is a high degree of trust among those involved.

The different forms of power structure being influenced also have a bearing on the most appropriate M&E/IA, as shown in Table 1. In a relatively open and pluralist system it may be possible to involve opinion formers or even decision makers in evaluating the success of different advocacy approaches. In a closed system with power controlled by élites, it will often be difficult to get access to information on how decisions are made, and evaluation is reliant on assessing the degree to which advocacy work is making progress according to the conceptual model of how advocacy can achieve change. There are even fewer opportunities to access decision makers in a system dominated by ideology. Change is often slow, discontinuous, and may take place over decades.

Table 1 outlines some of the implications of different forms of power structure for the type of advocacy work undertaken and possible approaches to M&E/IA.

Table 1: How power analysis affects M&E/IA approaches			
System of power	Key characteristics of power structure	Possible advocacy approaches	Possible M&E/IA approaches
Pluralist system	• Relatively open, access defined by level of resources (e.g. many democracies) • Competition between interest groups on the basis of political and economic leverage • Powerlessness of poor and minorities	• Professional research and lobbying • Public-interest lobbying on defined issues • Influence over democratic processes/voting • Public campaigning to demonstrate public support	• Use available information, including public records of decision making • Involve wide range of stakeholders, possibly including opinion formers and/or decision makers • Possible joint evaluation between coalition partners • Include intermediate measures of political change, capacity building, and degree of participation
Elitist system	• Closed access, limited to the powerful élite (e.g. Burma) • Exclusion of issues and groups • Systematic forms of repression and exploitation	• Mobilisation of excluded groups in coalitions • Underground and secretive opposition movements • Strategies to de-legitimise the power of the élite • Important role of symbols of repression • Expand space for civil society to organise and influence	• In the absence of information on decision-making processes, M&E should assess progress on key influence pathways and test assumptions about how to achieve change • Involve coalition allies in participatory M&E where possible • Include evaluation of capacity building, scope of civil society involvement, and degree of participation
Ideological system	• Hidden forms of oppression arising from ideological non-conformity (e.g. institutional racism) • Hegemony of ideas perpetrated through formal structures of society • Dissenting voices stifled and ridiculed	• Popular education and building critical thought • Development of public understanding, through literature, arts, culture, etc. • Promote analysis and understanding of alternatives • Build a coalition among the powerless (e.g. the poor excluded from market ideology)	• Recognise even longer timeframes in achieving identifiable change • Assess the extent and nature of public understanding • Include evaluation of capacity building, scope of civil society involvement, exposure of different public audiences, changes in public perceptions

Assess the whole, not just the parts

A third principle that should guide the choice of M&E for advocacy is to be holistic. As shown in this paper, advocacy work is complex, multi-layered, and evolving rapidly. The traditional tools used in planning, monitoring, and evaluation, with their emphasis on limited timeframes, logical frameworks, annual objectives, periodic reviews, and lengthy reports, are often inappropriate. A recent review of M&E/IA approaches to advocacy illustrates that NGOs often look at part of this complex 'elephant', and not at the whole (Davies 2001). New approaches are required, recognising the huge diversity in advocacy work.

M&E must be an integral part of the advocacy process itself. This means that M&E is not a separate exercise carried out after a campaign is finished, an audit or a source of good news stories for funders. The timeframes for the campaign and the rapidity with which it evolves dictate how frequently activities and plans need to be reviewed. Flexibility is often important. A successful campaign is one that takes advantage of new opportunities or responds to new threats as they arise. Therefore, a successful M&E approach must be flexible enough not only to adapt to external events, but to be a tool in reshaping the campaign.

There are few answers available 'off the shelf'. The authors are involved in several initiatives that are developing aspects of M&E work. The World Development Movement (WDM), a UK-based membership network, is part of an international network of civil society groups campaigning on the General Agreement on Trade in Services (GATS). The overall campaign is multi-layered in tackling national governments, national and international corporate lobby groups, and international institutions (primarily the WTO); allies range from small community-based protest groups in the South fighting for local control over natural resources to international trade unions opposing privatisation of public services; the methods of campaigning are diverse and external events are moving quickly; and the systems of power are a mix of relatively pluralist, élitist, and ideological. M&E is difficult.

The approach used by WDM has been to develop a conceptual map of the advocacy process, identifying the decision makers to be influenced, the campaign outcomes that would benefit the poor and disadvantaged communities, and the pathways to do so. These campaigns typically use a combination of research and analysis to win the arguments and influence opinion makers; public education, mobilisation, and media coverage to create political pressure; and work with others to support their actions. The pathways therefore comprise a number of tracks which contribute to the overall goal.

At periodic intervals, the map is reviewed, progress discussed, and changes made to future plans. The conceptual map thereby provides a framework not only for planning, but for monitoring progress on each of the pathways for change and towards the overall influence target. Where there are often long time lags between the activity and the result, it is essential to be able to assess progress on each step of the advocacy path. Some indications of change can be ascertained from official positions, documents (especially those that are leaked!) and discussions, shared among allies. This framework has yet to be fully developed as an M&E/IA approach, but shows promise as a flexible and practical means to ensure that the assessment of the parts to a campaign contribute to the effective assessment of the whole.

Make impact assessment an organisational priority

A final principle, which could guide the development of M&E/IA of advocacy, is to make this process an organisational priority. At its best, M&E work should be about supporting institutional learning, encouraging reflection and adaptive work practices, and ensuring a voice and accountability to those people whose lives are most affected by NGO advocacy. For this to happen, M&E and IA have to transcend their specialist boxes and become a live and kicking part of the way an organisation works and relates to its stakeholders. Some NGOs are waking up to this challenge (Roche 1999; Chapman and Wameyo 2001). For example, the development of the Accountability, Learning and Planning System (ALPS) within ActionAid has created the potential for this to happen (see also the article by Patta Scott-Villiers in this volume). In essence, this new system simply details processes for appraisals, strategy formation, and programme review across the organisation. Yet it does more than this. It places emphasis on accountability to poor people at all levels of the organisation. It promotes ongoing reflection and learning as a key element of everyone's work. And, importantly, it explicitly recognises the influence that M&E/IA procedures have on the success or failure of ongoing work.

How does this affect the M&E/IA of advocacy? While it is too soon to judge the new ALPS system (indeed, there is currently a gap between intention and practice), it has provided the impetus for the organisation to seek greater clarity about what it is trying to achieve in its advocacy and how it measures this. There is a long way to go. A long-term action-research project (led by Jenny Chapman) is currently being developed, which explores how best to involve local women, men, and project partners at local, national, and international levels in the assessment of influencing, advocacy, and social change.[1] The work will be carried out with partners and activists in Uganda, Ghana, Nepal, and Brazil (ActionAid 2000b). While this work is in its infancy, it has two interesting elements. The first is the intention to involve central actors in identifying how they want to monitor and evaluate their own work in ways that are culturally appropriate and empowering, and which they find useful. The second is the intention to open up to the chaotic nature and full range of advocacy rather than close it down. The essential principle is that to be most useful M&E/IA has to be led by those engaged in advocacy themselves.

Conclusion

The most fundamental problem in undertaking M&E/IA of advocacy work is failing fully to understand the nature of the advocacy process – its multiple aims, multi-layered structures, shifting timeframes, and the nature of the power structures it aims to influence. While many NGOs are increasingly recognising the issue of power, there is little evidence of M&E/IA systems for advocacy that are explicitly designed to analyse change in the particular context. Consequently, NGOs sometimes collect a lot of information about particular aspects of an advocacy process, but rarely look at the whole. M&E/IA is often seen as a requirement imposed by donors, rather than as a dynamic system for learning that helps inform and guide the advocacy process itself. New approaches are required.

An important factor to consider in designing the most appropriate M&E/IA approach for a particular advocacy process is to start by ensuring that the most important aims are included. This means that less visible and long-term aims should not be forgotten or undervalued – such as capacity building, opening up democratic space for civil society, and including the participation of those most affected. Second, the methodologies used for M&E/IA need to be tailored to the nature of the advocacy itself, the power structure, and particularly the type of relationship that advocates have with influence targets. Third, advocacy planning and management should use frameworks that allow M&E/IA to assess the way that the various parts of the advocacy work fit together in order to achieve its aims. And, finally, M&E/IA must be an integral element of the advocacy process and the wider organisation. There are no 'off-the-shelf' answers; no easy solutions. Those of us who want to use M&E/IA tools to contribute to effective and accountable advocacy need to work together to develop new approaches.

Note

1 This research is co-funded by DfID and Comic Relief.

References

ActionAid (2000b) 'Innovative methodologies for assessing the impact of participatory policy work', unpublished full proposal for DfID submitted by ActionAid, London: ActionAid.

Brown, L. David and Jonathan Fox (1999) 'Transnational civil society coalitions and the World Bank: lessons from project and policy influence campaigns', paper presented at the 'Conference on NGOs in a Global Future', Birmingham, 10–13 January.

Chapman, Jennifer and Thomas Fisher (2000) 'The effectiveness of NGO campaigning: lessons from practice', *Development in Practice* 10(2):152–157.

Chapman, Jennifer and Amboka Wameyo (2001) 'Monitoring and Evaluating Advocacy: A Scoping Study', unpublished ActionAid Working Paper series, January 2001, London: ActionAid.

Davies, Rick (2001) 'Evaluating the effectiveness of DfID's influence with multilaterals: a review of NGO approaches to the evaluation of advocacy work', unpublished paper for the Department for International Development, August 2001, London: DfID.

Development Initiatives (1996) '1995 NGO aid cuts campaign: evaluation of impact', report to Inter-Agency Coalition, unpublished paper, Frome: Development Initiatives.

Gaventa, John (1995) 'Citizen knowledge, citizen competence and democracy building', in Stephen L. Elkin and Karol Edward Soltan (eds.), *Citizen Competence and Democratic Institutions*, Pennsylvania: Pennsylvania State University Press.

Harding, David (2000) 'Report on an Interim Review of the International Food Rights Campaign', unpublished report, London: ActionAid.

Miller, Valerie (1997) *Advocacy Sourcebook*, Boston, MA: Institute of Development Research.

Roche, Chris (1999) *Impact Assessment for Development Agencies: Learning to Value Change*, Oxford: Oxfam GB.

Watson, Gabrielle (2001) 'Advocacy case studies', in David Cohen, Rosa de la Vega and Gabrielle Watson, *Advocacy for Social Justice: A Global Action and Reflection Guide*, West Harcourt, CT: Kumarian Press.

This article was first published in Development in Practice *(12/3&4:530–541) in 2002.*

Resources

While all contributors to this volume are focused on the relevance of contemporary definitions of the learning organisation to development, they draw on a range of sources; some theoretical, and others grounded in empirical or organisation-specific experience. A number of the papers illustrate the difficulties faced, and the potential released, when organisations go beyond restructuring to more a more radical overhaul of working practices, sometimes referred to as 're-tooling'. It is clear, however, that although much of the cutting-edge thinking on the topic is evolving within development organisations, mainly in the non-government sector, the lessons are often not shared more widely even as 'grey literature' outside the organisation in question, even among its own Southern 'partners'. Worse still, the lessons are not distilled in such a way as to enable participatory learning to become part of the organisational fabric. Several contributors illustrate that good practice may develop in one region or at one hierarchical level, but not be transferred across to other areas – the most obvious divide is between advocacy, development, and humanitarian work. There are also cultural practices and ideologies that can undermine the capacity of an organisation to put its ideas into practice.

Conscious that this is a highly selective listing, we have first picked out a few key experts in the field and classic works of general application, and then followed the broad headings under which the essays are grouped to suggest further resources. The resources list has been compiled and annotated by Deborah Eade and Alina Rocha Menocal, Editor and Reviews Editor respectively of Development in Practice, with advice and input from Jethro Pettit and Laura Roper.

Leading experts in the field

Chris Argyris is an organisational psychologist whose work on the behaviour of groups and the individuals within them has significantly furthered our understanding of team dynamics and group conflict. His work on dialogue and organisational learning is based on the premise that individuals are resistant to change and will adopt defensive routines if they feel threatened. In addition, there usually is a significant gap between what people say they will do and what they actually do. Such behaviour, which helps to perpetuate cover-ups and defensive routines, hinders the learning required to bring about desirable individual and organisational change.

However, believing in the potential of individuals to learn and to effect change, Argyris developed his theory of *double-loop learning* in 1976. This involves learning to challenge the assumptions that underlie existing views, and publicly testing hypotheses about behaviour. The process should lead to more effective decision making and better acceptance of failures and mistakes. A second key concept is the *ladder of inference* – the progressive process of making observations, gathering information, making assumptions, and deciding action. Argyris believes that people tend to climb this ladder too fast. When a similar dynamic occurs within an organisational setting, it may well generate tension and escalate conflict. Much of Argyris' work was undertaken in collaboration with Donald Schön. For a detailed bibliography, see www.enhanced-designs.com/actnet/argbib.htm.

Robert Chambers is based at the Institute of Development Studies at the University of Sussex, where he is a member of the Participation Group. A prolific writer, he has become one of the most influential proponents of participatory development. His latest book, *Participatory Workshops: a Sourcebook of 21 Sets of Ideas and Activities* (London and Sterling, VA: Earthscan 2002), is a guide to interactive learning. His previous works, including *Rural Development: Putting the Last First* (1983) and *Whose Reality Counts? Putting the First Last* (1997), criticise top-down models of development in favour of participatory approaches and methods that view farmers in resource-poor areas as innovators and adapters, and recognise that their agendas and priorities should be central to development research and thinking. A proponent of Participatory Rural Appraisal (PRA), which has since given rise to numerous adaptations, Chambers argues that the poor will be empowered only if personal, professional, and institutional changes take place within development and donor agencies.

Peter Drucker has since 1971 been Clarke Professor of Social Science and Management at the Claremont Graduate School in Claremont, California, whose Graduate Management Center is named after him. Drucker is now a consultant specialising in strategy and policy in the corporate, non-profit, and public sectors. A hugely prolific writer, Drucker has identified and examined some of the most important issues confronting contemporary managers, from corporate strategy and management style to social change. For 20 years a columnist for *The Wall Street Journal*, Drucker's many works on economics, politics, and management have been translated into more than 20 languages. Some well-known titles include *The End of Economic Man* (1939, 1995), *The Future of Industrial Man* (1942, 1994), and *The New Society* (1949, 1992). Other relevant works include *Managing in Turbulent Times* (1980, 1992) and *Managing the Nonprofit Organization* (1990). For a full bibliographic listing, see www.peter-drucker.com

Paulo Freire was a leading figure in the struggle to empower the dispossessed through education, and his ideas have left an indelible mark in the fields of development and popular organisation. He believed that education was not merely about teaching decontextualised literacy skills ('banking education'), but about encouraging participation in the political process through knowledge of reading and writing ('conscientisation' and 'reading the world'). These radical ideas led the military government in Brazil to expel him in the early 1960s, not to return until 1979, when the country was returning to democratic rule.

Freire's most famous work, *Pedagogy of the Oppressed* (New York, NY: Continuum, 1970), remains the best introduction to his critique of conventional education and a manifesto for his ideas. Other works include *Pedagogy of Hope* (New York, NY: Continuum, 1994), *A Pedagogy for Liberation: Dialogues on Transforming Education.* (with Ira Shor, Massachusetts: Bergin & Garvey, 1987), and *We Make the Road by Walking: Conversations on Education and Social Change* (with Myles Horton, Philadelphia, PA: Temple University Press, 1990). Further information on the life and work of Freire, including further reading, references, and links can be found at www.infed.org/thinkers/et-freir.htm and other websites.

Henry Mintzberg is Cleghorn Professor of Management Studies at McGill University in Montreal and Visiting Scholar at INSEAD in Fontainbleau, France. An expert in the areas of managerial work, strategy formation, and forms of organising, he has worked in collaboration with a multicultural team to develop approaches to management education that help managers learn from their own experience.

In *Developing Managers, not MBAs* (forthcoming), Mintzberg summarises his thinking on education and the development of managers; *Why I Hate Flying* (New York, NY and London: Texere, 2001) is a humorous critique of the flying and the managing businesses, and of commercialism in general; *The Rise and Fall of Strategic Planning: Reconceiving Roles for Planning, Plans, Planners* (New York, NY: Free Press, 1994) is a critique of how organisations mistake planning for management, and hence cease to operate strategically. *Strategy Safari: A Guided Tour through the Wilds of Strategic Management* (co-authored with Bruce Ahlstrand and Joe Lampel) (New York, NY: Free Press and Prentice-Hall International, 1989) identifies ten different schools of thought on strategy formation (for example, as a process of conception, as a process of negotiation, or as a reactive process). For each school, they discuss the leading figures behind it and provide a critique of its main contributions and limitations. Web: www.henrymintzberg.com

Gareth Morgan teaches at the Schulich School of Business at York University in Toronto and is a leading thinker and writer in the field of organisational learning. Focusing on the transition to an information age, Morgan believes that new approaches to organising and managing our roles in the workplace are the only way to meet the challenges. Much of his work has centred upon how to release creativity and innovation, how to design and manage decentralised networks, and how to use theories of paradox and self-organisation to find better methods of managing change. Recent works include *Images of Organization* (Thousand Oaks, CA: Sage Publications, 1997), and *Imaginization: New Mindsets for Seeing, Organizing, and Managing* (San Francisco, CA: Berrett-Koehler, 1997)

Reg Revans was a pioneer of *action learning*. While working for the Cavendish Laboratories in Cambridge in the 1920s, Revans 'learned to learn' by taking part in weekly seminars where researchers were allowed only to describe what was *not* working with their projects. Through 'sharing ignorance' with his colleagues,

Revans concluded that 'Learning = Knowledge + Questioning', where 'Knowledge' is defined in static terms as the traditional instruction 'fed' to learners. True learning takes place outside the safety of the traditional knowledge base, in the 'Questioning' zone. His most influential book, in which he describes in detail the processes involved in action learning, is *The ABC of Action Learning* (Bromley, VT: Chartwell-Bratt, 1983). For more information, visit the International Foundation for Action Learning website: www.ifal.org.uk

Donald Schön was a philosopher by profession, but was committed to being an effective educator and helping other practitioners to be more effective too. His varied career spanned teaching urban studies, architecture, and planning at Massachusetts Institute of Technology, as well as co-founding and directing the Organization for Social and Technical Innovation (OSTI), a non-profit social research and development company based in the Boston area. Working in close association with Chris Argyris, Schön's best-known works include *Beyond the Stable State* (London: Maurice Temple Smith, 1971), and *Educating the Reflective Practitioner* (San Francisco, CA: Jossey-Bass, 1990).

Peter Senge is based at the Sloan School of Management at the Massachusetts Institute of Technology. A pioneer in the field of organisational learning in the private sector, Senge specialises in the ways in which organisations can develop learning capabilities in a world that is increasingly complex and subject to change. He chaired the Society for Organizational Learning, which aimed to 'discover, integrate, and implement theories and practices for the interdependent development of people and their institutions' until it closed in 1999. Senge's best-selling work *The Fifth Discipline: The Art and Practice of the Learning Organization* (New York, NY: Doubleday/Currency, 1990) presents tools and principles to help managers understand the structures and dynamics underlying organisational problems. His most recent work, *The Dance of Change* (New York, NY:Doubleday, 1999), argues that sustaining growth requires a fundamental shift in thinking. Contact details: psenge@sloan.mit.edu

Books

General

Clarkson, Petruska: *Change in Organisations,* London: Whurr Publishers, 1995, ISBN: 1897635338, 170 pp.

Intended for clinical, occupational, and counselling psychologists, this study explores the experience of working with or within organisations. Clarkson offers conceptual frameworks for understanding such experience, as well as practical advice on the ways in which its possibilities can be transformed.

Cooke, Bill and Uma Kothari, eds.: *Participation: The New Tyranny?* London and New Jersey: Zed Books, 2001, ISBN: 1 85649 794 1, 207 pp.

The current trend for participatory development makes it ever more important to examine the concept of participation and ask whether it can live up to the expectations placed upon it. This provocative book asks what happens if participatory processes degenerate into tyranny and the unjust and illegitimate exercise of power. The contributors, all social scientists and development specialists, come from a range of disciplines and represent a wide variety of hands-on experience. Warning about the potential pitfalls and limitations of participatory development, they challenge practitioners and theorists to reassess their own roles in promoting practices that may be naïve in the way they presume to understand power relations, and serve to reinforce existing inequalities.

Kaplan, **Allan**: *Development Practitioners and Social Process: Artists of the Invisible*, London and Sterling, VA: Pluto Press, 2002, ISBN: 0 7453 1019 2, 214 pp.

Kaplan's holistic approach to social development views it as a complex process of social transformation rather than as a technical operation. Drawing on his extensive experience as a development consultant in Africa and Europe, as well as on work of Goethe and Karl Jung, the author argues that intentional social change is possible, and that learning is the path to self-discovery and self-awareness, 'enabl[ing] both the organism and the world with which it interacts to be lifted to a new level of existence'.

Robinson, **Dorcas**, **Tom Hewitt**, **and John Harriss**, **eds.**: *Managing Development: Understanding Inter-Organizational Relationships*, London: Sage Publications (in association with The Open University) 1999, ISBN: 0 76196 479 7, 360 pp.

This book sets out to explain the dynamics of inter-organisational relationships in the development context. Moving beyond concepts of cooperation and partnership, contributors explore a wide variety of issues, including how diverse relationships can be; how competition, coordination, and cooperation are all constantly at play; how changes in institutional imperatives, terminology, and political agendas have yielded new types of organisational relationships; and how inter-organisational relationships can be worked out in practice. The volume also provides examples and case studies of ways of managing the real-life complexities of the development process.

Scott, **W. Richard**: *Institutions and Organizations*, Thousand Oaks, CA: Sage, 2001 (2nd edn.), ISBN: 0 76192 001 3, 278 pp.

This revised and expanded second edition provides a comprehensive overview of the institutionalist approach to organisation theory. The book presents a historical overview of the theoretical literature, an integrative analysis of current institutional approaches, and a review of empirical research related to institutions and organisations. Scott also provides an extensive review and critique of institutional analysis in sociology, political science, and economics as it relates to recent theory and research on organisations.

World Bank: *World Development Report: Knowledge for Development*, Oxford: OUP, 1998, ISBN: 0 8213 4107 3, 252 pp.

This twenty-first annual edition of the *World Development Report* focuses on knowledge, information, and learning as key factors affecting development. It examines both the benefits and the risks of a rapidly increasing stock of global knowledge, as well as the role of the public sector and international organisations in promoting knowledge and facilitating learning. The full report can be accessed electronically at www.worldbank.org/wdr/wdr98/index.htm

Challenges to learning

Blackburn, James with Jeremy Holland: *Who Changes? Institutionalizing Participation in Development,* London: ITDG Publishing, 1998, ISBN: 1 85339 420 3, 192 pp.

How can development projects become more genuinely participatory and empowering from the bottom up? This book explores the institutional changes that need to happen within the international development community to make participation a reality. Drawing together lessons and experiences from key development agencies worldwide, the book looks at the main issues confronting development professionals involved in Participatory Rural Appraisal (PRA) practices. How can they, for example, adapt PRA methods for large organisations? And how can they identify and implement the kinds of organisational changes needed to implement PRA effectively? In addition, the book offers a checklist of practical considerations (including training, culture, monitoring, etc.) to be taken into account when promoting a participatory approach to development. For a full review of this book, see *Development in Practice* 9(1):212—213.

Davidson, Marilyn J. and Ronald J. Burke, eds.: *Women in Management: Current Research Issues,* London: Sage Publications, 2000, 0 7619 6603 X, 336 pp.

This is the second volume of the highly successful *Women in Management: Current Research Issues* that first appeared in 1994, and reviews the latest research on women in management in a globalised context. Contributors examine contemporary issues confronting women in management, as well as their individual, organisational, and governmental dimensions. Key topics include: networking, leadership, race, gender, the 'glass ceiling', the 'management of diversity' approach, masculinity in management issues, and future organisational and governmental initiatives to strengthen women in management.

Goetz, Anne Marie, ed.: *Getting Institutions Right for Women in Development,* London and New Jersey: Zed Books, 1997, ISBN: 1 85649 526 4, 248 pp.

Gender and Development (GAD) or Women in Development (WID) initiatives have been promoted for almost three decades. However, while the material condition of women may have improved, such initiatives have not succeeded in dismantling the power structures that continue to subordinate women in the family and in the economy. This book offers a gendered analysis of development organisations in a range of institutional arenas. It builds a conceptual framework for exploring the internal politics and procedures of institutions that design and implement policy, and then applies this framework to analyse empirical case-study material. Topics addressed include how to help organisations internalise or institutionalise gender equity, and how to make accountability to women a routine part of development practice. For a full review of this book, see *Development in Practice* 9(1):204—206.

Lewis, David: *The Management of Non-Governmental Development Organizations: An Introduction*, London: Routledge, 2001, ISBN: 0 4152 0759 2, 242 pp.

Are NGOs equipped to manage their ever-increasing responsibilities in effective and efficient ways? In this book, Lewis explores the emerging field of NGO management. Analysing the internal structure of NGOs, their activities, and their linkages to the outside world, the author develops a composite model of NGO management that seeks to understand and articulate the particular challenges that these organisations face. For a full review of this book, see *Development in Practice* 12(1):110—111.

Lewis, David and Tina Wallace, eds.: *New Roles and Relevance: Development NGOs and the Challenge of Change*, Bloomfield, CT: Kumarian Press, 2000, ISBN: 1 56549 120 3, 272 pp.

As development NGOs become increasingly relevant in anti-poverty initiatives, they also need to ensure that their independence and integrity are not compromised. The contributors, who include both researchers and practitioners, argue that it is only through engagement at all levels and through effective learning strategies that NGOs will make a real and sustainable contribution to poverty-reduction efforts worldwide. For a full review of this book, see *Development in Practice* 11(4):538.

Lindenberg, Marc and Coralie Bryant: *Going Global: Transforming Relief and Development NGOs*, Bloomfield, CT: Kumarian Press, 2001, ISBN: 1 5654 9135 1, 271 pp.

Based on extensive international fieldwork and group discussions with NGO leaders, the authors argue that the major Northern-based NGOs in international relief and development are at the cusp of a process of re-definition and transformation. Changes in the international arena and the forces of globalisation are re-shaping the landscape NGOs inhabit, presenting them with new challenges and opportunities. If they seize these challenges creatively, Lindenberg and Bryant suggest, they may become yet more influential and effective in their efforts to eradicate poverty and expand their work into new areas (such as peace building and advocacy). However, if they fail to respond to the challenge, they risk becoming outdated or even obsolete.

Tools and methods

Brinkerhoff, Derick W. and Benjamin L. Crosby: *Managing Policy Reform: Concepts and Tools for Decision-Makers in Developing and Transitioning Countries*, Bloomfield, CT: Kumarian Press, 2002, ISBN: 1 56549 142 4, 270 pp.

While technocrats and sectional specialists in international donor agencies and developing countries may know what sound policy reforms should look like, they know much less about how to implement them. In this book, the authors argue that policy is a process, and hence successful policy outcomes depend not simply upon designing good policies but upon managing their implementation. Part I provides an in-depth analysis of the key concerns involved in policy change and policy-reform implementation. Part II offers a tool kit to enable policy reformers and managers learn how to plan and manage policy reforms strategically and thereby facilitate their success.

Brown, David L.: *Social Learning in South-North Coalitions,* Boston, MA: IDR 1998.

This report focuses on social learning as a process that creates new perspectives and behaviours at the social system level. It explores tools and methods that may help to turn potential organisational discord into a beneficial process of social learning. The report also explores how differences among members of an inter-organisational network can be used to develop new knowledge and improved practices.

Chopra, A.J.: *Managing the People Side of Innovation: 8 Rules for Changing Minds and Hearts,* West Harcourt, CT: Kumarian Press 1999, ISBN: 1 56549 098 3, 244 pp.

How do innovative ideas emerge in the face of deep-rooted organisational inertia and resistance to change? Chopra argues that such ideas will not be adopted without leadership, human energy, collaboration, and motivation. This 'how to' guide lists eight commonsense, though not always obvious, rules to change hearts and minds, and turns them into a series of tools aimed at facilitating change and innovation.

Coghlan, David and Teresa Brannick: *Doing Action Research in Your Own Organization,* London: Sage, 2000, ISBN: 0 7619 6887 3, 152 pp.

This primer on action research and how to use it to understand organisations is structured in two parts. Part I covers the foundations of action research, including the research skills needed to undertake research, while Part II covers the implementation of an action-research project. The book addresses the advantages and potential pitfalls of undertaking action research in one's own organisation, as well as the politics and ethics involved. It also offers practical advice on such matters as selecting and implementing an action-research project. Each chapter includes exercises, examples, and clear summaries.

Dixon, Nancy: *The Organizational Learning Cycle: How we can learn collectively,* Maidenhead: McGraw Hill, 1994, ISBN: 0 0770 7937 X, 176 pp.

Dixon analyses organisational learning as a powerful tool of self-transformation arguing that, while organisations and individuals can learn independently of each other, growth is best achieved when organisational and personal development are combined and integrated. Thus, organisational learning requires the active involvement of the organisation's members in establishing the direction of change and in inventing the means to achieve it. To illustrate the different stages and types of learning involved, Dixon uses the Organisational Learning Cycle, whose four steps are the generation of information; the integration of new information into the organisational context; the collective interpretation of that information; and the authority to act based on the interpreted meaning.

Eade, Deborah: *Capacity Building: An Approach to People-Centred Development,* Oxford: Oxfam, 1997, ISBN: 0 85598 366 3, 226 pp.

While the stated mission of international development agencies is to lift people out of poverty and to help them sharpen the skills they need to participate in the development of their own societies, there is a real danger that such efforts will result in dependence rather than in empowerment, especially if the agencies ignore the existing strengths of the communities involved. In this book, Eade analyses the concept of capacity building and examines why it is such an integral part of development. Providing insights into training and the development of a variety of skills and activities, the book explores specific and practical ways in which NGOs can work with people and their organisations to enable them to strengthen the capacities they already possess. Particular attention is paid to the need to use a capacity-building approach in emergency situations.

Edwards, Michael: *Future Positive and Global Citizen Action,* London: Earthscan, 2002, ISBN: 1 8538 3631 1, 292 pp.

In a world of globalising markets, eroding state sovereignty, expanding citizen action, and growing uncertainty about fundamental truths, what is the best way to tackle problems of global poverty and violence? Here, Edwards attempts to chart a 'third way' of promoting development that falls between heavy-handed state interventionism and complete *laissez faire* politics. The author reviews ways in which the international system operates, the pressures it faces, and the changes it must undergo, including the pressing need to create a new framework of international relations and foreign aid. Divided into two sections, Part I analyses the evolution of the current international system, while Part II examines the opportunities for change in the twenty-first century. For further details see: www.futurepositive.org

Edwards, Michael and Alan Fowler, eds.: *The Earthscan Reader on NGO Management,* London and Sterling, VA: Earthscan, 2002, ISBN: 1 85383 848 9, 464 pp.

NGOs are today a major force for transformation in both the political and the economic arena. But their role as key intermediaries between governments and civil society has also brought with it increasing responsibilities and a growing need for effective internal management. With contributors including academics, practitioners, and policy makers in the North and the South, this volume covers ten areas of management that are critical to the success of NGOs involved in international development. One section is devoted to the importance of becoming a Learning Organisation, while the remaining parts cover issues ranging from the management of growth and change to organisational accountability and good development practice. The overarching theme is the exploration of ways in which NGOs can best go about achieving maximum impact and effectiveness in their work.

Foster, Marie-Claude: *Management Skills for Project Leaders: What to do when you do not know what to do,* Basel: Birkhäuser Publishing, 2001, ISBN: 3 7643 6423 8, 202 pp.

Based on logical, rational reasoning, traditional models of management work best in situations characterised by simplicity, linearity, and continuity. However, in a world where chaos and uncertainty are the norm rather than the exception, such management models have become obsolete. Aimed at managers and project leaders working in development in low- and middle-income countries, this book outlines the critical skills that are needed to succeed in this increasingly complex field. A central theme running through the book is the importance of continuous learning among development workers and change agents.

Fowler, Alan: *Striking a Balance: A guide to enhancing the effectiveness of non-governmental organisations in international development,* London: Earthscan in association with INTRAC, 1997, ISBN: 1 8538 3325 8, 298 pp.

At a time of rapid global change, non-governmental development organisations (NGDOs) are confronted with simultaneous demands to increase their impact, diversify their activities, respond to long-term humanitarian crises, and improve their performance. This book seeks to provide a practical guide to help NGDOs better meet these expectations. Written for NGDO leaders, managers, donors, and scholars, the book summarises the major tasks of sustainable people-centred development, describing five key factors that influence effectiveness: suitable organisational design; competent leadership and human resources; appropriate external relationships; mobilisation of high quality finance; and the measurement of performance coupled to 'learning for leverage'. The book also includes details of the ways in which these factors can be acquired and improved. For a full review of this book, see *Development in Practice* 8(1):102—104.

Guijt, Irene and Meera Kaul Shah: *The Myth of Community: Gender Issues in Participatory Development,* London: ITDG Publications, 1998, ISBN: 1 8533 9421 1, 282 pp.

This book explores the ways in which women can become more appropriately and equally involved in participatory development projects, and how gender issues can be more meaningfully addressed. Containing contributions from Asia, Africa, Latin America, and Europe, this book provides a variety of viewpoints and perspectives from those most closely involved in participatory approaches to development, with a particular emphasis on the need to avoid assuming that community members share homogenous interests.

Leeuwis, Cees and Rhiannon Pyburn, eds.: *Wheelbarrows Full of Frogs: Social learning in rural resource management,* Assen: Koninklijke van Gorcum, 2002, ISBN: 90 232 3850 8, 480 pp.

The title of this book, taken from a Dutch metaphor, is used to illustrate the difficulties involved in social learning: how to keep all the frogs (i.e. the multiple stakeholders) inside a wheelbarrow (i.e. a platform for social learning), while manoeuvring across difficult terrain (i.e. resource-management dilemmas)? Contributors argue that success requires commitment, presence of mind, flexibility, and stability. Unlike interventions based solely on technological or economic grounds, social learning is 'an interactive process moving from multiple cognition to collective or distributed cognition'. The shared learning of interdependent stakeholders is therefore critical to reaching better outcomes in rural resource management. Following a theoretical overview, the book addresses a variety of issues, including social learning in action in agriculture, and social learning and institutional change.

Macdonald, Mandy, Ellen Sprenger, and Ireen Dubel: *Gender and Organizational Change: Bridging the Gap between Theory and Practice,* The Hague: Royal Tropical Institute, 1997, ISBN: 90 6832 709 7, 156 pp.

How can organisations in both North and South become more gender-aware and more gender-sensitive? Illustrated with experiences of gender interventions in numerous organisations, this book presents a practical approach to changing gender dynamics that is built on consensus. It includes a 'road map' for organisational change; material on organisational culture, the change agent, and gender; strategies for developing more gender-sensitive practice; and guidelines for a gender assessment of an organisation. For a full review, see *Development in Practice* 8(2):247—248.

Osborne, Stephen: *Voluntary Organizations and Innovation in the Public Services,* London: Routledge, 1998 (in association with Humanitarianism and War Project and IDRC) 2001, ISBN: 0 415 18256 5.

Based on research carried out in the UK, this volume seeks to assess the innovative capacity of voluntary organisations. Testing potential causal explanations for the development of such capacity, the author builds a theory of innovation under non-market and non-profit conditions. He also draws out a list of recommendations to help managers in government and the voluntary sector become more creative and inventive.

Rao, Aruna, Rieky Stuart, and David Kelleher: *Gender at Work: Organizational Change for Equality,* West Harcourt, CT: Kumarian Press, 1999, ISBN: 1 56549 102 5, 272 pp.

This volume analyses institutional barriers to gender equality and provides insights into how gender relations can be transformed. In-depth examples from diverse organisations and countries lay out strategies and approaches for transforming organisations into cultures expressing gender equity, and raise new questions about how gender-responsive policies and practices can best be advocated.

Roche, Chris: *Impact Assessment for Development Agencies: Learning to Value Change,* Oxford: Oxfam (in association with Novib), 1999, ISBN: 0 85598 418 X, 160 pp.

This book focuses on the centrality of impact assessment to all stages of development programmes. Its basic premise is that impact assessment should not be limited to the immediate outputs of a project or programme, but should incorporate any lasting or significant changes that it brought about. After providing a theoretical overview, the author discusses the design of impact-assessment processes and then illustrates their use in development, in emergencies, and in advocacy work. Roche ends by exploring ways in which different organisations have attempted to institutionalise impact-assessment processes and the challenges they have encountered in doing so. For a full review of this book, see *Development in Practice* 10(2):261–262.

Suzuki, Naoki: *Inside NGOs: Learning to manage conflicts between headquarters and field offices,* London: ITDG Publishing, 1998, ISBN 1 8533 9413 0, 224 pp.

Acknowledging that NGOs are often complex entities that have multiple offices staffed by diverse members with diverse values, this book concentrates on the tensions that inevitably arise between headquarters and field offices and suggests ways to resolve areas of conflict. Drawing on the voices of NGO practitioners to improve international development efforts, the book presents concrete strategies to address practical problems. For a full review of this book, see *Development in Practice* 8(4):486–487.

Tennyson, Ros: *Managing Partnerships: Tools for Mobilising the Public Sector, Business and Civil Society as Partners in Development,* London: The Prince of Wales International Business Leaders Forum, 1998, ISBN: 1 8991 5984 3, 124 pp.

This book seeks to provide development practitioners with the skills, confidence, and encouragement they need to develop cross-sectoral initiatives with the public sector, business, and civil society. Topics covered include how to plan and resource partnerships; how to develop cross-sector working relationships; how to build partnership organisations; how to develop action learning and sharing programmes; how to manage the partnership-building process and overcome obstacles; and how to measure the impact of partnership activity. The appendices offer checklists and prompts for practitioners involved in resource mobilisation, tips on how to manage cross-sector encounters, and notes on action research and impact assessment.

(Multi-)institutional initiatives and organisational case studies

Alsop, Ruth, Elon Gilbert, John Farrington, and Rajiv Khandelwal: *Coalitions of Interest: Partnerships for Processes of Agricultural Change,* New Delhi: Sage Publications, 2000, ISBN: 81 7036 890 1, 308 pp.

While significant rural policy reforms have been carried out in India, large sections of the agricultural population have not benefited from them. This book examines the agricultural scenario in the semi-arid region of Rajasthan and establishes the need for what the authors call process monitoring (PM), or the interaction and collaboration between different stakeholders: various levels of government, NGOs, and farmers' groups. The authors conclude that practical mechanisms are needed to bring about the consensus necessary to effect change through multiple stakeholder interaction; and argue that PM is the key tool to enable such coalitions to work.

Eade, Deborah, Tom Hewitt, and Hazel Johnson, eds.: *Development and Management: Experiences in Value-Based Conflict,* Oxford: Oxfam (in association with The Open University), 2000, ISBN: 0 85598 429 5, 320 pp.

Development is a complex process of negotiation over meanings, values, and social goals within the sphere of public action, not merely a question of project-based interventions, or of quantifiable inputs and outputs. This volume draws on The Open University's path-breaking work in the field of development management, and includes in-depth accounts by academics and development managers on topics that range from civil society organisations in Brazil and NGO workers in Egypt to government departments in Tanzania and black feminist activists in the UK.

Estrella, Marisol, ed., with Jutta Blauert, Dindo Campilan, John Gaventa, Julian Gonsalves, Irene Guijt, Deb Johnson, and Roger Ricafort: *Learning from Change: Issues and Experiences in Participatory Monitoring and Evaluation,* London: ITDG Publishing, 2000, ISBN: 1 85339 469 6, 288pp.

A compilation of case studies and discussions drawn from an international workshop on participatory monitoring and evaluation (PM&E) held in the Philippines in 2000, this volume provides an overview of relevant themes and experiences in this field. Part I offers a literature review of methodological innovations in PM&E practice worldwide. Part II presents case studies that illustrate the diversity of settings in which PM&E has been undertaken. Finally, Part III raises key questions and challenges arising from the case studies and the workshop proceedings, identifying areas for further research and action.

Hanna, Nagy and Robert Picciotto: *Making Development Work: Development Learning in a World of Poverty and Wealth,* Washington, DC: Transaction Publishers, 2002, ISBN: 0 7658 0915 X, 372 pp.

The World Bank's Comprehensive Development Framework (CDF) initiative has been launched in 12 developing countries. Its four key principles are: a holistic long-term vision of development; domestic ownership of development programmes; a results-oriented approach; and stronger partnerships and collaboration between government, the private sector, and civil society. Section I of this volume describes the evolution in development thinking that culminated in the CDF. Section II focuses on country ownership of development policies and programmes. Section III looks at results and at the ways in which aid agencies might enhance their impact on development. Section IV focuses on partnerships between aid agencies and their beneficiaries. The concluding chapter identifies key lessons learned, and proposes that multi-faceted approaches that incorporate 'client empowerment' and social learning should replace top-down, 'one-size-fits-all' prescriptions.

Jackson, Edward and Yusuf Kassam: *Knowledge Shared: Participatory Evaluation in Development Cooperation,* West Hartford, CT: Kumarian Press, 1998, ISBN: 1 56549 085 1, 272 pp.

The authors analyse the theory and practice of participatory evaluation around the world, arguing that it is a key ingredient in development because it helps mobilise local knowledge in conjunction with outside expertise to make development interventions more effective. With case studies from Bangladesh, El Salvador, Ghana, India, Indonesia, Kenya, Mexico, Nepal, and St Vincent, the book is a guide to a community-based approach to evaluation that is at once a learning process, a means of taking action, and a catalyst for empowerment.

Kanji, Nasneen and L Greenwood: *Participatory Approaches to Research and Development in IIED: Learning from Experience,* London: IIED, 2001, 62 pp.

Part of IIED's Policy and Planning Processes series, this volume is the result of a year-long exercise of participatory learning within the organisation. Reflecting on past experiences and acknowledging internal problems and weaknesses, the report is aimed at making IIED more transparent and at encouraging other organisations to carry out similar exercises. In particular, it illustrates the complexities involved in 'practising what you preach' and exemplifies the difficulty in adhering to the values that underpin 'participation' in a demanding and competitive environment.

Kelleher, D. and K. McLaren: *Grabbing the Tiger by the Tail: NGOs Learning for Organizational Change,* Ottawa: Canadian Council for International Cooperation, 1996, ISBN: 1 8966 2200 3, 190 pp.

In the face of declining resources, NGOs have had to address difficult issues of restructuring, downsizing, and rationalisation. This book proposes an approach to these organisational changes that will equip NGOs with the necessary skills to resolve their problems and rejuvenate their organisations. It describes in clear detail the experiences of several Canadian NGOs that have successfully undertaken structural reforms and draws lessons from their example. A video version of this book also exists, and both the book and the video are available in French.

Khor, Martin and Lim Li Lin, eds.: *Good Practices and Innovative Experiences in the South: Economic, Environmental and Sustainable Livelihoods Initiatives (vol. 1); Good Practices and Innovative Experiences in the South: Social Policies, Indigenous Knowledge and Appropriate Technology (vol. 2); Good Practices and Innovative Experiences in the South: Citizen Initiatives in Social Services, Popular Education and Human Rights (vol. 3)*, London and New York, NY: Zed Books, 2001, ISBN: 1 84277 129 9, 255 pp. (vol.1); ISBN: 1 84277 131 0, 215 pp. (vol. 2); ISBN: 1 84277 133 7, 260 pp. (vol. 3)

These three volumes constitute an attempt by Third World Network and UNDP's Special Unit for Technical Cooperation among Developing Countries to compile information on some of the best practices and innovative ideas that are being pioneered at the governmental, NGO, and community levels in developing countries. While the areas of experimentation are fairly diverse, all the experiences recounted here rely on the same basic principles: respect for local knowledge systems; harmony with the environment; equity; and democratic, participatory involvement. Providing examples of successful development efforts in Asia, Latin America, and Africa, the editors seek to contribute to the process of learning and replication elsewhere.

Murthy, Ranjani K., ed.: *Building Women's Capacities: Interventions in Gender Transformation*, New Delhi: Sage Publications, 2001, ISBN 81 7829 012 X, 383 pp.

Addressing the question of female empowerment in India, this volume examines how women's capacities can be strengthened so that they are better able to confront the challenges that face them, and how to go about sensitising men to gender issues. Contributors describe the difficulties they encountered, and the strategies they adopted to overcome them, in promoting gender training and participation and in building gender-transformative capacities. Viewing empowerment as part of a wider process of social change and not as an isolated phenomenon, the case studies demonstrate that empowerment needs to occur in multiple arenas, including the personal (e.g. control over one's own body), the social (e.g. an individual's standing in the community), the economic (e.g. control over resources), and the political (e.g. participation in decision making).

di Notarbartolo Villarosa, Francesco: *Information, Management and Participation: A New Approach from Public Health in Brazil*, London: Frank Cass, 1998, ISBN: 0 7146 4353 X.

Development projects aimed at improving general well-being need to be able to reach the most vulnerable groups. However, official 'top-down' information is often incapable of identifying, prioritising, and 'marking out' these groups at the local level, and the result may be an unfair, inefficient, and ineffective allocation and use of resources. Based on an in-depth analysis of a development health project carried out in Brazil in the 1990s, this book argues that a 'process approach' is necessary to generate relevant knowledge about local needs, especially in poor urban areas. Such an approach fosters flexibility and adaptability to the local context.

Smillie, Ian and John Hailey: *Managing for Change: Leadership, Strategy and Management in Asian NGOs,* London and Sterling, VA: Earthscan, 2001, ISBN: 1 85383 721 0, 193 pp.

As the number of NGOs increases, so they need to work harder at preserving their distinctiveness and effectiveness. Based on their analysis of how nine successful NGOs in Asia are managed, the authors seek to identify the key characteristics of a sustained growth process, and the strategies, management styles, and organisational structures that are more likely to lead to success. For a full review, see *Development in Practice* 12(3&4):549–551.

The Sphere Project: *The Sphere Handbook: Humanitarian Charter and Minimum Standards in Disaster Response,* Geneva: The Sphere Project, 2000, ISBN: 9 2913 9059 3, 322 pp.

An international initiative aimed at improving the effectiveness and accountability of disaster response, the Sphere Humanitarian Charter and Minimum Standards in Disaster Response spells out the rights and minimum standards that organisations providing humanitarian assistance should guarantee to those affected by natural disasters. The Humanitarian Charter is based on the principles and provisions of international humanitarian, human rights, and refugee law, and on the principles of the Red Cross and the NGO Code of Conduct. The Handbook then sets out minimum standards in five core sectors: water supply and sanitation; nutrition; food aid; shelter and site planning; and health services. Available also in French, Russian, and Spanish, the full text is available at www.sphereproject.org/handbook_index.htm

Uphoff, Norman, Milton Esman, and Anirudh Krishna: *Reasons for Success: Learning from Instructive Experiences in Rural Development,* West Hartford, CT: Kumarian Press, 1998, ISBN: 1 56549 076 2, 236 pp.

A sequel to *Reasons for Hope* published in 1996, this volume is informed by the authors' concern that rural development is increasingly neglected in economic development circles. They seek to demonstrate, however, that improving rural living standards depends more on ideas, leadership, and appropriate methods than on financial resources as such.

Wood, Adrian, Raymond Apthorpe, and John Borton, eds.: *Evaluating International Humanitarian Action: Reflections from Practitioners,* London and New Jersey: Zed Books, 2001, ISBN: 1 85649 976 6, 224 pp.

This book analyses humanitarian assistance both in terms of how it is (and should be) delivered, and in terms of how it is (and should be) evaluated, and draws upon the experiences of those engaged in humanitarian programme evaluations and the lessons they learned in the process. Compiled by the Active Learning Network for Accountability and Performance in Humanitarian Assistance (ALNAP), the case studies are drawn from four continents, including Central Asia and the Balkans, and illustrate the different kinds of emergencies that have afflicted so many people over the past decade. The volume addresses the context in which evaluations of humanitarian assistance take place; the process of doing evaluations; and lessons to improve the conduct of evaluations in future. For a full review, see *Development in Practice* 12 (3&4):551–553.

Journals

Professional schools, especially those in management and business administration, are a natural home for journals featuring the latest thinking on learning and organisational development. While it would be impossible to list all of these publications, two particularly prominent examples are the *Harvard Business Review* (ISSN: 0017 8012) and the *MIT Sloan Management Review Quarterly* (ISSN: 1532 9194), which have become trusted sources of useful and innovative ideas on organisational learning and managerial excellence. Their regular contributors include business-management innovators like Peter Drucker, Henry Mintzberg, and Peter Senge (see above). Although these journals naturally focus on the corporate sector, they are increasingly paying attention to learning and management innovation in the non-profit sector.

Development in Practice, published five times a year: Carfax/Taylor & Francis on behalf of Oxfam GB. Editor: Deborah Eade, ISSN: 0961 4524

This is a multi-disciplinary journal of practice-based analysis and research concerning the social dimensions of development and humanitarianism. It acts as a forum for debate and the exchange of ideas among practitioners, policy makers, and academics worldwide. The journal seeks to challenge current assumptions, stimulate new thinking, and shape future ways of working.
www.developmentinpractice.org

International Journal of Cross Cultural Management, published three times a year: Sage Publications. Editors: Terence Jackson, ESCP-EAP European School of Management, Paris-Oxford-Berlin-Madrid, and Zeynep Aycan, Koç University, Istanbul, Turkey, ISSN: 1470 5958

This journal seeks to provide a specialized academic forum for the discussion and dissemination of research on inter-cultural and trans-cultural aspects of management, work, and organisation. In particular, it explores the ways in which culture influences management theory and practice. The journal is linked with three international organisations: the Centre for Cross Cultural Management Research, the International Organizational Network (ION), and the International Society for the Study of Work and Organizational Values (ISSWOV).
www.sagepub.co.uk/journals

Journal of Organizational Change Management, published bi-monthly: Emerald Insight. Editor: David M. Boje, Management Department, New Mexico State University, USA, ISSN: 0953 4814

An interdisciplinary forum to analyse and discuss the latest theoretical approaches and practices underpinning successful organisational change, this journal focuses on how organisations can manage change positively and implement it effectively.
www.emeraldinsight.com/journals/jocm/jourinfo.htm

The Learning Organization – An International Journal, published bi-monthly: Emerald Insight. Editor: Jim Grieves, Teeside School of Business and Management, University of Teeside, UK, ISSN: 0969 6474

Committed to furthering research and knowledge on what the learning organisation is and does, this journal presents ideas, generates debate, and offers case-study material and practical examples to practitioners, consultants, researchers, and students worldwide. Its aim is to illustrate how a culture of learning can be implemented, so that an organisation never ceases to grow. www.emeraldinsight.com/tlo.htm

Management Learning, published quarterly: Sage Publications. Editors-in-Chief: Christopher Grey, University of Cambridge, UK, and Elena Antonacopoulou, Manchester Business School, UK, ISSN: 1350 5076

Through the publication of creative enquiry and the promotion of dialogue and debate, this journal addresses fundamental issues in management and organisational learning. Chris Argyris (above) describes it as '[a] journal full of insights and actionable ideas that are useful for practitioners and scholars.' Themes covered include the nature of management learning, the process of learning, and learning outcomes. www.sagepub.co.uk/journals

Nonprofit Management and Leadership, published quarterly: Jossey-Bass on behalf of the Mandel Center for Nonprofit Organizations. Editor: Roger A. Lohmann, Mandel Center for Nonprofit Organizations, Case Western Reserve University, USA, ISSN: 1048 6682

The only journal to focus exclusively on the problems faced by the non-profit sector, it offers state-of-the-art thinking on issues such as fundraising, strategic planning, governance, human resources, financial resource development and management, management of change and innovation, and organisational effectiveness. www.wileyeurope.com/cda/sec/0,,6160,00.html

PLA Notes, published three times a year: IIED.

An informal journal focusing on participatory approaches and methods, which offers a forum for practitioners to share field experiences, conceptual reflections, and methodological innovations. Free of charge for non-OECD subscribers. The first 40 issues of *PLA Notes* are also available on CD ROM. www.planotes.org

Public Administration and Development, published five times a year: John Wiley & Sons. Editor: P. Collins, Institute for International Policy Analysis, University of Bath, UK, ISSN: 0271 2075

Focusing on development issues in less industrialised and transitional economies, this journal reports, reviews, and assesses the practice and implications of public administration at all levels. It gives special attention to research on the management of all phases of public policy formulation and implementation, as well as to questions of development management in the NGO sector. *Public Administration and Development* also produces selected abstracts on key themes, drawn from a variety of journals. Its February 2002 issue was devoted to the topic of 'Government-Nonprofit Relations in Comparative Perspective'. Other special

issues have included 'Development Training' (February 1999) and 'The Challenges of State Transformation in South Africa' (May 2000).
www.interscience.wiley.com/jpages/0271-2075/

World Development, published monthly: Elsevier Science. Editor: Janet L. Craswell, American University, USA, ISSN: 0305 750 X

Recognising 'development' as a process of change involving nations, economies, political alliances, institutions, groups, and individuals, the journal is dedicated to examining potential solutions to the key problems of development, including poverty, environmental degradation, inadequate scientific and technological resources, international debt, gender and ethnic discrimination, civil conflict, and lack of popular participation in economic and political life.
www.elsevier.com/locate/issn/0305750X

Organisations, networks, and websites

Active Learning Network for Accountability and Performance in Humanitarian Action (ALNAP) is an active-learning international membership network of development organisations and practitioners committed to 'improving the accountability and quality of humanitarian action by sharing lessons, identifying common problems, and, where appropriate, building consensus'. Its 2002 Annual Review, *Humanitarian Action: Improving performance through improved learning*, based on the main findings and recommendations of more than 50 evaluations of humanitarian action, maps current learning practice within the humanitarian sector; considers key constraints to learning; and offers an agenda for action.
www.alnap.org

Alforja: the Alforja network is a regional initiative that brings together the work of seven NGOs in Mexico and Central America committed to popular education. Alforja focuses on two programmes in particular, one devoted to democracy, the other to development. The democracy programme seeks to empower the popular sectors and increase their influence and participation in the political process. The development programme is striving to elaborate an Integrated Human Development Paradigm that incorporates concrete experiences in the urban and the rural sectors and contributes to the elaboration of alternative development ideas and proposals.
www.alforja.org

Asociación Latinoamericana de Organizaciones de Promoción (ALOP): composed of developmental NGOs from 20 Latin American countries, ALOP embodies one of the most durable efforts toward the integration of NGOs in the region. Its main objectives are to facilitate the interchange of lessons and experiences among the organisations, promote regional projects, and ultimately strengthen the effectiveness and capacity of its member organisations, both individually and as a group.
www.alop.or.cr

Ashoka – Innovators for the Public provides financial and professional support and promotes 'social entrepreneurship' by encouraging individual pioneers in their efforts to solve social problems. Changemakers.net is Ashoka's online newsletter, including *Creative Resourcing Network,* which is a forum for social entrepreneurs and civil society activists to exchange ideas on local resource mobilisation. www.ashoka.org or www.changemakers.net

Bangladesh Rural Advancement Committee (BRAC) is an established development organisation committed to alleviating poverty and to empowering people living in extreme poverty. Recognising that development is a complex process requiring a strong dedication to learning, knowledge-sharing, and responsiveness to the needs of the poor, BRAC places a strong emphasis on organisational development and capacity building. It has recently established its own university. www.brac.net

BRINT Institute is a virtual network dedicated to the development of thinking and practice on information, technology, and knowledge-management issues to facilitate organisational and individual performance and success. The Institute's content and community portals provide the latest resources and information on key topics of interest; one portal, for example, is dedicated to 'Knowledge Management, Organisational Learning, and Learning Organisations'. www.brint.com/press/

Center for Alternative Development Initiatives (CADI) is a Philippines-based organisation, dedicated to promoting sustainable development through 'threefolding' – a process whereby government, civil society, and business are all stakeholders in development plans and initiatives. Another focus is the advancing of 'cultural renewal' through innovative educational activities, and the support for civil society. CADI also engages in publishing and networking in the international arena. E-mail: cadi@info.com.ph Web: www.cadi.ph

Center for Gender in Organizations (CGO) is an international resource for innovative thinking and practice in the field of gender, work, and organisations. Understanding gender as a construct that works simultaneously with race, class, ethnicity, age, and sexual orientation in shaping organisational systems, cultures, and practices as well as individuals' identities and experiences at work, CGO seeks to promote both gender equity and organisational effectiveness in learning and support organisations. CGO works at the intersection of research and practice and focuses annually on a specific learning theme, the research results of which are widely published in CGO's working papers, academic journals, *CGO Insights,* and other publications. www.simmons.edu/gsm/cgo

Community Development Resource Association (CDRA) is an NGO based in South Africa that is committed to the conscious and continuous learning about development processes and the art of intervention. CDRA carries out a broad range of activities, including organisational interventions, training, accompanied learning, collaborative explorations, and the dissemination of experiences and lessons learned. Some of the association's relevant publications include *Action Learning for Development: Use your experience to improve your effectiveness* (1997), and *Action Learning Series: Case studies and lessons from development practice* (2 vols., 1998 and 1999). www.cdra.org.za

Comparative Research Programme on Poverty (CROP) is a response from the academic community to the problem of poverty, organised around an extensive international and multidisciplinary research network. Its main focus is on multidisciplinary and multi-cultural research, with the principal purpose of producing reliable knowledge that can serve as a basis for poverty reduction. CROP also organises regional workshops, international conferences, and projects that bring researchers together to discuss topics of mutual interest.
www.crop.org

Evaluating Capacity Development is a website established to facilitate the exchange of information among individuals interested in the evaluation of organisational capacity-development efforts. The primary users are project participants – i.e., organisations focused on evaluating capacity development in research and on development more generally. The site provides useful information on key concepts, terms, and links.
www.isnar.cgiar.org/ecd/index.htm

IBASE (Brazilian Institute of Social and Economic Analyses) is an organisation committed to strengthening the quality of democracy in Brazil by promoting justice, equality, respect for human rights, social development, and the active participation of all Brazilians in the decision-making process. To increase awareness and encourage citizen involvement in the political process, IBASE engages in a wide range of activities, including research, dissemination of information, public debates, and the defence of public interests. To maximise its impact, IBASE also works in conjunction and partnership with civil society organisations and movements, universities, and governmental bodies.
www.ibase.org.br

IFAD IFAD's mission is to enable the rural poor to overcome their poverty through agricultural and rural development supported by loans and grants for innovative approaches. Much of its work is geared to influencing pro-poor policies and on promoting institutions that serve and represent the rural poor. Defining itself as a knowledge institution, IFAD is committed to mutual learning and lesson-sharing with others active in this field. To this effect, it has recently established a Knowledge-Management Facilitation and Support Unit, which includes a pilot knowledge base on Gender and Household Food Security.
www.ifad.org

International Development Research Centre (IDRC) is a Canadian public corporation that was created to help developing countries find lasting solutions to the social, economic, and environmental problems that confront them. Founded on the premise that science and technology are powerful tools to promote economic growth and development, IDRC focuses on knowledge gained through research as a means of empowering the people of the South. Some of its main objectives include: assisting scientists in developing countries identify sustainable solutions to pressing development problems; mobilising and strengthening the research capacity of developing countries; and disseminating research results worldwide, in

particular through developing and strengthening the electronic networking capacity of institutions in recipient countries.
www.idrc.ca

International NGO Training and Research Centre (INTRAC) Recognising and supporting the commitment of the NGO sector to values that promote sustainable development, social justice, empowerment, and participation, INTRAC seeks to strengthen the organisational, management capacity, and institutional development of NGOs. Its focus on training, consultancy, research, and learning underpins its publishing programme. Relevant recent books include: *People and Change: Exploring Capacity-Building in African NGOs* (2002); *Knowledge, Power and Development Agendas: NGOs North and South* (2002); and *Striking a Balance* (see **Books** above). E-mail: intrac@gn.apc.org Web: www.intrac.org/

International Organization for Cooperation in Evaluation (IOCE) is a loose coalition of regional and national evaluation organisations from around the world that is dedicated to building leadership and capacity in developing countries, fostering the cross-fertilisation of evaluation theory and practice, and encouraging the evaluation profession to take a more global approach to problem solving.
www.internationalevaluation.com

Monitoring and Evaluation News (MandE News) is a news service that focuses on the latest developments in monitoring and evaluation methods relevant to development work, and is supported by Oxfam GB, Save the Children Fund, ActionAid, Christian Aid, CAFOD, CIIR, IDRC, World Vision, and WWF, via Bond. MandE's website includes an Open Forum in which all visitors are actively invited to participate in seeking and/or sharing information relating to monitoring and evaluation theory or practice. The news service also posts information on events, work in progress, new documents, and books of interest. Links to other specialist M&E websites, evaluation centres, and evaluation networks are available as well. E-mail: Editor@mande.co.uk Web: www.mande.co.uk

Resource Centres for Participatory Learning and Action Network (RCPLA) Maintained by the International Institute for Environment and Development (IIED), the RCPLA Network brings together 14 organisations from around the world committed to information sharing and networking on issues pertaining to participatory methodologies and approaches. The documentation held at IIED consists mainly of unpublished literature, case studies, and reports, and features material in more than ten languages. The network's ultimate goal is to supply reliable information and training support to Southern organisations, as well as to meet a growing demand for it in both non-OECD and OECD countries. The *PLA Notes* series (see **Journals** above) is an integral component of the IIED's network. E-mail: resource.centre@iied.org Web: www.iied.org/resource/index.html

Society for Organizational Learning (SoL) is an action-learning community composed of a heterogeneous group of corporations, NGOs, governmental institutions, and individuals from all over the world, founded by Peter Senge (see **Leading experts in the field** above). Its main objective is to generate knowledge

about and build capacity for fundamental innovation and change through collaborative action-inquiry projects. Reflecting on such issues as the benefits and shortfalls of globalisation, economic growth, and the development of human capital, SoL is a global, enabling network where dialogue, research, collaborative action, and learning take place at multiple levels.
www.solonline.org

Southern and Eastern Africa Policy Research Network (SEAPREN) is a network of six African research institutions engaged in strengthening policy analysis in their home countries. SEAPREN seeks to collaborate on national and regional research projects and capacity building; exchange best practices and mutual learning in research as well as institutional management; and monitor international developments and new approaches within the field of policy analysis. Among the issues and problems the network focuses on are regional and international trade, poverty alleviation, governance, and economic development.
www.seapren.kabissa.org

World Neighbors works with the rural poor in 18 countries in Asia, Africa, and Latin America to strengthen the capacity of individuals and communities in confronting problems related to hunger, poverty, and disease, and in identifying and developing home-grown solutions. World Neighbors' programmes integrate local capacity-building, improved sustainable agriculture, community-based health, reproductive health, gender awareness and the empowerment of women, environmental conservation, water and sanitation, and livelihood strategies, including savings and credit. The organisation also has a publishing branch with many titles of interest, including, for example, 'Evaluating an Integrated Reproductive Health Program: India Case Study' (2002), and *From the Roots Up: Strengthening Organizational Capacity through Guided Self-Assessment* (2000, 2nd ed.).
www.wn.org

WWW Virtual Library: Evaluation This virtual library is an online database of Internet resources related to social policy evaluation The database includes brief descriptions and links to hundreds of websites. The library's catalogue can be browsed by subject area.
http://vlib.org

Addresses of publishers

Birkhäuser Publishing
Viaduktstrasse 42, CH-4051 Basel,
Switzerland.
www.birkhauser.ch

**Canadian Council for International
Cooperation**
1 Nicholas Street, Suite 300,
Ottawa, Ontario K1N 7B7, Canada.
www.ccic.ca

Carfax/Taylor & Francis
4 Park Square, Milton Park,
Abingdon, OX14 4RN, UK.
www.tandf.co.uk/journals

Earthscan Publications
120 Pentonville Road,
London N1 9JN, UK.
www.earthscan.co.uk

Elsevier Science
P.O. Box 211, 1000 AE, Amsterdam,
The Netherlands.
www.elsevier.nl

Emerald Insight
60/62 Toller Lane,
Bradford, BD8 9BY, UK.
www.emeraldinsight.com/academic

Frank Cass
Crown House, 47 Chase Side,
London N14 5BP, UK.
www.frankcass.com

John Wiley & Sons
The Atrium, Southern Gate, Chichester,
West Sussex PO19 8SQ, UK.
www.wileyeurope.com

Jossey-Bass
c/o John Wiley & Sons, Ltd.,
The Atrium, Southern Gate,
Chichester, West Sussex
PO19 8SQ, UK.
www.josseybass.com

Institute for Development Research
44 Farnsworth Street, Boston,
MA 02210-1211, USA.
www.jsi.com/idr

IIED
3 Endsleigh Street,
London WC1H 0DD, UK.
www.iied.org

INTRAC
PO Box 563, Oxford, OX2 6RZ, UK.
www.intrac.org

ITDG Publishing
103–105 Southampton Row,
London WC1B 4HL, UK.
www.itdgpublishing.org.uk

Koninklijke van Gorcum
Industrieweg 38, 9403 AB Assen,
The Netherlands.
www.vangorcum.nl

Kumarian Press
14 Oakwood Avenue,
West Hartford, CT 06119 2127, USA.
www.kpbooks.com

McGraw Hill
2 Penn Plaza, 12th Floor, New York,
NY 10121–2298, USA.
http://books.mcgraw-hill.com

Oxford University Press
Walton Street, Oxford OX2 6DT, UK.
www.oup.co.uk

Oxfam Publishing
274 Banbury Road,
Oxford OX2 7DZ, UK.
www.oxfam.org.uk/publications

Pluto Press
345 Archway Road, London N6 5AA, UK.
www.plutobooks.com

**The Prince of Wales International
Business Leaders Forum (IBLF)**
15–16 Cornwall Terrace, Regent's Park,
London, NW1 4QP, UK.
www.iblf.org

The Sphere Project
P.O. Box 372, 1211 Geneva 19,
Switzerland.
www.sphereproject.org

Transaction Publishers
390 Campus Drive, Somerset,
NJ 07830, USA.
www.transactionpub.com

Routledge
11 New Fetter Lane,
London EC4P 4EE, UK.
www.routledge.com

Royal Tropical Institute
Mauritskade 63 (main entrance),
P.O.Box 95001, 1090 HA Amsterdam,
The Netherlands.
www.kit.nl

Sage Publications
2455 Teller Road, Thousand Oaks,
CA 91320, USA.
www.sagepub.com

Whurr Publishers
Blackhorse Road,
Letchworth SG6 1HN, UK.
www.whurr.co.uk

Zed Books
7 Cynthia Street, London N1 9JF, UK.
www.zedbooks.demon.co.uk

Index

Association for Women's Rights in
Development (AWID) 76
authoritarian model 278
autonomy-compatible assistance, and
open learning 47–50
Awareness Raising Campaigns (ARC)
use in Kenya 158–9
results 161

BAIF (NGO in India)
founder-leader (Dr Desai) 198, 202
as learning organisation 194, 196
research by 198
balanced scorecard concept 212
Bangladesh Rural Advancement
Committee (BRAC) 406
and evaluation of diploma
programme 10, 16, 124–9
founder-leader (Dr Abed) 195–6,
197, 200, 202
gender equality improvement
programme 82–5
Gender Quality Action Learning
(GQAL) programme 83, 84
in Global Partnership 122
internal democracy 83
as learning organisation 124, 194,
195–6, 197, 200
permeability to outside ideas and
influences 83
research by 124, 198
Research and Evaluation Division
124, 200
resolving contradictions 84
teamwork in 83
tools and processes for
organisational learning 84
training resources 197
Bangladeshi NGOs
disaster mitigation policies 296,
297, 301
disaster terminology used 300
as learning organisations 124, 194,
195–6, 197, 200
management 301
sources of information on disaster
mitigation 299

Barot, Nafisa (founder-leader of
Utthan) 61, 62, 66–7
Batten, John (executive director of
ActionAid) 235
behavioural change, and Outcome
Mapping 358, 359
Belgian Administration for
Development Cooperation,
programme logic model used by
367
'best practice' model, in
academic–NGO collaboration 114
'best practices', tendency to adopt
universal 46
bicultural collaboration 16, 132–51
bilateral programmes
institutionalising participation in
152–68
and organisational learning
principles 10
Body Shop International 178, 179
books
as information sources on disaster
mitigation 298
bottom-up development, case study 22
bottom-up learning (BUL) 25–9
barriers to 31–6
benefits 38
and changes in structure, systems
and culture 27
contrasted with organisational
pragmatism 27–8
core strength of 28
and partnerships with local NGOs
31, 37
rejection of top-down development
programmes 28
theoretical underpinnings 28–9
BRAC see Bangladesh Rural
Advancement Committee
brand values 178–9
branded knowledge, as dogma 40–3
Brazil, women's health NGO 284
Brazilian Association of NGOs
(ABONG), charter of principles
281, 283
BRINT Institute 406

double-loop learning 3, 9, 76, 212, 220, 282, 367, 389
   example question 220
   in Temporal Logic Model 370
downward accountability 36, 100
   operational and political implications 37
Doyle, Michael 360, 363
Drucker, Peter 389
Dutch–Kenyan bilateral programmes 154–66
   see also Keiyo Marakwet case study

Easterby-Smith, Mark, review article by 2, 4
ecology of knowledge 41–2
economic environment, effect on NGOs 191
education
   in Kenya 263–4
   valuing of 6
Edwards, Michael 9, 23, 280
elitist system
   advocacy approaches 378, 383
   characteristics of power structure 377, 383
   M&E/IA approaches 382, 383
Elmore, R. 50
empowerment
   after organisational learning intervention 289
   and monitoring and evaluation 352–3
empowerment of community
   in bilateral ASAL programme 163
   effect on INGO's operations 25
empowerment of farmers 187
empowerment of staff 353
engendering mechanisms 58, 64–71
ETC East Africa 164
ethical performance standards 211, 219
Ethiopia
   INGOs in, monitoring and evaluation policies and practices 332–55
   self-help institutions 354n[9]
European Commission, programme logic model used by 367

Evaluating Capacity Development (website) 407
evaluation
   of GP NLM diploma programme 122–30
   for learning 121–31
   online database on 409
   see also monitoring and evaluation
evaluation logic model, see Logical Framework Analysis
expert-consultant model, in academic–NGO collaboration 113
expert-trainer model, in academic–NGO collaboration 114
exploration stage, in creation of learning organisation 104, 105
external sources, learning from 197

fair trade
   in cocoa, practical details 179, 181, 188n[4]
   in coffee 177
   definition in consumer marketing 180
   meaning of term 188n[4]
   public support for 182–3
   reaction of multinational companies 179–80, 186
   in USA 183
   see also Cafédirect; Day Chocolate; Twin Trading
farmers
   lack of support for 169, 180
   support of 173
feedback loops
   discouragement of 42
   lack of 35
   see also double-loop learning
feedback mechanisms, in monitoring and evaluation systems 335, 348–50
feedback workshops, Local Capacities for Peace Project 307–9
field contact, lacking in upper management 35
field diaries 348
field practice, not used at organisational level 30

International Women's Health
  Coalition (IWHC) 277, 285
inter-organisational relationships 132,
  135
IUCN (NGO in Pakistan), learning in
  194

Jacobin–Bolshevik strategy 47
Jagawat, Harnath and Sharmistha
  (founder-leaders of Sadguru) 195,
  197, 200, 202
Japan International Cooperation
  Agency, programme logic model
  used by 367
joint evaluation 342
  of Global Partnership NLM
    Postgraduate Diploma
    Programme 16, 122–31
joint-learning model in
  academic–NGO collaboration 114,
  117–19
  criteria for success 118–19
journals
  as information sources on disaster
    mitigation 298
  references listed 403–5

Kant, Immanuel 51, 55n[4]
Keiyo Marakwet case study (Kenya) 10,
  152–68
  background 153–7
  District Development Committee
    155, 166n[4]
  criticised by local community
    159
  political implications of
    Transect Area Approach
    strategy 157, 163
  feedback and training 160–1
  process of institutionalising
    participation
    effect on government officials
      162–3
    management of outcomes 161–3
    outcomes 161
    participatory planning 159–60
    people's inputs 158–9

steps 157–61
strategy 157–8
team formation 157
Project Management Committee
  161
selection of concentrated Transect
  Areas 158
Transect Area Approach strategy
  157
Transect Area Committee 160, 161,
  166n[4]
see also ASAL programme
Kenya
  ASAL programmes 153–61, 163,
    164
  educational system 263–4
  school-based nutrition project 16,
    261–76
    agriculture teaching 267
    community involvement 267–8,
      270–3
    data collection 264, 267
    educational system 263–4
    initial planning 265
    participatory aspects 269–73
    practical problems encountered
      272–3
    pupil involvement 16, 269–70
    reaction of Educational Officers
      271–2
    results 268–9
    study area 263
    study population 263
    teacher selection and training
      265–6
knowledge
  as key resource 192
  origins 77–8
knowledge-based development
  assistance 41
Kuapa Kokoo (Ghanaian cocoa
  farmers') cooperative 173–6
  assistance from NGOs 174, 175,
    177–8
  attitude to external (foreign)
    supporters 175
  educational links 182

in academic–NGO collaborations
114, 117–19
learning practices, of newcomers 145–8
learning programmes, modelling
366–72
level-one issues 144
resolution of 144, *145*
level-two issues 144
management in case study 146
mis-recognition as level-one issues
144
resolution of *145*
Lewin, Kurt 89, 95
livestock distribution, by Heifer
International 242
Lloyd, G.E.R. 52
Local Capacities for Peace Project
(LCPP) 13, 14, 303–15
consultations 309–10, 313
Do No Harm Framework 308
barriers to uptake of 311
implementation of 309
and organisational learning 312
Do No Harm (work-in-progress)
booklet 307, 315n[4]
experience-based learning phases
case studies 305–7
feedback workshops 307–9
funding 314n[1]
implementation phase 309–10
inductive process used 13, 16, 304–5
learning process and Do No Harm
Framework 310–11
mainstreaming phase 310–13
origins 303–4
local experimentation and verification
49
LogFrame approach 32, 343
Logical Framework Analysis (LFA) 343,
366, 367–8
criticisms 368, 370
disruptive influences recorded in 370
extension to represent changes over
time 368–71
favoured by funding agencies
343–4, 367
model *368*

'machines' view of organisations 153,
155, 164
McLaren, Kate 86
Mahiti (community-based organisation
in India) 60, 61
mainstreaming
of disaster mitigation and
preparedness 301
of Local Capacities for Peace Project
311–13
meaning of term 58
Malaysia, cocoa production in 170
management by objectives (MbO) 92,
93
management by participation 92, 100
management framework (in strategic
planning) 212
developing 213–14
example (CARE International)
215–19
management structure
meaning of term 90
optimum for development work 98
and social-systemic model of
organisation 97–9
and three-way compatibility test 91
management style, and gender equity
66
management system
culture compatibility in *91*, 92–3
meaning of term 90
model compatibility in 91–2, *91*
practice compatibility in *91*, 93–4
reasons for success 90–4
and social-systemic model of
organisation 97, 99–100
and three-way compatibility test 90,
91, 94
management values
meaning of term 91
and social-systemic model of
organisation 97, 100–2
and three-way compatibility test *91*
marketplace-of-ideas concept 50
master's-level programmes 120, 122
Max Havelaar Foundation 188n[3]
mechanistic use of participation 163

Nagaland Empowerment of People Through Economic Development Programme (NEPED) 360, 364n[3]
National Committee for Responsive Philanthropy (NCRP) 35
natural disasters
  cost in lives and money 294, 296
  meaning of term 302n[1]
Navajo case study 10, 134–50
Navajo culture
  and entrepreneurial activity 141
  and profit generation 140
Navajo economic development project
  Canyon Inn enterprise 137
  evolution of project 138–43
  host organisation 136–7
  inter-organisational relationships 135
  roles and activities of inter-organisational relationship members 135–6
Nestlé, on fair trade chocolate 179
Netherlands Development Organisation (SNV) 177
  programmes
    ASAL programme in Kenya 155, 164
    cocoa farmers in Ghana 173, 174, 177
networking, of cocoa farmers 182, 186
neutrality principle
  in humanitarian organisations 322, 327
  and organisational policies 328
  renegotiation of 318
NGO Leadership and Management (NLM) Postgraduate Diploma Programme 121, 122
  evaluation of 122–31
    learning from evaluation process 128–30
    learning from results 127–8
    methodology 122
    objectives of evaluation 122
Nicaraguan NGOs
  disaster planners/managers 301
  disaster terminology used 300
non-dogmatism 53–4

non-profit organisations, compared with for-profit organisations 23–4
non-rational decision making 78
Norwegian Agency for Development, programme logic model used by 367
nutrition project, school-based, in Kenya 16, 261–76
Nyerere, Julius 6

OECD, poverty-reduction targets 205, 211, 213, 215, 219
'Official Views'
  and clients 41
  debate on 42
  and loyalty to organisation 40–1
Ombudsman Project (for humanitarian organisations) 329
'One Best Way', as pseudo-scientific approach 44
onion model of organisation 247
open learning model
  and autonomy-compatible assistance 47–50
  and competing options 50–3
open system
  development programmes as part of 361
  organisation as 94, 95
opportunity-cost doctrine 52–3
Organisation of Rural Associations for Progress (ORAP) 122
organisational analysis, in creation of learning organisation 104
organisational change
  in ActionAid 225–41
organisational culture, in humanitarian organisations 317, 320–1
organisational development (OD)
  methodology 95
  basic principles 102–3
  S-P-A model 95
organisational learning 3–5, 277–9
  barriers to 31–6, 40–7, 297–8, 328, 356
  bottom-up learning 25–9

pest control, by plant-based sprays 266
Philippine NGOs
    disaster terminology used 300
    sources of information 299
planning
    cyclical nature of 360–2
    for external results and internal
        performance 359–60
    as learning 210–12
planning/monitoring/evaluation
    cyclical nature of 358, 360–2
    inappropriate tools for 230–3,
        282–3, 384
pluralist system
    advocacy approaches 378, 383
    characteristics of power structure
        377, 383
    M&E/IA approaches 382, 383
political dynamics, learning affected by
    17, 166
political empowerment, in
    participation strategy 157, 158, 164,
        165
political environment, effect on NGOs
    191
political systems, organisations as 153
poor, as source of organisational
    learning 195
Popper, Karl 42
Poverty Reduction Strategy Papers
    (PRSPs) 223n[1]
poverty-reduction targets, adoption by
    CARE International 205, 211, 213,
        215, 219
practice, learning from 195–6
practice compatibility 91, 93–4
preparedness, meaning of term 299,
        302n[3]
Preskill, H. 123
preventive logic 298
principles
    humanitarian 317–20
    organisational 320, 321–2
private sector accountability 11
proactive orientation 94
probing, as calibrating act 145–6
process of learning 37

producer organisations
    in Ghana 173–6
    purpose and context 183–4
programme planning and reporting
    systems, as barriers 32–3
programme planning stage, in
    Temporal Logic Model 368, 369
programme 'tunnel vision', as result of
    using LFA tool 370
programme/project goals/objectives,
    obsession with quantitative targets
        22, 164, 196
progressing acts, in cross-cultural
    context 135, 146–8
PROSHIKA (NGO in Bangladesh)
    as learning organisation 194, 195,
        196, 197
    monitoring of work 198
    training by 197
public criticism, constructive role of
    50–1
public relations
    alternatives 34–5
    as a barrier 33–4, 46
purdah (seclusion) system, effects 67
purpose of development 237–8

qualitative data, in evaluation of
    training programme 130
qualitative indicators 345–6
quantitative indicators 345

rage to conclude 45
Rashomon effect 55n[5]
Red Cross movement 316
reflection process, and Outcome
    Mapping 358, 363
reflection sessions/workshops (in
    organisational learning) 129, 130, 286
reporting systems
    alternatives 33
    as barriers 32–3
research
    combined with community
        development 274
    learning through 124, 198
    see also action-research

Resource Centres for Participatory
Learning and Action (RCPLA)
Network 408
Revans, Reg 191, 390–1
Roche, Chris 281
Rogers, Everett 49
role models, NGOs as 7–8
Rosenburg, Leon 367

Sadguru (NGO in India)
founder-leaders (Harnath and
Sharmistha Jagawat) 195, 197,
200, 202
as learning organisation 194, 195,
196, 197
Schön, Donald A. 46, 111, 115, 212, 391
school gardens, in Kenya 267, 269
School for International Training (SIT)
120
and evaluation of diploma
programme 10, 16, 124–9
in Global Partnership 122
orientation to organisational
learning 124
science
methodology 48
as source of dogmas 44
second-order learning 37
self-assessment, and Outcome
Mapping 358, 360, 362–3
self-development by communities 31
self-directed learning, discouragement
of 43
self-governance skills 31, 36
self-help institutions, in Ethiopia
354n[9]
self-improvement aspects 3
Semi-Arid Rural Development
Programme (SARDEP) 163–5
Senge, Peter 2, 192, 278, 360, 362, 391,
408
on role of leaders in learning
organisations 199, 201
Shetty, Salil (executive director of
ActionAid) 235
short-term measurable/visible results
23, 25, 164

single-loop learning 3, 9, 282, 367
example question 220
Smillie, Ian 192
Smutylo, Terry 356
SNV *see* Netherlands Development
Organisation
Snyder, William 24, 25
social policy evaluation, online
database on 409
social science, as dogma 44–5
social-systemic model of organisation
91, 92
leadership styles to be changed 100
and learning organisation 96–7
management structure 97–9
management system 97, 99–100
management values 97, 100–2
relevance in development
organisations and programmes
97–102
Society for Organizational Learning
(SoL) 391, 408–9
Socratic ignorance 54
Socraticism 51, 56n[8]
solidarity with the poor 28
SOS-Sahel, extension package 350
South Asian NGOs
organisational learning in 15,
190–204
see also Bangladesh Rural
Advancement Committee
(BRAC)
Southern and Eastern Africa Policy
Research Network (SEAPREN) 409
Southern NGOs
disaster responses 297
increase in size and capacity 373,
376
Sphere Project 329
handbook on 402
spiritual aspects 86
SRSC (NGO in Pakistan), learning in
194
staff participation, learning through
196
staff turnover
effects 301, 321, 328

in voluntary humanitarian
organisations 14, 321
strategic learning 212
strategic planning
in CARE International 211–12
commonly used models 223n[3]
factors affecting 206
Heifer International Cornerstones
Model used 248, 249, 250–1
strategy implementation
alternative approach 211–12
cascade method 210
problems with 210–11
strategy-map concept 212
structural adjustment programmes
(SAPs)
effects on farmers 169, 171–2
research on export-led growth 176
response of cocoa farmers 172–3
structural level of NGO, gender equity
issues 64–71
structures–processes–acts (S-P-A)
model 95
user-friendly approaches to
exploration 105
substantive level of NGO, gender
equity issues 63–4
success (in developmental sense),
contrasted with self-preservation of
INGO 24–5
successful NGOs, how they learn 194–8
Sumatra 246
see also Heifer Project Indonesia
programme
Sungi (NGO in Pakistan), learning in
194
sustainable development, behavioural
change as key to 358
sustainable strategies, and Temporal
Logic Model 371
Swedish International Development
Agency, programme logic model
used by 367
Sweetman, C. 64
system intelligence, user-friendly
approaches to exploration 105
systems and procedures

alternatives 33
as barriers 32–3
for disaster planning 296–7
systems theory approach 94, 278, 360

Taylor, J. 121
team-based structures 98–9
teams, compared with groups 99
teamwork 98
and organisational learning 83
Temporal Logic Model (TLM) 368–71
monitoring stages 369
programme context row 369
programme design rows 369, 370
programme planning stage 368, 369
terminology, on disaster mitigation
299–300
theory-development model, in
academic–NGO collaboration 114
Third World Network 376
book compiled by 401
time resource constraints 14, 297, 349,
361
tools and methods for learning 332–87
books covering 394–9
Torres, R.T. 123
total quality management (TQM),
failure rate 90
trade liberalisation
response of Ghanaian cocoa
growers to 172–3, 181
social effects 171–2
training
agricultural/horticultural 267
formal, learning from 197
transformation to learning
organisation 15–17
transformative impact of learning
organisations 8
transformative power of learning 6
transformative thinking 2
Transnational Institute 176
transparency of organisation 322
'triple bottom line', for private sector
companies 11
trust between organisations, in
evaluation activities 125

tutelage 49, 55n[4]
TWIN (UK-based NGO), and cocoa
    farmers in Ghana 10–11, 173, 174, 177
Twin Trading 176, 177, 179

Underwood, Barry (chief executive of
    AKRSPI) 195, 200
UNDP, Special Unit for Technical
    Cooperation among Developing
    Countries, book compiled by 401
United Nations Development Fund for
    Women (UNIFEM) 76
USAID
    Matching Grants 243, 244
    programme logic model used by 367
Utthan (NGO in India) 58–75
    background 60–1
    childcare and support facilities 69
    cultural level 71–3
    founder-leader (Nafisa Barot) 61,
        62, 66–7
    funding 62
    gender issues 63–71
    gender-sensitisation training 71
        assessing organisational impact
        72–3
    gender-sensitive leadership 66–7
    gender-sensitive organisational
        practice 73–4
    mission statement 64
    mobility of women staff members 68
    organisational structure 61–3
    resources for gender-equity focus
        70–1
    roles and responsibilities 69–70
    staff recruitment 67–8

Valença, Antônio Carlos 279
value, meaning of term 92
value conflicts 93
    in NGOs 23, 30, 281
value differences
    in cross-cultural interactions 143
    resolution of 143–5

Value For Money Audit (VFMA) 164
values-based approach to learning 19,
    280
values of NGOs
    and actual behaviour 280–1
        reasons for differences 281–3
    and measuring impact of advocacy
        381
vegetables, traditional, growing and
    use in Kenya 267–8, 269
volunteers, in humanitarian relief
    work 316, 323

war
    and impacts of aid 303
    rules of 318
water collection systems 60, 61
Weick, Karl 277
women's health, NGO in Brazil 284
Women's Learning Partnership,
    (WLP) 76
work–family issues, and organisational
    learning 85
work pressures
    and information sourcing 298
    as obstacles to uptake of new
        approaches 297
World Alliance for Citizen
    Participation (CIVICUS) 76
World Development Movement
    (WDM) 13, 384
World Neighbors 409
World Trade Organization (WTO)
    negotiations, campaign against
        376, 380, 382
    trade rules 375–6
WWW Virtual Library, on social policy
    evaluation 409

Zimbabwean NGOs
    disaster terminology used 300
    management 301
    sources of information on disaster
        mitigation 299

Development in Practice Readers

Development in Practice Readers draw on the contents of the acclaimed international journal *Development in Practice.*

> '*The great strength of the* Development in Practice Readers *is their concentrated focus. For the reader interested in a specific topic ... each title provides a systematic collation of a range of the most interesting things practitioners have had to say on that topic. It ... lets busy readers get on with their lives, better informed and better able to deal with relevant tasks.*'

(Paddy Reilly, Director, Development Studies Centre, Dublin)

The series presents cutting-edge contributions from practitioners, policy makers, scholars, and activists on important topics in development. Recent titles have covered themes as diverse as advocacy, NGOs and civil society, management, cities, gender, and armed conflict.

There are two types of book in the series: thematic collections of papers from past issues of the journal on a topic of current interest, and reprints of single issues of the journal, guest-edited by specialists in their field, on a chosen theme or topic.

Each book is introduced by an overview of the subject, written by an internationally recognised practitioner, researcher, or thinker, and each contains a specially commissioned annotated list of current and classic books and journals, plus information about organisations, websites, and other electronic information sources – in all, an essential reading list on the chosen topic. New titles also contain a detailed index. *Development in Practice Readers* are ideal as introductions to current thinking on key topics in development for students, researchers, and practitioners.

For an up-to-date list of titles available in the series, contact any of the following:

- the Oxfam Publishing website at www.oxfam.org.uk/publications
- the *Development in Practice* website at www.developmentinpractice.org
- Oxfam Publishing by email at publish@oxfam.org.uk
- Oxfam Publishing at 274 Banbury Road, Oxford OX2 7DZ, UK.

> '*This book* [Development, NGOs, and Civil Society] *will be useful for practitioners seeking to make sense of a complex subject, as well as for teachers and students looking for a good, topical introduction to the subject. There is a comprehensive annotated bibliography included for further exploration of many of the issues.*'

(David Lewis, Centre for Civil Society at The London School of Economics, writing in *Community Development Journal* 36/2)

Development in Practice

'A wonderful journal – a real "one stop must-read" on social development issues.'

(Patrick Mulvany, Intermediate Technology Development Group, UK)

Development in Practice is an international peer-reviewed journal. It offers practice-based analysis and research on the social dimensions of development and humanitarianism, and provides a forum for debate and the exchange of ideas among practitioners, policy makers, academics, and activists worldwide.

Development in Practice challenges current assumptions, stimulates new thinking, and seeks to shape future ways of working.

It offers a wide range of content: full-length and short articles, practical notes, conference reports, a round-up of current research, and an extensive reviews section.

Development in Practice publishes a minimum of five issues in each annual volume: at least one of the issues is a 'double', focused on a key topic and guest-edited by an acknowledged expert in the field. There is a special reduced subscription for readers in middle- and low-income countries, and all subscriptions include on-line access.

For more information, to request a free sample copy, or to subscribe, write to Oxfam Publishing, 274 Banbury Road, Oxford OX2 7DZ, UK, or visit: www.developmentinpractice.org, where you will find abstracts (written in English, French, Portuguese, and Spanish) of everything published in the journal, and selected materials from recent issues.

Development in Practice is published for Oxfam GB by Carfax, Taylor and Francis.

'Development in Practice *is the premier journal for practitioners and scholars in the humanitarian field who are interested in both practical insights and academic rigour.'*

(Joseph G Block, American Refugee Committee, USA)